REIMAGINING HOME

MORLING PRESS

 A catalogue record for this book is available from the National Library of Australia

The 5th Conference of the Australian
Association for Mission Studies,
Whitley College, Melbourne,
2–5 July 2017

REIMAGINING HOME

Understanding, reconciling and
engaging with God's stories together

Edited by:
Darrell Jackson
Darren Cronshaw
Rosemary Dewerse

 MORLING PRESS

REIMAGINING HOME

The 5th Conference of the Australian Association for Mission Studies, Whitley College, Melbourne, 2–5 July 2017

© Darrell Jackson, Darren Cronshaw and Rosemary Dewerse 2019

First published in Australia in 2019

Morling Press
122 Herring Rd
Macquarie Park NSW 2113 Australia
Phone: +61 2 9878 0201
Email: enquiries@morling.edu.au
www.morlingcollege.com/morlingpress

The publication is copyright. Other than for the purposes of study and subject to the conditions of the Copyright Act, no part of this book in any form or by any means (electronic, mechanical, micro-copying, photocopying or otherwise) may be reproduced, stored in a retrieval system, communicated or transmitted without prior written permission.

All Scripture quotations, unless otherwise indicated, are taken from the Holy Bible, New International Version® Anglicised (NIVUK), NIV®. Copyright ©1979, 1984, 2011 by Biblica, Inc.™ Used by permission. All rights reserved worldwide.

ISBN: 978-0-9945725-8-5 (paperback)
ISBN: 978-0-9945725-9-2 (e-book)

Designed by Brugel Creative www.brugel.com.au

CONTENTS

FOREWORD
René Erwich ix

INTRODUCTION
Come On In! The Making of Many Homes
Darrell Jackson xi

SECTION ONE: INCARNATION AND FRAGILITY: NEGOTIATING HOME IN THE FACE OF OVERWHELMING ODDS

CHAPTER 1
Negotiating 'Home' in an Age of Uncertainty
Seforosa Carroll 3

CHAPTER 2
Earth as Home–Place: Ecotheology and the Incarnation
Deborah Guess 21

CHAPTER 3
Reimagining Home Economics:
The Missiological Imperative of Embodied Economic Witness in Twenty-First-Century Australia
Jonathan Cornford 37

CHAPTER 4
Home and Homelessness in the Anthropocene
Mick Pope 55

SECTION TWO: MIGRANT NARRATIVES OF HOME

CHAPTER 5
Relocating in Christ:
Churches and Migration in Rural Australia
Mark Short and Monica Short 77

CHAPTER 6
A Century and a Half to Call this 'Home':
Chinese Churches in Sydney
Michael Chu 97

CHAPTER 7
Migration: Finding Hope and Home in a Foreign Land
Sharmila Blair 120

CHAPTER 8
Reconciling Church for Second-Generation Chinese Australians
Graham R. Scott 130

CHAPTER 9
Sehnsucht, Home and the Second-Generation Migrant
Stephen Said 142

CHAPTER 10
**Envisioning a Home for the Gospel
among Australia's Urban Hidden Peoples**
Edward James 152

SECTION THREE: IMAGINATION AND REIMAGINATION: FINDING HOME IN THE BIBLICAL TEXT

CHAPTER 11
Preserving Home: Seeking *Shalom*
Deborah Storie 171

CHAPTER 12
Indigenous Homemaking as Public Theology
Steve Taylor 188

CHAPTER 13
Reading Romans in Multicultural Australia
Siu Fung Wu 208

CHAPTER 14
**A 'Steam Boat' Theology of Home:
Reading the Gospel of Luke with Chinese Eyes**
Xiaoli Yang 227

CHAPTER 15
The Lord's Home in Isaiah
Eleonora Scott 247

CHAPTER 16
***Polis* and *Topos*: Reimagining 'Home' in Mark's Narrative**
Keith Dyer 261

SECTION FOUR: HOME AND THE MISSIONARY EXPERIENCE

CHAPTER 17
Making Bengal Home, 1882–1931
Rosalind M. Gooden *273*

CHAPTER 18
Overseas Missionaries and Their Families:
Can the Homecomings for Those Affected by Trauma be Reimagined?
Linda Devereux *290*

CHAPTER 19
Building Church Homes across Cultural Barriers:
Biblical Guidelines with Examples from the Muslim World
J. Dudley Woodberry *310*

CONCLUSION

Advance Australia Home?
Darren Cronshaw *323*

Information about Our Contributors and Editors
Reimagining Home *332*

Foreword

René Erwich

Reading the various chapters in this wonderful multi-perspective volume on the 'home-discourse', I was reminded of Mackay's analysis of Australian society and culture. He characterises it with reference to social and economic inequality, the eroding of trust in institutions, technological and sociological changes, and increasing domestic violence. According to Mackay, this has led to a deeply disruptive disconnection between people and groups of people.[1]

More than ever we are 'online', but do we really connect to each other? Churches and communities are not in the 'centre of everything', and we notice the struggle in finding adequate answers in the midst of widely reported massive cultural changes. Churches and communities are struggling as well, because many of their assumed 'jewels' are now provided by other religious and non-religious providers such as chaplaincy providers, retreat centres with a variety of spirituality offerings, cinemas and other media.

This 'liquefaction' of the church presents both a crisis and an opportunity in our society and for our communities. It is a serious crisis if we complain about it and interpret it only as a loss and a sign that the church in her mission is going downhill (morally, ethically, etc.). It presents an opportunity if we have the courage to reinterpret and reconfigure the core message of Jesus in connection with the search for what it means to be human. In this respect, much of the challenge lies in the extent to which we will be able to develop new views on *human dignity* in the twenty-first century, both in collective and individual perspectives.

I believe that this current volume, *Reimagining Home*, crafted in a deep theological engagement with real questions about what 'home' means, touches the core of the matter: what does it mean, theologically and missiologically, to be human and to be woven into the local web of life? The quest for human dignity should be at the heart of the theological and missiological enterprise, otherwise both theology and missiology become harmless. They call out for a prophetic voice and this voice is clearly present in this book.

The more we engage with the stories of God and people, the more we recognise that we live with borrowed breath. It is a great joy to recommend this book, especially because it is the fruit of many years of intense cooperation on

---

1   Hugh Mackay, *Australia Reimagined: Towards a More Compassionate, Less Anxious Society* (Sydney: Pan Macmillan Australia, 2018).

the platform that AAMS provides for the scholarly study of God's mission in this world. Whitley College is proud to be partnering with AAMS in this ongoing discourse to open doors to be at home with God and each other.

Parkville, October 2018

Introduction

COME ON IN! THE MAKING OF MANY HOMES

Darrell Jackson

For many Australians, the popular notion of 'home' is on view in the iconic Australian movie, *The Castle* (1997). Its memorable one-liners are often quoted with a smile, even though we know they are poking fun at our addiction to bricks and mortar. Darryl Kerrigan's famous, 'It's the serenity of the place', does nothing to undermine the association of 'home' with 'house'. As the authors of *Reimagining Home* demonstrate, this is a one-sided and inadequate association.

To reimagine home, the task they set themselves here, is to throw open the metaphorical windows, doors and skylights, and to allow in the fresh breeze of new ideas, voices and participants in the making of many homes. The authors in this modest volume invite you, the reader, to 'come on in!' and to join them in reimagining home as we each respond to God's mission to, among and with us.

A concern for God's mission remains central to the Australian Association for Mission Studies and its support of the scholarly study of God's mission is the rationale for its existence. However, the triennial conferences of the Australian Association for Mission Studies (AAMS) have no fixed abode. Institutional partners in Melbourne, Canberra, Adelaide and Sydney have each hosted an AAMS Conference over the last ten years and AAMS, established in 2006, has operated from administrative bases in Melbourne and Sydney for the last twelve years. These facts point to the sense that our association must look to others in its making of a 'home', given our own limited facility and resources.

What for AAMS is of relatively minor consequence, is for the many individuals and families who have been uprooted and struggle to establish home in a new land, of much greater consequence. AAMS has found its 'place' over the last twelve years within the family of similar associations known as the International Association for Mission Studies and gratitude and hopefulness characterise this current adolescent phase of its life. Such attitudes are also common among the many individuals and families who are given new opportunities to reimagine home in a new place.

However, AAMS has also faced periods when the future has been less than certain. The loss of key members of the family, financial vulnerability, the impermanence of membership; each of these has generated periods of anxiety, frustration, and fearfulness. Reimagining home, for those who must do so, can be accompanied by its own sense of anxiety, frustration and fearfulness. This collection of chapters remains sensitively pastoral and radically oriented to the narratives shared here, of people who have had to reimagine home in a wide, sometimes bewildering, range of new situations and circumstances.

Reimagining Home: Understanding, Reconciling and Engaging with God's Stories Together

Our fourth AAMS triennial conference in 2017 was hosted and co-organised with Whitley College, Melbourne. Whitley has a keen and ongoing commitment to contextual mission training and has been a strong supporter of AAMS since hosting the 2005 Australian Missiology Conference that led to the formation of AAMS one year later. Whitley was a key institutional partner in helping to establish AAMS in the early years, providing an institutional base for the first secretary of AAMS, Rev Professor Ross Langmead.

The initial planning for the conference began in 2014 and collaboration continued throughout 2015 and 2016. The conference theme was proposed by the AAMS Committee at the July meeting in 2016, and Whitley partners endorsed this at a joint meeting in August 2016. At the conference, held from July 2–5, 2017, 107 scholars and students of mission gathered to present and listen to papers addressing the conference theme in one of seven thematic streams. This current volume is one of the fruits of the conference, with selected chapters edited and selected according to four thematically arranged sections.

Introducing our Nineteen Contributors

The first four contributors alert the reader to the dangers of equating 'home' with little more than bricks and mortar. In section one, chapters are arranged to illustrate an investigation of the themes of 'Incarnation and Fragility: Negotiating home in the face of overwhelming odds'. This section takes something of a lead from the biblical witness to Jesus of Nazareth as the Son of Man who embraced the created order as an embodied human being, yet who had no permanent place in which 'to lay down his head' and call home.

In her opening chapter, one of the conference's plenary speakers, Seforosa Carroll, carefully scrutinises the concept of 'home'. Her rich and colourful portrait points to the problematics involved in talking of Australia as home, the need for a more ethnically diverse understanding of home, and then to the subversive notion of understanding journeying as 'home'. She develops a careful argument for understanding homemaking as the activity that works towards establishing places of permanence, hospitality, affiliation and belonging, among others. In sum, she envisages a place that encourages the flourishing of all human and non-human life, a place which we can imagine the Lord of all creation being pleased to call home.

In their respective chapters, Mick Pope and Deborah Guess, orient their discussion of home towards an understanding of planet earth as a home for humanity. For Guess, an ecological focus points decisively away from purely individualistic understandings of home. Earth as 'home' is the most widely shared home that any of us will ever inhabit. She points to the problem of a Christian tradition that places the sole emphasis upon sojourn and homelessness as a virtue of discipleship that is oriented towards the future reign of God. Guess challenges us to read the incarnation of Jesus as God's divine 'yes!' to the planetary 'home–place' that we call 'the earth'.

In contrast, Pope's chapter may appear somewhat ironic. He suggests that collective human activity has the very real potential to render humanity homeless, through making uninhabitable an increasingly fragile earth. Pope is a meteorologist and his attention to the detail of the Pacific region adds authenticity to his discussion of human impact upon climate change in a 'disrupted world'. Pope suggests that a new concept of ecomission is required to persuade humanity to discover new ways of making home in a disrupted world. His development of the theme of a homeless people living with the eschatological hope of home is a compelling call to ecomission.

In his contribution to this section, Jonathan Cornford outlines an embodied economic witness that takes home seriously as an important context for the shaping and sustaining of this kind of alternative economic understanding. He issues a call for a biblically-informed 'true materiality' that subverts a 'consumer materiality' informed only by capitalism. Cornford points to incarnation and creation as central theological resources for developing this new, whole of life, economic vision.

In the second section, 'Migrant Narratives of Home', six contributors deal with highly topical themes that illustrate the ways that Australia is becoming home to various groups of people, both inside and outside of the church.

Mark and Monica Short explore this theme through the lens of Anglican rural parishes that must minister to the medium- to long-term rural populations of Australia alongside the recent arrivals of refugees located to the country within the scope of the UN's humanitarian resettlement program. They set this within a discussion of the tendency of globalisation to create shared spaces, or virtual homes. The Shorts suggest that this is often far from being a real home of welcome, connection, participation and belonging. To achieve this, they point to an understanding of Christian mission that works towards a new, real and reimagined home.

Michael Chu is a first-generation Chinese migrant pastor, living in Sydney for over thirty years. Chu tells a little-known story of Chinese churches in Sydney, pointing back to a continuous presence for almost 130 years. He sets his discussion against the wider background of Chinese migration and presence in Sydney over the same period. The final challenges he leaves for his own church community is whether their churches are still seen as a 'home' for second- and third-generation Chinese young people who are Australian-born or Australian-raised.

Sharmila Blair makes important connections between her own experience and the biblical narratives of Ruth, the fifth chapter of Mark's Gospel, and the story of the Samaritan woman in John chapter four. She reads these texts from the perspective of the 'other' and offers her readings as a way to facilitate those 'outside' being invited to belong 'inside' the family of God.

Graham Scott writes, as does Michael Chu, about aspects of church as experienced by second-generation Chinese Australians. He understands 'home' as a helpful metaphor to describe a group of Australian-born and Australian-raised Chinese youth becoming a community and a church. This is a vital step, because according to Scott, church is the collective experience by which the Chinese young people interpret their own experiences of life in their Australian home.

Stephen Said writes out of the orienting theological insight that he is living between two worlds and yet is not fully at home in either. Set against what he describes as a 'joyless' childhood, Said imagines a way for the church to engage more profitably with second- and third-generation migrants.

The final contribution to this section is the work of a missiologist, Edward James, who explores the missiological consequences of the increasingly ethnically diverse cities of Australia. He suggests that whereas formerly, missionaries left the shores of Australia in search of people who had yet to hear the gospel, now there are countless opportunities to encounter such people in our cities. This requires a reconceptualisation of the task of mission, trying to understand it with reference to a reimagining of home for people considered 'least reached'.

In the third section, 'Imagination and Reimagination—Finding home in the biblical texts', attention is switched to biblical narratives that are offered by the six contributors as a key theological resource for the task of reimagining home in a world in which there exist multiple options that might be considered 'home'.

Deborah Storie reads Luke 19:1–27 (the story of Zacchaeus) using a form of intercultural exegesis which enables her to reimagine the Jericho parables, identifying the power structures laid bare in the text, and which she argues are intended to exclude and alienate. By doing so, Storie offers resources for a more adequate Christian response to the crises prompted by immigration and other social phenomenon.

Steve Taylor sets out to introduce the reader to the Maori leader and 'Kingmaker', Wiremu Tamihana, who developed a way of reading key biblical texts (particularly the Epistle to the Ephesians) that allowed him to reposition his own Maori people as the true and rightful inheritors of traditional Maori lands, as partners with equal rights to making home as their British co-signatories to the Waitangi Treaty of 1840. In sum, drawing on this historical account, Taylor offers the notion of a biblically-informed practice of 'homemaking' as a public missiology.

In his chapter, Siu Fung Wu outlines a typically careful reading of Romans with reference to multicultural contexts of first-century Rome and twenty-first-century Melbourne. He does so by evoking the Pauline metaphors of familial relationship, drawing the significance of sibling love as a basis for social cohesion as well as for Christian community.

Xiaoli Yang reads the Gospel of Luke to develop a characteristically Chinese way of understanding home with reference to a steam boat, or 'hot pot' theology. With reference to Chinese table meals, Yang draws our attention to the instances in Luke's Gospel of Jesus eating with friends, neighbours and other contemporaries. Her reading is subversive of some elements of Chinese cultural table practice, but she is no less critical of Western assumptions. However, her primary concern is to illuminate community, hospitality and the ministry of Jesus within the setting of the kingdom of God and to do so with a concern to better inform our practice of inclusion and welcome.

Eleonora Scott turns the focus onto the Old Testament texts of Isaiah. She introduces the Hebrew concepts of house, home and temple as ways of talking about the home of the Lord in Isaiah, which allow her to make application to contemporary church and mission practices. Central to her reading of the Lord's home is its function as a place of instruction, refuge, justice and holiness. When this home is no longer identified with a particular people, God looks for other peoples, committed to faithful and holy observance of God's will and purposes, and among whom he can presence himself to make a home.

Keith Dyer delivered the plenary Bible studies at the conference and here he offers a reading of home as '*polis*' and '*topos*' from Mark's Gospel. Dyer ponders the absence of direct gospel references to the places (or *topoi*) of either Sepphoris or Tiberias, Hippus, and Scytholopis, cities of note at the time of Jesus. He suggests that the absence of references to these places represents a rejection of the material culture of Herod and the Caesars. In rejecting kingdom and empire, Jesus offered instead the banquet of the wealthy and powerful to five thousand people seated in the fields overlooking the Sea of Galilee. Home for Jesus is to be found precisely in such places, not in the comfortable palaces and villas of either kingdom or empire.

In section four, 'Home and the Missionary Experience', three authors point to the experience of finding and making home in the context of missionary service. Much of what they write is core to the identity of many AAMS members. This basic experience of making home in another culture explains, in part, the personal and existential commitment to the theme of the book demonstrated in these final three chapters.

In chapter seventeen, Rosalind Gooden introduces the pioneering Australian women who entered missionary service in Bengal during the late nineteenth and early twentieth centuries. Having left homes, they had to make new homes in a culture that had no concept of the single career female. Among married missionary colleagues, they struggled for acceptance and had to negotiate for separate living quarters, having been initially billeted with married missionary couples. Despite such challenges, Gooden observes that many of these single women became highly regarded, finding a sense of home as 'mothers in the Lord'.

Linda Deveraux was raised in a missionary family based in the Democratic Republic of the Congo during the violent periods of political instability in the 1950s and 60s. Her experiences set the backdrop for a more formal study of the various traumas experienced by missionary families, an under-examined area of formal research. Deveraux discusses the main reasons for missionary trauma, introduces the problematic aspects of categorising the children of missionaries using categories that 'other' the so-called 'third-culture kids' and calls for a more adequate response to those who have returned to the countries from which they were sent, traumatised, and who may no longer be able to name their country of birth, 'home'.

In the final chapter of this book, plenary conference speaker, J. Dudley Woodberry, draws on his significant understanding and experience of mission among Muslims. He highlights the points of correspondence between Christianity and Islam and suggests ways in which Christians might adapt new customs and practices that foster acceptance by Muslims in a 'shared home'. Woodberry points beyond this initial welcome and social encounter to multiple instances of Muslims seeking a spiritual home beyond the militant religiosity of some forms of Islam.

'Come On In!': Hosts and Guests

Throughout this book, an ongoing conversation is underway. In it, our various contributors engage in an exploration of who gets to define 'home', the host or the guest? They make frequent reference to the various ways in which home is described, and experienced; whether relationally, dynamically, or with reference to our global home. The discussion they encourage and energise takes equally seriously the competing claims of home owner and home dweller. As theologians, they consider carefully what it means for humans to be 'at home' and discuss with equal care, the implications of understanding the incarnation as the divine experience of 'coming home'.

Each, in their own way, is a testimony to the reality of a God in whose mission we are called to participate. In doing so, the contributors to this volume remind us that in taking flesh, the incarnate Word of God, Jesus of Nazareth, came to dwell among those who were his own kith and kin, but that his own ultimately rejected him. This book contains a call to persevere in this mission. This is deeply paradoxical, for mission is a call to homelessness in a world in which the spirit of God continues to make resident the divine presence in every human culture that opens its homes and hearts to welcome the coming King of kings.

SECTION ONE:
INCARNATION AND FRAGILITY: NEGOTIATING HOME IN THE FACE OF OVERWHELMING ODDS

Chapter 1

NEGOTIATING 'HOME' IN AN AGE OF UNCERTAINTY[1]

Seforosa Carroll

Traveling with Jesus means leaving the static places of home and challenging the status quo.[2]

Jorge Rieger, *Traveling*

I am a Pacific Island migrant, and as is often the case for many migrants, home becomes a central and critical point of reflection at some point in our lives. I left my home in Lautoka, Fiji, thirty years ago, the year I finished my University Entrance (Year 12 equivalent).

I had received two scholarships to study at the University of the South Pacific. However, at the time I felt that freedom for a young woman lay beyond the Pacific shores. It took me twenty years to figure out that the reason I left home was to find home. Through varying experiences, writers, communities, family and friends, I began to make sense of that twenty-year journey and learnt to embrace

---

1   Some aspects of this chapter appear in an earlier article titled 'Homemaking: Reclaiming the Ideal of Home as a Framework for Hosting Cultural and Religious Diversity', in *Colonial Contexts and Postcolonial Theologies: Storyweaving in the Asia–Pacific*, eds. Mark Brett and Jione Havea (Palgrave, 2014).
2   Jorge Rieger, *Traveling* (Minneapolis: Fortress Press, 2011), 39.

my not-at-homeness as a way of being at home. For me, one significant insight is that home, or being at home, is possible even in displacement and dislocation.

Over time I began to celebrate and embrace my identity as an outsider–insider, to find 'home' and to be at home within that space—both in Australia and through my current work with church partners in the Pacific. There is pain, celebration and opportunity in both ways of being.

What I have learnt from this is that the idea of home is always a constant negotiation. Elaine Padilla encapsulates this beautifully in saying that '*not-at-home*ness becomes a state of becoming that actualises a sense of home-self but always with the residue of that which is to come'.[3]

My interest in the concept of home came about through Jacques Derrida, who raised the question of whether hospitality would be possible if one were homeless—particularly as 'hospitality is fundamentally connected to place—to a space bounded by commitments, values and meanings'.[4] Derrida's question continued to haunt me, prompting me to consider the notion of home and homemaking as an alternative against the experience of displacement and dislocation in the diaspora.

What Is 'Home'?

At the best of times, 'home' is a fraught concept. It is an ambiguous notion. It can mean a range of things—a house, a street address, land, country and religion, through to feelings of security and belonging. In fact, home is inclusive of all these things. Home is an actual lived location, a residence, an identifiable position on a map—as well as a place of identity, hospitality and potential shelter. Home is both an ideal (idea, concept, metaphor) and a lived reality. It is evident that a simple approach to the concept of home is not adequate; there is a need for critical scrutiny.

Sara Ahmed highlights three registers against which 'home' can be measured or defined—(i) your country of birth, (ii) the address at which you currently live; and (iii) the country in which you currently reside.[5] In using these registers, Ahmed emphasises the ambiguous nature of home, highlighting that one could have multiple homes. Thus, it could be said that home is affective and symbolic, and is evoked by memory and experience; home is not limited to a fixed physical dwelling. Home is more than just a fixed geographical location on a map.

---

3   Elaine Padilla, 'Border-Crossing and Exile: A Latina's Theological Encounter with Shekinah', *CrossCurrents* 60, no.4 (December 2010): 530.
4   Christine D. Pohl, *Making Room: Recovering Hospitality as a Christian Tradition* (Grand Rapids, MI: W. B. Eerdmans, 1999), 136.
5   Sara Ahmed, *Strange Encounters: Embodied Others in Post-Coloniality* (London: Routledge, 2000), 86.

Ideally, home is a place where there is a deep sense of belonging, and subsequently, security, acceptance and connection, without fear or shame.[6] Laura Gross maintains that 'as a human family, most of us have a conception of home as a sense of place that ideally connects us with others and the space we share'.[7] Alison Blunt claims that home is usually the place 'invested with meanings, emotions, experiences and relationships that lie at the heart of human life'.[8] Simply put, home is where primary relationships, identity and notions of the other are formed, and where hospitality is practised.

But home is also both a site of integration and difference. It is a place where identity is formed and challenged. Roopa Nair, in her study of Gujarati immigrant women in suburban Montreal, noted the following:

> For immigrants, the home not only reflects and mirrors identity but it is an important space that is used to create particular home experiences. In addition to being an important physical space, home embodies metaphoric meanings that are especially important for persons struggling to belong in a new society.[9]

Home embodies both the private/domestic and public/political spheres. Any discussion of home almost inevitably gives rise to gender considerations. Fiona Allon notes that, for the most part, the home has been seen and understood as existing only in the private/domestic sphere.[10] This tendency is to be expected given that the language of home is often associated with the domestic sphere—the place that society has specifically designated for women. The divide between the private and public spheres—commonly known as the 'separate spheres ideology'—was a theoretical framework used to describe gender roles.

Home has very much been the domain to which women are assigned, and feminists have shown that the home can be a place of exclusion, oppression and

---

6 Michael Mitton, *Dreaming of Home: Homecoming as a Model for Renewal and Mission* (Abingdon: Bible Reading Fellowship, 2012), 136.
7 Lora Gross, 'Resistance as Earth-Healing: Coming Home in an Ecological Age', *Currents in Theology and Mission* 28, nos. 3–4 (2001): 287.
8 Alison Blunt, 'Cultural Geography: Cultural Geographies of Home', *Progress in Human Geography* 29, no. 4 (2005): 506.
9 Roopa Nair, *Renegotiating Home and Identity: Experiences of Gujarati Immigrant Women in Suburban Montreal* (Master of Arts, McGill University Montreal, 1998), 16.
10 Fiona Allon, *Home as Cultural Translation: John Howard's Earlwood* (Communal/Plural, 5, 1–25, 1997), 1–13.

violence. It can very easily be a site of patriarchy and kyriarchy.[11] Iris Marion Young, however, argues that despite home being a place of exclusion and oppression for women, home has its redemptive qualities.[12] This feminist reading blurs the private and public spheres, with the resounding reminder that home is relational and can be a place where difference and otherness is affirmed and nurtured.

One of the most significant contributions of second-wave feminism to the separate spheres debate is the pertinent insight that the personal is political. Allon, an Australian sociologist and political analyst, has identified a particular aspect of this insight, insisting that home is not constrained to the personal—it is also political. Allon observes that 'home, now, more than ever, is seen as firmly connected to the world of politics and economics, as actively shaped and defined by the public sphere rather than existing simply as a refuge from it'.[13]

Homemaking in Australia

The idea of Australia being *home* is not without its difficulties. The idea of Australia as home, both as metaphor and as lived experience and history is grounded in a troublesome history.

Whose home is this? Who determines which practices should be the norm? How do we determine who is *one of us* and how should we regard the other?

This set of questions is played out within an unfolding history of contested discovery, invasion, the White Australia policy (and its subsequent repeal and slow death), and the advent of a religiously and culturally diverse Australia.

Therefore, how we engage with the other does not happen in a vacuum. It takes place within a flow of history and cultural 'homemaking' practices that are subject to change. By extension, nations are homes that are formed through certain narratives and stories or homemaking practices.

Australia has been shaped by a particular narrative; this has continued to influence how the country has been home to those who have migrated here. It is also characterised by a 'paranoid and aggressive nationalism' that manifests as obsessive border control, and anxiety and fear of the non–Anglo-Celtic other.

---

11 Elisabeth Schussler Fiorenza, *Jesus: Miriam's Child, Sophia's Prophet: Critical Issues in Feminist Christology* (New York: Continuum, 1994); Biddy Martin and Chandra Talpade Mohanty, 'Feminist Politics: What's Home Got to Do With It?', In *Feminist Studies: Critical Studies*, ed. T. D. Lauretis (Bloomington: Indiana University Press, 1986), 191–212; Iris Marion Young, *Intersecting Voices: Dilemmas of Gender, Political Philosophy and Policy* (Princeton: Princeton University Press, 1997).

12 Young, *Intersecting Voices*.

13 Allon, *Home as Cultural Translation*, 1.

This paranoia undergirds the vision of Federation and the subsequent White Australia policy.

Clement Due and Damien Riggs argue that home in the Australian context is 'structured around the desire of white people to retain Australia as a "white nation"'.[14] Due and Riggs maintain that home in this context is:

> frequently drawn upon in relation to both how people perceive the way in which they, and others belong in a country, and this raises questions surrounding who is legitimately able to call Australia home. Such discourses of home evoke feelings of ownership in people who feel that they have a legitimate claim to a country for reasons primarily of race or location.[15]

This concern for being at home in a new land is strikingly set out in J. M. Arthur's *The Default Country: A Lexical Cartography of 20th-Century Australia*.[16] Arthur's work is concerned with language and its relationship with space and place. Arthur is concerned with the place of Australia, 'as imagined and understood by non-indigenous "Australians"—those members of the occupying society in the dominant language of that society—through their words'.[17] This study of 'Australian English' (the settler's language) explores the relationship between the settler, their imagination and their relationship to place. Arthur looks at how language was used to consolidate and legitimise colonial belonging in Australia.[18] She also examines the colonising process of imagining and its impact on place through the projection of words, showing how words can be used to convey ownership. She skilfully demonstrates how Australia is changed both through the coloniser's relationship with place and the image projected by the coloniser onto the place.[19] In Australia's case:

> English became a language that did not return home but found a new home; it was used for relocating the community within a colonized territory, for attaching the exiles to the place and imagining it as, making it, home.[20]

---

14 Clemence Due and Damien Riggs, '"We Grew Here You Flew Here": Claims to Home in the Cronulla Riots', *Colloquy* 16 (2008): 211, http://arts.monash.edu.au/ecps/colloquy/journal/issue016/due-riggs.pdf.
15 Due and Riggs, 'We Grew Here You Flew Here', 211.
16 J. M. Arthur, *The Default Country: A Lexical Cartography of Twentieth-Century Australia*. NSW, Australia: UNSW Press, 2003.
17 Arthur, *The Default Country*, 8.
18 Arthur, *The Default Country*, 8.
19 Arthur, *The Default Country*, 7.
20 Arthur, *The Default Country*, 3.

Nations are, as Benedict Anderson defines, 'imagined political communities'.[21] They are formed by narratives and are constituted through language. These narratives have to do with ideas that 'construct and inform our value systems and belongings'.[22] Language and imagination are inextricably linked.

Language became the way of inscribing and imagining the nation through a process of what Arthur terms 'imaginative construction', where imaginative construction is a mapping process that intentionally

> constructs a relation between an occupying culture and the place it has occupied. These constructions weave the assumptions, hopes, imaginings, of the place into the colonialists' experience of Australia.[23]

Drawing on Edward Relph's insight that the perception of place is drawn from the 'intentions of the inhabitants', Arthur asserts that the intention in this instance was to legitimise the colonialist's belonging on invaded land. Although certain homemaking practices can attempt to assign a narrative to spaces that seemingly exist without one, the tension between space (spatial history that can be mapped) and geography (lived experience of the place) means that the 'colonialist's perception and rewriting of place cannot be fixed and will always be reforming'.[24] The discrepancy between space and geography does not allow Australia as a concept to be fixed, but instead enables the reforming and reimagining of Australia. Thus, '"Australia" as an identity has always been an uneasy construction in the minds of Australians'.[25]

Home, nation and empire have deep and longstanding connections. An empire's narrative and home practices shape a nation and influence the private or domestic sphere of the nation, the home. A nation's narrative and homemaking practices influence the values and worldviews that are nurtured in the home. Home is a storied place shaped by homemaking practices that take the form of stories or narratives, memory, and practices or ritual—'home is a dwelling made familiar and particular by the stories that have shaped it'.[26] In *Renovation Nation: Our Obsession with Home*, Fiona Allon states that the 'concept of home has long been

---

21   Benedict Anderson, *Imagined Communities: Reflections on the Origin and Spread of Nationalism*, rev. ed. (London, New York: Verso, 1983), 5.
22   Laurie Duggan, *Ghost Nation: Imagined Space and Australian Visual Culture* (St Lucia, Queensland: University of Queensland Press, 2001), xi.
23   Arthur, *The Default Country*, 7.
24   Arthur, *The Default Country*, 8.
25   Arthur, *The Default Country*, 8.
26   Steven Bouma-Prediger and Brian J. Walsh, *Beyond Homelessness: Christian Faith in a Culture of Displacement* (Grand Rapids: William B. Eerdmans, 2008), 65.

a staple of politics, used to connect the individual's experience with the larger community of the nation'.[27]

Allon 'connects the (Australian) domestic story—what [goes] on in our private homes—with the national story, seeing them as ultimately impossible to separate'.[28] She suggests that 'our obsession with home not only transforms the houses we live in and the cities, places and communities around us, but has profound consequences for how we understand our identity (who we are) and our place in the world (where we belong)'.[29] Allon notes that 'the obsession with home ownership [in Australia] configures both the domestic and the national home as islands of sanctuary and refuge, with renovation as a practice that keeps the nation looking inward'.[30] She makes the point that in a climate of anxiety, uncertainty and globalisation, Australians have opted to focus on creating and maintaining their own private sanctuary and refuge through obsessive home renovations. Allon links this obsession with Liberal Prime Minister John Howard who not only promoted Australia as a nation of shareholders and homeowners but appealed to the nostalgia of the 1950s. Allon claims that

> the real key to the success of the politics of John Howard was that he developed a language of comfort and cohesion that directly countered such challenges, and connected the individual to the family home and to the neighbourhood and to the nation in a reassuring framework of belonging.[31]

This was a vision of home that appealed to a past of exclusion, insecurity and fear of the other. It reinforced and re-engaged fantasies of white supremacy—the 'private domestic home and the national home began to look remarkably alike: they became fortresses inside which Australians worried about safety, security and protecting our wealth'.[32] This conflation of the private and national home was emphasised in Howard's memorable assertion in his 2001 election campaign speech, insisting that 'we will decide who comes into this country and the circumstances in which they come'.[33] This was both a proclamation of fear and an assertion of ownership.

---

27 Fiona Allon, *Renovation Nation: Our Obsession with Home* (Sydney: University of New South Wales Press, 2008), 88.
28 Allon, *Renovation Nation*, 3.
29 Allon, *Renovation Nation*, 3.
30 Allon, *Renovation Nation*, 3.
31 Allon, *Renovation Nation*, 109.
32 Allon, *Renovation Nation*, 3.
33 John Howard, John Howard's 2001 Election Campaign Policy Launch Speech, accessed November 15, 2012, http://museumvictoria.com.au/immigrationmuseum/discoverycentre/identity/videos/politics-videos/john-howards-2001-election-campaign-policy-launch-speech/.

Similarly, Pauline Hanson and the One Nation party demonstrated how the private and political homes are easily collapsed into one, with each of these spheres as the extension of the other. In her maiden speech to Parliament in 1996, Hanson proclaimed, 'If I can invite whom I want into my home, then I should have the right to have a say in who comes into my country'.[34] What is particularly interesting about Pauline Hanson is her portrayal as a kind of mother to a nation. As Ien Ang observes:

> Pauline Hanson, a white Australian single mother of four, once famously represented herself as the 'Mother' of Australia, and the Australian people as her 'children'. But for her, not all people living in Australia belong to the 'Australian people'. Her proverbial hostility toward Aborigines and Asians is well known, and was arguably a major reason for her popular success in the closing years of the twentieth century. And while by 2001 Pauline Hanson's role on the Australian political stage seems well and truly finished, her quick and spectacular rise and fall should remind us that what she stands for—the anxieties and prejudices of White Australia—has not fully disappeared from the Australian landscape.[35]

Hanson's political career continues to be controversial. Hanson lost her federal seat in the 1998 election. In 2002 she was expelled from the One Nation party. In 2003 she was convicted of electoral fraud and spent eleven weeks in jail prior to her appeal being heard and overturned. Hanson re-entered Australian politics in 2016. At the 2016 Australian federal election Hanson was elected to the Senate, together with three other representatives from the state of Queensland. In addition to One Nation's existing anti-multiculturalism, anti-immigration policy, Hanson included an anti-Islam policy. At the foundation of the policy is a recommendation for a ban on Australian companies and businesses from paying the Halal Certification tax on food and other items.

> Ban the burqa and any other full face covering in public and government buildings. No more building of mosques and Islamic schools until an inquiry is held into Islam, to determine whether it is a

---

34 Pauline Hanson, Maiden Speech in the House of Representatives, accessed November 15, 2012, http://australianpolitics.com/1996/09/10/pauline-hanson-maiden-speech.html.

35 Ien Ang, 'From White Australia to Fortress Australia: The Anxious Nation in the New Century', In *Legacies of White Australia: Race, Culture and Nation*, eds. Laksiri Jayasuriya, David Walker and Jan Gothard (Western Australia: University of Western Australia Press 2003), 51–69.

religion or totalitarian political ideology undermining our democracy and way of life.[36]

Homeward Bound

What we have explored here is one version of being homeward bound that presupposes an Anglo-Celtic imaginary. In terms of faith, this vision of being homeward bound assumes the Judeo-Christian tradition or secular indifference. It is a vision of home that is bound by cultural prejudice, theories of racial purity and superiority of one civilisation over another. It is a vision of being homeward bound that is essentially self-contained and that depends upon legal restrictions and migration policies favouring those who are already like us. In his book *What Was It All For? The Reshaping of Australia*, Don Aitkin contends that the Australia of the future will need a new dream that reflects the diversity of the Australian people.[37] This new dream necessitates an engagement with our history and the necessary interrogation of the kind of memory that we as a nation possess. Bell Hooks claims that:

> the past can be a resource that can serve as a foundation for us to revision and to renew our commitment to the present, to making the world where all people can live fully and well, where everyone can belong.[38]

Perhaps we ought to pay more attention to the Indo-European root word for home, 'haunt'. Geraldine Brooks in *The Idea of Home*[39] reminds us of the need to take stock every now and then, to clean the house or home of the ghosts of the past. Without addressing invasion or the ghosts of the past, we cannot fully be at peace; and because we feel that we do not fully belong, we cannot make room for others. Brooks defines home as a place we can head towards—a goal, or a destination. In this sense, (the ideal of) home is a source of inspiration where the 'past is allowed to haunt and illuminate'.[40]

The ideas of home—both as a metaphor and reality—and homemaking need to be reframed. Reframing the notion of home as movement and relational, rather than as fixed or impermeable, may open up alternative ways of understanding,

---

36 One Nation Party, One Nation Policies, accessed September 5, 2018, https://http://www.onenation.org.au/policies/halal-certification-and-islam/.
37 Don Aitkin, *What Was It All For? The Reshaping of Australia* (Crows Nest, NSW: Allen & Unwin, 2005), 244.
38 Hooks, 2009, 5.
39 Geraldine Brooks, *The Idea of Home* (Sydney: ABC Books, 2011).
40 Brooks, *The Idea of Home*, 105.

engaging and becoming. Steven Bouma-Prediger and Brian J. Walsh identify eight characteristics of what they believe is exhibited in the phenomenology of home.[41]

Bouma-Prediger and Walsh's first criterion is that home is a place of permanence, and that permanence is not defined by simply having shelter over your head. Permanence, in this instance, intimates a sense of rootedness to a place in a way that enables one to belong to a community and place in a meaningful way. Home also implies connectedness to a place and people, rather than simply to a structure. For example, one can belong to a nomadic tribe and still have a sense of home. This can be so because the nomadic wanderer is being sustained by a web of cultural relationships and support. These meaningful relationships create, nurture and sustain home as a place of permanence. Alternatively, one can have a shelter under a bridge or on the steps of a cathedral, but this way of being does not necessarily create a sense of home. In these circumstances, access to resources is very limited and there is a disconnection from meaningful relationships. The absence of such makes being at home impossible as permanence is defined by meaningful connections to place and people and not necessarily to structural dwellings.

The second criterion in Bouma-Prediger and Walsh's phenomenology of home has to do with dwelling. They argue that home is a dwelling place, emphasising the difference between a house and a home: 'A house is a building, whereas a home is an abode'.[42] Dwelling in a home is distinctively different to living in a house. You can live in a house and not dwell. A house can be a space devoid of any meaning, while a home is a place filled with memory and relationships. To dwell is to live in a meaningful and connected way with others and place.

> Home is a relationship that is created and evolved over time; it is not consumed like the products of economic process.[43]

In sum, a home is not a commodity in the way that a house is seen as property or as an investment. On this aspect of home Simon Holt adds that our obsession with home as a commodity makes it impossible to dwell or to inhabit.[44] The Samoan *fale*, for example, is more than just a building structure. It embodies community relationships, their worldview and values.

Thirdly, home is considered to be a storied place. Homemaking practices through story and memory transforms space into place—'At home, the stories

---

[41] Bouma-Prediger and Walsh, *Beyond Homelessness*.
[42] Bouma-Prediger and Walsh, *Beyond Homelessness*, 57.
[43] Bouma-Prediger and Walsh, *Beyond Homelessness*, 57–58.
[44] Simon Carey Holt, *God Next Door: Spirituality and Mission in the Neighbourhood* (Brunswick, Victoria: Acorn Books, 2007), 80.

we remember recall our common past and infuse our hoped-for future'.[45] A home is created and maintained through relationships that embody stories that tell of experience and history. A house becomes a home when it is transformed by memory. Stories and memory endow a space with meaning. This suggests that home is not fixed or impermeable and neither is it the creation of one person, but rather a family, a community, a people.

The fourth criterion developed by Bouma-Prediger and Walsh is one that envisages home as a safe resting place. It is a place 'constructed in such a way that we are safe to rest'.[46] In this sense home is a refuge. It is a place from which one can safely explore the world, as well as a place to which one can retreat or return to for rest, regeneration and the nurture of self-identity.[47]

Fifthly, home is seen as a place of hospitality. It is where we have the freedom to welcome family and friends, and to extend our welcome to the stranger. Fiona Allon states that it is 'a place we sometimes need to declare open, a place where we invite others in and offer them hospitality'.[48] This offering of hospitality stems from a 'fundamental feeling of security and belonging'.[49]

The sixth is that home is a place of embodied inhabitation. Home is a two-way street—'We not only shape a place according to our homemaking ways, but we are shaped by the places we inhabit'.[50] Home 'requires care and cultivation, but that care and cultivation is always located in a particular place'.[51]

The seventh characteristic is that home is a place of orientation. It provides us with an 'anchor that prevents us from being set adrift amidst the flow... It is to have roots in a place, a secure point from which to look out into the world, a firm grasp of one's position in the order of things . . . Being at home is a mode of being whereby we are oriented within a spatial, temporal and sociocultural order we understand'.[52]

Finally, home is a place of affiliation and belonging. Home is where we find our place and gain our identity. It is a 'place of belonging, of recognition and acceptance' where we feel we are included and accepted for who we are.[53]

---

45 Bouma-Prediger and Walsh, *Beyond Homelessness*, 65.
46 Bouma-Prediger and Walsh, *Beyond Homelessness*, 59.
47 Bouma-Prediger and Walsh, *Beyond Homelessness*, 59.
48 Allon, *Renovation Nation*, 211.
49 Bouma-Prediger and Walsh, *Beyond Homelessness*, 57.
50 Bouma-Prediger and Walsh, *Beyond Homelessness*, 62.
51 Bouma-Prediger and Walsh, *Beyond Homelessness*, 62.
52 Bouma-Prediger and Walsh, *Beyond Homelessness*, 63.
53 Bouma-Prediger and Walsh, *Beyond Homelessness*, 64.

Redeeming and reframing the understanding of home requires a radical redefinition of this term. The home must become dynamic and relational. It should not be fixed or static. For Nelle Morton home is a journey. She declares:

> I have come to know home was not a place. Home is a movement, a quality of relationship, a state where people seek to be 'their own', and increasingly responsible for the world.[54]

This task of creating the ideal of home requires appropriate practices. The focus falls upon the art of homemaking. Homemaking practices enable the creation and nurture of home.

There are at least three basic key assumptions that homemaking is dependent upon. The first is that home is not fixed, impermeable or permanent; it is relational and involves movement, which is manifested through homemaking practices. This movement—the act of creating or re-creating home based on the values of an ideal home—is homemaking. Home is in the struggle, the uncertainty, the ambiguity, and in the gaps.

The second assumption is that home is about dwelling. To dwell in a place means to inhabit. Home is not just somewhere with bricks and mortar. At its core, home is about relationships with people and place. Inhabiting, or *being at home* as Ahmed maintains, means that the subject and space leak into each other, inhabit each other.[55] Spaces become significant places of meaning, memory and meaning when the inhabitants embody the stories, create new meaning and set down new roots. Being at home is a process of inhabitation or dwelling. Inhabitation is a matter of embodied being. It is a two-way process whereby we are shaped by place and where place is shaped by the relationship that we have with it.[56]

John Inge develops this link between inhabiting and its relationship with dwelling and building further.[57] Inge draws upon Martin Heideigger's etymological explication of the word 'building', which has its origins from the Old English and High German word for building, *bauen*, meaning to dwell. To dwell signifies to remain, to stay in place. According to Heideigger, a covert trace of the word has been retained in the German word for neighbour (*nachbar*). The German *nachbar* contains the Old English *neahgehur*, which is a combination of *neah*, near and *gebur*, dweller. The *nachbar* is the *nachgebur*, the *nachgebauer*, the near-

---

54 Nelle Morton, *The Journey is Home* (Boston: Beacon, 1985), xix.
55 Ahmed, *Strange Encounters*, 89.
56 Bouma-Prediger and Walsh, *Beyond Homelessness*, 62.
57 John Inge, *A Christian Theology of Place* (Aldershot, Hampshire, England; Burlington, VT, USA: Ashgate, 2003).

dweller—he who dwells nearby.[58] This suggests that a proper understanding of the word 'building' would require a look at its etymological roots, 'dwelling'.[59] This dwelling would involve a sense of continuity, community and of being at home. Inge maintains inhabiting requires that one be aware of the importance of place.

The third assumption is that homemaking involves intentional practices that create the *habitus* for home. There is a correlating relationship between habitat and habit as habits are created by repetitive practices. These repetitive practices in turn create, shape and form the habitat. Mary McClintock Fulkerson defines homemaking as 'the distinctive ways the community maintains itself as a physical place, for maintenance or upkeep, but also as a liveable place—a real homeplace where people offer each other material, emotional, and spiritual support'.[60]

The ideal of home can only be made possible through intentional homemaking practices. For Daniel Kemmis, inhabiting a place is to dwell there in a practised way. It is a way that relies upon certain regular, trusted habits of behaviour. Kemmis argues that our capacity to live well in a place might depend on our ability to relate to neighbours—especially neighbours who have a different lifestyle based on shared habits of behaviour. Homemaking practices enable and nurture the creation of a *habitus* for meaningful inhabitation where both human and non-human life is nourished.[61] It is creating and re-creating spaces into meaningful shared-storied places and providing opportunities to open up conversations with indigenous and non-indigenous people who identity this place as home. It is the ability to create new spaces by transforming them into places endowed with meaning and value (i.e. homes). Robert Ginsberg captures this capacity well in saying that human beings are inherently 'home-makers'. He writes:

> We make our homes. Not necessarily by constructing them, although some people do that. We build the intimate shell of our lives by the organization and furnishing of space in which we live. How we function as persons is linked to how we make ourselves at home. We need time to make our dwelling into a home . . . Our residence is where we live, but our home is how we live.[62]

---

58 Martin Heideigger, *Building, Dwelling, Thinking Poetry, Language, Thought* (New York: Harper Perennial Modern Classics, 2013).
59 Inge, *A Christian Theology of Place*, 19, 31.
60 Mary McClintock Fulkerson, *Places of Redemption: Theology for a Worldly Church* (Oxford: Oxford University Press, 2010), 127.
61 Bouma-Prediger and Walsh, *Beyond Homelessness*, 62, 141–43.
62 Robert Ginsberg, 'Meditations on Homelessness and Being at Home: In the Form of a Dialogue', In *The Ethics of Homelessness: Philosophical Perspectives*, ed. J. M. Abbarno (Amsterdam: Rodopi B. V.), 31.

For Ginsberg, our home is how we live. It is how we structure the household by the housekeeping rules that we choose to be governed by, and by the stories and symbols that we choose to represent who we are.

The play and use of the idea of home lend themselves to the practice of homemaking and *oikeiôsis*.

Travelling Home

Home and homemaking are in the journeying that is *home*. Home is the journey. Ernst Conradie describes this journeying as *oikeiôsis*.[63] Conradie wrote with an ecological purpose in mind, with the conviction that humans are not yet at home on the earth. He coined the word *oikeiôsis* to describe the journey towards reconciliation with ourselves and our place in the larger scheme of things—God's *oikonomia*.

Within this setting, home is not so much about a goal or an arrival at a destination; home is to be found in the actual journeying or movement in and through which we ourselves are changed. In a very broad sense, home is about how we choose to faithfully live out our Christian discipleship and also how we respectfully *manage* our relationships with others and place in the here and now. What we do here and now matters.

The eschatological necessity directs our gaze beyond history and current cultural religious practice. It transcends the present. Nevertheless, we live in a particular here and now. It is within space and time that we are to put *oikeiôsis* into practice. The critical step is to put into place appropriate homemaking practices that nurture the journey.

Homemaking creates space for the other through hospitality, enabling the other to tell their story and allowing them room in our home (the nation, church or community) to display the symbols of their story. The relating of such stories through the practice of compassionate listening creates and makes room for the other. It is a way of listening and paying attention.

Sheryl Kujawa-Holbrook has discerned five underlying assumptions of such listening. The first is the need to listen to the other, for we cannot ever assume that we know how it is to be another. The second is the imperative need to refrain from changing the other, as the other should be loved and welcomed for who they are. The third recognises that long-term peace comes from acknowledging the humanity and suffering of the other and that conflict and violence are a result of unhealed wounds. The fourth assumption is trusting that when people feel they

---

63 Ernst M. Conradie, *An Ecological Christian Anthropology: At Home on Earth?* (Aldershot, UK: Ashgate, 2005), 6.

are truly heard that they will be more open to listen to the stories of those they disagree with. Finally, compassionate listening is a practice of reconciliation which is grounded in the belief that 'mutually understanding and respect are the foundations for building communities across the borders of difference'.[64]

The redemptive, transformative task of homemaking is one of reconciling, renewing and transforming spaces, narratives and exercising out prophetic roles in the public domain. As a sent people or a sent community, we are tasked with a mission of reconciliation. This mission calls us to serving, healing, and reconciling a divided, wounded community *and earth*.[65] Following Thomas Tweed's[66] understanding of religion as crossing and dwelling, the church is called to a journey of relationship. This journey of relationship is one of partnership exercised in the form of reconciliation and healing of the wider *okoinomia*. It is mission. It is homemaking. It is a collective call to all to create an inhabitable, safe place for all. As such, mission is *homemaking*. It is engaging in the action and process of making home for all. Homemaking is concerned with the flourishing of God's household.

The task of 'making home' is a collective shared effort. It cannot fall primarily on either the government or on religious or cultural communities. Diana Eck states that community and belonging is not something religions can create on their own: 'the question is how do we go it together'.[67] In her reading of what is required, she insists:

> The aim is not mutual understanding, but mutual self-understanding and mutual transformation. What we must be able to do, however, is to recognize and clearly articulate our deep guiding values, our criteria and place them in clear, critical conversation with others. At its deepest level, the dialogue that will undergird a pluralist society is the encounter of commitments as well as the encounter of criteria.[68]

In this journey and in our life together with others in the earthly home, we are sojourners in this time and place. It matters then how we live and manage the resources entrusted to us. The home we create for future generations will be

---

64 Sheryl, A. Kujawa-Holbrook, *God Beyond Borders: Interreligious Learning among Faith Communities* (Eugene, Oregon: Pickwick, 2014), 34–37.

65 David Bosch, *Transforming Mission:Paradigm Shifts in Theology of Mission* (Maryknoll, New York: Orbis, 1991), 494.

66 Thomas A. Tweed, *Crossing and Dwelling: A Theory of Religion* (Cambridge, MA: Harvard University Press, 2006).

67 Diana Eck, *Encountering God: A Spiritual Journey from Bozeman to Banaras* (Boston: Beacon Press, 1993),190.

68 Eck, *Encountering God*, 189.

influenced by the homemaking practices that we choose to adopt and adapt to now. Homemaking is the journey of making the ideal of home possible, so that all human and non-human beings can flourish. Good household management considers the whole inhabited earth and its people. Stewardship or custodianship of the whole inhabited earth does not just mean caring only for the Christian household. The invitation to care or manage is a vision for a shared home for all.

But in the light of the impacts of climate change and in the dawn of the Anthropocene, home takes on a new meaning and requires us to further renegotiate. The Pacific is among a number of countries in the world on the forefront of climate change. Although my small island of Rotuma, or my hometown in Lautoka, Fiji, are not directly under threat from climate change (yet), many members of my wider Pacific family are. For those in Tuvalu, Kiribati, Marshall Islands, Tokelau and the Maldives, time is already running out for them. Their future is uncertain. They are destined to lose their home. It is no longer a matter of if but of when. For ecological migrants, the permanent absence of a physical home, or the reality of not having a home to return to, raises questions of identity, culture and faith. What does it mean to be at home in the permanent absence of a physical home? What does it mean to be a Tuvuluan when there is no longer a Tuvalu? What is the meaning of home, identity and faith in the advent of the Anthropocene?

BIBLIOGRAPHY

Ahmed, Sara. *Strange Encounters: Embodied Others in Post-Coloniality*. London: Routledge, 2000.

Aitkin, Don. *What Was It All For? The Reshaping of Australia*. Crows Nest, NSW: Allen & Unwin, 2005.

Allon, Fiona. *Home as Cultural Translation: John Howard's Earlwood*. Communal/Plural, 5, 1–25, 1997.

Allon, Fiona. *Renovation Nation: Our Obsession with Home*. Sydney: University of New South Wales Press, 2008.

Anderson, Benedict. *Imagined Communities: Reflections on the Origin and Spread of Nationalism*, rev. ed. London, New York: Verso, 1983.

Ang, Ien. 'From White Australia to Fortress Australia: The Anxious Nation in the New Century.' In *Legacies of White Australia: Race, Culture and Nation*, edited by Laksiri Jayasuriya, David Walker and Jan Gothard, 51–69. Western Australia: University of Western Australia Press, 2003.

Arthur, J. M. *The Default Country: A Lexical Cartography of Twentieth-Century Australia*. NSW, Australia: UNSW Press, 2003.

Blunt, Alison. 'Cultural Geography: Cultural Geographies of Home.' *Progress in Human Geography* 29, no. 4 (2005): 505–15.

Bosch, David. *Transforming Mission: Paradigm Shifts in Theology of Mission*. Maryknoll, New York: Orbis, 1991.

Bouma-Prediger, Steven, and Brian J. Walsh. *Beyond Homelessness: Christian Faith in a Culture of Displacement*. Grand Rapids: William B. Eerdmans, 2008.

Brooks, Geraldine. *The Idea of Home*. Sydney: ABC Books, 2011.

Conradie, Ernst M. *An Ecological Christian Anthropology: At Home on Earth?* Aldershot, UK: Ashgate, 2005.

Due, Clemence, and Damien Riggs. '"We Grew Here You Flew Here": Claims to Home in the Cronulla Riots.' *Colloquy* 16 (2008): 210–28. http://arts.monash.edu.au/ecps/colloquy/journal/issue016/due-riggs.pdf.

Duggan, Laurie. *Ghost Nation: Imagined Space and Australian Visual Culture*. St Lucia, Queensland: University of Queensland Press, 2001.

Eck, Diana. *Encountering God: A Spiritual Journey from Bozeman to Banaras*. Boston: Beacon Press, 1993.

Fiorenza, Elisabeth Schussler. *Jesus: Miriam's Child, Sophia's Prophet: Critical Issues in Feminist Christology*. New York: Continuum, 1994.

Fulkerson, Mary McClintock. *Places of Redemption: Theology for a Worldly Church*. Oxford: Oxford University Press, 2010.

Ginsberg, Robert. 'Meditations on Homelessness and Being at Home: In the Form of a Dialogue.' In *The Ethics of Homelessness: Philosophical Perspectives*, edited by J. M. Abbarno, 29–40. Amsterdam: Rodopi B. V., 1999.

Gross, Lora. 'Resistance as Earth-Healing: Coming Home in an Ecological Age.' *Currents in Theology and Mission* 28, nos. 3–4 (2001): 285–91.

Hanson, Pauline. Maiden Speech in the House of Representatives. Accessed November 15, 2012. http://australianpolitics.com/1996/09/10/pauline-hanson-maiden-speech.html.

Heideigger, Martin. *Building, Dwelling, Thinking Poetry, Language, Thought*. New York: Harper Perennial Modern Classics, 2013.

Holt, Simon Carey. *God Next Door: Spirituality and Mission in the Neighbourhood*. Brunswick, Victoria: Acorn Books, 2007.

Howard, John. John Howard's 2001 Election Campaign Policy Launch Speech. Accessed November 15, 2012. http://museumvictoria.com.au/immigrationmuseum/discoverycentre/identity/videos/politics-videos/john-howards-2001-election-campaign-policy-launch-speech/.

Inge, John. *A Christian Theology of Place*. Aldershot, Hampshire, England; Burlington, VT, USA: Ashgate, 2003.

Kujawa-Holbrook, Sheryl, A. *God Beyond Borders: Interreligious Learning among Faith Communities*. Eugene, Oregon: Pickwick, 2014.

Martin, Biddy, and Chandra Talpade Mohanty. 'Feminist Politics: What's Home Got to Do With It?' In *Feminist Studies: Critical Studies*, edited by T. D. Lauretis, 191–212. Bloomington: Indiana University Press, 1986.

Mitton, Michael. *Dreaming of Home: Homecoming as a Model for Renewal and Mission*. Abingdon: Bible Reading Fellowship, 2012.

Morton, Nelle. *The Journey is Home*. Boston: Beacon, 1985.

Nair, Roopa. *Renegotiating Home and Identity: Experiences of Gujarati Immigrant Women in Suburban Montreal*. Master of Arts, McGill University Montreal, 1998.

One Nation Party. One Nation Policies. Accessed September 5, 2018. https://http://www.onenation.org.au/policies/halal-certification-and-islam/.

Padilla, Elaine. 'Border-Crossing and Exile: A Latina's Theological Encounter with Shekinah.' *CrossCurrents* 60, no. 4 (2010): 526–48.

Pohl, Christine D. *Making Room: Recovering Hospitality as a Christian Tradition*. Grand Rapids, MI: W. B. Eerdmans, 1999.

Reiger, Joerg. *Traveling*. Minneapolis, Fortress Press, 2011.

Tweed, Thomas A. *Crossing and Dwelling: A Theory of Religion*. Cambridge, MA: Harvard University Press, 2006.

Young, Iris Marion. *Intersecting Voices: Dilemmas of Gender, Political Philosophy and Policy*. Princeton: Princeton University Press, 1997.

Chapter 2

EARTH AS HOME–PLACE: ECOTHEOLOGY AND THE INCARNATION

Deborah Guess

With ecological questions occupying an increasingly central place in public discourse, it is becoming clearer that complex phenomena such as anthropogenic (human-induced) climate change need to be approached from a wide range of disciplinary perspectives: not only science, economics and politics but also psychology, philosophy and theology. Philosophy and theology are especially significant because of the extent to which they inform worldviews, which in turn tend to fashion behaviour: in the words of Alfred North Whitehead, 'as we think, we live'.[1] How human beings see themselves, the divine and the biophysical world significantly influences how they respond to climate change, a phenomenon which is arguably the overarching moral and existential issue of our time.

The topic of home is interesting for ecological theology. Fundamentally, each entity in the more-than-human earth community[2] requires adequate space and an appropriate habitat in order to survive and thrive. Spaces are fought over—

---

1   Alfred North Whitehead, *Modes of Thought* (New York, NY: The Free Press, 1938), 63.
2   The term 'more-than-human' is a shorthand way of expressing the entire biophysical world, both human and other-than-human. It has the useful ecological function of affirming the interrelatedness of humankind with the rest of living (and non-living) parts of Earth. It also implicitly expresses the anti-anthropocentric stance of an ecological ethos by decentring the human.

changes in ecological systems are often the consequence of a struggle for place and space between competing species and with individuals. Within the human community, environmental, social and political issues are also often intricately related to the occupation of place and space. The global human population (now at over seven billion) has more than doubled since the 1950s, with its concomitant space-occupying features including housing, transport, commerce and twenty-six billion animals serving the meat and dairy industries. Every piece of space occupied by a human being, an artefact or piece of technology, or a farm animal, is inevitably a space from which the habitat of other living entities has been displaced or eliminated. Habitat is usually more fragile for other-than-human species than it is for humans. This is because animals and plants often have a more restricted requirement in terms of the type of space they need, whereas human beings, who have the ability to build dwellings and to make clothes, for example, are more adaptable to changed places and circumstances. Yet human beings are only able to survive within a certain temperature range and can only tolerate a certain degree of contamination of soil, air and water: we too are what Michael Northcott calls 'phenomenologically place-bound'.[3] All species, including the human, need a healthy and well-functioning planet as their essential place, as their home.

The famous 'blue marble' image of Earth taken from Apollo 17 in 1972 has often been used in ecospiritual discourse to evoke the idea of Earth as our home–place. The image is also frequently used in conjunction with the statement made the previous year by Edgar Mitchell, the pilot of Apollo 14, as he looked at Earth:

> Suddenly, from behind the rim of the Moon, in long, slow-motion moments of immense majesty, there emerges a sparkling blue and white jewel, a light, delicate sky-blue sphere laced with slowly swirling veils of white, rising gradually like a small pearl in a thick sea of black mystery. It takes more than a moment to fully realize this is Earth . . . home.[4]

The present ecological situation (by which is meant not only climate change *per se*, but also related phenomena such as deforestation, overfishing, deteriorating soil quality and loss of biodiversity) indicates that a dichotomy exists in current human understanding whereby on the one hand (like Edgar Mitchell) we affirm Earth as our home and on the other (like the space project itself) we treat Earth instrumentally and exploitatively as if it is a mere resource and garbage tip. In this

---

[3] Michael S. Northcott, *Place, Ecology and the Sacred: The Moral Geography of Sustainable Communities* (London: Bloomsbury, 2015), 169.

[4] New Mexico Museum of Space History: A Division of the New Mexico Department of Cultural Affairs, 'International Space Hall of Fame', http://www.nmspacemuseum.org/halloffame/detail.php?id=45.

chapter, I will suggest that an emphasis on the 'home' part of that dichotomy has value for understanding, and responding to, the present ecological situation. I will discuss some of the complex and ambiguous views about home–place and Earth in Christian and Western understandings and then suggest that the doctrine and event of the incarnation is fruitful for an understanding of Earth as our 'home–place' in a general way and for affirming the value of particular home–place/s, understandings which can speak to an ecological sensibility.

Home and Place

Today in the West, 'home' is generally thought of in a positive way as a private place providing identity, safety and relaxation for one or more people, often associated particularly with the nuclear family. Its strong affective and personal connotations are indicated by the large number of clichés associated with it: 'I feel at home here', or 'Home is where the heart is'. Australians might cite (with or without irony) a line from the film *The Castle*: 'it's not a house, it's a home'.[5]

But despite its common usage, the term 'home' does not necessarily have a clear or single meaning. In ecotheological discourse the etymology of 'ecology' is often evoked with a reminder that *oikos* is the ancient Greek equivalent of a house, household, family or dwelling place—terms that might automatically be seen as coterminous with 'home'. Yet Halvor Moxnes argues that the current understanding of 'home' is essentially recent, its modern usage indicated by the way that over the last two hundred years English-language Bibles (such as the KJV) have increasingly replaced phrases previously translated as 'house' with 'home'.[6] Before the modern era people would be more likely to describe the place they lived using terms such as 'house' or 'household', denoting a location of shared work and resources, usually under a patriarchal structure.[7] If Moxnes is correct, then the powerful urge for settling down has perhaps become greater in the highly mobile and globalised modern and postmodern eras.

The concept of 'home' can also have negative or problematic associations. It can evoke a backward-looking or fortress mentality, the primary intention of which is to exclude others. Related terms such as 'homeland' can trigger hostile and

---

5   A famous line from 'The Castle', an iconic and popular Australian film about place and displacement.

6   Moxnes notes that the seventeenth-century KJV translates *oikos/oikia* in the Synoptic Gospels almost exclusively as 'house' and only four times as 'home', whereas nineteenth- and twentieth-century KJVs show 'a steady increase in the use of "home"'. Halvor Moxnes, *Putting Jesus in His Place: A Radical Vision of Household and Kingdom* (Louisville, London: Westminster John Knox Press, 2003), 25–26.

7   Moxnes, *Putting Jesus in His Place*, 25.

reactionary responses which express xenophobia and racism. Home is a concept related to wealth: today home ownership is a telling indicator of one's position on the wealth-poverty spectrum. And, like the ancient *oikos*, home today can be a location of male dominance, where women and children can experience inequality, oppression, abuse and violence. In one-person households, home might also be a place associated with loneliness or neglect.

For Western people raised in a culture of individualism, the generally desirable associations of home are merged with a sense that it is somewhere we wish or need to move away from. Moxnes notes that leaving home for Westerners has become a 'rite-of-passage . . . part of the way in which a modern individual constructs himself or herself' in a way that contrasts to ancient and non-Western cultures where identity was and is located more firmly in the household, with its embedded roles: ' . . . to a Mediterranean mind in the first century, "household" and "self" were not two separate entities, but two aspects of the same condition. The self was located in the group . . .'[8]

To complicate the question further, a lack of home can be valorised or seen as noble: the heroic, romanticised figure of the self-autonomous (usually male) individual who lives an itinerant life unencumbered by domestic attachments has been a significant part of the Western imaginary, and perhaps this has contributed to the way that a neoliberal culture can portray homelessness as a 'lifestyle' choice, something which people could avoid if they so wished. It may also influence the way we perceive Jesus's itinerant way of living. A valorisation of homelessness may not only be a recent and Western tendency, however. In ancient religious, heroic and folk literature, itinerancy is commonly seen in the figure of the wandering quester, warrior, adventurer or pilgrim. As Erazim Kohák notes: 'Stoics understood the strategy of the wayfarer as clearly as the Romantics understood the strategy of the dweller'.[9] In the words of the philosopher of place, Edward Casey: 'If it is distinctively postmodern to wish to return to place, this is so even if the most promising patterns for the return are often distinctively premodern in inspiration'.[10]

Despite the complexity associated with the idea of home, today the desire for home seems to be an undeniably powerful, and perhaps insufficiently discussed, aspect of how humans see themselves and the world. Geographer Doreen Massey, seeking to establish a contemporary definition of 'place', notes the longing that

---

8   Moxnes, *Putting Jesus in His Place*, 57.
9   Erazim Kohák, 'Of Dwelling and Wayfaring: A Quest for Metaphors', in *The Longing for Home*, ed. Leroy S. Rouner (Notre Dame, IN: University of Notre Dame Press, 1996), 39.
10 Edward S. Casey, *Getting Back into Place: Toward a Renewed Understanding of the Place-World*, 2nd ed. (Bloomington, IN: Indiana University Press, 1993), xiv.

exists for 'the coherent and homogenous communities of the past'.[11] This longing is not necessarily reactionary or romantic—a profound and powerful yearning for something that is familiar and localised in a more positive sense can be seen as inherent to human beings: as the geographer Yi-Fu Tuan notes, there is an 'affective bond between people and place'.[12] At the very least it may be said that human beings today, living within the complex context of globalisation, have a profound need to 'belong' in a lived location, a site where we experience integration and meaning: in short, home.

The longing for home can be valuable for ecological discourse because a commitment to a place of home can be seen as a reaction to, and an implicit protest towards, the radically globalised, standardised, fast-paced and ecologically culpable culture which much of the world now experiences or aspires to. An understanding that Earth is, at least on one level, our 'home', the place we wish to care for and the place on which we are dependent (biophysically, but also to some degree spiritually, psychologically and emotionally) is conducive to an ecological ethos. To degrade and destroy the world is to degrade and destroy ourselves because we are an unavoidably integral part of creation, and our encounters with places that are local, concrete and personal are the means by which we enter community with other animals, plants, land and sea. Edward Casey notes that in a context of 'gathering ecological disaster' place becomes even more important not only as a possible location of safety to retreat to from the 'unknown' but as a sanctuary in a more positive way: 'Place is increasingly regarded as a natural reserve in which to care for existing life-forms—to be sure that they will be nurtured and protected despite the encroaching environmental threats'.[13]

Our unprecedented ecological situation has led to the development of a new term which is relevant to a study of home. 'Solastalgia' has been coined by Glenn Albrecht to describe the distress and loss of psychic stability experienced by people in relation to an impoverished environment.[14] The term combines 'nostalgia' with 'a lack of solace or comfort' in relation to one's ecologically deteriorated surroundings. Albrecht notes that up to the middle of the twentieth century nostalgia was a medically diagnosable psycho-physiological disease denoting a melancholia or homesickness experienced by people distant from their home and that the cure (e.g. for soldiers in war) was to return home. Nostalgia

---

11   Citation of paper by geographer Doreen Massey in Tim Cresswell, *Place: A Short Introduction* (Malden, MA: Blackwell, 2004), 68, 63.
12   Cited in Cresswell, *Place: A Short Introduction*, 20.
13   Casey, *Getting Back into Place*, xxviii.
14   Glenn Albrecht, 'Solastalgia: A New Concept in Health and Identity', *PAN: Philosophy, Activism, Nature*, no. 3 (2005): 45.

today has lost its geographical association with a place of home and suggests instead 'a "looking back", a desire to be connected with a positively perceived period in the past': Albrecht draws together both meanings of nostalgia to refer to a longing both for lost time and place.[15] The 'solace' aspect of the concept of solastalgia describes a lack of solace experienced not only in relation to a distant or lost home–place (as in nostalgia) but also to a sense of distress or desolation caused by ecological degradation of the place where one is currently dwelling. Solastalgia then is 'a form of homesickness one gets when one is still at "home"' where the identity of one's home is seen as being challenged or compromised.[16] Because human wellbeing and ecological sustainability are inextricably linked, the healing of a sense of solastalgia calls for the creation of a new future which calls on the innate human desire to be connected with life and with the natural world 'by finding an earthly "home" in the connection with living things and life processed on this planet'.[17]

Therefore, although human beings have an innate urge for a sense of belonging or identification with a particular location which we name as 'home', today people also encounter a destroyed or degraded ecology and thereby experience 'solastalgia'. In light of this, to avoid reactionary, introverted or overly romantic associations of 'home', it is helpful to link 'home' with the more neutral word 'place', understood here as 'a particular, unique, point of . . . intersection . . . a *meeting* place . . . [with] links with the wider world, which integrates in a positive way the global and the local'.[18]

The conjunction of the positive sense of 'home' as a location which gives a sense of belonging and identity, with the more neutral term 'place', follows the practice in some other ecotheologies and ecophilosophies. Ecotheologian Sallie McFague uses 'home' and 'place' somewhat interchangeably. She says it is the concept of place, the understanding that a location is our home, which grounds the ecologically indispensable identification of ourselves as Earth-beings: 'we need to realise that the earth is our home, that we belong here, that this is not only our space but our *place*'.[19] Ecophilosopher Freya Mathews also unites 'home' and 'place' by proposing that people connect with the natural world by identifying with and caring for a place which they consider, for whatever reason, to be their home–place: when people connect intensely and passionately to a place they

---

15 Albrecht, 'Solastalgia: A New Concept in Health and Identity', 45–47.
16 Albrecht, 'Solastalgia: A New Concept in Health and Identity', 48.
17 Albrecht, 'Solastalgia: A New Concept in Health and Identity', 59.
18 Cresswell, *Place: A Short Introduction*, 69.
19 Sallie McFague, *The Body of God: An Ecological Theology* (Minneapolis, MN: Fortress, 1993), 100–102.

become 'recharged' because 'they plug into the sustaining energies and spiritual solace inherent in a psychically activated world'.[20] Similarly for Val Plumwood, placelessness is reversed by 'a deep acquaintance with some place, or perhaps a group of places'.[21] Plumwood's use of the plural is helpful because in a globalised, pluralistic world where the birthplace of many, if not most, people is no longer their current dwelling place, human beings are more likely to have multiple homes and multiple identities.

Home–Places and the Western and Christian Tradition

The current longing for a home–place or places is a reflection of a fundamentally displaced culture. In the words of Bouma-Prediger and Walsh: 'To "diss" place. That's our current place'.[22] In non-Western culture the massive human displacement which is evident in the global refugee crisis can often be traced to historic factors such as colonialism or war, as well as to environmental factors such as climate change. In the West displacement is perhaps more closely associated with massive social and economic movement but is also philosophically linked with the twentieth- and twenty-first-century human experience of spiritual or intellectual *anomie:* from others, from God, from oneself and from the natural world. In a circular fashion, human loss of a sense of home–place both contributes to, and reflects, the profoundly connected dual phenomena of ecological decline and spiritual or existential fragmentation, at least within Western culture. John Haught says: 'The origins of our ecological crisis may lie, in part at least, in a deeply entrenched suspicion by humans that the cosmos is not really our home'.[23]

The idea that humankind does not really belong to or in the physical and biological world has been traced to ancient (early Greek) roots,[24] albeit radically exacerbated by philosophical, scientific and political-economic developments of the modern and postmodern era such as nominalism, the rise of Western science, the Enlightenment, and capitalist-industrial development. In the words of ecophilosopher Val Plumwood: 'Our current debacle is the fruit of a human- and

---

20 Freya Mathews, *Reinhabiting Reality: Towards a Recovery of Culture* (Albany, NY: State University of New York Press, 2005), 68.
21 Val Plumwood, *Environmental Culture: The Ecological Crisis of Reason* (London and New York: Routledge, 2002), 231–33.
22 Steven Bouma-Prediger and Brian J. Walsh, *Beyond Homelessness: Christian Faith in a Culture of Displacement* (Grand Rapids, MI: Eerdmans, 2008), xii.
23 John F. Haught, *The Promise of Nature: Ecology and Cosmic Purpose* (New York and Mahwah, NJ: Paulist Press, 1993), 40.
24 See Clifford Chalmers Cain, *An Ecological Theology: Reunderstanding Our Relation to Nature*, vol. 98, Toronto Studies in Theology (Lewiston, Queenston and Lampeter: The Edwin Mellen Press, 2009), 21–34.

reason-centred culture that is at least a couple of millennia old, whose contrived blindness to ecological relationships is the fundamental condition underlying our destructive and insensitive technology and behaviour'.[25] Admittedly, it is not a unidirectional process: the sense of a human–nature divide which was influenced by the Enlightenment's rational and scientific approach evoked the countervailing Romantic turn towards an affective and aesthetic engagement with nature. Along with its US counterpart, transcendentalism, Romanticism influenced movements of conservation and preservation in Europe and the US in the late nineteenth and twentieth centuries—precursors to the environmental movement—and sought to resituate humankind more intimately in the natural world, to affirm nature as the human home–place/s.

Like Western thought, the Christian tradition is complex and at times ambiguous in relation to home–place/s. On the one hand, the biblical narrative is usually grounded (literally) in specific, named places, and the theme of land is an undeniably powerful and central motif in the Hebrew Bible (also, some argue, this is implicitly the case in the New Testament).[26] Yet this positive notion of home–places is potentially undermined by the scriptural narrative's concurrent theme of homelessness. It might be argued that the itinerant way of living which is often presented in the Pentateuch, as a human sojourn towards the Promised Land, might be understood as affirming the value of home–places, yet there remains a sense of spiritual homelessness in which Yahweh 'refuses to be bound by any geographical locale'.[27] In the latter parts of the Hebrew Bible from the exilic and post-exilic periods, mention of the land becomes less common, reflecting changed circumstances as the exiled nation is scattered, the connection with the land weakened, apocalyptic thought (in which the establishment of the kingdom of God involves the destruction of earthly kingdoms) becomes more prominent, and as urbanisation and Hellenisation increased.

The orientation away from land as a home–place becomes even stronger in the New Testament where the gospel narrative often seems to reject home–place and to valorise homelessness. Even though Jesus's actions and teachings are usually identified with particular regions or places in the Gospels, these are, arguably, subordinated to the transient nature of his mission, to negative (if somewhat enigmatic) statements about home–place and family, and especially to the explicit

---

25   Plumwood, *Environmental Culture*, 8.

26   Geoffrey Lilburne argues that the lives of Jesus and of the early Christian community were grounded in Jewish faith in which the concept of land was extremely significant. Geoffrey R. Lilburne, *A Sense of Place: A Christian Theology of the Land* (Nashville, TN: Abingdon, 1989), 53–54.

27   Belden Lane (1992) cited by John Inge, *A Christian Theology of Place: Explorations in Practical, Pastoral and Empirical Theology* (Farnham: Ashgate, 2003), 41.

association with homelessness in Matthew 8:20 and Luke 9:58. In some Gospel stories, such as that of the woman at the well (John 4:21–24), geographical location is specifically de-emphasised in favour of a symbolic meaning.[28] In other parts of the New Testament spiritual significance predominates over location: as John Inge has observed, in Paul 'any "geographical identity" became "subordinated to that of being in Christ"'.[29] In Acts and in the Epistles the theme of the geographical expansion of the Christian faith serves to exacerbate a valorisation of homelessness, a sense that the true human home is in an 'other' world. Some parts of the Christian tradition (such as doctrines associated with eschatology and the monastic mystical tradition) have emphasised the value of withdrawal from one's home–place as a vital part of the journey of spiritual growth.[30] H. Paul Santmire has demonstrated that, taken as a whole, Christian texts and traditions contain ecologically positive aspects along with ecologically negative ones, as well as many other aspects that are neither positive nor negative: Christianity is in many ways ambiguous in relation to the topic of home–place and in general to an ecological sensibility.[31]

The tendency for Christianity (and other religious traditions) to valorise homelessness has been identified as problematic by ecotheologians such as John Haught who argued that 'the single most problematic feature of the main religions is their dubious connection to the spirit of "cosmic homelessness"'.[32] For Haught, religions have often fostered the idea that humans 'do not really belong here in the cosmos or on the earth [and this] leads many devout people to regard the natural environment as something from which to disassociate themselves in the name of religious integrity'.[33] Similarly, Sallie McFague argues that 'Christians have often not been allowed to feel at home on the earth, convinced after centuries of emphasis on otherworldliness that they belong somewhere else—in heaven or another world'.[34] For Ernst Conradie, Christianity 'has been guilty of instigating, reinforcing and legitimising [an] alienation of human beings from the rest of the earth community'.[35] Christianity, then, has endorsed the idea that humankind is

---

28 Dorothy A. Lee, *The Symbolic Narrative of the Fourth Gospel: The Interplay of Form and Meaning* (Sheffield: Sheffield Academic Press, 1994), 83.
29 The thought of W. D. Davies summarised by Inge, *A Christian Theology of Place*, 48.
30 However, some types of mystical theology (e.g. Evelyn Underhill) see an important dimension of religious experience in its ability to translate into tangible, earthly ends.
31 H. Paul Santmire, *The Travail of Nature: The Ambiguous Ecological Promise of Christian Theology* (Minneapolis, MN: Fortress, 1985).
32 Haught, *The Promise of Nature*, 40.
33 Haught, *The Promise of Nature*, 40.
34 McFague, *The Body of God*, 102.
35 Ernst M. Conradie, *An Ecological Christian Anthropology: At Home on Earth?* (Aldershot: Ashgate, 2005), 26.

alone, separated from Earth; that our true home–place is in heaven and not here. Earth may be the place in which the non-human (flora and fauna, hills and seas) belongs, but we do not truly belong.

This critique from ecotheology undoubtedly has validity, but it highlights the central difficulty for ecotheological reflection on home–places which is that religious traditions are fundamentally oriented towards spirit or transcendence. As Leroy S. Rouner has said, 'The world's great religious traditions think of the self as not being at home in this world'.[36] Even in Confucianism in which the primary religious aim is 'humanness' it is an ultimately unattainable aim and remains a 'transcendent ideal'.[37] Within Christianity too, there is a deep sense that we ultimately belong in, with, or close to, the divine. Despite the fact of its difficult ecological implications, a certain degree of *spiritual* homelessness seems indispensable: as Leroy S. Rouner puts it, 'Christianity is blatantly nostalgic for this home where we have never been'. The yearning for a spiritual home–place is emphasised in highly varied parts of the Christian tradition, including mysticism and Protestantism, and dates back at least to Augustine's prayer that 'our hearts are restless till they find their rest in thee'.[38] Even prior to the Christian tradition it can be argued that in Plato 'the self is not at home in its present historical situation'.[39] While an ecological sensibility will inevitably focus on the biophysical Earth in general and on particular located earth–places, a background acknowledgement must be made that the concept of 'home–place' will always include not only the lived earthly places that we know but also the places that we know of only intuitively. John Haught acknowledges this and seeks to make a distinction between two types of homelessness—spiritual (the underlying sojourning, exilic character of religion) and cosmic (the ecologically problematic claim that we do not really belong on Earth and should distance ourselves from it).[40] For Haught it is possible to hold the two together. Therefore it is not necessary to:

> . . . simply abandon the disturbingly exciting ideas about the fundamental homelessness of our being. To do so would be a violation of some of the most sacred, and ultimately fulfilling, features of the traditions we have inherited . . . Ecological theology cannot be purchased at the price of this precious imperative . . . We can, at least in principle, preserve the lofty ideal of religious homelessness without

---

36 Leroy S. Rouner, ed. 'Home Is Where We've Never Been: Experience and Transcendence', in *The Longing for Home* (Notre Dame, IN: University of Notre Dame Press, 1996), 81.

37 Rouner, 'Home Is Where We've Never Been: Experience and Transcendence', 81.

38 Rouner, 'Home Is Where We've Never Been: Experience and Transcendence', 81.

39 Rouner, 'Home Is Where We've Never Been: Experience and Transcendence', 81.

40 Haught, *The Promise of Nature*, 40–41.

requiring the environmentally unhealthy conviction that we do not belong to the universe.[41]

In summary, the Christian and Western traditions articulate a complex and ambiguous relationship between humankind and their home–places. The distinction between spiritual and cosmic homelessness helps to avoid a one-sided ecological theology which ignores the spiritual foundation of the Christian tradition.

The Incarnation

It was previously argued that the problematic and contestable notion of cosmic homelessness relates to the concept of solastalgia, which is experienced by people in relation to the situation of the Earth as a whole and to the ecological change and decay that occurs in those places in which we feel that we belong. Cosmic homelessness and solastalgia can begin to be addressed by acknowledging that the ecological ambiguity expressed in Christian texts and traditions (noted earlier) in itself creates something of an open, potentially fruitful space within which the complex and rich Christian tradition can be explored for an understanding of home–places which resonates with an ecological sensibility.

One part of the tradition with the potential to bear fruit for exploration, retrieval and revision is the doctrine and event of the incarnation.[42] The incarnation is a good starting point for many kinds of theological discussions because the person and event of Jesus Christ occupies a normative and unifying position in Christian thought and practice. In conjunction with the doctrine of the Trinity with which it is so intricately connected, the incarnation makes a foundational statement about the meaning of Christianity and has been pivotal for Christian thought as it has developed over the centuries. Christianity may even be said to be: ' . . . the religion of the incarnation *par excellence*'.[43]

As well as being of central importance in the tradition, the incarnation is also rich in meaning for ecological theology. In the early decades of ecotheology the incarnation was a relatively neglected topic, largely because Christian thought had tended to express the doctrine exclusively in terms of God taking on *human* form, thereby affirming (explicitly or implicitly) a human-centredness

---

41 Haught, *The Promise of Nature*, 47.
42 The 'incarnation' is used in this chapter in its broader sense to refer to God's enfleshment in Jesus Christ, represented in the entire life, ministry, death and resurrection of Jesus.
43 McFague, *The Body of God*, 14.

(anthropocentrism[44]) which ecotheology has critiqued. In more recent decades ecologically sympathetic understandings of the incarnation have been articulated which avoid an anthropocentric stance and inherently affirm the notion of Earth as home–place. One of the most important of these emphases is the fleshly aspect of the incarnation.

Enfleshment is the root meaning of 'incarnation'. The anthropocentric assumption that divine enfleshment must automatically or exclusively be read as occurring in human flesh is contested, not by seeking to deny the obvious fact that Jesus was a human being, but by suggesting that fleshliness can be seen in broader, more-than-human categories, such as living being, vertebrate or mammal. The 'fleshly' aspect of the incarnation has ancient roots deriving from John 1:14 and patristic thought. Duncan Reid argues that the Johannine prologue 'together with the oblique reference to it in the Creed' sees the human being as part of, rather than the essence of, flesh or Earth.[45] A fleshly theology holds promise for ecological Christology because it situates humankind within the more-than-human earth community, emphasising the interconnectedness between humans and other entities and systems, a key affirmation for ecological discourse.[46]

Reid's understanding that 'flesh' implicitly extends beyond the human to include the animal kingdom has been extended to refer to all matter. For Ernst Conradie the incarnation serves to dignify all life and affirms 'the goodness and integrity of creation in time and space'.[47] This recognition takes the notion of the Word out of the category of a disconnected idea or a human construction and into a concrete message of God through Jesus Christ: 'The gospel can prove to be a liberating word only if the relationship between language and reality can be clarified in material, biological, ecological and Christological terms. Only then can the Word who became flesh allow all flesh to flourish'.[48]

---

44   'Anthropocentrism' is not used here in its philosophically 'trivial' or tautological sense, which claims that anything said or done by a human being is inevitably anthropocentric. Instead the term is used in the stronger sense of describing and critiquing a form of egocentrism or selfishness of a species, especially when it unquestioningly places human interests above the interests of the non-human other. Peter Singer's term 'speciesism' articulates the problematic nature of species-centredness rather effectively because it calls to mind the better-known terms 'sexism' and 'racism' which are already accepted and commonly used critical terms.

45   Duncan Reid, 'Enfleshing the Human: An Earth-Revealing, Earth-Healing Christology', in *Earth Revealing–Earth Healing: Ecology and Christian Theology*, ed. Denis Edwards (Collegeville, MN: Liturgical Press, 2001), 72.

46   The principle of interconnectedness is the second of six principles undergirding the Earth Bible Series. The Earth Bible Team, 'Guiding Ecojustice Principles', in *Readings from the Perspective of Earth*, ed. Norman C. Habel (Sheffield: Sheffield Academic Press, 2000), 44–46.

47   Conradie, *An Ecological Christian Anthropology*, 178.

48   Conradie, *An Ecological Christian Anthropology*, 178.

Between them, Reid and Conradie ascribe an inherent value to flesh and matter, implying a dignity not only to human beings but to the entire created world. The idea has been developed further by Niels Gregersen who echoes Reid and Conradie, noting that even though Paul says Christ was 'bearing human likeness',[49] the New Testament does not say that God became human but that he took on flesh.[50] In the person of Christ 'the divine Logos assumed the entire realm of humanity, biological existence, earth and soil'.[51] Jesus Christ reveals the divine Logos through and in himself, holding all things together '*within* the matrix of materiality that we share with other living beings'.[52] In Gregersen's theology the event of Jesus Christ occurs so profoundly within creation that a connection can be made between Jesus and the entire organic and inorganic world, a connection so profound that Gregersen draws on the concepts of deep ecology (humans are embedded within ecological systems) and deep history (which emphasises the things that we share with animals and plants) to coin the theological term 'Deep Incarnation'.[53] God's enfleshment in Christ is 'deep' because it is 'an incarnation into the very tissue of biological existence, and system of nature'.[54] All things participate in God, and God and the world are united in Christ, although they are not identified (as in pantheism): the triune God has a breadth that Gregersen calls a 'stretch', meaning that the Father is transcendent to creation, that the Son becomes flesh and that the Spirit vivifies.[55]

A deep incarnational approach revises human-centred understandings of Jesus's (and implicitly, our own) genealogies. Using a contemporary evolutionary understanding, Gregersen goes beyond Jesus's human genealogies that are presented by the Gospels of Matthew and Luke to note 'the ancestral bonds of Jesus with other creatures'.[56] The fleshly, deep incarnation approach invites human beings to move beyond the limitations of themselves as 'only' human and enables us to see ourselves in other more Earth-based categories: as animals, vertebrates, carbon, matter, etc. If the location (home–place) of divine embodiment is the entire

---

49 Phil 2:7.

50 Niels Henrik Gregersen, 'Christology', in *Systematic Theology and Climate Change: Ecumenical Perspectives*, eds. Michael S. Northcott and Peter M. Scott (London: Routledge, 2014), 45–46.

51 Gregersen, 'Christology', 45.

52 Gregersen, 'Christology', 36.

53 Gregersen, 'Christology', 40. The idea of deep incarnation has subsequently been developed by Elizabeth Johnson, Celia Deane-Drummond, Denis Edwards and others.

54 Niels Gregersen, 'The Cross of Christ in an Evolutionary World', *Dialog: A Journal of Theology* 40 (2001): 205.

55 But 'where the Son and the Spirit is, there is also the Father'. Gregersen, 'Christology', 38.

56 Gregersen, 'Christology', 39.

more-than-human Earth then a higher status can be attributed to all of matter, to the entire biophysical world. Although this idea has a new dimension to the extent that it utilises ecological and evolutionary understandings, it also has ancient trajectories, which are especially familiar to the Eastern Orthodox tradition, for example, in John of Damascus's claim that matter must be honoured 'because God has filled it with His grace and power'.[57]

The claim that God indwells matter is neither to be mistaken for a pantheist claim that it is the only place of divine indwelling, nor is it to claim that Earth is the only location in which human beings may long to have their home–places. As was discussed previously, the experience of transcendence in religious traditions is too deeply held and too widespread to entirely deny spiritual yearnings for a deeply-intuited 'place', that cannot be identified with a geographical location. But it does contest the idea of cosmic homelessness, that Earth is to be denied, rejected or resisted as our true home. It challenges the idea that we are merely sojourners on Earth ('Pilgrim through this barren land' as the well-known hymn has it). Despite instances in the Christian tradition where cosmic homelessness has been endorsed, the high status of earthly matter implied through the event and doctrine of the incarnation resonates with an ecological claim that the material world is to be honoured, respected and valued. It also resonates with the way that the biophysical occupies a highly significant place within the Christian narrative and tradition: the specific and tangible dimension of Christian sacraments; the biological aspect of the activities of healing and feeding which are seen so prominently in Jesus's ministry; the bodily death and resurrection of Jesus; and the motif of the church as the body of Christ.

To conclude, an ecotheology which emphasises the fleshly and material aspects of the incarnation coheres with an ecological ethos by challenging the idea of cosmic homelessness and reaffirming the value of Earth as the place of divine embodiment. In praxis terms, this means that a Christian might validly claim a theological basis for identifying with one or more home–places on Earth and make a theologically-grounded decision to live or work in a particular home–place, acknowledging and responding to the problem of 'solastalgia' and seeking to restore ecological health and stability through acts of ecological protection and restoration.

---

57 St John of Damascus, *On the Divine Images: Three Apologies against Those Who Attack the Divine Images*, trans. David Anderson (Crestwood, NY: St Vladimir's Seminary Press, 2000), 23.

BIBLIOGRAPHY

Affairs, New Mexico Museum of Space History: A Division of the New Mexico Department of Cultural. 'International Space Hall of Fame.' http://www.nmspacemuseum.org/halloffame/detail.php?id=45.

Albrecht, Glenn. 'Solastalgia: A New Concept in Health and Identity.' *PAN: Philosophy, Activism, Nature*, no. 3 (2005): 44–59.

Bouma-Prediger, Steven, and Brian J. Walsh. *Beyond Homelessness: Christian Faith in a Culture of Displacement*. Grand Rapids, MI: Eerdmans, 2008.

Cain, Clifford Chalmers. *An Ecological Theology: Reunderstanding Our Relation to Nature*. Vol. 98. Toronto Studies in Theology. Lewiston, Queenston and Lampeter: The Edwin Mellen Press, 2009.

Casey, Edward S. *Getting Back into Place: Toward a Renewed Understanding of the Place–World*. 2nd ed. Bloomington, IN: Indiana University Press, 1993.

Conradie, Ernst M. *An Ecological Christian Anthropology: At Home on Earth?* Aldershot: Ashgate, 2005.

Cresswell, Tim. *Place: A Short Introduction*. Malden, MA: Blackwell, 2004.

Damascus, St John of. *On the Divine Images: Three Apologies against Those Who Attack the Divine Images*. Translated by David Anderson. Crestwood, NY: St Vladimir's Seminary Press, 2000.

Gregersen, Niels. 'The Cross of Christ in an Evolutionary World.' *Dialog: A Journal of Theology* 40 (2001): 192–207.

Gregersen, Niels Henrik. 'Christology.' In *Systematic Theology and Climate Change: Ecumenical Perspectives*, edited by Michael S. Northcott and Peter M. Scott, 33–50. London: Routledge, 2014.

Haught, John F. *The Promise of Nature: Ecology and Cosmic Purpose*. New York and Mahwah, NJ: Paulist Press, 1993.

Inge, John. *A Christian Theology of Place: Explorations in Practical, Pastoral and Empirical Theology*. Farnham: Ashgate, 2003.

Kohák, Erazim. 'Of Dwelling and Wayfaring: A Quest for Metaphors.' In *The Longing for Home*, edited by Leroy S. Rouner, 30–46. Notre Dame, IN: University of Notre Dame Press, 1996.

Lee, Dorothy A. *The Symbolic Narrative of the Fourth Gospel: The Interplay of Form and Meaning*. Sheffield: Sheffield Academic Press, 1994.

Lilburne, Geoffrey R. *A Sense of Place: A Christian Theology of the Land*. Nashville, TN: Abingdon, 1989.

Mathews, Freya. *Reinhabiting Reality: Towards a Recovery of Culture*. Albany, NY: State University of New York Press, 2005.

McFague, Sallie. *The Body of God: An Ecological Theology*. Minneapolis, MN: Fortress, 1993.

Moxnes, Halvor. *Putting Jesus in His Place: A Radical Vision of Household and Kingdom*. Louisville, London: Westminster John Knox Press, 2003.

Northcott, Michael S. *Place, Ecology and the Sacred: The Moral Geography of Sustainable Communities*. London: Bloomsbury, 2015.

Plumwood, Val. *Environmental Culture: The Ecological Crisis of Reason*. London and New York: Routledge, 2002.

Reid, Duncan. 'Enfleshing the Human: An Earth-Revealing, Earth-Healing Christology.' In *Earth Revealing–Earth Healing: Ecology and Christian Theology*, edited by Denis Edwards, 69–84. Collegeville, MN: Liturgical Press, 2001.

Rouner, Leroy S. 'Home Is Where We've Never Been: Experience and Transcendence.' In *The Longing for Home*, edited by Leroy S. Rouner, 81–94. Notre Dame, IN: University of Notre Dame Press, 1996.

Santmire, H. Paul. *The Travail of Nature: The Ambiguous Ecological Promise of Christian Theology*. Minneapolis, MN: Fortress, 1985.

Team, The Earth Bible. 'Guiding Ecojustice Principles.' In *Readings from the Perspective of Earth*, edited by Norman C. Habel, 38–53. Sheffield: Sheffield Academic Press, 2000.

Whitehead, Alfred North. *Modes of Thought*. New York, NY: The Free Press, 1938.

Chapter 3

REIMAGINING HOME ECONOMICS: THE MISSIOLOGICAL IMPERATIVE OF EMBODIED ECONOMIC WITNESS IN TWENTY-FIRST-CENTURY AUSTRALIA

Jonathan Cornford[1]

In my first year of high school in the 1980s, Home Economics ('Home Ec') was a compulsory subject that everyone did for one semester. It involved us making a macramé owl, sewing a pencil case, cooking a meal of chicken chow mein and baking a chocolate cake. It was what was known amongst the students as a 'bludge subject'. As a fairly chauvinistic young male with an academic bent, Home Ec was a subject I held in low esteem, along with the girls (and it was only girls) who went on to choose it as an elective in the following years. (It didn't help that my chocolate cake, about which I was secretly quite excited, completely failed.) So, there is not a small amount of irony in the fact that I have now come to the conclusion that home economics is central to the reconciling of economics and ecology that lies at the heart of humanity's great challenge in the twenty-first century. More than that,

---

[1] Jonathan Cornford is the co-founder of Manna Gum, a ministry in 'good news economics'. Jonathan is a member of the Centre for Research in Religion and Social Policy (RASP) at the University of Divinity, Melbourne. He has a doctorate in political economy and is currently undertaking a doctorate in theology.

I have also come to the conclusion that a renewed practice of home economics is central to the health and witness of Christianity in Australia this century.

When forming any overall picture of the challenge of Christian witness within twenty-first-century Australia, two dimensions that must be central to consideration are, firstly, the role of consumer capitalism in shaping the social, economic, political, ecological and spiritual fabric of the nation; and secondly, by contrast, the increasing marginality of the Christian church. In this chapter, I argue that within a context of a destructive economics and cultural hostility, a reclaimed practice of *embodied economic witness* will be essential to the church's missiological effectiveness in twenty-first-century Australia. I further argue that the central site of such a witness must be the household and that a reimagined countercultural practice of household economics offers the possibility of a witness that integrates social justice and ecological concerns with evangelical possibility and political integrity.

Christian Witness in the Midst of Consumer Capitalism

The concrete tasks of Christian mission need to be elaborated in relation to the specific shape of the cultures and societies to which God's people are sent. The call to repentance (*metanoia*)—the renewal of one's mind—that is fundamental to Christian discipleship is, in the New Testament, inextricably linked to a necessary practice of social nonconformity. This is most pithily summed up by Paul in Romans 12:1–2. But it is an idea that is clearly present in most of the Pauline Epistles, as well as in some of the Pastoral Epistles (especially 1 Peter), and it is an idea that is central to the world-inverting teachings of Jesus.[2] More shall be said about the witness of social nonconformity later; for now it is enough to note that *cultural critique* is implicit to the performance of Christian witness.

How, then, do we understand the form of society and culture in twenty-first-century Australia? There are many frames that can and should be used; however, perhaps one of the most powerful descriptors comes through the frame of *consumer capitalism*. 'Capitalism' describes the mode of economic organisation within which, since the 'great transformation' of modernity,[3] society and culture has been embedded and shaped. It is a form of economic organisation founded on the goal of endless accumulation, which works through the process of the commodification of all things and is driven and disciplined by the engine of

---

[2] For a classic statement of this understanding, see John Howard Yoder, *The Politics of Jesus* (Grand Rapids, MI: Eerdmans, 1972), especially chapter 8.

[3] See Karl Polanyi, *The Great Transformation* (London: Beacon Press, 1963). For Polanyi, this took place in the eighteenth century; for many others the sixteenth century was the key moment.

competition.[4] 'Consumer capitalism' describes both the late modern variant of this form of economic organisation—in which the fate of the global economy has become staked to the ever-expanding high-consumption lifestyles of the top 20 percent of the world's population—as well as providing a sociological descriptor of deep significance. In this sense, 'consumerism' serves as a powerful placeholder for a series of beliefs, aspirations and behaviours which could be said to describe *the spirit* of our culture, whether we mean that in Weberian or Pauline terms.[5]

For Daniel Bell, capitalism is not so much a material order, but rather it 'has everything to do with spirit'.[6] He describes consumer capitalism as *an economy of desire*: it shapes our preferences about how life is ordered and to what particular ends or purposes this occurs.

> [C]apitalism is nothing less than a theological revolution, involving radical changes not only in the circulation of material things but also in the nature of desire and its relation to its supernatural (spiritual, theological) end.[7]

> Capitalism does not deny the spirit by grounding desire in the material but instead effects a horizontal displacement of desire by constantly misdirecting desire from its true (vertical) home in God, by means of the enchantments of consumerism.[8]

Consumer capitalism is predicated on societies and social groups with high purchasing power and therefore with high material standards of living. Australia's status as a nation with one of the highest material living standards in the world encapsulates a multiplicity of dimensions that need to be taken into consideration when we think about Christian witness within the Australian context. Here I will list four:

---

[4] See Immanuel Wallerstein, *Historical Capitalism* (London: Verso, 2014).

[5] Weber uses 'spirit' as a sociological descriptor to denote a collective ethic. Paul's usage of the term (for example, Eph 2:1–2) may be seen to include such a sociological understanding, but clearly goes much further. As Wink argues, it describes 'the invisible dominion or realm created by the sum of total choices'. That is, 'the spirit of the age' describes a dominating and oppressive force. Walter Wink, *Naming the Powers: The Language of Power in the New Testament* (Philadelphia: Fortress Press, 1984), 82–84.

[6] Daniel Bell, *The Economy of Desire: Christianity and Capitalism in a Postmodern World (The Church and Postmodern Culture)*, ed. James K. A. Smith (Grand Rapids, MI: Baker Publishing Group, 2012), 140.

[7] Bell, *The Economy of Desire*, 90.

[8] Bell, *The Economy of Desire*, 140.

Responsibility for Planetary Ecological Crisis

As one of the highest consuming, highest carbon-emitting and most wasteful nations on earth, Australians (along with all their English-speaking cousins) bear a greater share of responsibility for the planetary ecological crisis that is unfolding this century. The 2016 *Living Planet Report* estimates that whereas the planet can sustain 1.2 'global hectares'[9] of consumption per person, the average Australian requires over 7 global hectares to support their lifestyle.[10] The implications of this go far beyond questions of equity and justice: it is now widely recognised that we are in the midst of an anthropogenic mass extinction event that has also raised serious questions about the continued viability of current human population levels. If we believe, as Ellen Davis does, that the command of Genesis 2:15 to 'work and keep' the earth represents a deep and primary human vocation, then this situation represents a human failure of the most profound kind.[11]

Economic Inequality

There is a clear link between the ecological crisis and radical economic inequality. Australian lifestyles are predicated on a global economy that systematically funnels wealth upwards. Since 1988, 80 percent of world income growth has accrued to the wealthiest 10 percent on the planet, a category that includes around 8 out of 10 Australian income earners. The bottom half of the planet's population (3.6 billion people) received only 1 percent of that income growth.[12] The historic processes by which this global economic structure has eventuated are complex and contested, but the behaviour of mining companies or garment companies in the developing world nevertheless demonstrate that Western purchasing power is sustained and even extended by unjust and unscrupulous exertions of power.

---

9   A global hectare is a way of expressing ecological footprint and biocapacity in a productivity-adjusted hectare-equivalent unit. One global hectare represents a biologically productive hectare with world-average productivity.

10   'Living Planet Report 2016: Risk and Resilience in a New Era' (Gland, Switzerland: World Wildlife Fund, 2016), 74–80.

11   Ellen Davis, *Scripture, Culture, and Agriculture: An Agrarian Reading of the Bible* (Cambridge: Cambridge University Press, 2009), chapter 2.

12   Oxfam, 'An Economy for the 1%', in *Oxfam Briefing Paper* (Oxford: Oxfam, 2016), 8–9.

High Consumption Lifestyles

The work of people such as Oliver James[13] and Clive Hamilton[14] has long suggested that high 'affluenza' to describe the way in which high-income countries have become beset with a range of relational, social, psychological and physiological maladies that all have some traceable connection to our material mode of living. A striking factor of such analyses has been the diagnosis by non-Christian writers of a deep *spiritual malaise* at the heart of Western society.

Consumer Capitalism

Finally, as Vincent Miller[15] and William Cavanaugh[16] argue, consumer capitalism has had deeply negative implications for the shape of Christian faith in the societies where it has taken root, effectively co-opting 'God language' into structures of individual gratification. As R. H. Tawney noted early last century, Christian accommodation of capitalism has 'enthroned religion within the privacy of the individual soul, not without some sighs of sober satisfaction at its abdication from society'.[17] But when Christian faith becomes merely an accoutrement to a deeper hermeneutic of self it is not surprising that recent generations have increasingly found it to be easily *dispensable*.[18]

In summary, if Christian witness in Australia is to be the bearer of good news in any meaningful sense, it must take into account that the dominant mode of material life in Australia is unsustainable, unjust and unhealthy, and is a barrier to a relationship with God. More than that, we can say that consumer capitalism

---

13   Oliver James, *The Selfish Capitalist: Origins of Affluenza* (London: Vermilion, 2008).
14   Clive Hamilton and Richard Dennis, *Affluenza: When Too Much Is Never Enough* (Sydney: Allen and Unwin, 2005).
15   Vincent J. Miller, *Consuming Religion: Christian Faith and Practice in a Consumer Culture* (London: Bloomsbury, 2005).
16   William T. Cavanaugh, *Being Consumed: Economics and Christian Desire* (Grand Rapids: Eerdmans, 2008).
17   R. H. Tawney, *Religion and the Rise of Capitalism* (London: Verso, 1926 [2015]), 223.
18   One of the core findings of the 2007 *Spirit of Generation Y* study was the depth with which gen Y, irrespective of religious belief or unbelief, refracted all life questions through the lens of self—almost a hyperindividualism. Michael Mason, Andrew Singleton, and Ruth Webber, *The Spirit of Generation Y: Young People's Spirituality in a Changing Australia* (Melbourne: John Garratt Publishing, 2007). Voas and Crockett have calculated that Christian faith in the UK has 'a half-life of one generation'; that is, the transmission rate of Christian faith from parent to child is about 50 percent. David Voas and Alasdair Crockett, 'Religion in Britain: Neither Believing nor Belonging', *Sociology* 39, no. 11 (2005):12. One of the authors of the *Spirit of Generation Y* study has indicated to me that he believes transmission rates in Australia to be even lower (personal communication).

represents a fundamental disordering of human desire and human economies within the scheme of creation. Finally, if we are to comprehend the full significance of these statements, we must also take account of the fact that consumer capitalism, as the dominant mode of material life in Australia, describes the mode of living of most Australian Christians.

The Marginality of Christianity in Australia

How can Australian Christians possibly have anything to say into this culture? For the moment we will put aside the question of Christian complicity and concentrate on the question of the scope for influence. Consumer capitalism is a pervasive, all-encompassing force within Australian culture, whereas, in comparison, Australian Christianity seems almost irrelevant. The Census figures for Christian affiliation in Australia (52 percent in the recent census) are seriously flawed and it is surprising that they are still being used by serious commentators.[19] The findings of the market and social research firm, McCrindle, seem much closer to the mark, suggesting that the number of 'active practisers' of Christian faith in Australia is around 7 percent of the population.[20] If we read this figure in conjunction with Miller's diagnosis of widespread 'religious consumerism' *amongst regular church attenders*,[21] then this suggests that the number of Christians who are hearers (let alone bearers) of the countercultural and transformative implications of the kingdom of God is quite small.

Moreover, not only are Christians numerically marginal within Australian society, it seems clear that Christianity is becoming less and less welcome within the broader Australian culture. While it has long been known that Australia is one of the most secular nations in the world, as a specifically *post-Christian culture* it seems that there is particular animus that is reserved for Christianity amongst cultural elites. Revelations of child abuse and subsequent cover-up within churches, and the acrimonious debate on same-sex marriage, have only sharpened this cultural hostility. McCrindle's research has found that the single greatest repellent to investigating Christianity amongst Australians *is hearing from public figures* who are Christian.[22] All this suggests that, in the current atmosphere, the

---

19   Gareth Hutchens, 'Australian Census: Religious Affiliation Falls as Population Changes Rapidly', *The Guardian (Australian Edition)* (June 27, 2017).

20   'Faith and Belief in Australia: A National Study on Religion, Spirituality and Worldview Trends' (Sydney: McCrindle, 2017), 9.

21   Although there are real differences between the religious contexts of the US and Australia, there is no reason to think that the core sociological dynamic described by Miller is much different in Australia.

22   'Faith and Belief in Australia', 9.

public voice of the Christian church tends to detract from its witness. Given that Christian witness in the areas of social justice and moral issues, and even to some extent in evangelism, has largely been conceived in terms of the *public voice* of the church, this poses some problems.

James Hunter's striking diagnosis of the cultural influence of the highly organised, cashed-up and numerically weighty American evangelical movement seems doubly true for the much more marginal Australian church: 'the whole (in terms of its influence in the larger political economy of cultural production) is significantly less than the sum of its parts. And thus the idea that American Christianity could influence the larger culture in ways that are healthy and humane is, for the time being, doubtful'.[23]

Speaking publicly within this cultural context has other difficulties: Hunter draws on George Steiner's work to point out that the cultural fragmentation of postmodernity is resulting in a breakdown of the basic trust in the correlation between words and the world of reality. That is, it is becoming increasingly difficult for communication about anything to do with what is 'good' or 'right' to tap into a common understanding or shared commitment. Rather, such language is increasingly subject to the suspicion that it is merely the vehicle of a sectarian interest.[24]

Therefore, when thinking about the task of Christian witness in Australia, we need to face up to the marginality of the church's cultural location. This means taking account of the fact that, to a large extent, Christians have less and less cultural permission to speak, and that public speech is less and less an effective bearer of meaning. As the McCrindle research shows, the Australian public are sceptical about the substance of meaning behind such speech and political leaders have long understood that the proclamations of church leaders do not necessarily reflect the views of their membership.[25]

Viewed from both a sociological and theological perspective, it is arguable that the public voice of the church in Australia is a largely *disembodied voice*it lacks a body. This represents not only a serious missiological problem for Christianity in

---

[23] James Davison Hunter, *To Change the World: The Irony, Tragedy, and Possibility of Christianity in the Late Modern World* (Oxford: Oxford University Press, 2010), 92.

[24] Hunter, *To Change the World*, 205–9.

[25] We should not confuse the prominence of Christian faith for a number of recent Australian Prime Ministers (Rudd, Abbott, Morrison) with the political influence of church leadership. Geoffrey Robinson, 'Christianity Does Not Play a Significant Role in Australian Politics, But Cultural Conservatism Does', *The Conversation* (May 31, 2017), theconversation.com, accessed October 16, 2018; Muriel Porter, 'Catholic Bishops Speak Out—But Is Anyone Listening?', *The Conversation* (May 19, 2016), theconversation.com, accessed October 16, 2018.

Australia, but one that is also ecclesiological in nature. The central witness of the New Testament is that God's Word becomes flesh—it requires the particularity and substance of a whole life, including death and resurrection, to communicate into the mess and brokenness of humanity. The description of the Christian community as the body of Christ—that is, the corporate enfleshment of the spirit of Christ's ongoing work in the world—reflects the extension of God's incarnational method to the church. This is amplified in Paul's insistence in Romans 12 that 'faith in Christ' requires 'bodies'—our material existence—that are to be given as ongoing lived sacrifices.[26]

In missiological terms, then, this suggests that perhaps the church needs to become silent for a season and to put its body where its proclamation is. It could be interesting to consider what this might mean in the context of Australia's all-encompassing consumer capitalism. If consumer capitalism is 'bad news' for creation, for humanity and for ourselves, what might the good news of the kingdom of God *look like* in the midst of this?

Embodied Economic Witness

It seems logical that if bad news is being driven by a material culture then good news must reflect a rejection of that culture and the embodiment of an alternative material culture. When combined with the constraints placed on effective Christian speech, all this suggests that embodied economic witness will be central to the church's missiological effectiveness in the twenty-first century and may even be central to the survival of Christian faith.

What do I mean by embodied economic witness? Foregrounding the cultural marginality of the church in Australia helps to identify such a witness with the exilic vocation of the people of God, which is described in various places in the Bible. In particular, it brings to mind the apocalyptic discernment in Revelation 18 of the people of God as exiles in the midst of Babylon the Great, and the cry of the angel to 'Come out of her, my people, so that you do not take part in her sins'.[27] A number of commentators have highlighted the richness of economic language and imagery within Revelation, and that a significant portion of the sins attributed to Babylon and the beasts of chapter 13 are *economic sins*.[28] In an analysis that bears striking resonances to contemporary economic structures, Bauckham shows that the image of Babylon (Rome) as a harlot reveals that the

---

26   Rom 12:1.
27   Rev 18:4.
28   For example, Richard Bauckham, *The Climax of Prophecy: Studies on the Book of Revelation* (Edinburgh: T&T Clark, 1993), chapter 10; Wes Howard-Brook and Anthony Gwyther, *Unveiling Empire: Reading Revelation Then and Now* (New York: Orbis Books, 1999).

seductive attractions of her wealth and power, in combination with the ideological power of the claims of *pax Romana*, in fact obscure a fundamentally exploitative set of economic relations.[29] This suggests that imagery of coming out of the sins of Babylon involves, somehow, seeking to become disentangled from the economic injustices and dislocations upon which she is founded.

But the imagery of Revelation is the stark polarity of light and dark, and while providing powerful shock treatment for our consciousness, it offers little practical help in the complexity of a globalised consumer economy. Here, Jeremiah's letter to the exiles within the historical Babylon offers more guidance: in the midst of a culturally and religiously hostile involvement, God's people are enjoined to build homes, plant gardens, marry and have children, and in and through these disarmingly simple acts, to pray and work for the shalom of the city.[30] The image is one of witness through the practice of a wholesome, life-affirming materiality. Holding Revelation 18 and Jeremiah 29 together in tension, we might say, then, that embodied economic witness requires, as much as is possible, disentanglement from the sins of *an economic system* whose spiritual core is anti-Christ. But doing this requires that we partake in life-giving economic expressions within the actual social and economic communities that we find ourselves in.

In a similar vein, Luke Bretherton points out that Paul's advocacy of the life of the Spirit is actually an advocacy of 'true materiality': it stresses 'neither an ethereal, otherworldly life nor an interior realm of consciousness, but a whole pattern of life which is truly material, truly itself, human life as part of creation healed and fulfilled'.[31] Paul's letters demonstrate a consistent concern that every aspect of bodily life—eating, drinking, use of money, work, thought and conversation, sexual and political relations—be conformed to Christ. Central to this is the understanding that new life in Christ represents a healing, or a turning from the distorting influence of the 'deceitful desire' that rules the life of the flesh:

> The converse of Paul's division between the fleshly life and the Spirit empowered life is that the bodily life can either be a witness to or a witness against God. For Paul, there is a battle over the shape and pattern of bodily life. It is a battle fought between the false authorities or principalities and powers of this age and the true and good lordship of Jesus Christ.[32]

---

29 Bauckham, *The Climax of Prophecy: Studies on the Book of Revelation*, 345–50.
30 Jer 29:1–7.
31 Luke Bretherton, 'Mundane Holiness: The Theology and Spirituality of Everyday Life', in *Remembering Our Future: Explorations in Deep Church*, eds. Andrew Walker and Luke Bretherton (London: Paternoster, 2007), 234.
32 Bretherton, 'Mundane Holiness', 235.

Thus, the Spirit of Christ works to transform desire such that the practical outworking of a reordered desire begins to transform our everyday material lives. Bretherton refers to this as the witness of 'mundane holiness': it is the realm of the mundane and the ordinary that represents the primary arena of our transformative encounter with God.

Such mundane holiness reflects not only the working out of the content of salvation—the materialisation of salvation, if you like—but it is also a primary form of *evangelical communication* with the world. It is through the practice of a wholesome and life-giving materiality that enables others to *see* the goodness behind words and concepts that they are otherwise unable to *hear*. Therefore, the translation of Spirit into material life is not just a process of personal sanctification and healing, or an expression of right relationship with neighbours and creation (although it is certainly both these things). It is also intrinsically an act of *communication*—the Word becoming flesh. It should come as no surprise, then, that McCrindle's research finds that the single greatest attraction to exploring Christianity in Australia is 'observing people who live out a genuine faith'.[33]

What has here been described as the transformative effect of the spirit of Christ on persons, should be further understood as an *ecclesiological vocation*. Daniel Bell has argued that the church, when it is faithful, is an *alternative economy of desire*, equipped with a range of practices and institutions for healing the idolatrous desires fostered by capitalism.[34] For John Howard Yoder, the church represents a new social reality whose imitation of Christ is most fully expressed in its social nonconformity and its independence from 'the Powers'. For Yoder, it is not the *effectiveness* of the church in influencing culture and politics that makes it an agent of the kingdom, but rather its *faithfulness* to the way of Jesus. Alan Kreider has argued that it is precisely this everyday social nonconformity of the early church—its mundane holiness—that explains its evangelical success in the first three centuries, in spite of a broader cultural context that was overwhelmingly hostile to it. This evangelical potency was itself the result of the deep conversion that early Christians underwent:

> Their concern was to maintain and nurture the character of the community, in the face of a hostile surrounding society. Conversion, they believed, began less at the level of belief than at the level of lifestyle. Only a person who was willing to change his or her 'conduct and habits' was 'capable of hearing the word'.[35]

---

33 'Faith and Belief in Australia', 9.
34 Bell, *The Economy of Desire*, chapter 5.
35 Alan Kreider, *Worship and Evangelism in Pre-Christendom* (Cambridge: Grove Books, 1995), 22.

And yet, despite what seems a demanding ethic, or perhaps *because* of it, early Christianity was attractive to a surprising number of people. As Minucius Felix described in the third century, 'Beauty of life causes strangers to join the ranks . . . We do not talk about great things; we live them'.[36]

Reimagining Home Economics

The embodiment of God's Word into everyday economic life is therefore properly to be thought of as a *witness*: it is a testimony of God's rule on earth, as it is in heaven. But what could such an embodied economic witness look like within the primarily urban and suburban social geography of Australia? Perhaps it goes without saying that this subject needs to be the topic of sustained and ongoing discernment, conversation, action and reflection. In what follows I will offer a sketch of the shape that an economic witness might take.

Firstly, as discussed, if it is to be the witness of the Christian body then responsibility cannot lie with professional Christians; it must be dispersed throughout the membership of the church. This suggests that the key unit of such a witness is the Christian household. The household is the core locus of our everyday economic practice—the unit for which money is earned and the primary unit in which money is consumed in the form of food, shelter, energy, water and material resources. This means that the household is also the core site of our use and abuse of the earth. And perhaps, for these reasons and more, the household, and not the Christian gathering, is also the most important location where faith is enacted or denied in a thousand different ways every day.

Below are a list of movements that, within our current context of capitalist hyperconsumption, might characterise a Christian approach to household economics. Ideally, each one would be explicated from a basis within biblical theology in a way that demonstrates the intertwining of ecclesiological, soteriological and missiological concerns, but there is not the space here for that. Instead, let me simply list some principles underlying the movements described below:

1. A reverence and enjoyment of the goodness of creation.
2. The discernment and embodied rejection of idols.
3. The centrality of renunciation as the way to fullness of life within Christ: to gain life one must first lose one's life.
4. That newness of life within Christ can be *experienced* in a still-fallen world—that it is actually *good news* in the midst of the bad news of

---

36 Quoted in Kreider, *Worship and Evangelism in Pre-Christendom*, 19.

consumer capitalism—and because fullness of life is visible to the world, it is itself a vehicle of evangelism.
5. The movement towards restoration of a right relationship—with our neighbour and within creation—is not merely an ethical obligation but part of the joy of salvation.
6. The centrality of the call to *faithfulness* in Christian witness, even when to us it seems not to be effective in achieving broader social or political change.
7. The communion of love between God, humanity and creation is the purpose—the *telos*—that should guide all action.

With these principles in mind, we might say that a Christian approach to household economics within twenty-first-century Australia might look something like this:

Downshifting

Downshifting is the voluntary commitment to live on a lower income and to live a more frugal life as the single most effective way of reducing the material throughput of households. This might be achieved either through voluntary income caps while in the midst of higher paying employment (effectively giving away any income above a nominated level); by embracing the lower wages of a particular job or profession as part of one's fulfilment of vocation; or by undertaking less paid employment within the household.

Reassessment of Work

This involves a reassessment of the idea of a career, where paid work becomes viewed firstly as a means to supplying the (simply assessed) bodily needs of the household, and secondly, where possible, an opportunity for serving the world, rather than a vehicle for earning high incomes and aggrandising a sense of self-worth. A decision to reduce the overall amount of paid work of a household also represents a release of more time and human energy to other areas of meaningful, unpaid endeavour.

Reassessment of the Household

A much more positive reassessment of the household economy as a site of creativity, productivity and meaningful work is endorsed, including the renewal of the idea of marriage as a vocation of *shared work*.[37] This especially requires a stronger re-engagement of men in the various labours and productive pursuits of the household.

Responsible Consumption

The inclusion of a sophisticated and nuanced practice of responsible consumption, where, as much as is possible, acts of consumption endeavour to support and care for our neighbours and for creation, including a preparedness to pay a higher price where necessary. Of course, when combined with a decision to live on a lower income, the decision to pay more requires a preparedness to consume less of certain things.

Household Economics

A developing understanding and practice of household economics as a miniature *ecology* with a cycle of water, energy, nutrient and material that is located within a much greater ecological cycle. This requires that serious attention be given to waste and to a practice of maintenance and restoration that shows a greater reverence for the intrinsic value of all material goods.

Essentially, I am arguing that in an age of excess, Christians should be exemplars of *voluntary simplicity*. In the midst of an overwhelming culture of acquisition and gratification, such a way of life is a visible and provocative form of communication that reflects Cardinal Souhard's description of the Christian vocation: 'To be a witness does not consist in engaging in propaganda, nor even in stirring people up, but in being a living mystery. It means to live in such a way that one's life would not make sense if God did not exist'.[38] Such a way of life will inevitably provoke questioning from 'the watching world', and such questioning provides a basis for evangelical conversation where none previously existed, especially if, as I believe, it is a way of life that will be attractive to some of those seeking a way out of the alienation and nihilism of consumer capitalism. Even without explicit conversation, the way of life outlined above is likely to communicate something of the character of the Christian God much more effectively than the current public voice of the church.

---

37 See the writing of Wendell Berry as a particularly profound expositor of this idea, especially, Wendell Berry, 'The Body and the Earth', in *The Art of the Commonplace: The Agrarian Essays of Wendell Berry*, ed. Norman Wirzba (Washington DC: Shoemaker and Hoard, 2002).
38 Quoted in John Berkman, 'An Introduction to the Hauerwas Reader', in *The Hauerwas Reader*, eds. John Berkman and Michael Cartwright (Durham: Duke University Press, 2001), 6.

Of course, such a way of life will not be attractive to all, and it will provoke hostility and derision from some quarters because it is also implicitly a form of *political communication*. Even if it is never framed in the form of public or policy pronouncements—and given what I have said above about the public voice of the church, such a temptation should perhaps be resisted—a commitment to voluntary simplicity amongst Christians would expose the lie that sits at the heart of Australian party politics: that it is the fundamental responsibility of the government to deliver continually rising material standards of living.[39] It is this political commitment that underlies the failure of Australian governments on climate change.[40]

Nevertheless, although the terminology of voluntary simplicity has the advantage of rooting a contemporary approach to household economics in an ancient Christian practice, it belies the fact that there is an immense amount of complexity that underlies each of the movements advocated above. The complexities are related both to the difficulty in actualising them within the structure of a globalised consumer economy, and also in the diversity and particularity of personal circumstances that must be negotiated. The devil is in the detail.

The complexity of actualising such a movement underscores the importance of the church as a site of *formation* into an alternative social reality and practice; it is ultimately not something that is possible for isolated Christian households to achieve on their own. This means that the gathered practices of the Christian community—its prayers, worship, reading and exposition of the Bible, baptism, sharing of the Eucharist—should all be practices, at least according to James Hunter, that strengthen the membership to 'stand in a position of critical resistance to late modernity and its dominant institutions and carriers; institutions like modern capitalism [and] liberalism'.[41] This does not involve being anti-modern or pre-modern, 'but rather a commitment to the modern world in that it envisions it differently'.[42]

Moreover, Christian communities will need to become repositories of experience and wisdom in the complexities of an alternative practice of household economics. In effect, it is suggested that one of the tasks of the church in the twenty-first century will be to rebuild a corpus of economic casuistry that grapples with the details of embodying the gospel into our present economic realities: How can a practice of responsible consumption avoid becoming a new legalism? How

---

39 This has been amply attested by many political commentators. See, for example Clive Hamilton and Richard Denniss, *Affluenza: When Too Much Is Never Enough*, 133–39; George Megalogenis, *The Longest Decade* (Melbourne: Scribe, 2006).

40 This is well evident in Verity Burgmann and Hans Baer, *Climate Politics and the Climate Movement in Australia* (Melbourne: Melbourne University Publishing, 2014).

41 Hunter, *To Change the World*, 235.

42 Hunter, *To Change the World*, 235.

do we negotiate the use of financial institutions given their centrality in destructive economics? What should a Christian attitude to debt be, especially given the astronomical pricing of houses? What should our attitudes and practices as Christians be towards investment?[43] Throughout such a body of casuistry it would be important to continually stress that the goal is neither moral purity nor perfect consistency—both of which are unachievable—but rather the continual struggle to orient one's self to the communion of love amidst the mess and complexity of a fallen world.

Conclusion

Thus, economic witness requires a transformative reimagining of household economics, where the Christian *oikos*—formed, located and joined within the wider *oikos* of God—is a site in which we strive for some reconciliation of the human *oikonomia* (economy) of production and consumption within the limits of the *oikologia* (ecology) of creation. In this sense, household economics is a primary field for the practise of shalom. Instead of being a form of works-based righteousness, it should be motivated by a vision of the fullness of life that accompanies the turning away from the idolatrous desires of consumer gratification and a turning into the communion of love that constitutes salvation. Rather than a gnostic flight from the material, it would reflect a healed materiality that can more fully appreciate the manifold goodness of creation, such that the truth of the third beatitude would be visibly apparent: (in the J. B. Phillip's rendering) 'Happy are those who claim nothing, for the whole earth will belong to them!'.[44]

In summary, a practice of household economics along the lines described above is a movement in the direction of disentanglement from the multifarious destructive predilections of consumer capitalism. It represents a movement towards a lower ecological footprint, a recognition of relationship with distant producers, a greater valuing and space for care and nurture within the household, a more cooperative and fulfilling structure to household life and relationships, and an opportunity to invest more *time* in acts of healing and grace in the world. Not only is such a practice of household economics an attempt to embody concerns for

---

43   R. H. Tawney has described how one of the casualties of the Reformation was the loss of the medieval church's large body of casuistry that provided detailed guidance in matters of economic ethics. Tawney, a Christian Socialist, called for the development of a new body of Christian economic casuistry. R. H. Tawney, *The Acquisitive Society* (Brighton: Wheatsheaf Books, 1921), 188–89. I have undertaken something of an attempt at such a casuistry in seven areas: work and leisure; consumption; sustainability; giving; savings and investment; debt; and hospitality. See Jonathan Cornford, *Coming Home: Towards a Christian Practice of Household Economics* (Morningstar Publications: Melbourne, forthcoming 2019).

44   Matt 5:5 (J. B. Phillips).

justice and ecology, it provides a visible and material foundation in support of the political advocacy that is required on issues such as climate change. But even more than that, I am convinced that it offers a site for a more abundant form of living than is possible in a glutted culture of overconsumption, and that this is something that will hold great evangelical appeal. As the apocryphal quote attributed to St. Francis says: 'Preach the gospel at all times, and, if necessary, use words'.

BIBLIOGRAPHY

Bauckham, Richard. *The Climax of Prophecy: Studies on the Book of Revelation.* Edinburgh: T&T Clark, 1993.

Bell, Daniel. *The Economy of Desire: Christianity and Capitalism in a Postmodern World* (*The Church and Postmodern Culture*), edited by James K. A. Smith. Grand Rapids, MI: Baker Publishing Group, 2012.

Berkman, John. 'An Introduction to the Hauerwas Reader.' In *The Hauerwas Reader*, edited by John Berkman and Michael Cartwright. Durham: Duke University Press, 2001.

Berry, Wendell. 'The Body and the Earth.' In *The Art of the Commonplace: The Agrarian Essays of Wendell Berry*, edited by Norman Wirzba, 93–134. Washington DC: Shoemaker and Hoard, 2002.

Bretherton, Luke. 'Mundane Holiness: The Theology and Spirituality of Everyday Life.' In *Remembering Our Future: Explorations in Deep Church*, edited by Andrew Walker and Luke Bretherton. London: Paternoster, 2007.

Burgmann, Verity, and Hans Baer. *Climate Politics and the Climate Movement in Australia.* Melbourne: Melbourne University Publishing, 2014.

Cavanaugh, William T. *Being Consumed: Economics and Christian Desire.* Grand Rapids: Eerdmans, 2008.

Davis, Ellen. *Scripture, Culture, and Agriculture: An Agrarian Reading of the Bible.* Cambridge: Cambridge University Press, 2009.

'An Economy for the 1%.' In *Oxfam Briefing Paper*. Oxford: Oxfam, 2016.

'Faith and Belief in Australia: A National Study on Religion, Spirituality and Worldview Trends.' Sydney: McCrindle, 2017.

Hamilton, Clive, and Richard Denniss. *Affluenza: When Too Much Is Never Enough.* Sydney: Allen and Unwin, 2005.

Howard-Brook, Wes, and Anthony Gwyther. *Unveiling Empire: Reading Revelation Then and Now.* New York: Orbis Books, 1999.

Hunter, James Davison. *To Change the World: The Irony, Tragedy, and Possibility of Christianity in the Late Modern World.* Oxford: Oxford University Press, 2010.

Hutchens, Gareth. 'Australian Census: Religious Affiliation Falls as Population Changes Rapidly.' *The Guardian (Australian Edition)*, 27 June 2017.

James, Oliver. *The Selfish Capitalist: Origins of Affluenza.* London: Vermilion, 2008.

Kreider, Alan. *Worship and Evangelism in Pre-Christendom.* Cambridge: Grove Books, 1995.

'Living Planet Report 2016: Risk and Resilience in a New Era.' Gland, Switzerland: World Wildlife Fund, 2016.

Mason, Michael, Andrew Singleton, and Ruth Webber. *The Spirit of Generation Y: Young People's Spirituality in a Changing Australia.* Melbourne: John Garratt Publishing, 2007.

Megalogenis, George. *The Longest Decade.* Melbourne: Scribe, 2006.

Miller, Vincent J. *Consuming Religion: Christian Faith and Practice in a Consumer Culture.* London: Bloomsbury, 2005.

Polanyi, Karl. *The Great Transformation*. London: Beacon Press, 1963.

Porter, Muriel. 'Catholic Bishops Speak Out—But Is Anyone Listening?' *The Conversation*. theconversation.com. Accessed October 16, 2018.

Robinson, Geoffrey. 'Christianity Does Not Play a Significant Role in Australian Politics, but Cultural Conservatism Does.' *The Conversation*. theconversation.com. Accessed October 16, 2018.

Tawney, R. H. *The Acquisitive Society*. Brighton: Wheatsheaf Books, 1921.

Tawney, R. H. *Religion and the Rise of Capitalism*. London: Verso, 1926 (2015).

Voas, David, and Alasdair Crockett. 'Religion in Britain: Neither Believing nor Belonging.' *Sociology* 39, no. 11 (2005).

Wallerstein, Immanuel. *Historical Capitalism*. London: Verso, 2014.

Wink, Walter. *Naming the Powers: The Language of Power in the New Testament*. Philadelphia: Fortress Press, 1984.

Yoder, John Howard. *The Politics of Jesus*. Grand Rapids, MI: Eerdmans, 1972.

Chapter 4

HOME AND HOMELESSNESS IN THE ANTHROPOCENE

Mick Pope

We live in a new geological age, the Anthropocene. We are at risk of becoming homeless due to our disruptive impact upon the earth. The biblical story is one of home and homelessness, from the expulsion from home in Genesis 2–4 to our new home described in Romans 8. In this chapter, I explore how the framework of Genesis 2–4 applies to mission in today's world as the Anthropocene unfolds. How have our actions abrogated the divine command to care for the earth? How do we understand the present crisis as our expulsion from the divine presence, and how do we make our home once more with God in our disrupted world?

The Anthropocene

Human influence on the earth has been so profound that a new geological epoch has been suggested: the Anthropocene.[1] While the definition of the Anthropocene has been debated, the most likely starting date is the period known as the 'Great Acceleration'.[2] This period is characterised by an increase in socio-economic trends such as rapid population growth, energy use and fertiliser consumption. The

---

1   Paul Crutzen, 'Geology of Mankind', *Nature* 415 (2002): 23.
2   Will Steffen et al., 'The Trajectory of the Anthropocene: The Great Acceleration', *The Anthropocene Review* 2 (2015): 1–18.

Great Acceleration is also marked by an increase in the human impact on the earth, including a rapid increase in greenhouse gas emissions, surface temperatures, ocean acidification, marine fish capture and extensive land clearing. The state of the earth as a whole can be quantified by nine planetary boundaries, which represent a safe operating space for humanity. It is estimated that we are disrupting seven of these boundaries, threatening our own existence.[3]

While Clive Hamilton is insistent that the Anthropocene represents a break with the past, requiring a new science to describe and explain it, the Anthropocene does not appear *ex nihilo* from history.[4] Lewis and Maslin have shown that the modern Anthropocene was preceded by a series of events of escalating scale and impact on the planet. The first was the Pleistocene extinctions of megafauna as humans migrated around the globe. The second, with its extensive land clearing and emissions in carbon dioxide and methane, was the origins of and intensification of farming. The third event was the European invasion of the Americas and the deaths of up to fifty million people due to European diseases, war, enslavement and famine. The resultant deaths produced a measurable drop in global carbon dioxide concentrations due to the collapse of agriculture. The last event was the beginning of the Industrial Revolution in 1760.[5] Even allowing for the Anthropocene beginning at a very early date, the Great Acceleration is fundamentally different to preceding stages, and may be referred to as the hyper-Anthropocene.[6] Hence, the Anthropocene and its antecedents are associated with changes in human interactions with the environment and the impacts upon humans themselves. This includes both the improvement of the human condition, albeit unevenly distributed, and our damage of and alienation from the rest of creation. Aspects of this process of damage and alienation will be examined below.

What does it mean to think about the Anthropocene missionally? Clive Hamilton observes that 'belonging to a certain cultural or religious group does not exempt one from what is happening on Anthropocene Earth'.[7] Missiology usually engages in contextualisation, focusing on local cultures, language groups and physical environments. What Hamilton makes clear for the missiologist is that there is a global context which we must all consider, that of the Anthropocene. While there may be local manifestations of this, no one group is immune from its

---

3 Will Steffen et al., 'Planetary Boundaries: Guiding Human Development on a Changing Planet', *Science* 347 (2015): 1–17.
4 Clive Hamilton, *Defiant Earth* (Melbourne: Allen and Unwin, 2017).
5 Simon L. Lewis and Mark A. Maslin, 'Defining the Anthropocene', *Nature* 519 (2015): 171–80.
6 James Hansen et al., 'Ice Melt, Sea Level Rise and Superstorms: Evidence from Paleoclimate Data, Climate Modeling, and Modern Observations that 2°C Global Warming is Highly Dangerous', *Atmospheric Chemistry and Physics Discussions* 15 (2015): 20059–179.
7 Hamilton, *Defiant Earth*, 38.

effects. One globally shared feature is that of homelessness, or the alienation from one place and the quest for a new home. Urbanisation represents the movement of people from rural to urban areas, including the urban development of formerly rural areas, or urban sprawl. In 2008, urbanisation reached 50 percent, i.e. as many people living in urban areas as in rural areas. If the current trend continues, more urban areas will be built between 2100 and 2130 than in all previous history, mostly driven by Asia and Africa.[8] The dynamics of urbanisation are complex, with factors including international capital flows, the informal economy, land use policy and generalised transport costs.[9] Increasingly, though, urbanisation and transnational migration are occurring due to climate change. In this latter sense, homelessness means that the local meets the global and then our local area, as people reach our borders. It is to this topic that we now turn.

Climate Change and Human Displacement

Linking climate change to forced migration and the conflict that drives it can be contentious, as the connections are often poorly understood and context specific.[10] A recent example of a complex situation involving climate change is the Syrian crisis.[11] Drought is not unknown in Syria and due to the low annual rainfall, and to the political tensions that exist with other countries over shared rivers, Syria is considered to be 'water scarce'.[12] Population growth and an inefficient use of flood irrigation has further stressed water supplies. From 2006 to 2011, Syria suffered a prolonged drought which has been described as the 'worst long-term drought and most severe set of crop failures since agricultural civilizations began in the Fertile Crescent many millennia ago'.[13] It is claimed that this drought resulted in agricultural failures, disruptions to the economy and population displacement of more than 1.5 million people from rural to urban areas. Suzanne Saleeby concludes that 'the regime's failure to put in place economic measures to alleviate the effects

---

8   Steffen et al, *The Great Acceleration*.

9   Karen C. Seto et al., 'A Meta-Analysis of Global Urban Land Expansion', *PLOS One* 6 (2011): e23777.

10 Michael Brzoska and Christiane Fröhlich, 'Climate Change, Migration and Violent Conflict: Vulnerabilities, Pathways and Adaptation Strategies', *Migration and Development* 5, no. 2 (2016): 190–210.

11 See for example, Mick Pope, *A Climate of Justice: Loving Your Neighbour in a Warming World* (Melbourne: Morning Star Publishing, 2017), chapter 4.

12 Water scarcity is the lack of sufficient available water resources to meet the demands of water usage.

13 Francesco Femia and Caitlin Werrell, 'Syria: Climate Change, Drought and Social Unrest', *The Center for Climate and Security* (February 29, 2012), https://climateandsecurity.org/2012/02/29/syria-climate-change-drought-and-social-unrest/.

of drought was a critical driver in propelling such massive mobilizations of dissent'.[14] In other words, drought was not the sole factor, but it was magnified by poor governance and planning, together with the high dependence on agriculture of those who were displaced. While this connection to climate is still being contested, a decrease in wintertime Mediterranean rainfall has likely occurred whose magnitude cannot be explained by natural changes. A connection between storm tracks over the Mediterranean and Indian Ocean temperatures has been suggested.[15]

In the Indian state of Assam, climate change has been linked to internal displacement related to the increase in flooding. River flows are driven by monsoonal rainfall and the seasonal melting of Himalayan glaciers upstream. Very heavy rainfall can cause the rivers to break their banks, and with climate change affecting the monsoon, causing rainfall to become more variable, there is a risk of this occurring. There is also more river flow during summer as rising temperatures in the Himalayas causes the melting of snow and ice. Floods destroy crops, houses and roads, and drown cattle. Damage caused to crop lands can be irreversible due to heavy silt deposits and salt deposition. Variable monsoonal rainfall also impacts crop yields, which have decreased with decreasing rainfall. Migration within India is a response to these changes, as males move to other districts to obtain jobs as semi-skilled workers, while the females tend to stay behind to care for the children and for the elderly. When this type of displacement happens, women are vulnerable to trafficking regardless of whether they migrate or stay behind.[16]

While flooding or drought can produce displacement, so can extremes of heat. A 2014 paper in the journal *Nature Climate Change* suggested that it was heat stress rather than flooding that most strongly correlated with migration in Pakistan. Uncharacteristically high temperatures reduce population wellbeing by lowering agricultural yields. Agricultural income suffers tremendously when temperatures are extremely high, wiping out over a third of farming income. The early maturity of wheat grains due to heat stress reduced Pakistani wheat yields by 13 percent in 2010. For the poor, the migration benefits following heat stress outweigh the moving costs, as they are not tied to land or assets which can be hard to sell.

---

14   Suzanne Saleeby, 'Sowing the Seeds of Dissent: Economic Grievances and the Syrian Social Contract's Unravelling', *Yadaliyya* (February 16, 2012), http://www.jadaliyya.com/pages/index/4383/sowing-the-seeds-of-dissent_economic-grievances-an.

15   Martin Hoerling et al., 'On the Increased Frequency of Mediterranean Drought', *Journal of Climate* 25 (2012): 2146–61.

16   Manipadma Jena, 'Women Bear the Brunt of Climate-Forced Migration', *India Climate Dialogue* (January 4, 2017), http://indiaclimatedialogue.net/2017/01/04/women-bear-brunt-climate-forced-migration/.

The risk of a male moving out of the village is eleven times more likely when temperatures are in the highest quartile.[17]

One of the clearest signs of the connection between migration and climate change, and in particular the need for permanent external migration, is sea level rise in Oceania (the Pacific). At only 1.5 metres above sea level at their highest point, the Carteret Islands are some of the first to succumb to the rising ocean tides. Here, as in many parts of Oceania, the sea is literally eating the ground.[18] In 1995, a storm surge cut one of the islands in half and the inundations left behind water for malaria-carrying mosquitos to breed. Storm surges associated with intense low pressure systems and tropical cyclones have washed away houses and vegetable gardens. With no cash economy on the Carterets, the only source of food is what people can grow for themselves. There are currently plans by the Carteret based group *Tulele Peisa* to relocate more than half of the population by 2020.

Sea level rise presents a large existential threat given the large percentage of the global population living within a few metres of sea level. By the end of the century, the Fifth Assessment Report of the Intergovernmental Panel on Climate Change expects sea level rise of somewhere between a half to one metre. More recent research suggests that this is an underestimate. A recent paper by James Hansen could not conclude with certainty that an increase in the temperature of the world of two degrees would produce multi-metre sea level rise. However, it did point out that the paleo climate record shows that during the Eemian, a period from 130,000 to 115,000 years ago when temperatures were not much warmer than the present, sea level reached six to nine metres above the present. Elevated temperatures persist for centuries, even for modest rises above pre-industrial values, providing enough time to melt the world's ice sheets.[19]

Solastalgia

Walter Brueggemann has observed that Western culture has 'a sense of being lost, displaced, and homeless'.[20] This sense does not imply that Western people are

---

17   Valerie Mueller, Clark Gray, and Katrina Kosec, 'Heat Stress Increases Long-Term Human Migration in Rural Pakistan', *Nature Climate Change* 4 (2014): 182–85.

18   The quote 'the sea is eating the ground' is from Simon Nazer, 'The Last Islanders: Rising Sea Levels in Papua New Guinea', UN Children's Fund (March 22, 2017), http://reliefweb.int/report/papua-new-guinea/last-islanders-rising-sea-levels-papua-new-guinea. For a theological reflection on this, see Mick Pope, 'The Sea is Eating the Ground: A Theology of Sea Level Rise', *Anglican Theological Review* 100, no. 1 (Winter 2018): 79–92.

19   James Hansen et al., 'Ice Melt, Sea Level Rise and Superstorms', *Atmospheric Chemistry and Physics* 16 (2016): 3761–812.

20   Walter Brueggemann, *The Land* (Philadelphia: Fortress Press, 1977), 1.

literally homeless, but that they feel placeless. However, a sense of impending homelessness is very real for the people of Oceania, where sea level rise threatens the future of entire nations. Consider for example, Tuvalu, a nation comprising of twenty-six square kilometres of coral islands and atolls with an average height above sea level of less than two metres. It is one of many nations threatened by rising sea levels. Like many, the threat of moving is not merely a physical issue of losing a home, but a matter of identity. As one Tuvaluan observes, 'Moving away from Tuvalu is not good for our culture and values. We want to live in our own land, our home, and where our forefathers have lived. Tuvaluan people don't like to be called refugees'. Note the connection between culture and place, but also between place and forefathers, i.e. a connection in time and space. Culture and values are shaped by a continuity with the past, and by a connection with the rest of creation. It is only Western culture that seeks to separate itself from its environment, producing the lostness Brueggemann writes of. For many in Oceania, this connection between place and values is also deeply theological; 'We don't want to leave this place . . . it's our land, our God-given land, it is our culture, we can't leave. People won't leave until the very last minute'.[21]

Similar feelings are expressed by Torres Strait Islander peoples. Joseph Elu, chairman of the Torres Strait Regional Authority (TSRA) understands the threat of rising sea level for the islands of the Torres Strait. The people of the region are not facing this threat helplessly, and the TSRA has been instrumental in contributing to plans to build adaptive capacity and resilience in the region. However, even he concedes that 'the last option I suppose is relocation but most of the island people don't want to do that'.[22] The attitude of Saibai elder Mebai Warusam is typical of those who do not wish to move: 'I will never move from this island. I will jump on my boat, tie that rope on a wongai tree. I will live here; I will die here'.[23] As with Tuvalu, migration may be a matter of physical survival, but it is at the expense of culture. As Elaine Kelley observes, 'the material damages expose a deeper and more profound cultural impact for Islander communities. The line

---

21 Friends of the Earth International, *Climate Change: Voices from Communities Affected by Climate Change* (Amsterdam: Friends of the Earth, 2007).

22 Nance Huxton, 'Calls for Detailed Climate Change Plan for Torres Strait Islands amid Projected Sea Level Rises', *ABC News* (January 5, 2015), http://www.abc.net.au/news/2015-01-05/call-for-torres-strait-climate-change-plan/6000646.

23 Saila Huusko, 'We're Sinking Here: Climate Change Laps at Front Door of Torres Strait Islands', *The Guardian* (December 8, 2016), https://www.theguardian.com/australia-news/2015/dec/08/were-sinking-here-climate-change-laps-at-front-door-of-torres-strait-islands.

between adapting and enduring loss is blurred in this situation, revealing a deeply troubling limit to adaptation'.[24]

The relationship between ecosystem distress and human distress has been termed 'solastalgia' by environmental philosopher Glenn Albrecht. Solastalgia is the concept of being homesick while still being at home[25] and it combines the ideas of solace and nostalgia.[26] Nostalgia was once linked to a diagnosable sickness associated with the homesickness people feel when distant from their homes. In modern usage nostalgia is more often associated with a fondness for a period in the past, a golden age where a person felt more culturally at home. Albrecht equates nostalgia not simply with a lost time, but also with a lost place, what one researcher describes as 'place pathology'. Such pathology has been identified among the Navajo in the US due to their displacement by Europeans, but it has also been observed among Europeans themselves in the US. Place pathology also occurs when people have lost their homes to natural disasters such as Cyclone Tracy in Darwin, 1974, or to flooding due to the building of dams.

However, Albrecht has also observed solastalgia in people who are still living at home but who are distressed by the changes that have been made to their home. These changes mean that people are unable to draw comfort or solace from being at home. Hence, Albrecht defines solastalgia as 'the pain or sickness caused by the loss or lack of solace and the sense of isolation connected to the present state of one's home and territory'. This lack of solace is caused by the recognition that the place one loves is under attack. Albrecht notes that the causes of solastalgia are varied: 'Drought, fire and flood can cause solastalgia, as can war, terrorism, land clearing, mining, rapid institutional change and the gentrification of older parts of cities'. Two examples Albrecht has examined are the impacts of open cut coal mining in the upper Hunter Valley of New South Wales and the environmental impacts of drought and its subsequent impacts on farmers in regions like the Western Australian Wheat Belt. Clearly climate change and associated impacts such as sea level rise and the threat of future dislocation also fall under this category.

Albrecht also notes that the concept of home can be expanded in an age of media and IT globalisation. We are now able to see in real time the impacts of humans on the planet, whether it is the disasters related to climate change or the

---

24 Elaine Kelly, 'Rising Seas Pose a Cultural Threat to Australia's "Forgotten People"', *The Conversation* (November 27, 2014), http://theconversation.com/rising-seas-pose-a-cultural-threat-to-australias-forgotten-people-34359.

25 Glenn Albrecht, 'The Age of Solastalgia', *The Conversation* (August 7, 2012), accessed June 3, 2017, https://theconversation.com/the-age-of-solastalgia-8337.

26 Glenn Albrecht, '"Solastalgia." A New Concept in Health and Identity', *PAN: Philosophy, Activism, Nature* 3 (2005): 44–59.

clearing of the Amazon Rainforest. Hence, Albrecht suggests that solastalgia is 'now possible for people who strongly empathise with the idea that the earth is their home and that witnessing events destroying endemic place identity (cultural and biological diversity) at any place on earth are personally distressing to them'. The rest of the chapter will address this issue of globalised solastalgia by firstly examining a biblical theology of home and homelessness and then by giving some brief suggestions on the shape of mission in the Anthropocene, particularly for an Australian context.

Home and Homelessness in Genesis

The theme of home and homelessness is pervasive throughout Scripture. Cynthia Edenburg identifies Genesis 2–4 as a literary unit that is post-exilic, and therefore has Israel's history, not some general history of the world, in its sights.[27] The parallels between the account of the man and woman in Genesis 2–3, and of Cain in Genesis 4 are shown in the table below. Edenburg suggests that the point of both these stories is that 'exile and alienation from YHWH is the inevitable consequence of violating YHWH's commandments and of failure to maintain essential social norms'. The divine command in Genesis 2 and 3 is explicitly not to eat of the tree. In Genesis 4, the test appears more arbitrary and Cain's sin is the abrogation of social norms in his act of fratricide.

	Gen 3	Gen 4
Divine command or warning	2:17, 3:1–5	4:6–7
Command abrogated	3:6–7	4:8
Confrontation and interrogation	3:9–13	4:9–10
Denial of guilt	3:12–13	4:9–10
Judgement and punishment	3:14–19	4:10–12
Break with land	3:18	4:12
Care for the transgressor	3:21	4:13–15
Expulsion east of Eden	3:23–24	4:16

Table 1: Parallels between Genesis 2–3 and Genesis 4 according to Cynthia Edenburg

---

27   Cynthia Edenburg, 'From Eden to Babylon: Reading Genesis 2–4 as a Paradigmatic Narrative', in *Pentateuch, Hexateuch, or Enneateuch : Identifying Literary Works in Genesis through Kings*, eds. Thomas B. Dozeman, Thomas Römer, and Konrad Schmid (Atlanta: Society of Biblical Literature, 2011): 155–67.

Identifying Genesis 2–4 as a post-exilic addition raises the issue of what the appropriate *inclusio* is for rounding off the literary unit. One possibility is 2 Kings 25:21, where Judah is exiled from the land. Another is Deuteronomy 30:15–20, where the threat of future exile is presented. Israel is given the choice between good and evil, life and death, dwelling in the land or exile. A third choice is Leviticus 26, with which Genesis 2–4 shares phrases and motifs. Ultimately, Edenburg observes that frames are constructed both by readers and authors. Edenburg's main point stands regardless, that Israel's history is marked by exile and alienation due to abrogating divine commands and social norms. Making Genesis 2–4 postexilic means that it is focused on Israel and not on world history. This might seem to make it difficult to apply its ideas of alienation to the contemporary issue of the Anthropocene. However, as Edenburg comments, when framing is thematic it can be more arbitrary. Ultimately, an eschatological and christological frame will be applied here.

Walter Brueggemann sees land as a central idea of Scripture, with land considered as place rather than space. For Brueggemann, space is often an assertion of independence and autonomy or freedom. Instead, place is space that has historical meanings and which provides community across the nations.[28] We saw this earlier in the understanding of the Tuvaluan's connection to their islands. Place is also space that embodies identity, vocation and the destiny of a group of people. This is seen clearly in the Abrahamic call of Genesis 12:1–3, where Abram's identity was to be the father of a great people in the place that YHWH would show him, whose vocation was to be a blessing to the nations and whose destiny was to be blessed. In grounding us (pun intended), 'place is indeed a protest against the unpromising pursuit of space. It is a declaration that our humanness cannot be found in escape, detachment, absence of commitment, and undefined freedom'.[29] As we shall argue below, it is this escape into undefined freedom which has led to the displacement of many and threatens the displacement of us all.

As far as Israel and the land is concerned, Brueggemann sees two stories in tension in Genesis. The first is the story of a landed people headed toward expulsion. We've already seen this in Genesis 2–4, but it continues through chapters 5–11, as escalating violence leads to the flood. The flood is an act of uncreation, undoing the ordering of chaos in Genesis 1, the setting of a homeless humanity adrift in the ark. The journey from landedness to landlessness in the first chapters of Genesis models the experience of Israel in the land during the monarchic period. According to Brueggemann, 'Israel's royal history in the land

---

28 Brueggemann, *The Land*, 5.
29 Brueggemann, *The Land*, 5.

moved inexorably toward exile',[30] due to their failure to manage the land correctly. He adds that the Torah 'consists in guidelines for land management'.[31] Now it would be anachronous to suggest that we can read back into the text modern ideas of environmentalism, but land management was part of Torah, including rest for land and domesticated animals, seen in the ideas of the Sabbath and Jubilee. The Sabbath reminded the Israelites that the land was a gift and hence 'not fully given over to our satiation'.[32] Land possessed its own rights.

However, land management is a broader concept in the Torah than merely landcare. Before the Sabbath and the recognition of the rights of land comes the prohibition of images. Images can be described as 'controllable representations of our best loyalties and visions'.[33] The idea of controllable representations relies upon the concept of continuity, i.e. that all things in existence are part of each other.[34] Hence, manipulation of an idol of Baal was said in turn to manipulate the storms, since Baal as storm God was identified with the storms. It is easy to see how an agrarian society could be tempted into seeking multiple ways to ensure the land continued to provide their needs, including turning to Baalism. Brueggemann identifies land as a temptation: the temptation for Israel was to forget that it was a gift and to believe that they had earned the land (Deuteronomy 8:11–17). The Israelites were tempted to forget who the giver of the land was and to seek after other gods.

The third aspect of land management is to care for our brother and sister; for the poor, stranger, sojourner, widow, orphan and Levite. When land is covenanted, all those who are landless within the land are to be treated as full members of the covenant, ensuring that they are included in the blessings of land. Brueggemann understands land as an opportunity to pervert justice, by excluding the landless. In particular, he identifies mismanagement of land by the monarchy of Israel as the chief source of injustice. The people had asked for a king like the other nations, and hence wanted the sort of security that other nations had in their human institutions. When YHWH acceded to Israel's request, it was on the condition that the king would have a different character to those of other nations (Deuteronomy 17:14–20). Israel's king was to be part of the covenant and bound by it, to regularly read the Torah and not to be given to the excesses of kingship. The history of kingship that followed is largely marked by the absence of this sort of character and hence it represents a journey to landlessness.

---

30   Brueggemann, *The Land*, 107.
31   Brueggemann, *The Land*, 60.
32   Brueggemann, *The Land*, 63.
33   Brueggemann, *The Land*, 62.
34   John N. Oswalt, *The Bible Among the Myths* (Grand Rapids, MI: Zondervan: 2009): 48.

How might we relate this to the present crisis of the Anthropocene and the impending homelessness of all humanity, anticipated by solastalgic feelings? Michael Northcott draws a connection between ecological disasters, exile and covenant unfaithfulness in Jeremiah 5:22–28.[35] There was a direct connection between building an empire, idolatry and ecological crises. The desire to be like the other nations necessarily meant raising a standing army and multiplying horses, despite injunctions against this in Deuteronomy 17. International diplomacy often took the form of the king taking foreign wives, and this lead to the adoption of their gods, as we see with Ahab or the ailing Solomon. Further, there was the temptation to bet each way with the land in order to ensure rains and fertility, clearly on show in 1 Kings 17–18. Land was managed by its acquisition from those to whom it had been covenanted (1 Kings 21, Isaiah 5:8), with a surplus required from the people to feed the standing armies and the court. Finally, the resulting lack of Sabbath rest meant that ecological collapse was an inevitable consequence. This shows us that the divine character is not merely external to creation but is also set into the character of creation.

The implication for the modern situation is that empire building by nation states has led inevitably to environmental degradation, the breaching of the planetary boundaries, and has accelerated the earth's entry into the Anthropocene. While the whole of humanity is not in covenant relationship with YHWH, as Israel was, there is a more general relationship between the Creator God and a creation made in God's image, or the *imago Dei*. As noted above, ecological collapse in Israel resulted from their failure to keep the Sabbath. The divinely imposed limits of land were not respected. Just as these limits reflected the divine character in the character of creation, as Northcott has suggested, so do the planetary boundaries in the present. Our lack of respect for planetary boundaries is in turn a lack of respect of God, which is resulting in the collapse of the key aspects of the earth's ability to support us.

There is debate as to whether the term Anthropocene apportions the blame too broadly. Without quibbling over terms, it should be recognised that the empires that have contributed most to the Anthropocene are Western ones, societies which have a Christian history, and therefore share some of the blame. Lynn White suggested that Western ideas of progress, development and prosperity are directly attributable to Christianity. Whether or not this represents the whole truth of the matter, the church has at times been subject to a kind of Babylonian captivity in terms of these ideas.[36]

---

35 Michael Northcott, *A Moral Climate: The Ethics of Global Warming* (New York: Orbis Books, 2007), 13.

36 Lynn White Jr., 'The Historical Roots of Our Ecologic Crisis', *Science* 155 (1967): 1203–7.

As Genesis 1–11 follows a landed people on their way to landlessness, so Genesis 12–50 is a landless people living in anticipation of becoming landed. The first experience of landlessness comes with the call of Abram itself, of being called out of the land into the Promised Land. The second experience is the wilderness wanderings between the Exodus and the period of conquest. The third is of course exile and with it the promise of return. Some scholars, such as Tom Wright suggest that many first-century Jews thought of themselves as still living in exile, because while they were landed once more, they were living under pagan rule. The Jews were still living in anticipation of a climactic moment of deliverance which might come at any moment and 'this continuing narrative was currently seen, on the basis of Daniel 9, as a long passage through a state of continuing "exile"'.[37]

This deliverance from exile is seen best in Paul's retelling of the history of Israel through her Messiah in Romans.[38] Those who are in the Messiah have been set free from slavery to sin (Romans 7:14–25) just as the Israelites had been set free from slavery in Egypt. Those who are in the Messiah are led by the Spirit (Romans 8:1–17) just as the people of God were led by the presence of God through the desert wanderings (e.g. Numbers 9:15–23). Finally, where Israel is led to the Promised Land (Joshua 1), Paul presents us with a renewed creation, where creation itself is set free from its own slavery (Romans 8:21). It is this eschatological hope of coming home which must frame our mission in the Anthropocene, a theme to which we will return soon.

Making Home in a Disrupted World

The existential and physical threat of the Anthropocene, together with the phenomena of solastalgia, presents a challenge to our concepts of mission. This would suggest that the church needs to expand its concept of mission to include the other parts of creation and our relationship to it, a term known as ecomission.

> [Eco-missiology] sees mission in terms of reconciliation at all levels. The gospel is broader than 'me and Jesus' because God is involved with the whole of creation, not just human beings. Eco-missiology is concerned for creation because God saves us *with* and not *from* creation. 'Eco-missiology is also a matter of eco-justice, since it is the global poor who face the worst effects of environmental degradation;

---

37 Tom Wright, *Justification: God's Plan and Paul's Vision* (Nottingham: IVP Academic, 2009).
38 For a discussion of this see Mick Pope, 'With Heads Craning Forward: The Eschaton and the Nonhuman Creation in Romans 8', in *Ecotheology in the Humanities: An Interdisciplinary Approach to Understanding the Divine and Nature*, ed. Melissa J. Brotton (Lanham: Lexington Books, 2016).

and includes eco-spirituality, which represents a new way of seeing creation, because it views caring for creation *in its own right* as a form of mission.[39]

This definition owes much to the work of Ross Langmead.[40] Notice that ecomission is multidimensional. We care for the creation because it has an impact on the lives of others, and because creation itself has value to God and has a future in Christ. The following is a brief list of ways in which ecomission in the Anthropocene can be conducted.

The first way in which ecomission for the Anthropocene can be carried out is by offering a home to the homeless. Even if we argue that climate change has not played a factor in the Syrian crisis, there are many groups threatened by future forced migration due to climate change. Indeed, with rising sea levels, it will be unavoidable in the Pacific. Current Australian policy on asylum seekers who come by boat is expressly designed as a deterrent, the conditions of which have been described as an 'international atrocity' by writer and activist Naomi Klein. She has pointed out that while the US wants to build a wall, Australia already has one: 'I think we shouldn't be so self-satisfied about it. You're actually doing it, he's [President Trump] just talking about it.'[41] Whether or not one accepts Klein's rhetoric, the policy of refusing entry and dealing with immigration issues offshore has a history going back over a decade and a half to the excising of offshore islands from Australian migration zones, and has been supported by both sides of politics. Offshore detention has left people in legal limbo and it has subjected them to all kinds of human rights abuses. Globally, nationalism is on the rise, with hardening attitudes towards refugees and asylum seekers.[42]

The mission of the church in the Anthropocene is then to act as salt and light, breaking the stereotypes that various interest groups engage in, supporting refugees in onshore detention and those living in our community. Groups like the *Asylum Seeker Resource Centre* provide care directly for people's needs. Further, the movement *Love Makes a Way* is in their own words 'a movement of Christians seeking an end to Australia's inhumane asylum seeker policies through prayer and nonviolent love in action'. Sam McLean, the former National Director of *GetUp!* has observed that *Love Makes a Way* cuts through the narrative that believes

---

39   Mick Pope, 'Preaching to the Birds? The Mission of the Church to Creation', in *Speaking of Mission Volume 2*, ed. Michael Frost (Morling College: Morling College Press, 2013).

40   For a review of his contribution to ecomissiology, see Mick Pope, 'The EcoTheology of Ross Langmead', *Australian Journal of Mission Studies* 10, no. 2 (2016): 19–25.

41   Georgina Mitchell, 'Q&A: Naomi Klein Says Australia No Better than "Insane and Racist" Donald Trump', *The Sydney Morning Herald* (November 8, 2016), accessed February 19, 2017.

42   Pope, *A Climate of Justice*, chapter 4.

cruelty is the best policy toward asylum seekers. Following on from Brueggemann, landcare in Australia means caring for the sojourner who is part of the creation covenant with us.

Quite apart from the fact that caring for refugees is a justice issue, the numbers of people currently seeking asylum in Australia is much smaller compared to those entering nations in Europe and North America, or indeed those living in refugee camps in the Middle East and Africa. As the planet warms and more people are displaced from their home due to rising seas and other climate change impacts, the relative trickle has the potential to become a flood. Australia and other Western countries will need to develop robust political and social systems to deal with those seeking a new home. Beyond this, there needs to be a fundamental change of attitude toward the 'other' in Australian society, so that the homeless seeking a home can find it here. Aside from the traumas that refugees face before resettling in a new country, an *Australian Centre for Child Protection* report notes that they may suffer from the following: disruption to sense of self, family and community, cultural dislocation, mental health problems, financial difficulties, poverty, social isolation, problems with adaptation to a new country, discrimination, language problems, change in profession, lack of recognition of educational qualifications, challenges to traditional patterns of family interaction, lack of validation of effective parenting practices, family upheaval and stress, interaction with community services and organisations, lack of awareness of formal supports, discomfort in seeking social support, marginalisation and minority status.[43] This opens up many missional avenues in collaboration with community services and immigrant churches, for example, to share the gospel by showing compassion to others in need of aid and home.

In the Australian context, offering home to the homeless impacted by the Anthropocene is further complicated by the fact that this is not our home. Before Europeans invaded, Aboriginal peoples had inhabited and flourished on this continent for at least 60,000 years. Likewise, Torres Strait Islander peoples have inhabited the region between mainland Australia and Papua New Guinea for over 5,000 years. Over two hundred years of occupation has seen a gap open up between Aboriginal and Torres Strait Islander peoples and non-indigenous Australians in key indicators such as health, education and employment. Aboriginal and Torres Strait Islander peoples have been made homeless in their own home: by removing children from their parents, closing remote communities, forbidding the teaching of their languages, granting of mining leases over native title, damaging sacred sites and by general everyday racism.

---

[43] Kerry Lewig, Fiona Arney, and Mary Salveron, *The Working with Refugee Families Project* (University of South Australia: Australian Centre for Child Protection, 2009), 26.

It is therefore impossible to move forward with a genuine theology that seeks to give home to those made homeless by the Anthropocene when the colonialism that underpins the Anthropocene goes undealt with in this country.[44] A full exposition of what this should look like is beyond the scope of this chapter, but I have explored it elsewhere.[45] In outline, it involves genuine justice by granting land rights not trumped by mining leases, reparations for harms inflicted and self-determination. The church can play a role in this in terms of advocacy and partnership with Aboriginal and Torres Strait Islander churches. A key thing that the church can do is listen. Firstly, we must listen to the accounts of injustices, including those in which the church has been complicit. Our response must be repentance. Secondly, we must learn from Aboriginal and Torres Strait Islander theologians as they develop a genuinely indigenous theology. Such a theology will deal with the home they extend as home to us, the invaders, as well as to other refugees. If we are seeking to welcome the homeless into Australia, we need to heed the words of Reverend Rronang Garrawurra:

> We are the First People, and as First People, it upsets me that we haven't been asked for our input on any of this. Should we be consulted, as we should—as Indigenous people, the first people of this land, we would think carefully about the problem, and offer our own solutions. [People seeking refuge] should be given their freedom, they should be welcomed here.[46]

Thirdly, we must learn land management techniques, such as fire management, from Aboriginal and Torres Strait Islander people. Traditional knowledge is embedded in action plans such as that of the Torres Strait Regional Authority. This is of course not separate from theological considerations.

A third area of mission in the Anthropocene deals directly with the ecological aspect, caring for the creation, in recognition that the land itself is homeless. As Paul notes in Romans 8:21: 'the creation itself will be set free from its bondage to decay and will obtain the freedom of the glory of the children of God (NRSV)'. The language of Romans 8 echoes that of the exodus and in this verse it is applied to the whole creation. Creation itself needs an exodus; it is homeless in search of

---

44 On carbon colonialism, see Pope, *A Climate of Justice*, chapter 5, and Mick Pope, 'Sacrificing the Sioux: Oil Pipelines, Girard, and the New Colonialism', *The Other Journal* 28 (2017), https://theotherjournal.com/2017/07/05/sacrificing-sioux-oil-pipelines-girard-new-colonialism/.

45 Pope, *A Climate of Justice*, chapter 5.

46 Tim Lam, 'Rev Rronang Garrawurra Honoured', *Crosslight* (November 5, 2015), http://crosslight.org.au/2015/11/05/rev-rronang-garrawurra-honoured/, accessed September 24, 2017.

a home. The future setting free of creation is an invitation to proleptic living, just as the promise of our own bodily resurrection and glorification is an invitation for living new lives in the present. The future bodily resurrection and renewed creation means that matter matters. The hope that the church offers in the face of the Anthropocene is not entirely in the future but reaches forward from the resurrection and backward from the eschaton. We are not to simply rely upon Christ to fix up our mess at his return but instead we should work as if the new creation had already begun, which indeed it has.

There are several ways to engage in ecomission in the Anthropocene, and some of these are outlined in *A Climate of Justice*.[47] There are a number of advocacy groups and campaigns, opportunities to walk alongside people of other faiths through groups like *Australian Religious Response to Climate Change (ARRCC)*, or with the largely secular groups. Christians have been involved in direct action, such as being chained up at coal mines, or forming a flotilla to blockade a coal port.[48] Of course direct action requires that choices are made carefully, given the possibility that it often involves taking actions leading to arrest. Christians of course can also make changes in their personal habits as part of individual discipleship. These acts may be necessary, without becoming pharisaical about which changes to make. However, our actions most actively reflect the mission of the church when done as the church. This requires a public witness within the community. The logic of the individual consumer at this point needs to be challenged.

This relates to the final aspect of ecomission in the Anthropocene that I will cover. It addresses the need for creation care as discussed above, but also Brueggemann's charge that Western culture is rootless. The modern or hyper-Anthropocene is a function of modernism, which together with its industrial and consumer complex, have separated us from place and land; there has been an uprooting. Our proper rooting to place will involve planting roots in the figurative and literal senses. The work of the Christian conservation organisation *A Rocha* is founded on the following five pillars: Christian faith, conservation, community, cross-cultural and cooperation. It does work that restores ecosystems, contributes to local economies and the wellbeing of people, and proclaims the gospel. Christians work within the local community to achieve these ends by putting down roots while planting roots. A *Rocha* is still in its infancy in Australia, but it continues to pursue projects in several states (see http://australia.arocha.org/).

---

47 Pope, *A Climate of Justice*, chapter 6.
48 Helen Davidson, 'Pacific Islanders Blockade Newcastle Coal Port to Protest Rising Sea Levels', *The Guardian* (October 17, 2014), https://www.theguardian.com/environment/2014/oct/17/pacific-islanders-blockade-newcastle-coal-port-to-protest-rising-sea-levels.

Another example of rootedness for people and plants comes in the form of community gardens. Miriam Pepper catalogued the variety of community gardens in the Uniting Church in a 2012 paper.[49] Churches can engage with gardens on a variety of scales and ownership models, from church owned and run to various partnership models. Gardens provide spaces for reconciliation, meditation, education and the opportunity to become rooted to place. Food can be shared within the church community, the wider community, or donated to various groups. Community gardens provide liminal or thin spaces to encounter God in, and proximity spaces forming a link between the 'sacred space' of the church and the 'secular space' of the world. Church gardens have the potential to change the outlook of a church to creation, retying it to the agricultural calendar. When the produce is the traditional food of immigrant Christians, church gardens have the potential to make a new home for the homeless by rooting them to place in figurative and literal senses.

The Anthropocene represents an existential and physical threat to humanity. People are now being made homeless, and there is the risk that the entirety of humanity and the whole of creation will be made homeless. The biblical narrative set out in Genesis tells this story of humanity at home on its way to homelessness, and a homeless people with the eschatological hope of home. This unique hope informs our ecomissional activities in the present. In the Australian context, we face the fourfold challenge of making a home for the homeless, recognising that we live in someone else's home, that we need to work for the rehoming of land, and ultimately that we need to make ourselves at home.

---

49   Miriam Pepper, 'Church-Based Community Gardening: Where Mission Meets Ecology in Local Contexts', *Australian Journal of Mission Studies* 6, no. 2 (2012): 54–59.

BIBLIOGRAPHY

Albrecht, Glenn. 'The Age of Solastalgia.' *The Conversation* (August 7, 2012). Accessed June 3, 2017. https://theconversation.com/the-age-of-solastalgia-8337.

Albrecht, Glenn. '"Solastalgia." A New Concept in Health and Identity.' *PAN: Philosophy, Activism, Nature* 3 (2005): 44–59.

Brueggemann, Walter. *The Land*. Philadelphia: Fortress Press, 1977.

Brzoska, Michael, and Christiane Fröhlich. 'Climate Change, Migration and Violent Conflict: Vulnerabilities, Pathways and Adaptation Strategies.' *Migration and Development* 5, no. 2 (2016): 190–210.

Crutzen, Paul. 'Geology of Mankind.' *Nature* 415 (2002): 23.

Davidson, Helen. 'Pacific Islanders Blockade Newcastle Coal Port to Protest Rising Sea Levels.' *The Guardian* (October 17, 2014). https://www.theguardian.com/environment/2014/oct/17/pacific-islanders-blockade-newcastle-coal-port-to-protest-rising-sea-levels.

Edenburg, Cynthia. 'From Eden to Babylon: Reading Genesis 2–4 as a Paradigmatic Narrative.' In *Pentateuch, Hexateuch, or Enneateuch: Identifying Literary Works in Genesis through Kings*, edited by Thomas B. Dozeman, Thomas Römer, and Konrad Schmid, 155–67. Atlanta: Society of Biblical Literature, 2011.

Femia, Francesco, and Caitlin Werrell. 'Syria: Climate Change, Drought and Social Unrest.' *The Center for Climate and Security* (February 29, 2012). https://climateandsecurity.org/2012/02/29/syria-climate-change-drought-and-social-unrest/.

Friends of the Earth International. *Climate Change: Voices from Communities Affected by Climate Change*. Amsterdam: Friends of the Earth, 2007.

Hamilton, Clive. *Defiant Earth*. Melbourne: Allen and Unwin, 2017.

Hansen, James, Mariko Sato, Paul Hearty, Reto Ruedy, Maxwell Kelley, Valerie Masson-Delmotte, Gary Russell, George Tselioudis, Junji Cao, Eric Rignot, Isabella Velicogna, Blair Tormey, Evgeniya Kandiano, Karina von Schuckmann, Pushker Kharecha, Allegra N. Legrande, Michael Bauer, and Kwok-Wai Lo. 'Ice Melt, Sea Level Rise and Superstorms: Evidence from Paleoclimate Data, Climate Modeling, and Modern Observations that 2°C Global Warming is Highly Dangerous.' *Atmospheric Chemistry and Physics Discussions* 15 (2015): 20059–179.

Hoerling, Martin, Jon Eischeid, Judith Perlwitz, Xiaowei Quan, Tao Zhang, and Philip Pegion. 'On the Increased Frequency of Mediterranean Drought.' *Journal of Climate* 25 (2012): 2146–61.

Huusko, Saila. 'We're Sinking Here: Climate Change Laps at Front Door of Torres Strait Islands.' *The Guardian* (December 8, 2016). https://www.theguardian.com/australia-news/2015/dec/08/were-sinking-here-climate-change-laps-at-front-door-of-torres-strait-islands.

Huxton, Nance. 'Calls for Detailed Climate Change Plan for Torres Strait Islands amid Projected Sea Level Rises.' *ABC News* (January 5, 2015). http://www.abc.net.au/news/2015-01-05/call-for-torres-strait-climate-change-plan/6000646.

Jena, Manipadma. 'Women Bear the Brunt of Climate-Forced Migration.' *India Climate Dialogue* (January 4, 2017). http://indiaclimatedialogue.net/2017/01/04/women-bear-brunt-climate-forced-migration/.

Kelly, Elaine. 'Rising Seas Pose a Cultural Threat to Australia's "Forgotten People."' *The Conversation* (November 27, 2014). http://theconversation.com/rising-seas-pose-a-cultural-threat-to-australias-forgotten-people-34359.

Lam, Tim. 'Rev Rronang Garrawurra Honoured.' *Crosslight* (November 5, 2015). http://crosslight.org.au/2015/11/05/rev-rronang-garrawurra-honoured/. Accessed September 24, 2017.

Lewig, Kerry, Fiona Arney, and Mary Salveron. *The Working with Refugee Families Project*. University of South Australia: Australian Centre for Child Protection, 2009.

Lewis, Simon L., and Mark A. Maslin. 'Defining the Anthropocene.' *Nature* 519 (2015): 171–80.

Mitchell, Georgina. 'Q&A: Naomi Klein Says Australia No Better than "Insane and Racist" Donald Trump.' *The Sydney Morning Herald* (November 8, 2016). Accessed February 19, 2017.

Mueller, Valerie, Clark Gray, and Katrina Kosec. 'Heat Stress Increases Long-Term Human Migration in Rural Pakistan.' *Nature Climate Change* 4 (2014): 182–85.

Nazer, Simon. 'The Last Islanders: Rising Sea Levels in Papua New Guinea.' UN Children's Fund (March 22, 2017). http://reliefweb.int/report/papua-new-guinea/last-islanders-rising-sea-levels-papua-new-guinea.

Northcott, Michael. *A Moral Climate: The Ethics of Global Warming*. New York: Orbis Books, 2007.

Oswalt, John, N. *The Bible Among the Myths*. Grand Rapids, MI: Zondervan: 2009.

Pepper, Miriam. 'Church-Based Community Gardening: Where Mission Meets Ecology in Local Contexts.' *Australian Journal of Mission Studies* 6, no 2 (2012): 54–59.

Pope, Mick. *A Climate of Justice: Loving Your Neighbour in a Warming World*. Melbourne: Morning Star Publishing, 2017.

Pope, Mick. 'The EcoTheology of Ross Langmead.' *Australian Journal of Mission Studies* 10, no. 2 (2016): 19–25.

Pope, Mick. 'Preaching to the Birds? The Mission of the Church to Creation.' In *Speaking of Mission Volume 2*, edited by Michael Frost. Morling College: Morling College Press: 2013.

Pope, Mick. 'Sacrificing the Sioux: Oil Pipelines, Girard, and the New Colonialism.' *The Other Journal* 28 (2017). https://theotherjournal.com/2017/07/05/sacrificing-sioux-oil-pipelines-girard-new-colonialism/.

Pope, Mick. 'The Sea is Eating the Ground: A Theology of Sea Level Rise.' *Anglican Theological Review* 100, no. 1 (Winter 2018): 79–92.

Pope, Mick. 'With Heads Craning Forward: The Eschaton and the Nonhuman Creation in Romans 8.' In *Ecotheology in the Humanities: An Interdisciplinary Approach to Understanding the Divine and Nature*, edited by Melissa J. Brotton. Lanham: Lexington Books, 2016.

Saleeby, Suzanne. 'Sowing the Seeds of Dissent: Economic Grievances and the Syrian Social Contract's Unravelling.' *Yadaliyya* (February 16, 2012). http://www.jadaliyya.com/pages/index/4383/sowing-the-seeds-of-dissent_economic-grievances-an.

Seto, Karen C., Michail Fragkias, Burak Güneralp, and Michael K. Reilly. 'A Meta-Analysis of Global Urban Land Expansion.' *PLOS One* 6 (2011): e23777.

Steffen, Will, Wendy Broadgate, Lisa Deutsch, Owen Gaffney, and Cornelia Ludwig. 'The Trajectory of the Anthropocene: The Great Acceleration.' *The Anthropocene Review* 2 (2015): 1–18.

Steffen, Will, Katherine Richardson, Johan Rockström, Sarah E. Cornell, Ingo Fetzer, Elena M. Bennett, Reinette Biggs, Stephen R. Carpenter, Wim de Vries, Cynthia A. de Wit, Carl Folke, Dieter Gerten, Jens Heinke, Georgina M. Mace, Linn M. Persson, Veerabhadran Ramanathan, Belinda Reyers, and Sverker Sörlin. 'Planetary Boundaries: Guiding Human Development on a Changing Planet.' *Science* 347 (2015): 1–17.

White Jr., Lynn. 'The Historical Roots of Our Ecologic Crisis.' *Science* 155 (1967): 1203–7.

Wright, Tom. *Justification: God's Plan and Paul's Vision*. Nottingham: IVP Academic: 2009.

SECTION TWO:
MIGRANT NARRATIVES OF HOME

Chapter 5

RELOCATING IN CHRIST: CHURCHES AND MIGRATION IN RURAL AUSTRALIA

Mark Short[a] and Monica Short[b]

The purpose of this chapter is to illuminate the theme of 'reimagining home' by exploring what faithful Christian mission looks like in a world where the very idea of a stable and secure home is challenged by the dislocating impact of globalisation. This chapter aims to inform and inspire Christians to overcome narratives of division and disconnection by cultivating a shared sense of home in Christ in their local churches and communities. It begins by exploring the impact of globalisation on two groups—medium- to long-term residents of rural Australia and people who have relocated to those areas originally as refugees under the humanitarian resettlement program. It then narrates the findings from two research projects, a cooperative inquiry and a collective case study, into the engagement between former refugees and Anglican churches in regional and rural Australia.[1] Through their stories we learn how the church can be an expanding shared space that creates connections and networks within the presence of God for the mutual

---

[1] Monica Short, *Three Anglican Churches Engaging with People from Culturally and Linguistically Diverse Backgrounds* (Sydney, NSW: BCA, 2015); Monica Short et al., 'Connecting to Belonging: A Cross-Disciplinary Inquiry into Rural Australian Anglican Church Engagements with People from Culturally and Linguistically Diverse Backgrounds', in *Journal of Contemporary Religion* 32, no. 1 (2017): 119–33.

benefit and spiritual wellbeing of all involved.[2] The chapter concludes with a theological reflection on the concept of 'relocation in Christ', pointing a way forward for faithful Christian engagement with a world of shifting borders and emerging walls.

The Opportunity and Challenge of Globalisation

It is widely recognised that globalisation represents one of the key challenges and opportunities for Christian mission in the early twenty-first century.[3] An issues paper prepared by the global evangelical Lausanne Committee defines globalisation as 'a set of complexly related historical processes by which local situations throughout the world are increasingly interconnected within a single, but often conflicted, social space'.[4] This social space is formed by the flow of people, capital, images and ideas across national and regional boundaries. Thomas Friedman describes this in terms of a flattening of the world driven by forces such as the fall of the Berlin Wall, the spread of the internet and the increased use of outsourcing by the manufacturing and technology sectors.[5] The creation of a single social space resonates with the idea of home, but whereas the traditional ideal of home is associated with themes of belonging, security and stability the 'space' of globalisation is characterised by fluidity, mobility and uncertainty.

Hence, while he is generally positive about the impact of globalisation, Friedman also recognises its potential to disenfranchise individuals and communities and in so doing to sow the seeds of its own demise. 'There are hundreds of millions of people on this planet who have been left behind by the flattening process or feel

---

[2] Short, *Three Anglican Churches Engaging with People from Culturally and Linguistically Diverse Backgrounds*, 33.

[3] For some recent discussions see Tormod Engelviksen, Erling Lundeby, and Dagfinn Solheim, eds., *The Church Going Global: Mission and Globalisation* (Oxford: Regnum, 2011); Ernst M. Conradie, 'Mission in a Globalised World: A New Vision of Christian Discipleship', *Australian Journal of Mission Studies* 8, no. 1 (2014): 3–9; Craig Ott, 'Globalisation and Contextualisation: Reframing the Task of Contextualisation in the Twenty-First Century', in *Missiology* 43, no. 1 (2015): 43–58; Daniel Groody, 'Migrants and Refugees: Christian Faith and the Globalization of Solidarity' in *International Review of Mission* 104, no. 2 (2015): 314–23. The latter paper draws out common themes from *Evangelii Gaudium* by Pope Francis, *Together Towards Life*, by the World Council of Churches, and *The Cape Town Commitment* by the Lausanne movement.

[4] Lausanne Committee for World Evangelization, *Globalization and the Gospel: Rethinking Mission in the Contemporary World*, Lausanne Occasional Paper, no. 30 (2004): 22.

[5] Thomas L. Friedman, *The World is Flat: A Brief History of the Twenty-First Century* (New York: Farrer, Straus and Giroux, 2005), 48–172.

overwhelmed by it, and some of them have enough access to the flattening tools to use them against the system, not on its behalf.'[6]

Globalisation has certainly brought opportunities for Christian mission. The migration of Christians across national boundaries has led to the establishment of new communities of faith and the renewal of existing ones.[7] International mission and humanitarian organisations have been a conduit for the sharing of resources and expertise.[8] New technologies have allowed the Christian message to be communicated in contests where physical person-to-person contact is difficult or impossible.

Nonetheless, the challenges of globalisation for Christian faith, witness and mission are also real. The cultural and ideological pluralism fostered by globalisation often encourages a rejection of any claims to a transcendent reality and the consequent restriction of matters of faith to the realm of the private and the individual. The tendency noted by Friedman above for globalisation to engender violent counteractions sometimes results in the persecution or marginalisation of Christians and other minority groups.[9]

For all of these reasons it is vital that Christians engage with an increasingly globalised world in a way that is consistent with fundamental commitments such as the love of God and the love of neighbour. This chapter will explore what this might look like, through the image of home and through the experiences of former refugees and residents of rural Australia.

Globalisation and rural Australia

In Christian discourse it is sometimes assumed that globalisation is primarily an urban phenomenon. For example, a recent textbook on Christian mission states:

> But it is in the city that perhaps an even more important missionary encounter is taking place with the most powerful global religion in our time . . . the urban revolution began in Western culture as it was driven

---

[6] Friedman, *The World is Flat: A Brief History of the Twenty-First Century*, 375.
[7] See for example the significant impact of Nigerian Christianity on churches in the West. Alan L. Effa, 'Releasing the Trigger: The Nigerian Factor in Global Christianity', *International Bulletin of Missionary Research* 37, no. 4 (2013): 214–18, or the worldwide impact of Hillsong. Tanya Riches, 'God's Brand is Love: Australian Pentecostalism in the United States of America', *Australian Journal of Mission Studies* 8, no. 1 (2014): 53–62.
[8] *Globalization and the Gospel*, 35–36.
[9] *Globalization and the Gospel*, 30–31.

by the Industrial Revolution. Much of the urban explosion in the Southern hemisphere is propelled by the dynamics of globalisation.[10]

The impact of globalisation on our cities and the degree to which those cities are in turn shaping a global culture is acknowledged here in this chapter, but it should also be recognised that restricting the discussion of globalisation to urban contexts risks excluding already marginalised groups and communities from conversations which shape their futures. From a Christian perspective, ignoring the rural context runs counter to the gospel witness of God's work being made manifest, even though this may seem small or insignificant from a human perspective.[11]

This chapter partially addresses this particular gap in the literature and in Christian discourses about globalisation and rurality. Furthermore, it explores the dislocating impact of globalisation on two groups—existing residents of rural and regional Australia, and former refugees who have moved to those areas and are establishing new homes. It then considers how the church can become a place of encounter between these two groups, where both reimagine a common location, or home, in Christ.

Rurality is a complex term and one that is not amenable to a single definition.[12] This research interchanges the term 'rural' with 'rural, regional and remote' and it means populations located outside capital cities or their immediate surrounding suburbs.[13] The rural archetype differs from the urban experience, in several respects, potentially including the experience of globalisation. For example, according to the United Nations, in 2016, the largest segment of the world's poor, though difficult to quantify, are people who reside in rural environments. These include subsistence farmers and herders, fishers and migrant workers, artisans and indigenous peoples.[14] This may indicate that people living in rural areas have been disproportionately excluded from any economic benefits arising from globalisation.

---

10 Michael Goheen, *Introducing Christian Mission Today: Scripture, History and Issues* (Downers Grove, IVP Academic, 2014), 376–77.

11 Cf. Jesus's teaching on the nature of God's kingdom in the parable of the Mustard Seed (Mark 4:30–34) and Paul's exploration of how the cross overturns human ideals of strength and significance in 1 Corinthians 1:18–31.

12 United Nations, *Population Density and Urbanisation* (2017), accessed June 15, 2017, https://www.mozilla.org/en-US/firefox/central/.

13 Short, *Three Anglican* Churches, 14; Regional Australia Institute, *Why a Regional Australia Institute?* Australia: Regional Australia Institute (2013), accessed May 25, 2014, http://www.regionalaustralia.org.au/wp-content/uploads/2013/08/RAI-Fact-Sheet-August-2013.pdf.

14 United Nations, *Rural Poverty* (2017), accessed June 15, 2017, http://www.un.org/en/sections/issues-depth/rural-poverty/index.html.

In the Australian context the impact of globalisation on rural or non-urban locations has been profound.[15] The dependence of the rural economy on highly trade-exposed sectors such as agriculture, mining and tourism means that movements in exchange rates and commodity prices have a disproportionate impact on employment levels, population movements and housing prices, and on rent in non-urban contexts. One example is the impact of movements in iron ore prices on the value of real estate in the Pilbara region of Western Australia, an area heavily dependent on the mining industry. Between December 2012 and December 2016, the iron ore spot price decreased from US$129 to US$79—a reduction of 39 percent.[16] Over the same time rents in some Pilbara communities decreased by 70 percent and housing prices by 60 percent.[17] While this of course increased housing affordability for new residents moving into these communities, it also created considerable stress for those long-term residents who had taken out mortgages and purchased investment properties at the height of the market. In addition, neoliberal policies adopted by Australian federal, state and local governments since the 1980s have favoured those sections of the rural economy which have been able to respond to globalisation through structural adjustments such as the merging of smaller farms into larger units, capital-intensive technological change and the adoption of flexible working arrangements such as Fly-in-Fly-Out employment in the mining industry.[18]

It is perhaps no surprise then that the most recent figures on the rate of structural economic change—as measured by the change in the industry employment mix between two points of time—shows that the pace of change increases with the remoteness of the location[19] (see Table 1).

---

[15] See Margaret Alston, '"You Don't Want to Be a Check-Out Chick All Your Life": The Out-Migration of Young People from Australia's Small Rural Towns', *Australian Journal of Social Issues* 39, no. 3 (2004): 299–313; Tony Sorensen, 'Imagining the Impact of Globalisation on the Future of Australia's Rural Communities', *Horizons in Geography* 81–82 (2012): 116–24.

[16] Information from www.marketindex.com.au/iron-ore, accessed June 15, 2017.

[17] Figures are for the towns of Port Hedland and Newman calculated from *Pilbara Housing and Land Snapshot, December 2016 Quarterly Report* 5, accessed June 15, 2017, www.pdc.wa.gov.au.

[18] For a discussion of some of these developments see Jennifer Moffat, *Engaging Rural and Remote Communities: A Practice Framework*, accessed May 31, 2017, www.queensland.gov.au/storage. For an overview of the impact of these changes on mining communities and the implications for Christian ministry see David Ferguson, 'Communities in Transition: Modelling their Dynamics and Implications for Ministry and Mission,' Australian Journal of Mission Studies 7, no. 1 (2013): 57–64.

[19] Calculated from data in, Department of Infrastructure and Regional Development, *Yearbook 2015: Progress in Australia's Regions* (Canberra: Commonwealth of Australia, 2015), 172–80.

Structural Change Index by Remoteness Class

(2006–2011)

Major Cities	3.6
Inner Regional	4.1
Outer Regional	4.3
Remote	6.2
Very Remote	15.5
AUSTRALIA	3.8

Table 1: Structural change by remoteness class[20]

Perhaps in relation to these changes there is now emerging evidence of the erosion of social capital in regional and remote Australia. The concept of social capital[21] refers to those formal and informal relationships, networks and shared norms which build trust, bind a community tougher and give it resilience in the face of external and internal challenges. It is these networks, relationships and norms which build a sense of 'home' that goes beyond an individual's dwelling to encompass a broader community.

Previous research has suggested that higher levels of social capital in rural locations have provided a 'buffer' between objective economic disadvantage and people's subjective sense of wellbeing.[22] To put it another way, the bush is a place where people know one another more intimately and are connected in multiple ways, so people there have a deeper sense of facing adversity 'together'. There are, however, signs that this situation may be changing. Table 2 below shows two key indicators of social capital—the percentage of people who are involved in a civic or political group and the percentage of people who agree or strongly agree that most people can be trusted.[23]

---

[20] Australian Government, *Yearbook 2015: Progress in Australia's Regions*, 172–80.

[21] Key works on social capital include Robert Putnam, *Bowling Alone: The Collapse and Revival of American Community* (Simon and Schuster, 2000) and David Halpern, *Social Capital* (Polity Press, 2005). Andrew Leigh, *Disconnected* (UNSW Press, 2010) applies this work to the Australian context.

[22] This was the conclusion of Tony Vinson, *Dropping Off the Edge: The Distribution of Disadvantage in Australia* (Jesuit Social Services, 2007).

[23] Australian Government, *Yearbook 2015: Progress in Australia's Regions*, 158–62.

Indicators of Social Capital by Remoteness Class (Percentage)

Group Involvement	2006 Percent %	2010 Percent %	2014 Percent %	2006–2014 Change Percent %
Major Cities	18.1	18.0	13.6	-4.5
Inner Regional	19.9	19.8	13.8	-6.1
Outer Regional and Remote	18.8	21.6	12.4	-6.4
Generalised Trust				
Major Cities	53.2	54.0	55.6	2.4
Inner Regional	56.3	55.7	52.3	-4.0
Outer Regional and Remote	55.4	51.9	50.8	-4.6

Table 2: Indicators of social capital by remoteness class[24]

The reduction in the group involvement of respondents and in their declared level of trust in other people was shown to be greatest for those living furthest away from major cities. Indeed, by 2014, according to the latter measure at least, the level of social capital decreased the further away respondents were from capital cities. Clearly, this trend will have major implications for the wellbeing of residents in rural locations if it persists.[25]

Globalisation and humanitarian refugees

Another aspect of globalisation is the dislocation of people from their home of origin. Currently the world is witnessing the highest levels of displacement on

---

24   Australian Government, *Yearbook 2015: Progress in Australia's Regions*, 158–62.
25   For an earlier reflection of the importance and fragility of social capital in a rural context see Margaret Alston, 'Social Capital in Rural Australia,' *Rural Society* 12, no. 2 (2002): 93–101. Alston argues that voluntary organisations in rural locations are struggling to counteract the erosion of social capital arising from the withdrawal of government services and the implementation of neo-liberal policies.

record.[26] In 2015, there existed approximately 244 million international migrants, of which 65.3 million people had been forcibly displaced.[27]

In Australia, in 2016, about 28.5 percent of Australia's estimated resident population (6.9 million people) were born overseas.[28] According to the Australian Parliament, the United Nations Convention and Protocol Relating to the Status of Refugees (1951) is the key international legal document defining refugees.[29] Article 1 A(2) of the Refugee Convention defines a refugee as someone who:

> Owing to well-founded fear of being persecuted for reasons of race, religion, nationality, membership of a particular social group or political opinion, is outside the country of his [her] nationality and is unable or, owing to such fear, is unwilling to avail himself of the protection of that country; or who, not having a nationality and being outside the country of his former habitual residence as a result of such events, is unable or, owing to such fear, is unwilling to return to it.[30]

In 2015 to 2016, the Australian Government granted 17,555 refugee and humanitarian visas,[31] allowing these people to call Australia home. While there are not easily obtainable figures on how many of these people have or will settle in rural Australia, anecdotal evidence suggests that many have or will settle outside urban centres.

What happens when residents of rural Australia and people who were formally refugees, both groups who have been impacted by globalisation, find themselves occupying the same social space? Can they find home together? One possible narrative is disengagement, where members of disparate groups retreat

---

26 United Nations, *Refugees* (2016), accessed June 15, 2017, http://www.un.org/en/sections/issues-depth/refugees/index.html.

27 Food and Agricultural Organisation of the United Nations, *Decent Rural Employment* (2017), accessed June 15, 2017, http://www.fao.org/rural-employment/resources/detail/en/c/433778/.

28 Australian Bureau of Statistics, *Migration, Australia, 2015–2016*, accessed June 15, 2017, http://www.abs.gov.au/ausstats/abs@.nsf/mf/3412.0/.

29 Parliament of Australia, *Refugee Resettlement to Australia: What are the Facts?* (2016), accessed June 15, 2017, http://www.aph.gov.au/About_Parliament/Parliamentary_Departments/Parliamentary_Library/pubs/rp/rp1617/RefugeeResettlement; United Nations High Commissioner for Refugees, *Convention and Protocol Relating to the Status of Refugees* (1951), accessed June 15, 2017, http://www.unhcr.org/en-au/3b66c2aa10.

30 United Nations High Commission for Refugees, *Convention and Protocol Relating to the Status of Refugees* (1951), accessed June 15, 2017, http://www.unhcr.org/en-au/3b66c2aa10.

31 Refugee Council of Australia *Australia's Refugee and Humanitarian Program Statistics* (2016), accessed June 15, 2017, http://www.refugeecouncil.org.au/getfacts/statistics/aust/australias-refugee-humanitarian-program-2/.

from a shared social space, further eroding social capital in a community.[32] Another possible narrative is conflict, where the newcomers are perceived as a threat or as competitors for scarce economic and social resources such as jobs, housing and access to government services. There are certainly instances of this narrative being expressed in rural Australia. For example, in 2006, there was a well-publicised incident when a council in a NSW rural city decided to reject the resettlement of five Sudanese families.[33] A second example is when a far-right political movement in a NSW regional centre sought to use the resettlement of refugees to generate local support.[34]

The rest of this chapter seeks to chart an alternative way forward for the people of God, first by reviewing some recent research on encounters between these groups through the ministries of rural Anglican churches and secondly by setting some aspects of those encounters in a broader theological and missiological framework.

Insights from recent research

Two recent research projects investigated perceptions about how rural Australian Anglican churches engaged with people from culturally and linguistically diverse backgrounds including but not limited to former refugees.[35] The first[36] was a cooperative inquiry conducted by three social workers and two theologians into the research question: 'What are the co-inquirers' perceptions about the Anglican Church of Australia's engagements with people from diverse cultural backgrounds in rural, regional, and remote Australia?'[37] It argued that the rural Anglican Church of Australia is part of an international Christian community transcending cultural distinctiveness, which gathers people, including former refugees, and serves and sends people out in the name of Jesus.[38] This research recognises that a warm hospitable welcome by an Anglican church which is associated with a sense of

---

32 There is an extensive literature on the relationship between cultural and ethnic diversity and social capital in a community. Putnam argued for a 'hunkering down' effect, whereby people respond to diversity by being less trusting and altruistic. For a more recent survey which argues that Putnam's conclusions may not be generalisable outside the US and Canada see Vilius Semenas, 'Ethnic Diversity and Social Capital at the Community Level: Effects and Implications for Policymakers', *Inquiries* 6, no. 4 (2014): 1–2.
33 For example, 'You're Not Welcome, Town Tells Refugees', *The Sydney Morning Herald* (December 15, 2006), accessed online May 31, 2017.
34 www.ausidentity.blogspot.com.au/2010/01/sudanese-refugees-wagga-wagga-gets-dose.html.
35 Short, *Three Anglican* Churches; Short et al., 'Connecting to Belonging', 119–33.
36 Short et al., 'Connecting to Belonging', 119.
37 Short et al., 'Connecting to Belonging', 120.
38 Short et al., 'Connecting to Belonging', 130.

connection can lead to positive, mutual and participatory relationships, and a sense of belonging for people from a culturally and linguistically diverse background.[39]

The second project was a collective case study investigating two research questions: 'How does the Anglican Church of Australia, outside capital cities, engage with people from diverse cultural backgrounds?', and 'What are the intentions, impacts and implications of these engagements?'[40] Twenty people from three churches were interviewed. It posits that engaging with the rural Anglican churches of Australia can be part of a migration experience, can mean access to safe public spaces which connect people with God and each other, can ensure a go-to place when people are experiencing exclusion by society, can uphold people's wellbeing and can build social capital.[41]

In both research projects it was apparent that people from culturally and linguistically diverse backgrounds perceived their churches in terms of home, as shown in the two quotes below—one from each research project.

> Some interviewees connected to church because it felt like a safe place for them and a window into the Australian community. Others consider it a place to meet people and make friends. Some thought of it as a home away from home; a kind, helpful and nurturing place. Others describe it as a place that helps them grow in their personal relationship with God.[42]

> In this Anglican congregation of about sixty people, there were over a dozen nationalities represented. The walls of the church building were decorated with the flags of different nations and it was clear that the church celebrated its multicultural identity. CALD people attending the church were generally skilled mining workers with excellent English, but they were nevertheless appreciative of the 'home away from home' they experienced there.[43]

In both projects this sense of home was linked with feeling loved and accepted. Tom (name anonymised), a former refugee living in a rural town, described the feeling below.

> We don't pay him [the minister]. All he does is through love. He gives some of his time . . . On behalf of parents and others he helps we are

---

39 Short et al., 'Connecting to Belonging', 130.
40 Short, *Three Anglican* Churches, 10.
41 Short, *Three Anglican* Churches, 7–8 and 33.
42 Short, *Three Anglican* Churches, 120.
43 Short, *Three Anglican* Churches, 126.

very, very grateful to have him. Whatever I say here is also related to his wife as well. All they do they do through love.

The sections below flesh out this emphasis on home by summarising stories collected during the research projects under headings which can encapsulate the various stages of establishing a shared social space or home—connection, welcome, participation and belonging. In each instance the intention is to narrate the experience from the perspective of both the former refugees and the existing residents of each location. Doing so allows insight into the reciprocal nature of the process whereby either party may find themselves acting as guest, or host, or both at any one time.

Connection

Connection can start with a single isolated contact and has the potential to form into a relationship.[44] A group of people who were former refugees who had made a regional town their home approached a rural church's parish council asking if they would partner with them in starting a language specific service.[45] This new initiative was challenging for parts of the church, which was predominately Anglo-Saxon, however, the service did start and the congregation eventually became a valuable part of the church.[46] It encouraged people from other culturally and linguistically diverse communities to attend the church[47] and it allowed the existing church to become connected to a significant part of the local community.[48]

Welcome

A group of people who were refugees resettled in a rural town and began establishing their family homes. They were made to feel very welcome at the local Anglican Church. The church sometimes organised meals after a church service to welcome new people to the congregation and to encourage the forming of relationships. A young woman, who we are calling Minni (name anonymised) commented on this. Minni stated:

> Everyone in the church is very nice and very helpful . . . They come to us and ask questions and talk to everyone. We have more confidence to

---

44 Short, *Three Anglican* Churches, 126.
45 Short, *Three Anglican* Churches, 126.
46 Short, *Three Anglican* Churches, 126.
47 Short, *Three Anglican* Churches, 126.
48 Short, *Three Anglican* Churches, 126.

> go to church... We sometimes have lunch after church. We bring food and share food together. I am so happy they like our food.[49]

Jill (name anonymised), a long-term resident of the town and leader in the same church recalled the initial and ongoing engagement between the former refugees in their homes and the congregation in the following terms:

> After that first day a friendship began to grow. On the next Sunday they all came and kissed me and said, 'You come to our house again'. For a long time I would go and we would muddle through ... I started to importune various people to get beds etc. for them because they had almost nothing. If there is someone without a bed they tell me now. So now a people who hadn't ever even seen a bed mostly have beds, and many of our [anonymised] have chairs and kitchen tables, and other things ... They know I have bad knees and help me out of a chair with much laughter, and lots of kisses. They are amazing people.

In the two quotes above we see how the experience of welcome both creates and arises out of a shared social space where both parties act as host and guest. For former refugees this social space allowed them both to give (through sharing their food, homes and culture and by expressing concern for Jill's wellbeing) and to receive (through practical assistance provided by the congregation). The same two-way relationship was experienced by the existing congregation members, who were welcomed into another culture (for example, through shared home-cooked meals) while also welcoming members of that culture (by helping them navigate a new church experience).

Participation

Participation allows people to move beyond dependence and recognises that they can contribute to their churches. People, former refugees, from a particular culture moved as a group to a rural town, established their new homes and a number began attending a rural Anglican church. The children needed help with their education. The church set up a homework group, helping the children with their reading, writing and maths. The church, at the same time, supported a young adult with his studies. He was accepted into university. This young man, called Joe (anonymised), started helping at the homework club and became part of the leadership team. Joe approached the church to set up a group for parents from his cultural group to teach

---

49   Short, *Three Anglican* Churches, 29.

them how to help children with their homework.[50] Joe has also started participating in other church activities. Joe describes his experience below.

> Talking as a student who comes from no English background countries, I think what this church does is very, very important, especially for the kids. I was not born here and English was my fourth language . . . I am not sure I would be at university studying social work at the moment if it was not for people willing to support me. I do believe what the church is doing will be very beneficial to the children . . . Especially if the children feel they do not get enough help from their parents. It also gives them confidence.

A long-term resident of the local town and leader within the church, Tilly (name anonymised) reflects below on the impact that this initiative had on her and other residents, most of whom are also church members.

> I try to get each tutor and chat when they arrive. Once a term we have tea together to build team spirit. They did not know each other but now have become a team. They help students and the students have helped them in their life journey. It is always wheels within wheels with this sort of stuff. One person likes craft, one supervises the homework table, one supervises the iPads. Rotating the others through reading or other activities. Seeing . . . people relate to children or [people] from another culture is amazing.

Common to these two quotes is the theme of growth through participation. For some of the former refugees this meant growing confidence in engaging with a new culture and language. For some existing residents and church members it meant a growing sense of being part of a team and a deeper awareness of how their particular skills and interests can make a difference to others. For both groups their participation in the homework club meant for a number of them a growing sense of how they could contribute to the building up of the people of God and of the people in their local community. Once again, this happens through the establishment and maintenance of a shared social space—in this instance, a homework club.

Belonging

Everyone who is a new creation in God belongs at church.[51] A young woman who we will call May (anonymised), moved with her husband and her family from a

---

50   Short, *Three Anglican* Churches, 42.
51   Short, *Three Anglican* Churches, 28.

refugee camp to rural Australia and established their new home there. On arrival, May found Australia very confusing. Her husband was able to find work in a regional centre. May found everyone in the regional centre very kind, however, she found it hard to have a sense of belonging in the new place until she went to church.[52] May states:

> In the human world we cannot speak English and we are not educated and I think when you look at [us through] the human eye a hierarchy exists like teacher, professional. Most of us do not understand what is going on when we ask for things in the local community. At church they are all nice to me. When I talk to someone at church, even if they are a teacher, they still treat me like a person. They love me. Most of the congregation have a professional job; they do not make me feel different to them.[53]

Jill (anonymised), a long-term resident of the town and leader talks fondly of her relationship with people from a particular cultural group and how the group make her feel like she belongs in all their gatherings and homes. She describes attending evening prayer led by people from the cultural group and being included in the service and the meal time below.

> We often meet on a Saturday night now to pray Evening Prayer in someone's house, and maybe to eat noodles together. On a Saturday night there can be four or five of the group who have pretty reasonable English. An [name of cultural group] person, usually designated by the matriarch, leads the group in [a native language] . . . When we reach the place for the sermon, I speak briefly about the gospel reading for the next morning's Eucharist. One of the group who has good English translates. It can all take time. I sometimes have to check I have heard them right. That works both ways . . . That's a joy.

Belonging can be a powerful, social and inclusive experience.[54] Here in these two quotes above, we see a depth of relationship that moves beyond shared activities to a shared experience of graces, such as love and joy. Once again, this is a mutual experience encompassing diverse groups who together develop a shared social space.

---

52   Short, *Three Anglican* Churches, 28.
53   Short, *Three Anglican* Churches, 28.
54   Monica Short, 'Belonging: Social Work, Sociological and Theological Insights into Engagements with People Living with Disabilities,' in *Swift: Newsletter of the Australian Association of Social Workers New South Wales Branch*, no. 1 (2017): 29.

Relocating in Christ

The section above has narrated and evaluated significant experiences of connection, welcome, participation and belonging encompassing former refugees and residents of rural Australia. This does not, however, directly answer the question of what makes these experiences an expression of Christian mission. Certainly, there are some who referred to their faith in Christ and/or their involvement with church as a motivation for their involvement, whether as former refugees or existing residents. It is also noteworthy that all of the shared social spaces which facilitated and arose from these experiences happened either within an existing community of faith or through new ventures sponsored by a community of faith. Nevertheless, it is possible that Christian faith could be seen as merely one amongst many ideologies that could potentially bind together individuals and communities from otherwise diverse backgrounds.[55]

One way forward is to identify analogies or parallels between the experiences outlined above and the witness of the foundational documents for Christian mission, namely the books which make up the New Testament. This section seeks to do so in a preliminary way through a consideration of one of those books.

Issues of globalisation and dislocation are not unique to the twenty-first century. Christians in the New Testament era were called to live faithfully as the might of the Roman Empire impacted their world. So, for, example, Carter's introduction to the New Testament and the Roman Empire states, 'This book recognises that Rome's Empire does not disappear or go away when it is not explicitly mentioned. It is always there. It forms the pervasive context of New Testament writings'.[56]

We see some of these dynamics in the letter of 1 Peter.[57] In Peter 1:1 the recipients of the letter are addressed as 'God's elect, exiles scattered throughout

---

55 That might be a conclusion drawn from Robert D. Putnam, and David E. Campbell, *American Grace: How Religion Divides and Unites Us* (New York: Simon and Schuster, 2010) which draws on survey analysis to argue that once the frequency and intensity of a person's congregational attendance is taken into account nothing about the specific content of their theological beliefs seems to impact on their propensity to be a good neighbour to others (467). For an alternative position which argues that specific theological beliefs do make a demonstrable difference to the generation of social capital see Robin Gill, *Society Shaped by Theology: Sociological Theory Volume 3* (Farnham: Ashgate, 2013), 125–76. For a recent overview of research on the role of local churches in building social capital see Wilma Gallett, 'Social Connectedness: The Role of the Local Church in Building Community', *Pointers* 26, no. 4 (2016): 1–5.

56 Warren Carter, *The Roman Empire and the New Testament: An Essential Guide* (Nashville: Abingdon Press, 2007), ix.

57 The teaching of 1 Peter especially as it relates to a new home or household in Christ has been explored in more detail in John H. Elliott, *A Home for the Homeless: A Sociological Exegesis*

the provinces of Pontus, Galatia, Cappadocia, Asia and Bithynia' and in 2:11 they are described as 'resident aliens and foreigners.' There is a double meaning here. On the one hand it reflects the fact that they had been dislocated geographically, perhaps from Rome to modern-day Turkey. It also reflects the religious and social dislocation that had happened when they turned to Christ.[58] Their faith had introduced them to trials (1:7), false accusations of wrongdoing (2:12), insults (3:9), abuse (4:4) and various types of suffering (4:13). They no longer felt at home in familiar places and amongst familiar faces.

In chapter two, however, the image of dislocation is reversed. Instead of being scattered, they have now come together, 'like living stones . . . being built into a spiritual house to be a holy priesthood, offering spiritual sacrifices acceptable to God through Jesus Christ' (2:5). They are relocated in Christ, established as the new people of God. In 1 Peter 2:9, we are given three characteristics of this people. First, they are a people of grace, 'a chosen people', their election grounded not in past performance or future potential but in the abundant mercy of God. Second, they are a royal and priestly people, 'a royal priesthood, a holy nation'.[59] Third, they are a deeply valued people, 'God's special possession'. Arising from this threefold identity is a specific vocation, 'To declare the praises of him who called you out of darkness into his wonderful light' (2:11). Their relocation in Christ does not remove either their geographical or social dislocation; rather it provides a new perspective on their dispersion among the nations since it now expresses and enables their central role in God's plan for all humanity.

Drawing on this New Testament teaching Richard Bauckham has noted that the concept of being exiles among the nations is one of the key missionary images for the Western church seeking to engage a post-Christian society.

> The church in the West may have to get used to the idea that its own centre in God, from which it goes out to others in proclamation and compassion, is actually a position of social and cultural marginality.

---

of 1 Peter, Its Situation and Strategy (Philadelphia: Fortress Press, 1981); and Shively T. J. Smith, *Strangers to Family: Diaspora and 1 Peter's Invention of God's Household* (Waco: Baylor University Press, 2016). For Elliott the incorporation of believers into the *oikos*, or home/household of God is the central metaphor of the letter (228–29). For Smith it is one image that forms part of a broader vision for God's people living faithfully in diverse locations while remaining separate from them (166–68).

58 Elliott, *A Home for the Homeless*, 38ff.

59 The language reflects that used of Israel in Exodus 19:1–6. Peter is 'applying the identification to the people of the new covenant in Christ, who are now ordained with the role of a royal priesthood mediating God in Christ to the nations'. Karen Jobes, *1 Peter* (Grand Rapids: Baker, 2010), 160.

This may improve its witness to the Christ who was himself usually also found at the margins.[60]

In this sense, the dislocating impact of globalisation can be seen as a providential gift as it makes clear to the people of God where their true home is to be found, that is in their election and vocation in Christ. Moreover, it is from this place that a shared space can be established to welcome others who are also dislocated. As outlined in the stories collected in the research, it is through a reciprocal process of connection, welcome, participation and belonging that home is reimagined in a new place and in a new way.

Conclusion

This chapter began by considering the opportunities and challenges of globalisation for Christian mission. It noted the tendency for globalisation to create a shared space, or virtual home, albeit one vulnerable to conflict and uncertainty. It then described the impact of globalisation on two potentially marginalised groups—residents of rural Australia and former refugees—as well as the potential for conflict, disengagement and the further erosion of social capital when those two groups come in contact with each other.

Through reflecting on stories from two research projects on rural Anglican churches engaging with people from culturally and linguistically diverse backgrounds, including former refugees, the chapter charted an alternative narrative characterised by a reciprocal process of connecting, welcoming, participating and belonging. The end point of the process was the establishment of new, shared social spaces where the 'imaginary' home of globalisation is replaced by a new, reimagined home.

A connection was made between this narrative and the teaching of 1 Peter, where the recipients' experience of dislocation is transformed as it becomes the opportunity for them to discover and express a new sense of home in Christ, as well as their sense of divine vocation. It has been suggested that this sense of mission from the place of dislocation has significant implications for the contemporary church. Even as globalisation pushes Christians to the margins it opens up the opportunity for them to encounter others who are similarly displaced, and in so doing, to build a new home in Christ where difference is not eliminated but celebrated, and where engagement and mutual understanding flourish in a changing world.

---

60   Richard Bauckham, 'Mission as Hermeneutic for Scriptural Interpretation,' in Michael Goheen, ed., *Reading the Bible Missionally* (Grand Rapids: Eerdmans, 2016), 37.

BIBLIOGRAPHY

Alston, Margaret. 'Social Capital in Rural Australia.' *Rural Society* 12, no. 2 (2002).

Alston, Margaret. '"You Don't Want to Be a Check-Out Chick All Your Life": The Out-Migration of Young People from Australia's Small Rural Towns.' *Australian Journal of Social Issues* 39, no. 3 (2004): 299–313.

Australian Bureau of Statistics. *Migration, Australia, 2015–2016*. Accessed June 15, 2017. http://www.abs.gov.au/ausstats/abs@.nsf/mf/3412.0/.

Australian Government, Department of Infrastructure and Regional Development. *Yearbook 2015: Progress in Australia's Regions* (Canberra: Commonwealth of Australia, 2015).

Bauckham, Richard. 'Mission as Hermeneutic for Scriptural Interpretation.' In *Reading the Bible Missionally*, edited by Michael Goheen (Grand Rapids: Eerdmans, 2016).

Carter, Warren. *The Roman Empire and the New Testament: An Essential Guide* (Nashville: Abingdon Press, 2007), ix.

Conradie, Ernst M. 'Mission in a Globalised World: A New Vision of Christian Discipleship.' *Australian Journal of Mission Studies* 8, no. 1 (2014): 3–9.

Effa, Alan L. 'Releasing the Trigger: The Nigerian Factor in Global Christianity.' *International Bulletin of Missionary Research* 37, no. 4 (2013).

Elliot, John H. *A Home for the Homeless: A Sociological Exegesis of 1 Peter, Its Situation and Strategy* (Philadelphia: Fortress Press, 1981).

Engelviksen, Tormod, Erling Lundeby, and Dagfinn Solheim, eds. *The Church Going Global: Mission and Globalisation* (Oxford: Regnum, 2011).

Ferguson, David. 'Communities in Transition: Modelling their Dynamics and Implications for Ministry and Mission.' *Australian Journal of Mission Studies* 7, no. 1 (2013): 57–64.

Food and Agricultural Organisation of the United Nations. *Decent Rural Employment 2017*. Accessed June 15, 2017. http://www.fao.org/rural-employment/resources/detail/en/c/433778/.

Friedman, Thomas L. *The World is Flat: A Brief History of the Twenty-First Century* (New York: Farrer, Straus and Giroux, 2005).

Gallett, Wilma. 'Social Connectedness: The Role of the Local Church in Building Community.' *Pointers* 26, no. 4 (2016): 1–5.

Gill, Robin. *Society Shaped by Theology: Sociological Theory Volume 3* (Farnham: Ashgate, 2013).

Goheen, Michael. *Introducing Christian Mission Today: Scripture, History and Issues* (Downers Grove, IVP Academic, 2014).

Groody, Daniel. 'Migrants and Refugees: Christian Faith and the Globalization of Solidarity.' In *International Review of Mission* 104, no. 2 (2015): 314–23.

Halpern, David. *Social Capital* (Polity Press, 2005).

Jobes, Karen. *1 Peter* (Grand Rapids: Baker, 2010).

Lausanne Committee for World Evangelization. *Globalization and the Gospel: Rethinking Mission in the Contemporary World*. Lausanne Occasional Paper, no. 30 (2004).

Leigh, Andrew. *Disconnected* (UNSW Press 2010).

Moffat, Jennifer. *Engaging Rural and Remote Communities: A Practice Framework.* Accessed on May 31, 2017. www.queensland.gov.au/storage.

Ott, Craig. 'Globalisation and Contextualisation: Reframing the Task of Contextualisation in the Twenty-First Century.' In *Missiology* 43, no. 1 (2015): 43–58.

Parliament of Australia. *Refugee Resettlement to Australia: What Are the Facts?* (2016). Accessed June 15, 2017. http://www.aph.gov.au/About_Parliament/Parliamentary_Departments/Parliamentary_Library/pubs/rp/rp1617/RefugeeResettlement.

Pilbara Housing and Land Snapshot. December 2016 Quarterly Report. Accessed June 15, 2017. www.pdc.wa.gov.au.

Putnam, Robert. *Bowling Alone: The Collapse and Revival of American Community* (Simon and Schuster, 2000).

Putnam, Robert, and David E. Campbell. *American Grace: How Religion Divides and Unites Us* (New York: Simon and Schuster, 2010).

Refugee Council of Australia. *Australia's Refugee and Humanitarian Program Statistics* (2016). Accessed June 15, 2017. http://www.refugeecouncil.org.au/getfacts/statistics/aust/australias-refugee-humanitarian-program-2/.

Riches, Tanya. 'God's Brand is Love: Australian Pentecostalism in the United States of America'. *Australian Journal of Mission Studies* 8, no. 1 (2014): 53–62.

Semenas, Vilius. 'Ethnic Diversity and Social Capital at the Community Level: Effects and Implications for Policymakers.' *Inquiries* 6, no. 4 (2014): 1–2.

Short, Monica. 'Belonging: Social Work, Sociological and Theological Insights into Engagements with People Living with Disabilities.' In *Swift: Newsletter of the Australian Association of Social Workers New South Wales Branch*, no. 1 (2017).

Short, Monica. *Three Anglican Churches Engaging with People from Culturally and Linguistically Diverse Backgrounds* (Sydney, NSW: BCA, 2015).

Short, Monica, Geoff Broughton, Mark Short, Yangi Ochala, and Bill Anscombe. 'Connecting to Belonging: A Cross-Disciplinary Inquiry into Rural Australian Anglican Church Engagements with People from Culturally and Linguistically Diverse Backgrounds.' In *Journal of Contemporary Religion* 32, no. 1 (2017): 119–33.

Smith, Shively, T. J. *Strangers to Family: Diaspora and 1 Peter's Invention of God's Household* (Waco: Baylor University Press, 2016).

Sorensen, Tony. 'Imagining the Impact of Globalisation on the Future of Australia's Rural Communities.' *Horizons in Geography* 81–82 (2012): 116–124.

Sydney Morning Herald. 'You're Not Welcome, Town Tells Refugees' (December 15, 2006). Accessed May 31, 2017. www.ausidentity.blogspot.com.au/2010/01/sudanese-refugees-wagga-wagga-gets-dose.html.

United Nations. *Population Density and Urbanisation* (2017). Accessed June 15, 2017. https://www.mozilla.org/en-US/firefox/central/.

United Nations. *Refugees* (2016). Accessed June 15, 2017. http://www.un.org/en/sections/issues-depth/refugees/index.html.

United Nations. *Rural Poverty* (2017). Accessed June 15, 2017. http://www.un.org/en/sections/issues-depth/rural-poverty/index.html.

United Nations High Commissioner for Refugees. *Convention and Protocol Relating to the Status of Refugees* (1951). Accessed June 15, 2017. http://www.unhcr.org/en-au/3b66c2aa10.

Vinson, Tony. *Dropping Off the Edge: The Distribution of Disadvantage in Australia* (Jesuit Social Services, 2007).

Chapter 6

A CENTURY AND A HALF TO CALL THIS 'HOME': CHINESE CHURCHES IN SYDNEY

Michael Chu

Chinese migrants from various parts of Asia started moving to Australia as early as the mid-nineteenth century. Out of fleeing poverty or striving for a better livelihood, they left their homelands and moved to Australia in search of a new home on new soil. In turn, some of these new Asian migrants started attending churches, searching for a spiritual home, marking the genesis of Chinese churches in Australia.

This chapter details a history of Chinese churches in Sydney. It considers the historical background of Chinese migrants, the size of Chinese migration, the development of Chinese churches and the fruit of Chinese churches. It also reveals certain aspects of social engagement between Chinese migrants and local Australians.

History of Chinese Migrants to Sydney

Australia is a multicultural nation of migrants. One in four of Australia's 22 million people were born overseas, from more than 270 ancestries. Nearly 50 percent of the population have at least one parent who was born overseas.[1]

---

1   Australian Human Rights Commission, 'Face the Facts: Cultural Diversity', accessed October 18, 2017, https://www.humanrights.gov.au/face-facts-cultural-diversity.

From 1851, with the discovery of gold at Ballarat, Chinese workers and migrants began to settle in Australia—first in Victoria, then in various regions of New South Wales, such as the Rocky River Goldfield and at Bathurst.[2] At the peak of the gold rush, the Chinese population in Australia totalled almost 40,000.[3] Choi's research reveals that 'not all the Chinese in goldfield areas were gold miners; some were scattered around mining towns managing small stores and groceries, or working in market gardens, or keeping cafes and boarding houses. The Chinese population in the capital cities was not large'.[4]

After the peak of the gold rush years, some Chinese miners returned to China, while other miners chose to move to Sydney, which soon became the city with the highest Chinese population. In 1901, there were 10,073 Chinese recorded in New South Wales.[5] 'Chinese were found in most of the suburbs in Sydney . . . in 1901, but the principal concentrations, both of residence and shops, were in the city centre . . . around the Haymarket-Dixon Street area . . .'[6]

After the gold rush, the number of Chinese migrants in Australia dropped, largely due to a change of government policy. The policy that initially affected migrants was the Immigration Restriction Act, one that was passed in 1901. This

---

[2] NSW Government State Records, 'Immigration from Many Lands', accessed 10 August 2015, http://www.records.nsw.gov.au/state-archives/research-topics/immigration/immigration-from-many-lands. Although the Gold Rush in Victoria was better known, other documents indicate that Chinese gold miners gathered in New South Wales as well. For example, as early as 1866, more than 120 Chinese miners at the Rocky River Goldfield sent a petition letter on April 18 to the Minister for Lands and Executive Council. They asked for the return of Commissioner Dalton as the Gold Commissioner, as they felt that Dalton's presence there could protect them from racial conflict. According to Choi, in the mid-nineteenth century, most Chinese settlers in Australia were in the gold field. 'In Victoria in 1861, the goldfield areas of Ararat, Ballarat, Beechworth, Castlemaine, Maryborough and Sandhurst had some 24,000 among a total Chinese population of 24,700. In New South Wales in the same year (1861), of a total 13,000 Chinese, about 12,200 of them were in the mining areas—Mount Braidwood, Bathurst, Bombala, Turon and Wellington'. C. Y. Choi, *Chinese Migration and Settlement in Australia* (University of Sydney, NSW: Sydney University Press, 1975); Lindsay Maxwell Smith, '*Hidden Dragons: The Archaeology of Mid to Late Nineteenth-Century Chinese Communities in Southeastern New South Wales*,' unpublished diss. (Canberra, ACT, The Australian National University, 2006), 209.

[3] Wendy Lu Mar, *So Great a Cloud of Witnesses: A History of the Chinese Presbyterian Church, Sydney 1893–1993* (Sydney, NSW: Chinese Presbyterian Church, Sydney, 1993), 1.

[4] C. Y. Choi, *Chinese Migration and Settlement in Australia*, 28.

[5] The figure is an addition of the settlers from China (9993) and Hong Kong (80). Australian Bureau of Statistics, 'Table 72. Population, Sex and Country of Birth, States and Territories, 1901 Census', accessed September 7, 2016, http://www.abs.gov.au/AUSSTATS/abs@.nsf/DetailsPage/3105.0.65.0012006?OpenDocument.

[6] C. Y. Choi, *Chinese Migration and Settlement in Australia*, 33.

later developed into the so-called 'White Australia' policy,[7] which forbade Chinese and Asian people to enter Sydney or into other parts of Australia.[8]

Moreover, the first group of Chinese in Australia were mostly men who had left their wives and children in their homelands.[9] The ratio of male and female migrants was disproportionally skewed towards the former. As the Chinese settlers grew old, most of them chose to return to their homeland and to reunite with their families in China.

In the early 1950s, the Australian government started to restore relationships with Asian nations and planned to erase the negative impressions caused by the White Australia policy.[10] Steps were taken to accept non-European migrants. In 1957, a policy was passed allowing non-Europeans who had resided in Australia for fifteen years to become Australian citizens.[11] Moreover, the infamous dictation test associated with citizenship was abolished. This allowed business migrants to enter Australia with their families[12] and for Chinese and their descendants to settle in Sydney for the long-term. With Chinese children being born in Sydney, biological growth was significant. 'Non-English-speaking-background' migrants

---

7   The White Australian Policy was developed as a national ideal, 'a vision of a future Australia inhabited only by "white" people'. Andrew Marcus, 'White Australia', in *The Oxford Companion to Australian History* (South Melbourne, VIC: Oxford University Press, 2001), 686. The superiority of white Australians to all non-European people 'was nurtured by racial theories, particularly Social Darwinism, at a time of apparent global dominance of the European civilisation. Marcus, 'White Australia', 687.

8   According to the 1901 Immigration Acts, all Asians attempting to enter Australia had to go through the infamous dictation test. It was a test of any European language (such as Italian, French or English). It was virtually impossible to prepare for the test beforehand. It became clear that, practically, no Chinese person could enter Australia anymore. NSW Migration Heritage Centre, '1901 Immigration Restriction Act', accessed September 7, 2016, http://www.migrationheritage.nsw.gov.au/exhibition/objectsthroughtime/immigration-restriction-act/.

9   In the early stages of the gold rush, the Immigration Restriction Act allowed the wives of migrants to enter Australia. However, in 1905, the clause allowing the entry of wives was cancelled. Alanna Kamp, 'Chinese Australian Women in White Australia: Utilising Available Sources to Overcome the Challenge of "Invisibility"', *Chinese Southern Diaspora Studies* 6 (2013): 79.

10 NSW Migration Heritage Centre, 'Object Through Time: Australian Migration History Timeline, 1945–1965', accessed September 7, 2016, http://www.migrationheritage.nsw.gov.au/exhibition/objectsthroughtime-history/1945-1965/.

11 Barry York, 'White Australia Policy—The Beginning of The End 50 Years Ago', *Museum of Australian Democracy at Old Parliament House*, accessed September 7, 2016, http://moadoph.gov.au/blog/white-australia-policy-the-beginning-of-the-end-50-years-ago/.

12 Mar, *So Great a Cloud of Witnesses*, 22.

thus grew gradually.¹³ Statistics show an increase of more than three thousand Chinese residing in Sydney in the period from 1954 to 1961.¹⁴

Major Factors of Chinese Migration to Sydney

After 1970, certain factors contributed to the growth of Chinese migration and settlements. Firstly, in the 1970s, the political instability in certain Asian countries, such as that following the fall of Vietnam in 1975, the civil war in Cambodia and the Indonesian annexation of East Timor in the mid-1970s, caused a lot of refugees to seek asylum in Australia.¹⁵

From the 1960s, the Australian government gradually began to abolish the White Australia policy, instead adopting a policy of multiculturalism.¹⁶ In the 1970s, the Whitlam government abolished university fees for overseas students and graduates were allowed to stay in Australia after their study. Thus, upon graduation, a great number of young, highly educated, bilingual (if not multilingual) and skilled professionals became Australian residents. These graduates stayed, worked and started their families in Australia. This particular policy was in effect until early in the 1980s.¹⁷

In addition, in the early 1980s, Britain and China started several rounds of negotiation on the future of Hong Kong.¹⁸ The Sino-British Joint Declaration was signed in 1984, stipulating that Britain would return Hong Kong to China

---

13 Mar, *So Great a Cloud of Witnesses*, 38; James Jupp, *Australian People: An Encyclopedia of the Nation, Its People and Their Origins* (North Ryde, NSW: Angus & Robertson Publishers, 1988), 121.
14 Mar, *So Great a Cloud of Witnesses*, 21.
15 Mar, *So Great a Cloud of Witnesses*, 38.
16 Department of Immigration and Citizenship, 'Fact Sheet 6—Australia's Multicultural Policy', *Australian Government, Department of Immigration and Citizenship*, accessed November 14, 2016, http://www.immi.gov.au/media/fact-sheets/06australias-multicultural-policy.htm.
17 Lyndon Megarrity, 'Under the Shadow of the White Australia Policy: Commonwealth Policies on Private Overseas Students 1945–1972', *Change: Transformations in Education* 6 (2005), 45–46.
18 The background of the negotiation between China and Britain has to be traced back to the mid-nineteenth century. In the mid-nineteenth century, several treaties were signed between Britain and China, leasing Hong Kong to Britain. As the lease of Hong Kong was to expire in 1997, the future of Hong Kong was uncertain in the 1980s. Thus, the negotiations were necessary and urgent.

on 1 July 1997. The signing of the declaration triggered a tide of migration.[19] Many young Cantonese-speaking families and educated professionals migrated to Sydney. According to statistics, there was a big increase of numbers in the Hong Kong migrant community in Sydney from 1971 to 2000.[20]

Towards the end of the 1980s, because of the Tiananmen Square massacre, the Australian government established a policy of accepting more Chinese migrants.[21] Thus, fifteen thousand Chinese students, mostly Mandarin speaking, were granted temporary visas.

From 1980 to the early 2000s, the number of Chinese migrants coming to Australia increased significantly. Figure 1 below shows that the increasing rate of migrants from Hong Kong's SAR[22] and from China was astonishing.

Year of Arrival in Australia	Number from Hong Kong (SAR of China)	Number from China (excl. SARs and Taiwan)
2001 to 9 Aug 2011	7,190	76,084
1991 to 2000	12,620	37,660
1981 to 1990	11,724	27,161
1971 to 1980	4,239	3,817
1961 to 1970	1,126	1,907
Arrived in 1960 or earlier	603	2,688

Figure 1: Number of Chinese migrants arriving in Australia by origin

---

19   The background of the tide of migration should be traced back to 1950. The Communist government ruled mainland China from 1949 and there were several waves of political unrest and social upheaval (such as the infamous Cultural Revolution). Many residents in China (mainly the wealthy and educated) were oppressed by and suffered at hands of the Communist government. Thus, they chose to escape from China to Hong Kong in the 1950s and 1960s. Now, as 1997 approached, the horrible memory of the past oppression triggered a strong urge to migrate to Australia and other Western countries.

20   NSW Government, 'Birthplace—China (excl. SARs and Taiwan), Year of Arrival', 2011, accessed July 30, 2015, http://multiculturalnsw.id.com.au/multiculturalnsw/birthplace-by-year-of-arrival?COIID=5038.

21   The Australian Prime Minister at the time, Bob Hawke, shedding tears at Parliament House after the Tiananmen Square massacre was broadcast on television. His sympathy for the Chinese students resulted in the policy of accepting more Chinese migrants. Greg Callaghan, 'Remembering Tiananmen', *The Australian* (2009), accessed September 2, 2016, http://www.theaustralian.com.au/news/remembering-tiananmen/story-e6frg6n6-1225712617852.

22   SAR stands for Special Administrative Region. Hong Kong returned to China in 1997 and has been renamed as Hong Kong Special Administrative Region. The reason for using SAR is that Hong Kong maintains a different political, judicial and economic system from the communist China.

Although migrants from mainland China, Taiwan, Hong Kong and other South-East Asian countries (such as Indonesia, Malaysia, Singapore, Vietnam and Cambodia) were all ethnic Chinese, their cultural constructs varied.[23] Before the 1980s, mainland China was politically and socially separated from the Western world. China had virtually no business dealings or interactions in the international arena. Migrants from mainland China remained culturally traditional. However, Hong Kong had been a British colony for more than a century and social and business interactions with the rest of the world were common practice. Additionally, the education system in Hong Kong maintained a British influence. The people of Hong Kong were thus culturally much less traditionally Chinese. Meanwhile, culturally, Taiwan was in between mainland China and Hong Kong. In this regard, the cultural constructs of Chinese migrants were quite diverse.

History of Chinese Churches in Sydney

THE ESTABLISHMENT OF THE CHINESE PRESBYTERIAN CHURCH

At the close of the nineteenth century, the leaders of the Sydney Presbyterian Church started noticing the number of Chinese workers and their need for the good news. With the continuous support of the Presbyterian Foreign Mission Committee,[24] the Chinese Presbyterian Church (CPC) came into existence in 1893. In subsequent decades, the Presbyterian Foreign Mission Committee provided support in two ways: one was with the purchasing of a church hall;[25] another was through recruiting Chinese-speaking pastors to minister to the congregation.[26] By the early 1960s, the two-hundred-member Chinese Presbyterian Church had its own minister and church building, and was totally self-supporting.[27]

23　It is noted that the demographic result of the survey shows that most of the pastors in Chinese churches are Cantonese speaking. It is plausible to suggest that the place of origin of many Cantonese-speaking pastors is from Hong Kong or the Canton province of China.

24　In August 1892, the Presbyterian Church in New South Wales held 'a grand missionary musical festival' in the Sydney Town Hall to raise funds to purchase a site for the Chinese Presbyterian Christians. Chinese Presbyterian Church, *Chinese Presbyterian Church: Centenary Magazine 1893–1993* (Sydney, NSW: Chinese Presbyterian Church, 1994).

25　The first church hall was purchased in 1893 in Foster Street, Surry Hills. In 1957, Fullerton Memorial Church was acquired by the Chinese Presbyterian Church. Mar, *So Great a Cloud of Witnesses*, 4, 22.

26　A few ministers were inducted and appointed, with Rev John Young Wai as the first minister, who also became the longest serving pastor of the Chinese Presbyterian Church. Mar, *So Great a Cloud of Witnesses*, 63.

27　Mar, *So Great a Cloud of Witnesses*, 25.

The two decades after 1960 were marked by continuous growth of the CPC. One of the contributing factors to the continuous growth was the faithful, devoted and vigorous service of two ministers, Rev David C. K. Tsai and Rev Philip Fong. They were enthusiastic in Bible proclamation and in gospel ministry. The service of these ministers improved the quality of ministry and the stability of the pastoral leadership.

Another factor was that Reverend Tsai could speak and preach in various Chinese dialects, such as Mandarin and Swatow, so that the congregation could have access to the Word of God in their heart language.[28]

Moreover, the stable membership also allowed the pastors to select and equip certain church members to become lay leaders. With the assistance of faithful lay leaders, the ministers could concentrate on preaching, teaching, leadership and pastoral care.

FORMATION OF CHINESE MINISTRY IN THE CENTRAL BAPTIST CHURCH

Before the Chinese Presbyterian Church was founded, a Baptist church was opened in Bathurst Street in 1836, with John Saunders, who had travelled from London to Sydney, as their first pastor.[29] The Bathurst Street Baptist Church later moved to 619 George Street, Sydney, and was renamed the Central Baptist Church on October 9, 1937.[30] As the location of the church was close to Chinatown and The University of Sydney, a Chinese fellowship for Chinese settlers and overseas students was formed at the Central Baptist Church, and gradually became a significant ministry.[31]

A few events proved to be milestones for the Chinese ministry at the Central Baptist Church. In 1964, about thirty members attended the first 'Chinese Sunday School', which for years was known as 'The Asian Department'. In 1971, Rev Edward Yu was ordained as the first Chinese minister and served the church until 1994. In 1993, the first Cantonese service commenced on Sunday mornings. Rev

---

28   Mar, *So Great a Cloud of Witnesses*, 27.

29   Alan C. Prior, *Some Fell on Good Ground: A History of the Beginnings and Development of the Baptist Church in New South Wales, Australia, 1831–1965* (Sydney, NSW: Baptist Union of New South Wales, 1966); Ken R. Manley, *In the Heart of Sydney: Central Baptist Church, 1836–1986* (Sydney, NSW: Central Baptist Church, 1987); Philip J. Hughes, *The Baptists in Australia* (Nunawading, VIC: Christian Research Association, 1996).

30   Roy Gilchrist and Ailsa Thompson, *A Brief History of Central Baptist Church* (Sydney, NSW: Central Baptist Church, 2001), 254. In late 1960s, small fellowship groups were set up in some Baptist churches, such as Stanmore Baptist Church, Ashfield Baptist Church and Randwick Baptist Church. Joseph Fung, *United Chinese Evangelism Committee (Brief History)*, (Sydney, NSW, n.d.).

31   In the late 1950s, the Chinese fellowship attracted some Chinese members and overseas Chinese students. Generally, about forty Chinese attended the fellowship regularly.

David Tse was appointed as the senior pastor in 1996 and has become the longest serving pastor of the church. It was remarkable that such an established and well-developed local Baptist church would appoint two ethnic Chinese pastors as their senior pastors. This was mainly due to the evangelistic and strategic foresight of the leaders and the faithful ministry of mission-minded members.[32]

THE CHINESE CHRISTIAN CHURCH AND THE WEST SYDNEY CHINESE CHRISTIAN CHURCH

In the mid-1960s, another Chinese church was formed. Four elders[33] from the Chinese Presbyterian Church observed the need for gospel proclamation and spiritual nurturing among the ever-increasing Chinese migrants. They also noticed that some converted Christians did not want to join a church with Presbyterian denominational background and beliefs.[34] As cited in one report:

> . . . because of denominational divisions, complacency and language difficulties, wonderful opportunities to cultivate spiritual advancements and Christian works among the believers were sadly missed, and organised efforts to spread the Gospel among the unbelievers were lacking. The need for an inter-denominational and independent Church to fulfil this urgent need weighed heavily in the hearts of many devoted Chinese Christians.[35]

In August 1965, the interdenominational Chinese Christian Church (CCC) was formed, which was a church with congregational governance.[36]

The church recorded fast growth in the first few years. In the first year, the church met at the AMP auditorium at Circular Quay and the attendance jumped to

---

32 Although Central Baptist Church has developed a strong Chinese ministry, the church has never claimed that they were a Chinese church. The Chinese congregation was simply a Chinese ministry among many ministries in the local Baptist church.

33 The four elders were T. Y. Lin, T. C. Chen, T. Liao and A. Wong. Chinese Christian Church, *Moving Forward: CCC Milsons Point 50 Anniversary Publication* (Sydney, NSW: Chinese Christian Church, 2015), 15.

34 As a matter of fact, some early leaders and members of the Chinese Christian Church were from a Baptist church background. The first baptism of the Chinese Christian Church was actually held at Central Baptist Church, instead of at the Chinese Presbyterian Church. Chinese Christian Church, *Moving Forward*, 15–18.

35 Chinese Christian Church, *Moving Forward*, 2.

36 Congregational governance signifies that the major decisions are made by the members in general meetings. The day-to-day decisions are made by the board of deacons or board of elders, which are led predominantly by the lay leaders. The pastors are expected to provide ministry guidance and advice only. Such church governance is adopted by most independent churches.

more than one hundred.[37] Gifted overseas preachers, such as Dr Leland Wang, Dr Hong Sit and Rev Wilson Wang were invited to proclaim the Bible message. The power of God's Word changed and transformed many people's lives.[38] In 1967, the Chinese Christian Church decided to purchase a church from the North Sydney Congregational Church at a price of $110,000.[39] A few years after the inception of the CCC, for various reasons, the four founding elders stepped down from the key leadership positions and younger members took over the leadership.[40] Dynamic, and with a strong background with the Overseas Christian Fellowship (OCF),[41] they laid a solid foundation for the newly established church.

In the early 1970s, the Chinese Christian Church's church hall became overcrowded—the attendance had increased from 150 in 1975 to 240 in 1977[42]—so the suggestion was made to plant a new church. As a result, the West Sydney Chinese Christian Church (WSCCC) was established at Strathfield to serve local Chinese migrants. In 1978, their first meeting was held at the Burwood Gospel Hall and in 1983 the Strathfield Uniting Church was bought as a new church venue. The West Sydney Chinese Christian Church became independent in January 1982[43] and the key leaders of the new church were Rev Wilfred Chee, Hock Leng Hiu, Peter Chen, Pak Lim Chu and Lim Kim Bew.[44]

Both the Chinese Christian Church and the West Sydney Chinese Christian Church started with a monolingual (English) service. In the 1980s and 1990s, as Chinese migrants continued to enter Sydney, the churches set up Cantonese and Mandarin services to meet the needs of Cantonese-speaking and Mandarin-speaking migrants.[45]

The process of establishing branch churches, and later becoming independent churches, was smooth and pleasant. Although the West Sydney Chinese Christian Church became independent, both the Chinese Christian Church and the West

---

37 Chinese Christian Church, *Moving Forward*, 20.
38 Chinese Christian Church, *Moving Forward*, 20–22.
39 Chinese Christian Church, *Moving Forward*, 27–28.
40 T. Y. Lin passed away in 1971. A. Wong returned to CPC and resumed his elder position. T. C. Chen and T. Liao decided not to serve in the key leadership team. Chinese Christian Church, *Moving Forward*, 33.
41 As recalled by Joseph Fung, the key ministry of the Overseas Christian Fellowship in the 1960s was Bible study. OCF members benefited from various faculty members of Moore Theological College (including Broughton Knox, Peter O'Brien, Peter Jensen and Alan Cole). OCF became a platform for leadership training. More discussion of OCF to follow below.
42 Chinese Christian Church, *Moving* Forward, 37.
43 Chinese Christian Church, *Moving Forward*, 38.
44 Information taken from a personal conversation with Rev Chris Chua on July 16, 2015, at North Rocks, NSW, Australia.
45 Chinese Christian Church, *Moving* Forward, 38.

Sydney Chinese Christian Church continued to work closely together for a number of years, undertaking joint ministries such as the Joint Missionary Committee.[46] The establishment of the West Sydney Chinese Christian Church was of critical significance to the Chinese churches in Sydney, so that establishing branch churches became a new paradigm or model for planting new churches.

PERIOD OF CHURCH PLANTING

By the end of the 1970s, the three existing Chinese churches (the Chinese Presbyterian Church, the Chinese Christian Church and the West Sydney Chinese Christian Church) had paved the way for many new churches. Since the early 1980s, the growth of Chinese churches in Sydney has been remarkable. By 2016, around one hundred new churches had been established, which included denominational churches such as Presbyterian, Alliance, Baptist, Anglican, Evangelical Free, Lutheran, Salvation Army, Uniting and the Ling Liang Church. The growth of independent congregational churches was also astonishing. Some churches were purely monolingual, either Cantonese or Mandarin. Many others were Cantonese speaking (or Mandarin speaking) with an English service for the young people of the second generation. Doctrinally, they ranged from evangelical Bible-believing churches to Pentecostal and charismatic churches.[47]

Many factors contributed to the church planting phenomenon. One was the ever-increasing growth of Chinese migration.[48] The huge needs of new migrants were visibly met by their attendance at Sunday services and various church meetings. Migrants were people in transition, undergoing drastic changes in life situation. Therefore, they became more open and receptive to Christianity and started attending church.[49] Churches were able to play a crucial role in providing

---

46 Chinese Christian Church, *Moving Forward*, 38.

47 Information taken from a personal conversation with Rev Joseph Fung on July 15, 2015 at Cremorne, NSW, and a conversation with Rev Chris Chua on July 16, 2015 at North Rocks, NSW.

48 NSW Government, 'Birthplace—China (excl. SARs and Taiwan), Year of Arrival' (2011), accessed July 30, 2015, http://multiculturalnsw.id.com.au/multiculturalnsw/birthplace-by-year-of-arrival?COIID=5038; NSW Government, 'Birthplace—Hong Kong (SAR of China), Year of Arrival' (2011), accessed July 30, 2015, http://multiculturalnsw.id.com.au/multiculturalnsw/birthplace-by-year-of-arrival?COIID=5039.

49 According to the diaspora missiology proposed by Wan and Tira, missions to migrants can be understood as 'missions at our doorstep'. The notion of 'missions at our doorstep' is characterised by such dimensions as accessibility to people, ample opportunity, a holistic ministry approach and partnership. These characteristics become the main driving forces in the rapid growth of Chinese churches. Enoch Wan and Sadiri Joy Tira, 'Diaspora Missiology and Missions in the Context of the Twenty-First Century', *Torch Trinity Journal* 13, no. 1 (2010): 51–52.

physical support and community connection for the migrants.[50] As most new migrants were yet to become acquainted with Australian culture, and were yet to learn English, they were virtual outsiders to Australian society. Thus, Chinese churches could be perceived as social safe havens, where they could maintain their Chinese traditions, language and culture. An immediate effect was that the existing number of churches could not cope with the increasing rate of growth. Hence many new churches were planted.

Another factor was the generous partnership and support from the pastors of Caucasian churches and the principals of local schools.[51] They were particularly crucial in the pioneering stage of newly-planted churches. Specifically, Caucasian pastors allowed the Chinese groups to meet in their church halls, even at the prime time of Sunday mornings. School principals made available their school halls and classrooms to Chinese churches, for them to use for Sunday services and Sunday school classes.[52] Although granting permission to use their premises certainly added extra administration for the churches and schools, their tolerance and support were a great help.

Fruits of Chinese Churches

FRUITS OF CHINESE CHURCHES: EVANGELISM AND MISSION

The thirty-year growth of the Chinese church in Sydney from the 1980s has not only been characterised by church planting.

---

50   Jackson and Passarelli discuss the role of the church extensively in their work, although the discussion is more within a European context. Darrell Jackson and Alessia Passarelli, *Mapping Migration, Mapping Churches' Responses in Europe: Belonging, Community and Integration: The Witness and Service of Churches in Europe* (Geneva, CH: Churches' Commission for Migrants in Europe and the World Council of Churches, 2016).

51   This is the concept of partnership in the diaspora missiology suggested by Wan and Tira. Wan and Tira, 'Diaspora Missiology and Missions', 45–56.

52   For example, the Chinese Australian Baptist Church West Ryde has been meeting at Marsden High School since 1986. In their early years, 1987 to 1992, Northern District Chinese Christian Church (NDCCC) was using Marsfield Community Church as a venue. Also, NDCCC has been using Epping North Public School for Sunday school classes since 1992 and Epping Boys High School for Sunday services since 2010. Various Sunday services of the Evangelical Free Church of Australia have been meeting at Chatswood Public School and Chatswood Church of Christ since 1987. Hills District Chinese Christian Church met at Castle Hill Baptist Church from 1992 to 1997. Beverly Hills Chinese Baptist Church used Kingsgrove Beverly Hills Baptist Church as a venue from 1995 to 2002. From 1993 to 2000, Livingstone Evangelical Free Church used Beecroft Primary School, Carlingford High School and North Rocks Primary School as venues for Sunday services. North Shore Chinese Christian Church met at Gordon Baptist Church from 2006 until 2013, when the church merged with Gordon Baptist Church.

From 1980 to 2016, the Chinese churches underwent a period of growth. Unchurched people were reached through evangelistic rallies, personal evangelism and local mission. Alongside evangelistic meetings arranged by individual churches, inter-church evangelistic rallies were organised.[53] Well-known gifted overseas evangelists were invited to speak at those rallies, and hundreds responded to altar calls.[54]

Various methods of personal evangelism were employed by churches, such as *Evangelism Explosion*, *Two Ways to Live* and *Four Spiritual Laws*. Pre-evangelism initiatives were also used to reach non-Christian friends.[55] These were complemented by loving care, new migrant support and constant prayer. As a result, numerous new converts joined the churches.

Chinese churches also became passionate about overseas missions. On June 3, 1990, a meeting on mission was organised by the Overseas Missionary Fellowship Australia (OMF) for Chinese churches.[56] The speaker, James Hudson Taylor III, challenged the 650 young people attending to 'go forth into battle' and to be involved in mission. Forty young men and women made commitments to do full-time mission ministry.[57]

A joint taskforce titled Chinese Churches for Mission was formed in 2004, initiated by Dr Calvin Ma, who was then the national director of OMF Australia. The taskforce was joined by representatives from various mission agencies[58] and the Sydney Chinese Christian Churches Association. It was set up to mobilise Chinese

---

53 Chinese Presbyterian Church, *Chinese Presbyterian Church: Centenary Magazine 1893–1993* (Sydney, NSW: Chinese Presbyterian Church, 1994), 3.

54 Major evangelistic rallies were jointly organised by Chinese churches once every two years through the Sydney Chinese Evangelistic Association (SCEA), which later developed into the Sydney Chinese Christian Churches Association (SCCCA). These rallies were held at various auditoriums with huge seating capacities, such as the Sydney Town Hall, Sydney Opera House and Sydney Showground. The above information is extracted from the minutes of the Sydney Chinese Christian Churches Association (SCCCA) meetings.

55 Christian movies and music, outings and picnics, soccer teams and other sports, and parenting and marriage seminars were employed to reach out. Some churches organised quality children's programs, which led many non-Christian parents to place their children in Chinese churches, as the parents wanted their children to make more Chinese childhood friends. Some churches were skilful enough to organise Christian parenting talks in parallel to the children's programs, at which the good news was shared to parents. As a result, the parents became Christians.

56 Joseph Fung, *UCEC Report on CIM (OMF) Centenary Thanksgiving Worship Service* (Sydney, NSW: United Chinese Evangelism Committee, 1990).

57 This is taken from a report to the United Chinese Evangelism Committee (which later became the Sydney Chinese Christian Churches Association) by Rev Joseph Fung to OMF, dated June 8, 1990.

58 OMF, SIM, Wycliffe, the Chinese Christian Mission Australia and the Far East Broadcasting Company.

churches for global mission. Surveys on mission involvement of Chinese churches in Sydney were conducted. Mission training days and mission conferences were organised in 2006 and 2007.[59] With all of these events and initiatives, from 1980 to 2000, almost twenty missionaries were sent overseas by Chinese churches.[60]

Moreover, regular short-term mission trips (one every two months) to rural New South Wales were organised by the Chinese Christian Mission Australia. Destinations included Penrith, Bathurst, Orange, Wagga Wagga, Canberra, Albury, Newcastle, Wollongong, Tamworth and Armidale. Every team was comprised of approximately ten members from various Chinese churches.

The above-mentioned results were the joint effort of pastors and members of various Chinese churches, as well as of certain passionate mission leaders and preachers, and the constant assistance of mission organisations. This resulted in multiple converts, who, in turn, became members of Chinese churches. It also resulted in sending many missionaries overseas.

FRUITS OF CHINESE CHURCHES: YOUNG PEOPLE'S MINISTRY

Another prominent result of the growth of Chinese churches was the development of young people's ministry, among both Chinese-speaking and English-speaking Christians.

The first annual Combined Chinese Youth Summer Conference (CCYSC) was held in 1991 with full enrolment. In subsequent years, 150 to 200 Cantonese-speaking young Christians from different churches gathered together to learn the Bible. Speakers were invited from overseas to preach expositional sermons.

One of the results of the conferences was the establishment of the Chinese Christian Fellowship (CCF) in 1992, both at the University of Sydney and at the

---

59 This information is taken from the CCFM meeting minutes, dated October 26, 2006 and May 12, 2007.

60 Just to name a few. Dr Patrick and Jenny Fung were sent to Pakistan and Dr Fung has now become international director of OMF International. Dr Garry and Maggie Fong were sent to East Asia, where Dr Fong works as a medical doctor among minority groups. Rev Daniel and Dominica Lai were sent to Kenya, in charge of all the administrative affairs. Rev David and Janice Zheng were sent to Hong Kong to do mission broadcasting into China. Rev Phil and Irene Nicholson, Rev Wayne and Angela Chen and Miss Christine Dillon were sent to Taiwan. Dr Lawrence and Liling Tan were sent to Bolivia. Johan and Debbie Linder were sent to Thailand. Jacob Yung was sent to Tasmania. After 2000, there were even more missionaries sent from Chinese churches in Sydney, such as Shirley Jim, Sharon Law, John and Bec Yeo, Rolf and Bonnie Lepelaar, Jacqui Ng, Aaron and Amy Koh, Andrew and Jo Wong, Alex and Naomi Fung, Peter and Kath Lau, Rita and Rohan Minehan, John and Denise Dickson, Mark and Susan Boyley, Calvin and Joyce Ma, Cathy Lau, Grace Chu, Allan and Bronwyn Lihou, Jason and Hiwin Tam, John and Regine Gill, Dave and Jan Martin, Vivian To, Susanna Tse, Hoi Yan Shea, David and Jenn Ng, Moses Truong, Yakim and Grace Morgan, Lee-On Tan, and Michael and Joyce Lee.

University of New South Wales, with the primary target group being Cantonese-speaking students from Hong Kong. From 1993 and 1994, CCF groups were also set up at Macquarie University, the University of Technology Sydney, the University of Western Sydney and the University of Sydney Cumberland Campus. The regular weekly meetings were well attended, ranging from forty to one hundred students. CCF was the evangelistic arm of the church, reaching out to the young people on campus. The evangelistic initiatives of the students brought many young members, leaders and pastors into the Chinese churches.[61]

The ministry to English-speaking students also bore fruit. Overseas Christian Fellowship (OCF) aimed at and reached out to Asian overseas students, mainly from Malaysia, Singapore and other English-speaking Asian countries.[62] Many overseas students became devoted Christians and mission-minded leaders, and were subsequently involved in Chinese churches as leaders, pastors and missionaries.[63] Also, groups of the Fellowship of Overseas Christian University Students (FOCUS) were set up at the University of Sydney[64] and at the University of New South Wales.[65] Weekly Bible-study groups helped Asian and Chinese students grow in their Christian faith. English-speaking students also benefited from the annual Katoomba Leadership Conference which helped raise up English-speaking leaders and pastors. These leaders were trained in local theological

---

[61] Many of the then young leaders become pastors in Chinese churches, such as Wilson Fong (CABC—West Ryde), Herbert Chan (CABC—Thornleigh), Daniel Chan (Grace Chinese Christian Church), David Truong (Northern District Chinese Christian Church), Andrew Tung (Gracepoint Chinese Presbyterian Church), Billy Lee (Campbelltown Chinese Christian Church) and Eric Lai (Christ Evangelical Centre).

[62] Mar, *So Great a Cloud of Witnesses*, 28.

[63] For example, John Ting later became a minister at CPC. Andrew Lu later became an elder and session clerk at CPC. Bruce Lin later became an elder at the Chinese Christian Church Sydney. Wilfred Chee was the first one from OCF to serve as a full-time minister. Lim Kim Bew later became a minister at the Chinese Christian Church. Joseph Fung planted a number of Chinese Baptist churches and served as a key leader in the Sydney Chinese Christian Churches Association.

[64] AFES, 'Evangelical Union Sydney University > Sydney,' accessed November 14, 2016, https://www.afes.org.au/campus/evangelical-union-sydney-university-sydney.

[65] AFES, 'FOCUS University of New South Wales > Kensington,' accessed November 14, 2016, https://www.afes.org.au/campus/focus-university-new-south-wales-kensington.

colleges. Over the years, almost forty English-speaking Chinese pastors have been trained to serve in various Chinese churches and to teach in Bible colleges.[66]

It is noted that all of the youth ministries mentioned above were conducted in two separate language streams, Chinese and English, however the young people of Chinese groups and English groups had virtually zero contact with each other. It was true that *ministry* was blossoming, but in the early days the seed of *non-communication* between Chinese and English was being sown.

FRUITS OF CHINESE CHURCHES: THE SYDNEY CHINESE CHRISTIAN CHURCHES ASSOCIATION

By 1966, the leaders of Chinese churches in Sydney realised the great need for collaboration. Although, at the time, there were only two Chinese churches and a few small Chinese fellowships affiliated with some local Baptist churches, they formed the Combined Sydney Chinese Christian Revival and Evangelism Committee. This was all under the leadership of Rev Wilson Wong, who was then the pastor of the Chinese Presbyterian Church. The Christians joined hands in organising regular open-air evangelistic meetings in Dixon Street, Chinatown. They also organised once-a-year evangelistic rallies and annual family retreats. Meetings were conducted according to the languages of the target groups.

In 1975, through the encouragement of Rev Thomas Wang[67] of the Chinese Congress of World Evangelisation (CCOWE), the Combined Sydney Chinese Christian Revival and Evangelism Committee was re-formed and renamed the United Chinese Evangelistic Committee (UCEC), under the leadership of Rev Philip Fong, who was the minister of the Chinese Presbyterian Church. In 1993, UCEC was again renamed—the Sydney Chinese Evangelistic Association (SCEA). In 2003, the association became a government registered body, and was renamed the Sydney Chinese Christian Churches Association (SCCCA), with seventy-five

---

66   Some of the names are: Kenny Liew, Sam Chan, Andrew Hong, Eugene Hor, Michael Leong, Steve Chong, Sam Mak, Ying Yee, Tom Tokura, Peter Ko, Gary Koo, Peter Lin, Ben Johnson, John Menzies, Duncan Chang, John Dickson, Joshua Ng, Brian Tung, Cam Phong, Denise Chee, Ernest Chiang, David Tsai, David Chen, Alby Lam, Owen Seto, Simon Wong, Andrew Ku, Thomas Lai, Steve Turner, David Martin, Simon Chiu, John Gurusamy, Anthony Dumbrell, Michael Kwan, Sam Chan, Dan Wu, Andy Chung, Kenny Liew, David Truong, Doug Fyfe and Andrew Tipps.

67   Rev Thomas Wang later became the first general secretary of the Chinese Coordination Centre of World Evangelism in 1976. Chinese Coordination Centre of World Evangelism, 'General Secretary,' *Chinese Coordination Centre of World Evangelism, 2016*, accessed November 14, 2016, http://www.cccowe.org/content.php?id=about_general_secretary.

members.[68] One of the objectives was 'To encourage, promote and support the proclamation of the Gospel among the Chinese in Australia and overseas'.[69]

In terms of operation, general meetings were held once every two months, with Cantonese as the main language, and Mandarin and English as the auxiliary languages. Three ministry teams were set up according to the languages, namely Cantonese youth ministry, Mandarin ministry and English ministry,[70] and each team organised activities and events to meet the specific need of their language congregation. For example, the Combined Chinese Youth Summer Conference had been organised in Cantonese since 1991. Yet in 2013, the conference was divided into two language groups, Cantonese and Mandarin, as the number of Mandarin-speaking youth was increasing.[71] The English ministry team also organised training days in various districts to equip youth leaders in Chinese churches.

On occasion, ministries were organised with the joint force of all three language teams. For example, in 2015 and 2016, as 'same-sex marriage' became a hot issue in the political arena and subsequently among Chinese churches, joint initiatives of the three language teams of the SCCCA were organised. A forum on 'same-sex marriage' was organised with speakers speaking in both English and Mandarin. Petition letters representing all three language churches were sent to the Prime Minister and to the Leader of the Opposition. A statement by SCCCA on 'same-sex marriage' was published in newspapers on June 18, 2016.[72]

With the assistance of SCEA and SCCCA, a few new ministries were established to reach out to the needs of specific groups in the Chinese community, such as the Restaurant Mission, Marriage and Family For Christ,[73] the First Light Care Association[74] and the Chinese Theological College of Australia.[75] In a sense, UCEC, SCEA and SCCCA were catalysts for developing collaboration between

---

68 Joseph Fung, 'SCCCA—History, Sydney Chinese Christian Churches Association', accessed November 14, 2016, http://sccca.org.au/history; Frankie Law, *Annual Report 2016: Sydney Chinese Christian Churches Association* (Sydney, NSW: Sydney Chinese Christian Churches Association, 2016).

69 Sydney Chinese Christian Churches Association, 'About SCCCA,' Sydney Chinese Christian Churches Association, accessed November 14, 2016, http://sccca.org.au/about.

70 The Cantonese youth ministry team was led by Billy Lee, the Mandarin ministry team by Rev David Zheng, and the English ministry team by Rev Ying Yee.

71 Meeting minutes of the SCCCA—CYM on December 12, 2011 and September 17, 2012.

72 Law, *Annual Report 2016: Sydney Chinese Christian Churches Association*, 2.

73 Marriage and Family For Christ, 'About Marriage and Family For Christ,' accessed November 14, 2016, http://www.mffc.org.au/en/about/mffcau/.

74 First Light Care Association, 'History of FLC,' accessed November 14, 2016, http://www.firstlightcare.org.au/aboutus#history.

75 Chinese Theological College Australia, 'The Birth of the Vision,' accessed September 8, 2016, http://www.ctca.org.au/en/the-birth-of-the-vision/.

Chinese churches, vehicles for promoting mission and platforms for uniting the language congregations of Chinese churches.

The above ministries would not have come into existence without the foresight of visionary pastors. The pastors were not overwhelmed by heavy ministry loads and busyness. Their constant prayerful attention to the needs of Chinese churches contributed to the prosperous development of the ministry. Moreover, such a ministry pattern was not limited to the first-generation pastors. There were a few second-generation English-speaking Chinese pastors working in a similar manner.

It is noted, however, that ministries in those days were organised separately by Chinese-speaking and English-speaking leaders. There was little routine interaction or communication organised between English-speaking and Chinese-speaking leaders.[76] Pastoral leaders from the two generations rarely communicated their concerns or shared their visions. Not only was there non-communication between these two groups of leaders at SCCCA level, there was also a lack of communication among Chinese-speaking and English-speaking pastors in Chinese churches. It is believed that if the English-speaking and Chinese-speaking pastors had communicated regularly, it would have minimised the unnecessary conflicts and disputes that arose within Chinese churches. It would also have demonstrated and developed a desirable, healthy model of pastoral ministry.

FRUITS OF CHINESE CHURCHES: THEOLOGICAL EDUCATION

Over the last thirty years, theological education has enhanced the growth of Chinese churches. At the same time, the growth of Chinese churches has also fostered the establishment of a new Chinese theological college.

Local theological colleges contributed to the development of Chinese churches by organising lay-leader training programs. Morling College (Baptist) began offering certificate subjects in Cantonese from 2002.[77] Moore Theological College (Anglican) has offered Chinese correspondence courses since 1995. They have even translated six course textbooks into Chinese, including Introduction to the Bible, Old Testament 1, New Testament 1, Romans, Theology 1 and Reformation Church History.[78] As early as 1990, the China Graduate School of Theology (from Hong Kong) offered up to four subjects in Sydney for Cantonese

---

76 The only exception was the issue of same-sex marriage. In the last two years, there were some joint seminars and interaction between the Chinese group and the English group.

77 In 2002, I taught the first class of Introduction to Old Testament, which was attended by fifty-five students.

78 I was part of the organising team and was responsible for marking papers, translating and proofreading the course textbooks.

lay leaders each year (biblical subjects and ministry subjects).[79] Although these courses offered solid Bible teaching to lay leaders, the need for training pastors was not overlooked. The local theological colleges in Sydney have trained many pastors for Chinese churches and some pastors have even received higher research degrees.[80] All this training, however, has been in English.

In 1991, as the number of Chinese churches increased, a group of leaders (from Chinese churches)[81] realised that there was a need to train new pastors in Chinese. Pastors who were not proficient in English could therefore be trained to serve in pastoral ministry. In the process of discussion, they negotiated with various local colleges to explore the opportunity of partnership. In 2000, after years of discussion and planning, it was decided to set up a new college, the Chinese Theological College of Australia,[82] with Chinese as the main teaching language.[83]

The Chinese Theological College of Australia has indeed met the theological training needs of students who have less proficiency in English. Unfortunately, however, when the graduates enter into pastoral ministry in Chinese churches, their communication and relationships with pastors of other languages can be difficult.

Reflection and Conclusion

In summary, what has been outlined above reflects how the Chinese church has grown in both quantity and quality. As of 2015, there were over one hundred Chinese churches, incorporating more than an estimated fifteen thousand members. The evangelistic enthusiasm and outreach activities of these Chinese churches have become strong. In the last century, Chinese churches have changed from being 'receivers' to 'givers', from 'inward-looking' to 'out-reaching'. The newly developed Chinese churches have shown vitality and signs of self-replicating, self-

---

79   Again, I was also part of the organising committee of the courses.
80   Elim Hiu was awarded a ThD through Morling College. Pius Li and Michael Chu were awarded their DMin through Morling College. Joe Mock was awarded an MTh from Presbyterian Theological Centre (Australian College of Theology, 2016). A few others were awarded MAs from various colleges in Sydney, such as Michael Chu, Bob Lee, Albert Leung, Sunny Tse, Joe Lin, Almon Li, Frankie Law, Chris Chua, Joshua Mak, Wai Kwan Fung and Daniel Lai.
81   The group of people included Joseph Fung, Dennis Law, Charles Cheung, Pamela Chan, Michael Wong and Peter Wongso.
82   The first president was Dr Peter Wongso and the first dean was Rev Ming Leung, who was formerly the dean of Alliance College in Canberra. Dennis Law, Charles Cheung and Joseph Fung became the board members of the college.
83   At CTCA, Mandarin was the official teaching language, with Cantonese as the auxiliary language. However, basic questions about the Chinese theological college are yet to be answered. Do the students in the Chinese theological college receive enough exposure to and training about Australian culture? Are they well equipped with intercultural competence, so as to enable them to serve well in the bi-cultural Chinese churches?

government and self-support. Partnerships with local churches and colleges have become indispensable. Chinese churches are no longer churches on foreign soil—they can now call Australia home.

In the course of the growth and development of Chinese churches in Sydney, the support from Australian churches and leaders has been invaluable. The virtually unlimited support of the mission committee of the Presbyterian church in the late nineteenth century brought the Chinese Presbyterian Church into existence. Many local schools and Australian churches allowed and even welcomed Chinese churches to meet in their premises. Such a continual provision greatly minimised the difficulties of the development of Chinese churches. Moreover, over the last few decades, the faculty of Bible colleges (such as Moore College and Morling College) offered substantial theological training and education of ministers and leaders for Chinese churches.

Nevertheless, in the historical portrait above, two separate language streams are noticeable. Most of the events and ministries were monolingual, targeting a monocultural people group. In terms of effectiveness, they were successful. However, the underlying disadvantage was that the two language groups did not know one another. There was no communication or relationships and no ministry interface or platform between the two language groups. This non-interaction stretched from pastors to lay leaders and members, becoming a norm, which no one would question. In fact, the phenomenon was undetected, covered over by the overwhelming success. The question now is: can the members of the same family, the Chinese church in Sydney, survive without communication and interaction?

Furthermore, the above historical account forces one to reflect on one specific dimension of the notion of a spiritual home: whose home is it? Can Chinese Christians, whether born overseas or born in Australia (or raised in Australia), all call their Chinese church their home? As the overseas-born Chinese and Australian-born Chinese are of different cultural roots, their worldview and cultural values vary.[84] Thus, these two groups of members in Chinese churches appear to come from two different cultural backgrounds. They have different ways of thinking and doing things; they speak different languages.

Is there a common language for communication at this spiritual home? The first language of the members from a traditional Chinese culture and from an Australian culture are different. They must communicate with one another with their broken second language, or they simply cannot and do not communicate with the second language at all. Without such a common language, some members (and usually the members of the minority group) do not find a home in the church. Even worse, in some situations, members and leaders of both cultural backgrounds fight for the ownership and governing rights of Chinese churches.

These questions must be explored and answered by members and leaders of both cultural backgrounds. Without honest reflection and candid inquiry, the foundation of such a spiritual home will be undermined, and its future put at risk.

---

84 The cultural roots of older overseas-born Chinese are founded in traditional Chinese culture, which stems from Confucianism. The core concept of Confucianism is *ren* (or *jen*), which refers to harmony and goodness in social relationships, parental and filial piety, and brotherly respect, which explains why traditional Chinese value relationships (*guanxi*) and avoid open disagreements and conflict. See Wing T. Chan, 'On Translating Certain Chinese Philosophical Terms,' in *Reflections on Things at Hand: The Neo-Confucian Anthology* (New York, NY: Columbia University Press, 1967), 359–69. The Australian-born Chinese are primarily immersed in and shaped by Western culture and the Western worldview. Thus, Australian-born Chinese tend to value knowledge, equality, individualism, competition and self-reliance. The characteristics of a Western worldview are considered as being openly confrontational, intolerant of ambiguity, unguarded in its expression of emotions and the stressing of one's rights. Paul Hiebert, *Transforming Worldviews: An Anthropological Understanding of How People Change* (Grand Rapids, MI: Baker Academic, 2008), 337–43; David Augsburger, *Pastoral Counseling Across Cultures* (Philadephia, PA: Westminster John Knox Press, 1986), 66–67.

BIBLIOGRAPHY

AFES. 'Evangelical Union Sydney University > Sydney.' Accessed November 14, 2016. https://www.afes.org.au/campus/evangelical-union-sydney-university-sydney.

AFES. 'FOCUS University of New South Wales > Kensington.' Accessed November 14, 2016. https://www.afes.org.au/campus/focus-university-new-south-wales-kensington.

Augsburger, David. *Pastoral Counseling Across Cultures*. Philadephia, PA: Westminster John Knox Press, 1986.

Australian Bureau of Statistics. 'Table 72. Population, Sex and Country of Birth, States and Territories, 1901 Census.' Accessed September 7, 2016. http://www.abs.gov.au/AUSSTATS/abs@.nsf/DetailsPage/3105.0.65.0012006?OpenDocument.

Australian Human Rights Commission. 'Face the Facts: Cultural Diversity.' Accessed October 18, 2017. https://www.humanrights.gov.au/face-facts-cultural-diversity.

Callaghan, Greg. 'Remembering Tiananmen.' *The Australian* (2009). Accessed September 2, 2016. http://www.theaustralian.com.au/news/remembering-tiananmen/story-e6frg6n6-1225712617852.

Chan, Wing T. 'On Translating Certain Chinese Philosophical Terms.' In *Reflections on Things at Hand: The Neo-Confucian Anthology*. New York, NY: Columbia University Press, 1967.

Chinese Christian Church. *Moving Forward: CCC Milsons Point 50 Anniversary Publication*. Sydney, NSW: Chinese Christian Church, 2015.

Chinese Coordination Centre of World Evangelism. 'General Secretary.' *Chinese Coordination Centre of World Evangelism, 2016*. Accessed November 14, 2016. http://www.cccowe.org/content.php?id=about_general_secretary.

Chinese Presbyterian Church. *Chinese Presbyterian Church: Centenary Magazine 1893–1993*. Sydney, NSW: Chinese Presbyterian Church, 1994.

Chinese Theological College Australia. 'The Birth of the Vision.' Accessed September 8, 2016. http://www.ctca.org.au/en/the-birth-of-the-vision/.

Choi, C. Y. *Chinese Migration and Settlement in Australia*. University of Sydney, NSW: Sydney University Press, 1975.

Department of Immigration and Citizenship. 'Fact Sheet 6—Australia's Multicultural Policy.' *Australian Government, Department of Immigration and Citizenship*. Accessed November 14, 2016. http://www.immi.gov.au/media/fact-sheets/06australias-multicultural-policy.htm.

First Light Care Association. 'History of FLC.' Accessed November 14, 2016. http://www.firstlightcare.org.au/aboutus#history.

Fung, Joseph. 'SCCCA—History, Sydney Chinese Christian Churches Association.' Accessed November 14, 2016. http://sccca.org.au/history.

Fung, Joseph. *UCEC Report on CIM (OMF) Centenary Thanksgiving Worship Service*. Sydney, NSW: United Chinese Evangelism Committee, 1990.

Gilchrist, Roy, and Ailsa Thompson, *A Brief History of Central Baptist Church*. Sydney, NSW: Central Baptist Church, 2001.

Hiebert, Paul. *Transforming Worldviews: An Anthropological Understanding of How People Change*. Grand Rapids, MI: Baker Academic, 2008.

Hughes, Philip J. *The Baptists in* Australia. Nunawading, VIC: Christian Research Association, 1996.

Jackson, Darrell, and Alessia Passarelli. *Mapping Migration, Mapping Churches' Responses in Europe: Belonging, Community and Integration: The Witness and Service of Churches in Europe*. Geneva, CH: Churches' Commission for Migrants in Europe and the World Council of Churches, 2016.

Jupp, James. *Australian People: An Encyclopedia of the Nation, Its People and Their Origins*. North Ryde, NSW: Angus & Robertson Publishers, 1988.

Kamp, Alanna. 'Chinese Australian Women in White Australia: Utilising Available Sources to Overcome the Challenge of "Invisibility."' *Chinese Southern Diaspora Studies* 6 (2013): 79.

Law, F. *Annual Report 2016: Sydney Chinese Christian Churches Association*. Sydney, NSW: Sydney Chinese Christian Churches Association, 2016.

Manley, Ken R. *In the Heart of Sydney: Central Baptist Church, 1836–1986*. Sydney, NSW: Central Baptist Church, 1987.

Mar, Wendy Lu. *So Great a Cloud of Witnesses: A History of the Chinese Presbyterian Church, Sydney 1893–1993*. Sydney, NSW: Chinese Presbyterian Church, Sydney, 1993.

Marcus, Andrew. 'White Australia.' In *The Oxford Companion to Australian History*. South Melbourne, VIC: Oxford University Press, 2001.

Marriage and Family For Christ. 'About Marriage and Family for Christ.' Accessed November 14, 2016. http://www.mffc.org.au/en/about/mffcau/.

Megarrity, Lyndon. 'Under the Shadow of the White Australia Policy: Commonwealth Policies on Private Overseas Students 1945–1972.' *Change: Transformations in Education* 6 (2005): 45–46.

NSW Government. 'Birthplace—China (excl. SARs and Taiwan), Year of Arrival' (2011). Accessed July 30, 2015. http://multiculturalnsw.id.com.au/multiculturalnsw/birthplace-by-year-of-arrival?COIID=5038.

NSW Government. 'Birthplace—Hong Kong (SAR of China), Year of Arrival' (2011). Accessed July 30, 2015. http://multiculturalnsw.id.com.au/multiculturalnsw/birthplace-by-year-of-arrival?COIID=5039.

NSW Government State Records. 'Immigration from Many Lands.' Accessed August 10, 2015. http://www.records.nsw.gov.au/state-archives/research-topics/immigration/immigration-from-many-lands.

NSW Migration Heritage Centre. '1901 Immigration Restriction Act.' Accessed September 7, 2016. http://www.migrationheritage.nsw.gov.au/exhibition/objectsthroughtime/immigration-restriction-act/.

NSW Migration Heritage Centre. 'Object Through Time: Australian Migration History Timeline, 1945–1965.' Accessed September 7, 2016. http://www.migrationheritage.nsw.gov.au/exhibition/objectsthroughtime-history/1945-1965/.

Prior, Alan C. *Some Fell on Good Ground: A History of the Beginnings and Development of the Baptist Church in New South Wales, Australia, 1831–1965*. Sydney, NSW: Baptist Union of New South Wales, 1966.

Smith, Lindsay Maxwell. '*Hidden Dragons: The Archaeology of Mid to Late Nineteenth-Century Chinese Communities in Southeastern New South Wales*.' Unpublished diss. Canberra, ACT: The Australian National University, 2006.

Sydney Chinese Christian Churches Association. 'About SCCCA.' Accessed November 14, 2016. http://sccca.org.au/about.

Wan, Enoch, and Sadiri Joy Tira. 'Diaspora Missiology and Missions in the Context of the Twenty-First Century.' *Torch Trinity Journal* 13, no. 1 (2010): 51–52.

York, Barry. 'White Australia Policy—The Beginning of The End 50 Years Ago.' *Museum of Australian Democracy at Old Parliament House*. Accessed September 7, 2016. http://moadoph.gov.au/blog/white-australia-policy-the-beginning-of-the-end-50-years-ago/.

Chapter 7

MIGRATION: FINDING HOPE AND HOME IN A FOREIGN LAND

Sharmila Blair

There is an ad by the New Zealand comedian and director Taika Waititi trending on YouTube[1] at the moment that takes a sarcastic shot at racism. 'Racism', says Waititi, 'needs your help to survive'. Like an ad for a charity he answers all the FAQs on 'how to keep racism alive'. 'If I only give a little bit to racism', he asks, 'will it be noticed?' To which he replies, 'To the people receiving the racism they'll be getting hundreds of small bits every day, so it will add up. It will be noticed!'

Waititi touches upon an important reality for the 'other', whether it be the migrant, indigenous peoples, people seeking asylum or refugees. Racism may not always be overt or obvious; it can be subtle. Those 'hundreds of small bits' do add up. They are the reminders that you are different to the rest, that you are unusual, a minority. They remind you that you are an outsider, that you belong elsewhere. You are a foreigner, an alien.

---

1   https://youtu.be/g9n_UPyVR5s.

Reading Christian Scripture through the Lens of the 'Other'

Despite having grown up in Australia and having spoken English all my life, I am still, on occasion, affirmed by well-intentioned people for 'speaking English very well'. I am a bit of an enigma. I sound 'Aussie' by way of my accent,[2] but I look 'foreign' because of the colour of my skin. I am a Malaysian-born Indian first-generation migrant. What does this lens bring to my reading of Scripture? In this chapter I hope to articulate the questions that arise from this particular reading site.

Firstly, I will draw on biblical narratives in which the 'other' is brought into community through acts of radical inclusion and hospitality. I will articulate how these stories also highlight themes of redemption and restoration, which are relevant to the inclusion of the new arrival today. Of course, the themes of 'insider' and 'outsider' arise frequently in Scripture. Three of the narratives stand out to me and I will use them to further explore these themes from a missiological perspective. The first is the story of Ruth the Moabitess which not only highlights the themes of inclusion and belonging, but also the question of redemption and restoration. The second is the New Testament story of the woman with the issue of blood from Mark 5, in which an outcast woman is restored not only through Jesus's radical act of healing, but through *naming*. Finally, the story of the woman at the well in John 4 highlights themes of ethnic difference and how Jesus breaks down these barriers to encounter the woman as she appeared in front of him.

Secondly, I will explore some of the ways in which these themes have resonated in my own experience as a migrant. I hope to demonstrate through these stories some of the ways in which the missiological questions may find some resolution, albeit in part.

Alienation and Restoration to Land: The *Go'el* Tradition

Throughout the book of Ruth there are 'hundreds of little reminders' of Ruth's outsider status. She is referred to throughout the book not only as Ruth, but as 'Ruth the Moabitess'.[3] The themes of 'insider' and 'outsider' run throughout this story. Ruth and Naomi are both foreigners; first, Naomi in Moab, then Ruth in Judah. In the story we are made to see the reality of the life of the other, moreover, the female other. As the story progresses it becomes apparent that there is little

---

[2] Which may or may not degenerate into Manglish (Malaysian English or Mangled English) in the presence of my Malaysian relatives.

[3] 'From the beginning the narrator calls her "the Moabitess". Her ethnic origin marks her out in Bethlehem.' Ellen van Wolde, *Ruth and Naomi* (Macon, GA: Smyth & Helwys, 1998), 49.

prospect for both of these women. Naomi is a woman past marrying age and a widow, for whom there are certain rights and protections, but she does not qualify for these. As a foreigner, Ruth has some basic rights (Lev 19:33, 34; 23:22), but she does not have the ability to inherit land, own land, or be admitted to the full assembly until the third generation (Deut 23:7).

The combined factors of Naomi's widowhood, the loss of her male sons, and her sojourn in Moab present her with some difficulties. Without a male family member, she is unable to claim the land of her husband, Elimelech, presumably left in the hands of tenant farmers. In Bethlehem, both Ruth and Naomi had lacked familial ties or protection within the land. Ellen Van Wolde writes:

> They go there as migrants, as resident aliens. At that time, being a migrant was a status with virtually no protection, midway between the full rights of the indigenous population and the lack of rights of the slave. Such an alien could not buy land and cultivate a property like the native population, but could enter the service of indigenous employers, usually land owners, and thus earn his living.[4]

Enter Boaz. Through Boaz, Ruth receives a kind of 'cultural guarantor'. Boaz was intentional about his role and he took responsibility for Ruth, ensuring a safe and secure future within the new land for both herself and Naomi. This was achieved through the role of 'kinsman redeemer' (Hebrew, *go'el*). This term originates in Israelite family law.

> [A] *go'el* or redeemer is a relative who had particular obligations within a clan. If someone had to sell his land out of economic need, a *go'el* is the one in the clan who was responsible for buying back the land so that the clan heritage remained intact. Boaz was Ruth's 'kinsman redeemer'. The function of the kinsman redeemer was to ensure they were not alienated from the land, that they belonged through this act of kinship.[5]

Josh Ketchum comments that 'this term is loaded with meaning legally, economically, socially, and spiritually'.[6] The role of the *go'el* was to 'indigenise' or acculturate a person to the land.

---

[4] Van Wolde, *Ruth and Naomi*, 7.
[5] Van Wolde, *Ruth and Naomi*, 32.
[6] Josh Ketchum, 'The Go'el Custom in Ruth: A Comparative Study', *Restoration Quarterly* 52, no. 4 (2010): 237–45.

Finding My *Go'el*

I migrated to Melbourne as a two-year old with my parents and younger brother in 1976, leaving behind all that we held familiar in Malaysia. Malaysia in the 1970s was a tense and violent place, especially for Indians and Chinese who were to lose out in the Bumiputera reforms that gave preferential treatment to the indigenous Malays and (effectively) pushed the Indian and Chinese communities to the edge. My parents discovered that for Indians it was going to become increasingly difficult to access higher education, or to gain employment, especially in the government sector. The message was clear, we were no longer welcome. It was time to get out. We were told that we were different, so my parents, in their wisdom decided that 1970s Australia would be the place to start again. Of course, fitting into this new community was as hard in Australia as it had become in Malaysia.

We struggled to fit in and find acceptance in Australian culture. My father used to tell us to 'blend in', whatever that meant to him. Feeling different characterised my experience in my early church-going years. I recall being the only dark-skinned child in my Sunday school class and at age four I remember singing together with my Sunday school class, '*Jesus loves the little children, all the children of the world*'. We all know the verse: '*Red and yellow, black and white, all are precious in his sight . . .*' My teacher had a perplexed look on her face seconds prior to this verse and had to think on her feet. She quickly inserted: 'Red, *brown*, yellow, black and white, all are precious in his sight'. I look back on her fumbling efforts to include me with deep gratitude, however awkward it made me feel!

But one family in particular went out of their way to embrace us as new migrants. They adopted us and showed us the ropes of Aussie culture. We were taught about Aussie Rules football, assigned a football team, invited to barbecues and shown how to cook a Sunday roast (which we believed to be an exotic delight). In a sense, they were acculturating us to the land, not in a controlling or dominating manner, but in a very genuine and loving way.

We were invited to call two older women, 'Aunty Kath' and 'Aunty Alma', and their mother, 'Nana O'Kain'. I had left my own beloved grandmother, great grandmother and my aunts back in Malaysia. I now had Aussie aunties and an Aussie nana here in Australia again. This radical act of welcome contributed to our sense of belonging as a family. By being included in their lives, we were not only made to feel that we belonged but that we were a part of a new family, and the family of God.

Fortunately, it was having our adoptee Australian family in our lives as cultural guides, which gave us a sense of security and hope. I recall my mother, who was struggling to juggle everything including my brother, myself and now my younger baby sister, dissolving into tears as she confided to our Aunty Kath that she was pregnant for the fourth time. My mother didn't know if she or dad could manage with another mouth to feed. I'll never forget our beautiful Australian Aunty Kath scoop my youngest sister into her arms whilst reassuring my mum, 'Don't worry, we will manage, you won't be doing it alone, we'll help'. True to her word, she was involved with our young family, babysitting and helping to cook meals. I remember once she took me out to see the movie, 'Annie,' complete with a sleepover at her house, and a train and tram ride into the city. I relished this quality time with her during what was a challenging time for my own family.

For us, as a newly arrived family, the sense of 'adoption' we received from them, their commitment to us, and their radical welcome of us into their extended family was in essence them fulfilling the role of *go'el* or kinsman redeemer in our lives.

Similarly, I think of an elderly Australian couple living in the south-eastern suburbs who have opened up their homes and lives to a young Muslim Hazara Afghani asylum seeker who has unofficially become their adopted son. Arriving here in Australia as an unaccompanied minor, Hassan knew little English and had a myriad of red tape to navigate in his bid to gain refugee status. Over the past couple of years they have supported him in this journey, in his learning of English and in obtaining his licence. Only recently, a family selfie on Facebook was taken to celebrate Hassan receiving his protection visa. For Hassan, 'John' and 'Susie' have fulfilled the function of kinsman redeemer in his life.

Mark Chapter 5: The Outcast is Reinstated

A sense of inclusion and family were the catalysts in my experience of feeling that I belonged.

In Mark's Gospel, the story of Jesus healing the bleeding woman (Mark 5:38–43) demonstrates an important aspect of Jesus's priority for the outsider. Mark carefully juxtaposes the story of Jairus's daughter alongside the story of the healing of the woman.[7] Jairus approaches Jesus to ask for his daughter to be healed. Based on the hierarchical system of the day in first-century Palestine, Jairus epitomised power and prestige in Jewish society. As an esteemed and respected leader of the synagogue, he should have been first in line to see Jesus.[8] Jairus had a name and a title which spelled out his connection to society and to his own family.

---

7   Mark 5:25–34.
8   Ched Myers, *Binding the Strong Man: A Political Reading of Mark's Story of Jesus* (Maryknoll, NY: Orbis Books, 1988), 198.

On the other hand, the woman who touched Jesus's cloak was unnamed, unclean and unconnected. Levitical law deemed her unclean in Jewish society and excluded her from participating in temple worship or ritual because of her longstanding illness. By prioritising the bleeding woman before Jairus, Jesus subverts society's expectations and replaces them with a 'new social order of the kingdom'.[9] In this case, the woman, alienated from family or social connections, relegated to the streets to beg because she had spent all she had on doctors, was singled out by Jesus from the crowd in order for him to reinstate her into the family of God and call her 'daughter'.

Jesus's public encounter with the woman symbolised her restoration and inclusion from outsider to insider. She could now fully participate as a member of her community once more without stigma or shame. Finally, she belonged to the family of God.

The Consciousness of Difference

My first day of school was an unforgettable experience for me. I was the only brown child in a predominantly white school in the Eastern Suburbs of Melbourne. The night before my father had stayed up late, preparing a cooked lunch for me which he packed into my lunchbox. As the clock ticked over to lunchtime the other children ran to their bags to pull out their sandwiches. I opened my own lunchbox to discover (much to my horror) fried rice. I burst into tears, immediately conscious of my difference. No one intended this, it was no one's fault, but those 'hundreds of small messages' had added up to make me feel, in that moment, that I was an outsider. My teacher didn't help matters either by proceeding to turn up her nose at my lunch saying, 'Hmm, you can't eat that!'

I wanted so desperately to be like everyone else, to be accepted by my Aussie peers. I cried because my dad had gone to such an effort to cook this meal for me. I cried because my lunch was different to all the other children. I cried because I felt like the outcast, alienated from Australian culture. As a young child the fear of not ever belonging was palpable and a real threat to my sense of security.

Another negative experience was being excluded from a birthday party because of my skin colour. To make matters worse, I was the only girl in my fourth-grade class who was not invited to a popular girl's birthday party. Even more hurtful was the fact that this message had come from my friend's mother, not my friend. The message I received that day was 'you don't make the cut. Your ethnicity excludes you from having a fun time with your friends'. As a young, impressionable eight-year-old, hearing this news translated as deep rejection, only

---

9   Myers, *Binding the Strong Man*, 199.

reinforcing my outcast status once again. Yet another message amidst the hundreds of small messages that I did not belong.

The above two experiences of feeling like an 'outsider' gives me some insight into the world of the woman in chapter five of Mark. The fact that I had the wrong coloured skin excluded me from participating with my friends. It felt deeply unfair. However, despite this, two of my friends stood with me that day, declaring they would boycott the birthday party. To an eight-year-old, this simple act meant the world to me! I had two friends willing to stand in solidarity with me. This communicated to me that I mattered, that I was important, that this situation of being excluded on the grounds of my skin colour was not okay.

In Jesus's encounter with the woman in Mark chapter 5 it is significant that he stopped, on the way to Jairus's house, in the midst of the crowds, in the push of the people; he stopped. In stopping he noticed, he saw, he spoke, and he named. This brief act suggests a solidarity—Jesus was 'in-tune' with the vulnerable and marginalised—to literally feel them in the throngs of people.

John Chapter 4:4–15—The Woman at the Well

The final narrative is one where Jesus engages once again with an outsider, the Samaritan woman in John chapter 4. Historically, Samaritans were despised by the Galilean Jews. They were the foreigners who came to occupy the central region of Palestine after the fall of the northern kingdom of Israel at the hands of the Assyrians in 721 BCE, after the exile of its Israelite inhabitants. These new arrivals were considered pagans, worshipping other gods and deities, polluting Jewish belief and practice. Consequently, in verse 9, we read in a note from our narrator, 'Judeans have no dealings with Samaritans'. The fractious nature of the often-tense relationship between the Judeans and the Samaritans is captured in the woman's statement, 'Our ancestors worshiped on this mountain, but you say that the place where people must worship is in Jerusalem' (v. 20).

In addition to this, we are told of this Samaritan woman's status as an outcast. It is likely that she was marginalised within her own Samaritan community, because she chose to draw water during the hottest part of the day; unlike other women who would gather to draw water in the cool of the evenings, catching up on the day's events. This woman experienced social isolation because of her relationship status, which rendered her an outcast within her own community. She had been dehumanised.

This passage revolves around two of the most basic needs for human survival: water and food (vv. 31–38). Jesus uses these most basic of human necessities to demonstrate something that is universal, that cuts across ethnic, racial and religious divisions: we all eat, we all drink, we are all human, we are all in this together. Without this lesson, the missional endeavour is meaningless: to whom would we otherwise proclaim? Jesus transforms these basic human necessities to illustrate a deeper, hidden need.

False perceptions can be barriers preventing us from relating on a human level with others. Recently, friends of ours who have an African foster son told a story which highlights this. 'Terry' is an 18-year-old African boy. Out and about one day he came across an elderly lady struggling to carry her groceries across the road. He asked her 'Excuse me ma'am, would you like a hand carrying those?', to which the woman replied, 'No thanks, I haven't got any money to give you'. Terry went away saddened at the false perception the woman had of him. In recent years, the African community in the City of Greater Dandenong has received a great deal of stigma. The commonly held perception at the time, and even now, is that African youth are involved in gangs, crime and generally 'up to no good'. During my ministry with Urban Neighbours of Hope, I encountered this perception on several occasions. It was not uncommon for police to be present around a group of Sudanese youth.

It was in going out to the local park that my husband and a fellow teammate were able to engage in a game of soccer with some of these Sudanese youth, which eventually led to a barbeque in the park every Friday evening. Here, our children, my husband and I, and our teammates would spend time together, eating, laughing, chatting and kicking around a soccer ball. The sense of community this generated provoked interest among other families who were also at the park.

Once, we were approached and asked if we were youth workers or something to that effect. We simply responded by saying that we were all simply friends hanging out together. It helped that my own migrant experience was something that these boys were able to relate to. This activity in the park wasn't a big, flashy kind of program, it was intended to be a starting point. We believed that what we needed to do was to humanise these young men, to treat them as equals and demonstrate that we were willing to trust them. We believed that we needed to rehumanise them before we did anything else. We did this around that most basic of human needs: food.

Conclusion

In our world today we are encountering many more displaced people. It is becoming increasingly important that we understand the experience of the new migrant, refugee, or asylum seeker. Our own Scriptures demonstrate a wealth of resources for understanding and responding to this, and this chapter only touches on a few.

For us, as Australian Christians, to enflesh a practical theology which welcomes the 'other' in our midst, we need to draw upon these resources and develop an appreciation of the text from the position of the 'outsider'. In reading these texts from the perspective of the 'other', we will gain valuable missiological insights as well as a better understanding of how to effectively minister to people from other countries.

The story of Ruth highlights issues of landlessness for the most vulnerable of the society of that time; the widow and the alien. This is a reality that is becoming increasingly common across the globe due to (amongst other things) conflicts, migration, forced evictions, natural disasters and climate change. The reality for so many people today is a rootless existence. In my own story I highlighted the family that adopted us and welcomed us to the country. They were our Boaz, our redeemers that restored us to this land. What will modern missions bring to the rootless and landless? How might the story of Ruth and Naomi inform our practice?

In Mark chapter 5, a marginalised woman is welcomed into the fold through a powerful encounter with Jesus. Jesus stops and stands in solidarity with her. How do we do this? How do we stand in solidarity with the marginalised? My friend's actions of boycotting the birthday party may not have been noticed, or even cared about, but this spoke powerfully to me.

Our own perceptions regarding those who are different could also be barriers preventing us from connecting on a deeper level with others. The story of Jesus's encounter with the Samaritan woman highlights the importance of seeing the person and relinquishing our preconceived notions of who they are. My young African friend encountered this in his experience with the elderly woman that day: no doubt yet another one of the many small reminders in his lifetime that he was 'different'.

What can we as Australian Christians learn from these stories? I was reminded by those I ministered to that these key biblical stories were indeed, their stories. They were stories of those on the 'outside' being invited to belong 'inside' the family of God.

Questions Raised By This Chapter Which May Be Useful for Practitioners to Think About:

- How do we do mission to displaced people in Australia? Is it possible?
- What are the implications for our faith communities if we re-read Scripture as Gentiles who find ourselves in a Jewish narrative?
- How does this then inform the way we relate to and *include* those from different countries, cultural backgrounds and faiths?

- What was the catalyst in these stories of people experiencing a sense of belonging?
- How can we as churches foster a sense of belonging and home for the 'other' in our midst?

BIBLIOGRAPHY

Ketchum, Josh. 'The Go'el Custom in Ruth: A Comparative Study.' *Restoration Quarterly*, 52, no. 4 (2010).

Myers, Ched. *Binding the Strong Man: A Political Reading of Mark's Story of Jesus*. Maryknoll, NY: Orbis Books, 1988.

Van Wolde, Ellen. *Ruth and Naomi*. Macon, GA: Smyth & Helwys, 1998.

Chapter 8

RECONCILING CHURCH FOR SECOND-GENERATION CHINESE AUSTRALIANS

Graham R. Scott

'I will dwell in the house of the Lord forever' (Psalm 23:6).

My wife and I have been on a journey over the last seven years with a congregation of second-generation Chinese Australians. By reflecting on our journey, I will explore the image of 'home' as a metaphor for our congregation's movement from being a little group gathered in a renovated carport, to now being a congregation with its own identity, vision and culture. They have journeyed from being a 'youth group' to realising their identity as a community and as a church. And it is in this sense that they have come 'home'.[1]

From conversations with others and my own observations I have good reason to believe that our congregation's experience is relatively common within migrant or ethnic churches in Australia. In any discussion of the second generation, there is an implicit first generation. In our case, these are friends who we count as brothers and sisters in Christ, and with whom we regularly fellowship, and who

---

1   A brief word about our context: our church context is an independent Chinese Christian church, founded by migrants from Hong Kong approximately thirty years ago, now with English and Chinese language congregations, and also now serving Mandarin speakers. Many of the English congregation have parents or even grandparents who worship in the Chinese congregation. Our location in an area away from the suburbs traditionally associated with Chinese immigration and business is both an isolating factor, as well as an opportunity.

have also been an integral part of our congregation's journey towards their home. It is all too easy to inadvertently, or otherwise, denigrate one generation when talking about another. In the use of generalisations I am aware of the potential for misunderstanding or miscommunication, and we have experienced more than enough along the way. I am convinced that the journey of the second generation is a far more fruitful and blessed venture when it demonstrates the living out of the Sermon of the Mount, and when it does not seek to reject or overthrow the other.

In reflecting on the issue of what church means and reimagining 'a church home' for second-generation Chinese Australians, I find the words of Moltmann encouraging—to be church is to grapple with 'the experiences of the Christian life' in such a way as to also 'interpret the experiences of this life'.[2]

Living in a House of Not Your Own Design or Construction

For second-generation Australians whose formative years are spent within migrant church contexts, church can represent both 'home' as well as a 'strange land'. Church is home in its familiarity, and church is also home in the sense of cultural solidarity, especially with others of the second generation. To be a young Christian in such a context also means feeling relatively at home with the faith practices associated with their parents' generation and their parents' home country. In these contexts, there is the promise that 'you are the future of the church'. At the same time church can also represent a 'strange land' because growing up in a migrant church community means experiencing a transplanted expression of faith and church, including imported forms of worship, fellowship, theologising and governance.

For these reasons, the metaphor of a journey towards home seems to fit the early experiences of second-generation ABCs (Australian-born-Chinese, which in this chapter also includes Australian-raised-Chinese).

House-sitting or visiting a relative is an interesting exercise as one unpacks and tries to settle into new surroundings. There is often the sense that there is not quite enough room. Whether it is the cupboard being too full for the clothes, or the bedside tables being fully covered, or other spaces throughout the house being full—other people's homes can be so full that it is hard to relax, because there just is not space enough to call one's own.

This is very much like the church experience of our congregation. The service of their parents' and grandparents' generation was familiar and known, but there was little room for them to articulate their faith, their hearts and spiritual

---

2   Jürgen Moltmann, *The Church in the Power of the Spirit: A Contribution to Messianic Ecclesiology*, trans. Margaret Kohl (Minneapolis: Fortress Press, 1993), 277.

gifts in ways that made sense to them. Indeed, the architecture of a church service is shaped by the demands of language, communication style, hierarchy, formality, familiarity, style of conflict resolution, and goals and vision. For our second-generation friends the architecture of the service and church life was laid out by the first generation, and so their first experiences of church were of being in a house that had been designed and occupied by others.

One caveat: the founding generation of the church is a diverse mix of Hong Kong immigrants who arrived in Australia as Christians and representing the denominations of their homeland. Others have come to faith since arriving in Australia. Our first and founding generation gathered first as a Bible study group, which coalesced into an independent church. As a faith community they too have experienced firsthand the stress and challenge of making a home. In many senses, their experience has been one of working it out as they went along.

For the second generation, living and worshipping in a house which they neither designed nor constructed has had fairly clear ramifications. Over the years the following have been observed:

- A sense of dislocation
- Weakened sense of ownership of the service or church ministries, and concomitantly varying levels of long-term commitment to church
- Passivity
- Attrition
- Sense of belonging derived from familial ties as much as commitment to faith and community of faith
- Tensions and miscommunications with the first generation
- Tensions and fractures within the second generation as it seeks to adapt and respond the best it can to its situation.

High levels of education, life achievement, changing roles as workers and adults as well as choice in personal lives can fuel a growing sense of discomfort and dissatisfaction. But the experience of the school-aged children in the group, and the arrival of the first members of the third generation have been a strong catalyst for the questions, 'Who are we? And where are we going?'

Whilst noting the 'negatives' of the second-generation experience, we must also acknowledge that there are 'positives' also, such as:

- An incredible patience
- A desire to keep the peace and to honour the older generation
- A will to make the best of their situation
- Adaptability (as might be expected of two-culture children)
- A sense of responsibility for their own generation
- A commitment to church as it was, despite the challenges.

And these positives have helped to shape a resilient group which is sure of its faith and commitment to each other and the church. They have become the architects who are designing and building a new home for their faith community, a place where there is room to live and grow, which honours the story of their parents, and which gives voice and form to their own story.

Learning to Tell New Stories of Home

Which story are we to tell? Is our story and our identity the story of the child, who in our parents' eyes will never grow up, never have enough experience or knowledge? Or is ours the story of adult professionals and growing families? The stories that we tell about ourselves shape our serving and ministry. A child cannot offer hospitality, unless they seek permission and it is mediated through their parents. As long as the story of faith and church is that of the child and parent, there is very limited sense of ownership and ability to do hospitality. The home is not one's own, but their parents'. And out of respect to parent and even grandparent, a child is cautious to invite others in. As an adult, however, there is a deep ownership and sense of empowerment to be hospitable—to welcome others into one's own home.

The story of a child is one imbued with promise and a hope for the future. For the children of immigrants, this is particularly so. In the stereotypical immigrant story, the first generation work incredibly diligently to establish a new life for their family. It is the second generation's responsibility to continue within that legacy—to work hard, to achieve the things that their parents could not achieve, for instance, status and approved career paths. Along with the responsibility to be successful, many second-generation children also feel the responsibility to be able to provide for not only their own spouse and children, but also their parents in the later years. Uniquely, though immigrant parents strive to protect their children as much as they can to maximise their educational opportunities, the children of immigrants also face unique responsibilities, as cultural guides and translators for their parents.

Another story that our congregation has inherited from their parents and grandparents and which they tell and grapple with is the story of the migrant outsider. Their parents tend to effectively live inside the Chinese diaspora, which though not necessarily geographic, means that their lives as workers and consumers of products, as well as entertainment and recreation, remains mostly within a Chinese language and cultural frame. This is an advantage for migrant groups who are large enough numerically to create their own home spaces within Australian urban areas. This enables those such as the Chinese community to enjoy a sense of comfort, familiarity, efficiency and safety as they work through what it means to live and dwell in the Australian context. Because these lives are not defined by geography, the reality is that none of our Chinese congregation lives in the same suburb and community as the one where they worship at church. This necessarily creates a sense that they are very much migrants within the suburb. Our location is a blessing, but there is no natural connection to our neighbours, local businesses, other churches, schools, or community organisations.

Of interest to this reflection is that the second generation has inherited this narrative and so has been shaped by their parents' stories as migrant-outsiders. Whilst they typically have attended school and university in their 'home' land and city and have consequently gone onto professional work in a range of industries, they still experience a sense of dislocation, just as their parents have. One friend commented and asked about sharing life and faith in the workplace, and made a comment something like, 'But don't they (Anglo-Australians) see us as too different to relate to?' As an Anglo-Australian, I was surprised by this, but again was reminded that for an ethnic majority differences with a minority are minimised, but that a minority feels those same differences as major. Throughout their lives, therefore, many Australian-born Chinese have a sense of displacement and dislocation, feeling a degree of differences with what is deemed 'typical' Aussie culture and life. And just like their parents' generation, they have little natural connection between the suburbs and communities in which they live and in the suburb in which they worship.

There is a further sense in which ABCs can experience a double dislocation. In addition to the dislocation within white Australian culture, there is also a sense of dislocation with their parents' story and lives. The internet is full of memes that tell the story of this dislocation between parents and children of Chinese diaspora families. One humorous example from within our congregation that illustrates this is a migrant parent unrelentingly telling their child to study hard, so they can get As and do well at school. The child responds, 'But mum, don't you know it's not hard to be smart in Australia?!' As children of migrants, Australian-born Chinese live on a bicultural bridge. They relate to their parents' stories, and at the same time, the stories of their Aussie friends, yet neither set of stories are their own. There is the need to establish and tell their own stories because the stories we tell about ourselves are an essential part of constructing and communicating our identity.

An essential element in identity formation and understanding our congregation's home has been to seek to understand and live within God's story of goodness and presence in our local area and the community in which we worship. Whilst the founding migrant generation of the church can identify God's blessing in the provision of our current property and give thanks for their journey from worshipping in a family garage, then a school hall, and then in our present location, there is still little sense of connection to that location and its wider community as home.

As a step forward for the church and especially for our congregation, we set about exploring the history of our local area to see where God had gone before us, and to understand where we might fit into his ongoing story of grace.

We were able to identify that our area was a place of God's provision and blessing for Yuggera and Gubbi Gubbi families and clans. Waterholes provided a good source of water and the area was blessed with abundant food. Later, the first non-indigenous immigrants arrived and settled in the area. In particular, German lay-missionaries settled and established a farm and mission, which provided a shelter and dwelling place for local indigenous people who were being marginalised under the pressures of settlers' greed, jealousy and political manoeuvring. A main road in the area is named after one of these German missionaries, and his Christian commitment is seen in his continued work and advocacy with the first peoples of the area even after state funding of the mission ended. These early Christians in our area represent God's guiding hand and are a real example of the power of lay people in God's kingdom. They were a blessing to the indigenous community at a time when many advocated injustice and even violence against indigenous Australians. And the German missionaries demonstrate that immigrants and their children have been a very real blessing in our local area, as we should be.

Not only can we identify God's blessing to the first people in our area, and through the lives and service of German missionaries, but we also identified a historic Chinese connection in our area. Chinese market gardeners leased land and grew vegetables which they sold to the local community. One elderly lady remembers as a little girl enjoying the fireworks that were part of the celebration of Chinese New Year.

The property and its main building were formerly an Anglican church, which was built on pastoral land, long used for Sunday school picnics, and an original Sunday school hall. As that Anglican church's doors closed, our community bought the property and has made it home for almost three decades. Thus, we have a deep connection to the place in which we meet and worship, and where our church has found its home. We may not always feel that connection, but we can be certain that God has gone before us and has been present in our neighbourhood long before we were present. God continues to be present and at work around us, in the local school, community groups, and in all the homes that make up the neighbourhood. This is the core of the story that we can tell. Now we have a story of identity within our local community, a deeper and longer story that we can connect to, and a narrative which we can further in our life together. This story, which we have realised together, now grants us the sense of permission that is needed internally to have the confidence to live and serve in our local community.

Plotting a Path Toward Home

Having established a sense of identity via historical connection to God's work in our context, we were able to reflect upon what we had been doing, and what we would like to be as a faith community.

As we mapped out a vision and planning process, we identified the values of the congregation. In any situation of cultural interaction, identifying values is a helpful step to being able to understand the other and resolve differences. As a group we drafted goals and purpose statements from our values' statement that reflected our values and heart. From this we can chart a course and direction for the coming days. Naturally this process is iterative and is ongoing. Any document derived from the process requires regular prayerful consideration, revision and refining. We are a community, not a monument; we are on a journey with God, not static or stationary; and thus, our eyes are set on our becoming with Jesus. We note the waypoints of our journey as learning lessons and opportunities for gratitude and praise.

Daring to Dream: Could We Build a House of Our Own?

The journey towards dreaming of their own house was not an automatic one. In fact, long before discussions about how their own worship could better reflect their faith, there were discussions about identity. For quite a while even this discussion was largely intellectual. Perhaps the underlying question in the early stages was, 'Would it even be possible?'

Interesting in this regard is the role of the emic and etic. In a congregation such as ours, the role of the emic perspective and endogenous knowledge has been crucial to its forward movement and journey towards home. As an outsider, I am unable to define what an effective faith home or expression of worship would be in our context. That was not a role in which I felt comfortable, or that I had sufficient understanding or knowledge for. But I can ask questions. And I can encourage the desire to risk and take a step. What we have realised as a community is the value of the dialogue between the emic and etic—a mutuality in learning from each other, understanding and listening to each other, and together seeking the direction that God has for the community.

Through such an approach, Sunday worship services gradually took shape. A very early point of departure from the traditional Cantonese service was the introduction of coffee time. For a group that generally does not arrive prior to the service starting, there was little time to catch up before the service. A mid-service pause to greet one another and grab a cup of coffee and a snack provided that time of fellowship, as well as providing a useful mental break before the learning time of the sermon. It was not clear how this was going to work when it began, but it made sense to all involved, and so we tried. Our coffee time quickly addressed an issue that had been identified—the need to grow deeper relationships across the group. The reaction from the traditional Cantonese congregation was to question why the English congregation was so hungry, and why they couldn't wait until the end of the service to eat! Coffee time continued for a couple of years until the group decided its purpose of providing fellowship time had been outgrown.

With healthy and growing relationships across the congregation, the group was ready for deeper fellowship and discussion, which now takes place immediately after the sermon. Small groups discuss how to put into action what they have heard through God's Word and the sermon. Freshly brewed coffee and snacks remain available during the service and now people just grab them when and as they like. Compared to how we started, the congregation is now characterised by close and supportive relationships and a strong sense of belonging.

This dialogical model between pastors and congregation has been incredibly productive. As we explored what it meant to be God's community together and focused on the essentials of faith, dreams for a home took shape.

Amartya Sen writes that being born into a particular ethnicity is not an act of freedom, because it does not represent a choice, however the decision to 'stay within the traditional mode' is a choice, just as is the decision to move away.[3] Thus each generation needs to work to choose and define its cultural identity.

Naturally, moving away from parents' culture and worship expression comes with resistance, both internally and externally. In many ways it has been a journey of exile. On the one hand there is the excitement of the path ahead, but on the other hand, there is the missing of the old, the desire for the certainty of what was known, and the fear of forsaking unity.

Of course, when you are on the path and the final destination is unclear, returning to your parents' house might seem like a reasonable option. Some differences with the founding generation's congregation will never be easily explained or justified to the satisfaction of some; they are just a fact of the new expression of worship and community life together.

---

[3] Amartya Sen, *Identity and Violence: The Illusion of Destiny* (New York: W. W. Norton, 2007), 157.

Coming Home: What Has It Meant?

Almost eight years down the road, where are we? We certainly have now experienced the joy of having a service and community which is shaped by the second generation's faith, identity and values.

A pivotal event in the life of our second-generation congregation was embarking on a building project to provide the congregation with its first 'real physical home' for services and gatherings. Prior to the new chapel, the congregation met in what was essentially a renovated carport. It did meet basic needs, but was quickly becoming much too small, and in summer was an oven. It did nothing to express the character and aesthetics of the group, and was not a place to invite others to visit.

Our first working bee on the building project was a long Saturday during which we completely demolished the space that was our church space. The next morning one of the toddlers arrived at church and declared, 'Oh no. You have to fix it. Put it back'. He mourned the loss of the only church space and home he had known. Truly this is a great metaphor for the challenge of the group's quest for church as home.

In the life of the congregation, the building project provided the group with the opportunity to not only participate in the design but also in the actual construction of their new space. This very literal act of building a new church home was transformative as the group bonded over helping out onsite, and particularly in the hours of painting and cleanup. Their physical work and financial sacrifice represented their commitment to their community, its worship together, and its future.

Integral to the building project, and now the use of the space as a physical home for the congregation, has been the continued task of reimagining what it means to call church 'home'.

To enter a physical worship space ought to engage the reality that God's story is our story. But more than that, God's story is also contained within the family of the church—in its stories of salvation, redemption, loss, pain, healing, grace and joy that are represented in the lives of the worshipping community.

Understanding the Desire for Home

The desire for home, both metaphorical and physical is a natural one. The metaphor of home represents the human need for psychological comfort, safety and a sense of belonging. The physical home represents a place to be comfortable, productive and engaged with others. It is important that we do not neglect the physical in our theological understanding of home. As embodied beings we have real physical needs, which we cannot ignore or reject out of a misplaced preference for the spiritual. It is easy to be critical of church properties and the resources which are spent upon them, and much of this criticism is justifiable. However, we cannot reject the need for shelter, the desire for physical spaces for our lives together and the importance of a sense of space which we can call home.

In terms of church as home, there is a felt-importance that the spaces in which we gather, worship, and welcome in others, reflect the aesthetics that are important to us as physical beings. In the experience of our second-generation Christian community, the move to a space which is uniquely theirs, and which reflects their aesthetics, and over which they have control, has been critical to group formation, identity and sense of ownership. Home is the place from which we launch out into the world.

Critics of church buildings and properties like to quote the words of Jesus in the Gospel of Matthew, 'Foxes have holes, and birds of the air have nests; but the Son of Man has nowhere to lay his head' (Matt 8:20). We do not want to deny the importance of taking up the cross of Christ, but we ought to see even Jesus's homelessness in context. His early life and most of his adulthood were spent in Nazareth, as the son of the carpenter, and thus presumably, engaged in such work and the typical life of the family and community. So too John the Baptist, or even Timothy, Paul tells us, was raised by his mother and grandmother, and that home experience was foundational for his Christian faith and ministry. And Jesus became home for the diverse group which formed around him. After the world-shattering events of that first Easter and then Pentecost, the disciples shaped a new home together in the presence of the Holy Spirit, through which they were empowered, supported and freed to take the gospel into the wider world.

Of course, the danger of the image of church as home is that we too easily forget that the church building can be viewed as the house of the Lord. This brings the risk of domesticating God's story and our faith, and so our faith story and its expression become about the self. The loss of the sense of God in a space and place means that the space and place can be possessed by us, and so we forget that we are mere caretakers, the holders of a trust much larger than ourselves.

But at its very best, 'church' represents home. From the community of faith the church is sent out into the world to be the light of Christ, having been nurtured and nourished. It is not a static home, but rather a dynamic growing place, an eschatological becoming of God's people in a particular place and time.

Conclusion

Every generation needs to learn how to be the community of God. Each generation finds itself in a new time and a new context. Thus, the importance and challenge of ongoing contextualisation for the church, and of discerning what it means to be a Christian in our context and place. Being willing to hear and ponder these big questions is a critical challenge, and the answers to these questions challenge and provoke us to avoid complacency and the status quo.

An example of this rethinking of what it means to be a church has been the discussion of whether the church is a public and private space.

If church is conceived as a private space, outsiders are invited in with caution, and only those with a certain pedigree are truly welcome. For a Cantonese church, welcoming Mainland Chinese requires the overcoming of not just linguistic barriers, but more importantly, historical and cultural boundaries. Early in my tenure, the chairperson of the church came running up to me after a service to tell me that a very tall Aussie guy had walked into the church hall, and I should come and work out who he was and what he wanted. When church is a private space, the outsider is unknown and is a potential threat. The large Aussie guy was, in fact, the pastor of a nearby church, who wanted to catch up with me.

By comparison, when church is a public space, all are invited, all are welcomed, and the physical space and the functions of the church are for all.

The journey towards church as home has meant coming to terms with the fact that home is neither solely the community, nor is home the building, but rather home is with God in his community. The confession of Jesus as Lord and the eschatological hope in Christ as Lord of all, function as both our present identity, as well as the horizon of our life together.[4]

As the second generation comes home at church, it continues to be part of the larger church organisation and family. In this regard our commitment to unity as a church seems stronger, but not because of our uniformity and heterogeneity. In the past this was at least a tacit goal for some. Now our unity is in our diversity. The journey towards home has led to a greater appreciation of all generations involved. That does not mean that there are no questions or hesitance. Our life together as a church family has, however, become an exercise in mutual trust as well as the acknowledgement that the Spirit is at work in the leadership and membership of the whole church. We can trust that the Spirit will lead all of us home.

---

4   Moltmann, *The Church in the Power of the Spirit*, 133.

BIBLIOGRAPHY

Moltmann, Jürgen. *The Church in the Power of the Spirit: A Contribution to Messianic Ecclesiology.* Translated by Margaret Kohl. Minneapolis: Fortress Press, 1993.

Sen, Amartya. *Identity and Violence: The Illusion of Destiny.* New York: W. W. Norton, 2007.

Chapter 9

SEHNSUCHT, HOME AND THE SECOND-GENERATION MIGRANT

Stephen Said

In his book 'Pilgrim's Regress', C. S. Lewis reaches for the German word *sehnsucht* to describe a complex phenomenon. It is an 'inconsolable longing' for 'we know not what', a 'longing for a far-off country, but not a particularly earthly land which we can identify. Furthermore, there is something in the experience which suggests this far-off country is very familiar and indicative of what we might otherwise call "home", even though we may never have been there'.

I discovered this multilayered phenomenon when asked to present a working definition of the kingdom of God at a conference. Being someone who likes a short and simple definition, I drew on Romans 14:17, 'the kingdom of God is not a matter of eating and drinking, but of righteousness, peace and joy'. Experiencing a childhood largely bereft of joy, I found myself in a quandary. It was a friend and colleague, Dave Andrews, who alerted me to the relationship between joy and trauma, as well as pointing me to Lewis.

As I explored joy with a view to presenting a pragmatic framework, the notion of a 'home' that I had never experienced, knew existed and would be the object of a lifelong obsessive pursuit until my dying day, has become a growing part of my consciousness. Lewis describes the phenomenon as a profound experience, one that often defies rational definition. For this reason, it is seldom an experience one can explore with others. Even though each individual feels as though this experience is unique largely due to the difficulty in finding suitable language to describe this phenomenon, Lewis insists that *sehnsucht* is a universal experience.

Sehnsucht, Consciousness and Never Going Home

What has since occupied my mind since my discovery of this concept is the degree to which one is conscious of the experience of *sehnsucht*. As I continued to explore the phenomenon, it seemed that this phenomenon is experienced in at least two discrete ways by the migrant who makes the transition from one world to another at an early age (migrant 1.5[1]) and those born of migrant parents (migrant 2.0[2]). I would suggest that the first peculiar way in which 1.5 and 2.0 migrants experience *sehnsucht* is a more conscious as opposed to an unconscious experience. The 'home' of the 1.5 and 2.0 migrant amongst family whilst being the primary place of nurture is simultaneously the home of their transplanted kin, and the home of the peoples and lands chosen to be their parents' adopted homeland. The experience of 1.5 and 2.0 migrants is that of living between two worlds: that of their ancestors; and that of the here and now web of relationships that include people for whom

---

1   'The term *1.5 generation* or *1.5G* refers to individuals who immigrate to a new country before or during their early teens. They earn the label the "*1.5 generation*" because they bring with them or maintain characteristics from their home country, meanwhile engaging in assimilation and socialization with their new country. Oftentimes, in the case of small children, a battle of linguistic comprehension occurs between their academic language and the language spoken at home. Their identity is, thus, a combination of new and old culture and tradition. Sociologist Ruben Rumbaut was among the first to use the term to examine outcomes among those arriving in the United States before adolescence, but since then the term has expanded to include foreign students, as well as other unique individuals.' Wikipedia, 'Immigrant Generations', accessed October 3, 2018, https://en.wikipedia.org/w/index.php?title=Immigrant_generations&oldid=862303414.

2   'The term "second-generation" extends the concept of *first-generation* by one generation. As such, the term exhibits the same type of ambiguity as "first-generation" as well as additional ones.

Like "first-generation immigrant" the term "second-generation" can refer to a member of either:

The second generation of a family to inhabit, but the first natively born in, a country, *or*

The second generation born in a country.

In the United States, among demographers and other social scientists, "second generation" refers to the U.S.–born children of foreign-born parents. The term *second-generation immigrant* attracts criticism due to it being an oxymoron. Namely, critics say, a "second-generation immigrant" is not an immigrant, since being "second-generation" means that the person is born in the country and the person's *parents* are the immigrants in question.' Wikipedia. 'Immigrant Generations.' In some missiological circles, the term 2.0 migrant is used interchangeably with the phrase second-generation immigrant. It is important because the bicultural phenomenon has significant effects upon the person's formation as discussed in the remainder of this chapter.

this place is already home, but not theirs. Whilst the 1.5 and 2.0 migrant is being formed in both contexts, the constant need to interpret the meaning of the signs and symbols of two different contexts creates this more conscious awareness.

The second peculiar way in which the 1.5 and 2.0 migrant experiences *sehnsucht* is as some kind of acknowledgement that this low-level experience of 'homelessness' will never be resolved in their lifetime. The way in which I have been best able to describe this phenomenon is the analogy of the 'mission trip'. When a church or Christian group participates in an exposure or mission trip, particularly where the difference in culture is significant, the powerlessness of being a minority possibly for the first time results in a feeling of culture shock. In a foreign context where the signs, symbols, language, architecture, bodily gestures and so much more are alien, the participant is necessarily on 'heightened alert'. Their senses and meaning-making apparatus are in overdrive. However, in some parts of the participant's psyche is the knowledge that eventually this heightened alert status will no longer be required, because eventually they will get to 'go home'. For the 1.5 and 2.0 migrant, the 'mission trip' is a life sentence. In short, they never get to 'go home'.

Critical Contextualisation: Missiological Task or Survival Skill?

By virtue of their lived experience, 1.5 and 2.0 migrants develop the advanced missional skill set of critical contextualisation. These skills create an opportunity for the migrant 1.5 and 2.0 Christian to discover and exercise the special call to read Scriptures through the lenses of multiple cultures.

The task of critical contextualisation is one that missiologist Paul Hiebert described as having several parts, of which I will focus upon three of the discrete iterative parts.[3] The first stage is a suspension of judgement regarding the observable part of the culture in question. The second stage is an examination of biblical material relating to the observed behaviour. The third and final stage is what Hiebert calls the building of an interpretive bridge.

In the first stage, the missionary is required to exercise restraint when confronted with something new. Whether it be food, an artistic expression or a behaviour, the missionary is required to achieve a state whereby they can objectively observe the new thing in question. For an individual that has crossed the boundary of their normative environment, this is a challenging proposition. As

---

3   Paul G. Hiebert, 'Critical Contextualization', *International Bulletin of Missionary Research* 11, no. 3 (1987): 104–12.

I have already suggested, the 1.5 and 2.0 migrant is at a distinct advantage in that the suspension of judgement is a necessary survival skill.

The second part of Hiebert's strategy is to reflect upon the biblical material that may be relevant in conjunction with the first step, because engaging and interpreting biblical material is an activity fraught with cultural danger. Hiebert suggests that there will be one of three outcomes at this stage. The biblical material will 1) deny the aspect of culture in question demanding some kind of transformation, 2) the biblical material will affirm the aspect of culture in question, or more often than not 3) the Bible will be silent on the matter.

At the conclusion of the first two stages, the missionary is then called to build an interpretive bridge between the current scenario and the preferred scenario which will include 1) an appropriate transformative strategy (if the biblical material calls for transformation), 2) a relevant and appropriate affirmation of the aspect of culture in question, or 3) do whatever internal work is necessary for the missionary to overcome their cultural prejudice.

For the purposes of illustrating the practice of critical contextualisation, I want to describe a scenario that occurred early on in my ministry formation when I was being taught this framework. It happened at a time some years ago when I was involved in the leadership of the youth and young adult ministry at a large regional suburban Pentecostal church. The church was contacted by a number of university students who were sharing a house. The students were experiencing strange supernatural activity and based on their experience of Christianity, one that was solely shaped by secular media, they concluded that they needed an exorcist to bless their rental property.

When two of the ministers who had visited the share house relayed the story to the eldership of the church, some of the more socially conservative elders expressed concern that unmarried males and females were sharing a house. At this point, as leaders of the young adult ministry directly interacting with the students, we felt that Hiebert's framework might be of assistance to us.

We worked with the elders in question, inviting them to suspend their judgement regarding university students living in a unisex arrangement, which to their credit they were able to do. We then looked to the Scriptures. It was difficult to find material condemning such a share house arrangement. To the contrary, we found biblical material (particularly Acts 2 which is a familiar passage to most Pentecostal denominations) encouraging caring for each other in the context of the pooling of physical resources. At one point, one of the elders suggested that the students might even be following the Scriptures more faithfully than those calling themselves Christians, as the students were practising a form of common purse.

Going through Hiebert's process, the Christian elders who were involved were able to identify their own cultural beliefs and practices, distinguishing them from what they assumed to be 'biblical beliefs' and consequently were able to create a hospitable welcome for young people who had no prior experience of a church.

I am mindful of Jesus's teaching regarding the speck and the log at a moment like this. It is easier for us to see the cultural bias (speck) of others. As we reflect upon the socially conservative elders who jumped to moralistic conclusions about unchurched Australian young adults, one can appreciate their awareness and repentance. To see the ways in which one can identify one's own cultural bias (log) is a far more difficult proposition.

Lesslie Newbigin, the missiologist who encouraged us to see Christendom as a comprehensive syncretistic blending of European mythologies with the gospel says, 'All reading of the Bible and all our Christian discipleship are necessarily shaped by the cultures which have formed us'.[4] In the example of the Pentecostal elders, that syncretism is clear, an attribution of nuclear family morality. That is the speck that we seek to remove from the eye of our brother. What is the log in our own?

'What Do We Do With the Children of Migrants?'

I have been in dialogue with many church leaders and I have been present in many conversations exploring this very question. What does the church do with the children of migrants who moved here as infants (1.5) and with the children of migrants (2.0) who were born here? In the context of this chapter, I suggest that the specific unconscious question being asked is: how does the church that has syncretised the Christian gospel with a collection of European mythologies, as well as more recent enlightenment mythologies, enculturate 1.5 and 2.0 migrants who do not fully embrace either the culture and mythology of their parents or the cultural and mythological milieu of Australia?

In one of the more creative works of recent fiction, the English science fiction and fantasy writer, Neil Gaiman, wrote 'American Gods'.[5] Its premise is that the old-world gods and mythological creatures exist as a result of the beliefs that early immigrants brought to America. However, the power of the gods wanes in modern times as America's beliefs and obsessions move towards media, celebrity, technology and various types of substance abuse. It is a powerfully creative and prophetic reflection upon the way in which syncretism has occurred to the degree that some American Christians can comfortably, and in good conscience, depict

---

4 Lesslie Newbigin, *The Gospel in a Pluralist Society* (Eerdmans, 1989), 196.
5 Neil Gaiman, *American Gods: A Novel* (William Morrow Paperbacks, 2017).

Jesus holding a shotgun whilst being draped in the American flag. Herein lies a profound opportunity for 1.5 and 2.0 migrants to play a redemptive role in the midst of a confused syncretism.

What Can the Children of Migrants Do With Us?

The American Franciscan Father, Richard Rohr, famously said, 'it is the things that you can't do anything with, and the things that you can't do anything about, that start to do something with you'.[6] In the same way, I suggest that in attempting to conceive of a way of forming faith amongst 1.5 and 2.0 migrants, we are asking the wrong question. I want to strongly assert that the question we should be asking and facilitating is: how can 1.5 and 2.0 migrants, armed with a significant set of missional skills and experiences, help the Australian church critically examine what we consider to be Christian discipleship, with a view to possibly finding and shaping a more faithful discipleship and witness in this unprecedented time of cultural conflict?

Reimagining Home

The Australian church is enmeshed in a dominant culture more accurately seen as a cultural construct, one that is 'home' to those who share the same worldview, whilst simultaneously alienating the 1.5 and 2.0 migrants who do not share the same worldview. The concept of a home for a faith community is not primarily a theological construct incarnated in a culture; rather it is a culture that the dominant ethnicities have unconsciously sought to affirm by ascribing to it biblical material that has been syncretistically observed and applied. Hence, the 'homelessness' that is experienced by 1.5 and 2.0 migrants is extended into the realm of the church and faith community.

When the 1.5 and 2.0 Migrant Reimagines Home

The 1.5 and 2.0 migrant experiencing a highly conscious form of *sehnsucht* can potentially play a profoundly important role in helping the church rehabilitate her sense of identity, missional vocation and ultimately her ability to reimagine home. However, the path to finding and living out such a vocation is not particularly straightforward.

---

6   Richard Rohr, *What the Mystics Know: Seven Pathways to Your Deeper Self* (Crossroad Publishing Company, 2015).

Making Our Way Back Home

Earlier on, I stated that the 1.5 and 2.0 migrant has the opportunity to discover and exercise the special call to read the Scriptures through the lenses of multiple cultures. This is an opportunity to be certain, but it is not a sure thing.

The first step in this possibility becoming a reality is receiving a language and a framework that describes and affirms the experience of a heightened sense of *sehnsucht*. My own personal experience of this was meeting with a Christian leader trained in missiology. In turn, I was introduced and became connected to a wider circle of missiologists. In that context, conversations about missiology and its various theories and frameworks was nothing short of a revelation. My experience of living between two worlds and finding a home in neither was described in many different ways. It was a deeply affirming experience. In particular, discovering the framework of critical contextualisation had deeply personal implications. Many missiologists and, in recent times, theologians consider this to be an increasingly valuable collection of skills and experiences. Therefore, the vital questions at this point are, what kinds of environments are required for 1.5 and 2.0 migrants to have initial encounters with missiology, and how can we facilitate their creation?

The second challenge is a reflection upon the process of theologising. There is great pressure on 1.5 and 2.0 migrants to gain an education and to 'do well'. The cultural pressure to take advantage of the previous generation's sacrifices to migrate and to create a new life, attaining the skills and experiences necessary to secure well-paying jobs and careers, is significant. The formal study of theology for 1.5 and 2.0 migrants is often not a path encouraged by the previous generation. This pressure exists before we even consider the systems whereby theological education is delivered. Primary, secondary and tertiary institutes in Australia are the consequence of years of cultural evolution; evolution of a particular culture that is alien to migrants who are neither European nor North American. This too is a significant barrier to the possibility of the 1.5 and 2.0 migrant discovering and exercising their particular calling and contribution. The question to ask at this stage is: how do we reimagine the institutions where theology is taught and where the practice of theologising is formed?[7]

---

[7] For me, this is a deeply painful and personal question. I have a growing number of former students from migrant backgrounds who just academically scrape through Whitley's NEXT program where I teach, who then need to return to a life of finding any kind of employment to support their migrant family, giving themselves to the present generation so that the subsequent one can flourish; a common migrant phenomenon. Many of these former students with 'the sight', and indeed their families, simply do not have the economic means or resilience to pursue further theological or missiological study. I am torn when I consider what is lost to the Australian church because of the economics of immigration.

The third challenge is trauma. Migration is a profound undertaking. I cannot overstate this enough. Often the pain of relocating is embraced because the pain of staying is greater. When families and communities migrate, it is reasonable to assume that there has been some form of trauma as a result of violence. When considering violence, one often limits it to experiences that are physical, sexual, emotional or psychological in nature. However, there are further categories which include spiritual, cultural, verbal, financial or neglectful violence. A person who is a 1.5 or 2.0 migrant frequently suffers the indirect trauma of several of these categories of violence through the previous generation's exposure to trauma that is often unprocessed. In the context of missiological study, traumatic wounds can be agitated and reopened. Therefore, reflection on the process of theological formation needs to consider these profound implications for all aspects of the ways in which theological formation occurs, from delivery strategies, through content and also to academics employed in the process.[8]

The fourth challenge is the process of the 1.5 and 2.0 migrant finding and using their voice. Being a minority can be challenging for the migrant community in the new land. Years of covert and overt racism takes its toll on those who do not have a direct connection to their ancestral culture and therefore the kind of resilience necessary to resist feelings of inferiority. The critical question at this stage is considering how to create environments of affirming welcome for the 1.5 and 2.0 migrant who wrestles with a profound existential experience of placelessness and homelessness.

How Do We Find Our Way Home?

After presenting these ideas in several contexts, I am aware that this enquiry creates more questions than it answers. I am asked, 'where to from here?' I don't yet know. It is a work in progress. I continue to consider responses, testing

---

8   When pursuing a postgraduate award, my supervisor directed me to material and ensuing conversation regarding kenotic theory. I was unaware of the impact that this material, which invited a self-emptying in imitation of Jesus, was having upon me, a survivor of domestic violence. Apparently, my supervisor did. He included in the material an article on kenosis and trauma. In this article, the writer reflected upon the destructive effects of inviting female victims of sexual abuse, women with a dysfunctional sense of agency, to reframe kenosis from an emptying, to kenosis as reconstruction of networks in Christian community. I vividly recall first reading this article in a public library where I was working on this research project and being moved to tears as her article spoke to my own sense of inherited trauma. My supervisor had the pastoral instinct to discern how the trajectory of my research was reopening old wounds, and with grace and skill, guided me to material that spoke to these wounds and through the theological task, became a mediator of healing. It is this kind of approach to teaching and supervising 1.5 and 2.0 migrants that needs to be part of the reconsideration that I am suggesting.

them both in the context of teaching in theological contexts and as part of my ongoing masters research. But we must try as there is much at stake. If we can give ourselves to the task of helping facilitate the 1.5 and 2.0 migrant to navigate these challenges, suddenly the church has at her disposal a community of people skilled and experienced at standing between two worlds with the ability to critically contextualise the gospel. As the Australian church struggles to navigate its relevance and indeed its inherited theology and mythology, a group of exiles in the form of these migrants who know the anxiety of dislocation can empathetically take the hand of the Australian people of God and act as guides into a future where we can reimagine home together, for all.

BIBLIOGRAPHY

Gaiman, Neil. *American Gods: A Novel*. Anniversary, Media Tie In Edition. William Morrow Paperbacks, 2017.

Hiebert, Paul G. 'Critical Contextualization.' *International Bulletin of Missionary Research* 11, no. 3 (1987): 104–12.

Newbigin, Lesslie. *The Gospel in a Pluralist Society*. Later Printing Used Edition. Eerdmans, 1989.

Rohr, Richard. *What the Mystics Know: Seven Pathways to Your Deeper Self*. Crossroad Publishing Company, 2015.

Wikipedia. The Free Encyclopedia. 'Immigrant Generations.' Accessed October 3, 2018. https://en.wikipedia.org/w/index.php?title=Immigrant_generations&oldid=862303414.

Chapter 10

ENVISIONING A HOME FOR THE GOSPEL AMONG AUSTRALIA'S URBAN HIDDEN PEOPLES

Edward James

Australia is becoming an increasingly diverse home for many people in terms of culture, language and religion. In 2016, the census reported that 21 percent of Australians speak a language other than English in their homes. The percentage of people speaking 'languages other than English' (LOTE) is even higher in large urban centres such as Sydney and Melbourne, where the percentage of LOTE speakers are 36 percent and 32 percent respectively.[1] Earlier immigration to Australia established large communities of Greek, Italian and Vietnamese speaking communities. There are now also many other growing immigrant communities with different cultures, languages and religions that are calling Australia home. The 2016 Census reports that more than three hundred different languages are spoken by people in Australia, including sixty-nine Australian indigenous languages, with more than one hundred speakers of each language.[2] Included in the diverse and growing immigrant population are also many sizeable and growing communities of what have often been referred to as 'least reached people groups' who have

---

1   www.profile.id.com.au/australia/language?WebID=10.
2   www.abs.gov.au/ausstats/abs@.nsf/lookup/Media%20Release3;
       www.abs.gov.au/ausstats/abs@.nsf/mediareleasesbyReleaseDate/
       1DBCFBCE6CACB75FCA25815400049DBA?OpenDocument.

little opportunity of hearing the gospel in their own language or in a culturally appropriate manner.[3]

Least Reached People Groups

People groups have been defined in various ways. The Joshua Project, which is an organisation that seeks to identify ethnic groups with the least followers of Jesus, defines a people group as:

> a significantly large grouping of individuals who perceive themselves to have a common affinity for one another because of their shared language, religion, ethnicity, residence, occupation, class or caste, situation, etc., or combinations of these.[4]

People groups have been further classified as 'reached' or 'unreached' according to the percentage of Christians within the people group.[5] According to the Joshua Project, for a group to be classified as least reached it needs to be 'less than 2 percent Evangelical and less than or equal to 5 percent Christian Adherent'.[6] According to these criteria there are approximately 16,300 people groups in the world today, of which 5,944 are classified as unreached or least reached. The term *least reached* may be a more appropriate descriptive term for these groups, one which I will use for the remainder of this chapter.[7]

---

3   Lausanne Strategy Workshop, Chicago, 1982, cited in Ralph Winter and Bruce Koch, 'Finishing the Task: The Unreached Peoples Challenge', in *Perspectives on the World Christian Movement*, eds. Ralph D. Winter and Stephen C. Hawthorne, 4th ed. (Pasadena: William Carey Library, 2009), 536.
4   www.joshuaproject.net/help/definitions.
5   Different people and organisations calculate and classify the status of unreached people groups differently. David Barret says that there are just under 9,000 (8,990) ethno-linguistic people groups in the world of which around 1,000 with less than 20 percent evangelised can be classified as unreached. David Barret, *World Christian Encyclopedia* (Oxford: Oxford University Press, 1982), 110. In the second edition of the encyclopedia the number of ethno-linguistic groups is increased to 12,600. David B. Barret, George T. Kurian, and Todd M. Johnson, *World Christian Encyclopaedia* (Oxford: Oxford University Press, 2001). Patrick Johnstone says that there are 16,350 people groups (10,340 when borders are ignored). Of this around 6,645 can be classified as least reached, having no viable church or are unengaged. Patrick Johnstone, *Operation World* (Downers Grove: Intervarsity Press, 2010), 25.
6   www.joshuaproject.net/assets/media/articles/why-include-adherents-when-defining-unreached.pdf.
7   Dave Datema, 'Defining "Unreached": A Short History', *International Journal of Frontier Missiology* 33, no. 2 (2016): 62, 64. The Joshua Project website gives a figure of 6,945 unreached people groups according to this criterion.

A Contested Notion: Unreached and Least Reached People Groups

The notion of people groups has been contested since the term was first introduced. Ralph Winter of the US Center for World Mission suggests that classifying least reached people groups according to the percentage of evangelical Christians or Christian adherents is unhelpful. Rather he says that the classification should take into account a community's 'ability' to evangelise itself and not just whether there are a certain percentage of Christians within the people group. Winter makes an important distinction, because although people might identify with others in a people group ethnically and linguistically, there can also be other sociocultural and religious differences which are barriers preventing people from engaging, communicating and communing with one another. Winter suggests that a group's ability to evangelise itself should be a key distinctive in a group being classified as reached or least reached.[8] For Winter, *'cultural distance'* is a major factor when considering a people's ability to evangelise other people in their own sociocultural, linguistic and religious community, as well as beyond.[9] Cultural distance refers to cultural, religious and linguistic differences that need to be crossed by Christians in order to communicate the gospel appropriately in another community, as well as the cultural and linguistic differences that would need to be crossed by potential believers in a community in order for them to feel at home in a local church.[10]

Others have questioned the very concept of people groups, saying that it is based on outdated theories of culture and missiology. Michael Rynkiewich, for one, suggests that due to 'global flows of objects, images, ideas and people', people's cultures, even in the remotest of places are no longer 'bounded' and 'integrated', but are instead 'fuzzy' and 'porous' due to the movement of people, ideas and objects.[11] Brian Howell also sees the rigidity of people group thinking as unhelpful for engaging with diasporic communities because it focuses on 'culture as a bounded, integrated, adaptive whole'.[12] It 'reifies culture as a singular entity'

---

8   Winter and Koch, 'Finishing the Task,' 538.
9   Winter developed the E-Scale and the P-Scale to express the idea of cultural distance. The E-Scale shows the 'cultural distances that Christians need to move in order to communicate the gospel'. The P-Scale shows the 'cultural distance that potential believers need to move in order to join the nearest church'. The E-Scale and P-Scale, however, may not be nuanced enough to describe the cultural distance of people within the same people group who belong to different religious communities. Winter and Koch, 'Finishing the Task', 532.
10   Winter and Koch, 'Finishing the Task', 532.
11   Michael Rynkiewich, 'The World in My Parish: Rethinking the Standard Missiological Model', *Missiology: An International Review* 30, no. 3 (July 2002), 315.
12   Brian Howell, 'Multiculturalism, Immigration and the North American Church: Rethinking Contextualisation,' *Missiology: An International Review* 39, no. 1 (January 2011), 81.

and does not take account of the impact of 'globalization, cultural change and hybridity'.¹³

A Call for Deep Engagement

The need to acknowledge and accept that cultures are always changing, and that people can have multiple sociocultural and linguistic identities is a welcome voice and a needed shift in thinking for appropriate and effective intercultural engagement. However, this does not mean that there is no longer value in continuing to identify and engage with people who share common affinities in terms of ethnicity, language, culture, heritage and religion, wherever they may be in the world. There remains a need to engage with people according to the language, culture and identity that they identify with, and which they feel most comfortable with, so that they can encounter the gospel not as a foreign entity, but as something that resonates with them and feels like home. At the same time we need to understand, as Rynkiewich suggests, that culture is always 'contingent, constructed and contested'.¹⁴ This means that instead of viewing all people from community X in a certain way, we need to take the time and effort to engage with them more deeply, understanding their individual stories, and their particular ways of seeing the world, rather than focusing our attention on idealised cultures, which in many ways only exist on paper.¹⁵

Hidden Peoples

Some people have referred to least reached communities living outside of their countries, regions and areas of origin as 'Hidden Peoples'.¹⁶ Hidden peoples is an appropriate term because many of these communities are living in large urban centres, far away from their traditional homes, but are not usually considered when it comes to Christian mission. Because of their religious heritage (they

---

13   Howell, 'Multiculturalism, Immigration and the North American Church', 81.
14   Rynkiewich, 'The World in My Parish,' 315.
15   Rynkiewich, 'The World in My Parish,' 315.
16   The term 'Hidden Peoples' was first suggested to Winter by Robert Coleman. Winter defined hidden peoples as 'the people of the world who cannot be drawn by E-1 methods into any existing, organized Christian fellowship', or alternatively, 'those E-2 and E-3 groups within which there is no culturally relevant church'. Cited in Datema, 'Defining "Unreached"', 52. 'Four out of five non-Christians in the world today', says Winter, 'are hidden, walled off by linguistic or cultural barriers from any existing missionary efforts'. By his estimates there are more than 16,000 hidden people groups; many are in India, China and the Muslim world. In all, more than two billion people are hidden and will not hear the gospel without pioneer missionary efforts. www.missionfrontiers.org/issue/article/waving-the-flag-for-hidden-peoples.

are predominantly Muslim, Hindu and Buddhist), they are also not among the ethnic groups that Christian denominations in large Western urban centres usually minister to because there are too few Christians among them. This means for the most part that they are out of sight and therefore remain largely unengaged.

For example, in Victoria, the Baptist Union has more than eighty-six LOTE churches (Languages Other Than English), as well as eight multiethnic churches. However, of the eighty-six LOTE churches only twenty different language groups are represented, which is well short of the three hundred plus languages that are spoken in Australia and recorded in the 2016 Census data.[17]

Theological Justification for Ministry to Hidden Peoples

The theological justification for seeking to engage with hidden peoples is based on a reading of the Old and the New Testament which shows that all of the nations, *ethne*, and family groups of the world are important to Yahweh. The blessing that was promised to Abraham and his descendants is something that is also intended for all the families of the earth (Genesis 12:1–3; 18:18; 22:18; 28:14). In Psalm 67 the nations are in view for the Psalmist as those who will be blessed, who will know God's saving power, will be glad, and who will offer their praises to Yahweh. Jesus also has the nations in his sights. In Matthew 24:14, Jesus tells his disciples that the good news of the kingdom is not just for the Jews, but that it needs to be proclaimed 'throughout the world' and 'to all nations', *ethnesin*. In the book of Revelation, John's eschatological vision includes an image of the heavenly throne room in which there is a multitude of people from every nation, *pantos ethnous*, tribes, *phylōn*, peoples, *laōn*, and languages, *glōssōn* (Revelation 7:9). In Revelation 21:3, we are told that the home of God will be among mortals and that they will be his 'peoples'. The use of the plural term 'peoples', *laoi,* is significant, as it shows again that the end goal is not uniformity through the removal of cultural and linguistic differences, but that cultural and linguistic diversity will remain even at the summation of this age.[18] This means that believers will be unified around the throne in their worship of Jesus, but not uniform, and that the different *peoples* will be recognisable from each other by their cultural and linguistic differences and will bring their unique worship to God.

Today, many people in least reached communities around the world have little chance of hearing the gospel because there are too few Christians in these communities who can share this with them. Where there are small numbers of Christians in least reached communities, often the cultural distance between

---

17   Meewon Yang, LOTE Church Diagram, Baptist Union of Victoria, 2017.
18   John Piper, www.desiringgod.org/articles/unreached-peoples#panta.

the Christians and the majority religious community is too great for effective communication and engagement to take place, which is why a focus on least reached communities continues to be relevant, as well as a just use of the resources of the church. Hidden peoples are diasporic members of these same least reached communities and, therefore, should be among the peoples who are seen by local churches and engaged with appropriately.

Least Reached People Groups > 1,000 in Australia[1]

	People Group	Population	Language Name	Religious Affinity	Percent of Christian Adherent	Percent of Evangelical Christian
1	Afghan, general	25,000	Dari	Islam	0	0
2	Arab, general	67,000	Arabic	Islam	0.5	0.3
3	Arab, Iraqi	67,000	Arabic	Islam	4	1
4	Bosniak	33,000	Bosnian	Islam	0.5	0.3
5	Burmese	12,000	Burmese	Buddhism	0.35	0.07
6	Cocos Islander/Kukus	1,200	Malay, Coco Island	Islam	0	0
7	Hazara	16,000	Hazaragi	Islam	0.03	0.03
8	Hmong Njua	2,100	Hmong Njua	Traditional Religion	4	2
9	Japanese	35,000	Japanese	Buddhism	5	1.6
10	Jew	115,000	English	Judaism	1	0.02
11	Khmer, Central	34,000	Khmer	Buddhism	5	1.4
12	Kurd, Kurmanji	4,300	Kurdish, Northern	Islam	1	0.7
13	Lao	11,000	Lao	Buddhism	3.5	1.9
14	Malay	138,000	Malay	Islam	0.3	0.25
15	Mandaean	4,000	Mardiac	Other	0	0
16	Pashtun, Northern	8,700	Pashto, Northern	Islam	0	0
17	Persian	58,000	Persian, Iranian	Islam	0.8	0.7
18	Sinhalese	110,000	Sinhala	Buddhism	0	0
19	Somali	14,176	Somali	Islam	>1	>1
20	Thai, Central	66,000	Thai	Buddhism	0.8	0.3
21	Turk	45,000	Turkish	Islam	0.2	0.15

1 www.joshuaproject.net/countries/AS.

How Many Hidden Peoples Are in Australia?

In Australia today, there are numerous groups of hidden peoples living in Australian urban centres. The Joshua Project database estimates that there are twenty-one least reached groups with more than one thousand people living in Australia.[19] Applying Ralph Winter's definition of least reached, the number of groups could increase by including communities with percentages of Christians larger than the parameters set by the Joshua Project. However, due to the cultural distance that exists between Christians and people of the majority religion in a community, ministry engagement is limited.

It is believed that a synergistic relationship between churches and cross-cultural sending agencies could change the situation so that hidden peoples can hear and experience the gospel in their own language and in a culturally appropriate manner within Australian urban centres.

In short, hidden people groups could have the opportunity to hear and experience the gospel by:
- Christians in Australian churches seeing the need and opportunity to engage with hidden peoples in Australian urban centres
- developing and implementing appropriate models of ministry
- equipping Christians in churches with the necessary *knowledge*, *awareness* and *skills* for intercultural ministry
- providing training, coaching, pastoral care, encouragement and prayer support for the teams and churches that undertake this ministry.

Models of Ministry for Engaging Hidden Peoples

Hidden peoples will not generally respond to traditional methods of Christian engagement and ministry because for many of them Christianity, as they see and understand it, is contrary to their own religious convictions, beliefs and practices. Furthermore, attending a Christian church would be for many somewhat like visiting another planet with practices and beliefs that are often considered strange, if not dangerous. This is the 'cultural distance' that Winter says impacts the ability of Christians and Christian churches to undertake evangelism to people from other sociocultural, linguistic and religious communities.[20] It is not that Christians and churches do not want to engage with these communities, it is just that the cultural distance between them and the communities which they seek to engage with is

---

19   www.joshuaproject.net/people groups/AS.
20   See Winter and Koch, 'Finishing the Task', 532.

generally too great to bridge with a traditional attractional model of ministry, which is prevalent in many Australian churches.

Primary Model of Doing Church in Australia

The primary model for ministry in most Christian churches in Australia, Baptist churches included, is an attractional model, which is based on the practice of drawing largely unconnected people together who have some shared affinities, particularly language and sociocultural, in order that they hear the Word of God, worship God and join in fellowship with others. What this effectively means is that people who attend need to embrace the language and culture of the dominant community in order to feel at home in these contexts. Many of the people who attend Christian churches in Australia meet for worship and other church related activities, but do not necessarily have organic relationships with one another. Because of this it is believed that ministry to hidden peoples will require churches to reimagine ministry, as the model that is currently the main stay of many Australian churches is not seen as the best vehicle for engaging hidden peoples with the gospel due to the social, cultural, linguistic and religious distance that exists between people in churches and the communities that they seek to engage with.

Attractional model: Unconnected people joining a new community

The attractional model of ministry has been shown not to be the most fruitful approach for reaching least reached communities with the gospel in their countries of origin.[21] The main reason for this is that the activity of drawing unconnected people together works against the existing natural affinities and social network orientation of people in many contexts.[22] The attractional model is also not seen as the best model for sharing the gospel with hidden peoples in the Australian context, or for that matter, with dominant culture Australians.[23]

---

21 Eric Adams, Don Allen, and Bob Fish, 'Seven Fruitful Branches', in *From Seed to Fruit: Global Trends, Fruitful Practices, and Emerging Issues among Muslims*, ed. J. Dudley Woodberry (Pasadena: William Carey Library, 2008), 3730.

22 Adams, Allen, and Fish, 'Seven Fruitful Branches', 3725.

23 Andrea Gray and Leath Gray, 'Attractional and Transformational Models of Planting', in *From Seed to Fruit: Global Trends, Fruitful Practices, and Emerging Issues among Muslims*, ed. J. Dudley Woodberry (Pasadena: William Carey Library, 2008), 5645ff.

Transformational model: Engaging people who are already socially connected

A more fruitful model for sharing the gospel with hidden peoples in Australian urban centres would be a transformational model of ministry, which is relationship centred, culturally and linguistically focused, religiously sensitive, and social-network orientated. This model of ministry has been referred to elsewhere in literature on the missional church movement as the incarnational approach and the organic church.[24] The transformational approach is essentially focused on others. Rather than calling people to leave their traditional cultural and linguistic homes in order to encounter and follow Jesus, it embraces the biblical principle that the gospel can be at home in any and every language and culture community. It also assumes that the best place for people to encounter Jesus is when they feel at home—relationally, linguistically, culturally and religiously.

CENTRAL IDEAS OF A TRANSFORMATIONAL MODEL

A central notion of the transformational model is that the flow of ministry movement is opposite to the attractional model. Instead of locating people and seeking to draw them into an existing church (someone else's home, which is a foreign social network), the transformational model encourages people from churches to move out of their homes, seeking to build authentic relationships with people in their existing social networks (in this case people in other sociocultural, linguistic and religious communities). In these new relationships, it is envisioned that people from Christian churches who are connecting with people in a least reached community will look for opportunities to share their hope in Jesus in culturally appropriate ways. Foundational and essential to a transformational model of ministry are deep, authentic, long-term relationships.

GOAL OF TRANSFORMATIONAL MODEL

The goal of the transformational model of ministry with hidden peoples is not to eventually persuade people to leave their own networked community and join an established church (another social network). Rather, it is to see a new community of faith born in a new home with people who have a strong *affinity* with one

---

[24] It is also referred to elsewhere in regard to missional church movements as the incarnational model. See Alan Hirsch, *The Forgotten Ways* (Grand Rapids: Brazos, 2006); Michael Frost and Alan Hirsch, *The Shaping of Things to Come* (Erina: Strand and Peabody: Hendrickson, 2003); and Neil Cole, *Organic Church: Growing Faith Where Life Happens* (San Francisco: Jossey-Bass, 2005).

another and who are already networked in some ways socially. In turn, the goal is to see people in a new faith community growing more like Jesus and sharing their faith and hope in Jesus throughout their social networks and beyond in a culturally appropriate manner.[25] A transformational model of ministry takes the sociocultural, linguistic and religious *affinities* of people seriously. It values their ideas and practices of home and works from the premise that the gospel must be fully translated across these barriers in order for people to encounter Jesus, make an allegiance shift to follow him, and share him authentically within and outside of their community.[26] People who adopt a transformational paradigm of ministry will seek to build real, deep, trust-filled, long-term relationships, in which they will have opportunities to tell their own life stories, listen to other people's life stories, share God's stories and to be engaged in long-term disciple-making activities with people who make an allegiance shift to Jesus.[27]

A key aspect of the transformational model of ministry is the ability of followers of Jesus to establish and sustain real friendships with people from communities who are socially, culturally, linguistically and religiously different to them. Evelyne Reisacher suggests that the type of friendship in which 'deep life sharing' takes place in least reached communities requires a high level of mutual human attachment.[28] This raises the obvious question: how can such deep level long-term relationships occur with people in our churches who do not (in most

---

25 Andrea Gray and Leath Gray, 'Transforming Social Networks by Planting the Gospel', in *From Seed to Fruit: Global Trends, Fruitful Practices, and Emerging Issues among Muslims*, ed. J. Dudley Woodberry (Pasadena: William Carey Library, 2008), 278.

26 Some missiologists believe that a homogenous approach to least reached diasporic communities is out of place in many urban contexts and that a multicultural approach is a more appropriate model. The multicultural model may be applicable with ethnic groups that are sympathetic or not hostile to Christianity and the church. However, where groups view Christianity and the church with suspicion, and even hostility, linguistic, cultural and religious distance needs to be narrowed in order to engage appropriately and effectively. See Howell, 'Multiculturalism, Immigration and the North American Church', and Datema, 'Defining "Unreached"'.

27 Jack Colgate, 'Making Storying Meaningful, Part 1: Relational Bible Storying and Scripture Use in Oral Muslim Contexts', *International Journal of Frontier Missiology* 25, no. 3 (Fall 2008), 137.

28 Such mutual attachment is developed over time through trusting, open relationships with our neighbours. In such relationships we will experience mutual joy, as well as times of sorrow and hurt. Deep lasting relationships can only occur, however, when there is a willingness and ability to restore a relationship when hurt, shamed or when sorrow has occurred between two people. Evelyne Reisacher, *Joyful Witness in the Muslim World: Sharing the Gospel in Everyday Encounters* (Grand Rapids: Baker Academic, 2016), 934.

cases) currently share natural affinity in terms of culture, language, worldview or religion with people in these communities?[29]

Such a list of obstacles can seem like an insurmountable barrier to engagement with people in these communities and could possibly deter people and churches from considering this ministry. However, with appropriate knowledge, awareness, opportunities, training and skills, churches and teams within churches could *appropriately*, *effectively* and *efficiently* begin to build language capacity, cultural understanding and cultural intelligence for such a ministry.

Tools, Awareness, Knowledge and Training

There is a need for partnerships between churches, Christian ministry training institutions and cross-cultural ministry sending organisations.

For example, the cross-cultural ministry sending organisation that I work with has appropriate short-term training programs and tools that are used to prepare people for cross-cultural ministry internationally, and which churches with a vision for engaging with hidden peoples could utilise. These include:

- a language acquisition program, that enables people without linguistic training to begin learning and developing capacity in any language[30]
- 'The Engaging Culture and Worldview Inquiry Program', which is a tool to begin understanding the cultures and worldviews of people in any community
- consultants in cross-cultural ministry, anthropology and linguistics who are skilled and who can give appropriate training to churches in many areas of intercultural ministry
- cross-cultural workers returning from working internationally who already have language and culture skills, cross-cultural ministry awareness and expertise, and who can use their skills, awareness and knowledge to help churches engage with different communities.

29　Affinity must be more than ethnolinguistic. For example, Somali people share 'ethnicity, culture, language, and religion', however, 'in reality' Somalians 'are divided by clan affiliations, the most important component of their identity'. Seth Kaplan, cited in Datema, 'Defining "Unreached"', 56.

30　This is known as the Growing Participator Approach. The same language program could also be used by churches and people without formal linguistic training to help migrants effectively learn English.

Why Not Just Do This in English?

Many new immigrants to Australia need and want to grow their English language skills to find work and to more fully participate in Australian life. English language classes are often used as a practical means of helping new immigrants and refugees and it gives an opportunity for people doing the teaching to build relationships with them. English language training is a great service that churches can provide to new immigrants and refugees. This service facilitates contact with people from new immigrant communities. It is a very practical way of helping people begin the long process of becoming settled in Australia and is a tangible way to express the love of Jesus for them. Engaging new immigrants in this manner should be one aspect of a ministry to hidden peoples, however, it should not be the only pathway for engagement.[31]

It has been shown in non-English speaking, international contexts, that the use of a community's heart language, as well as their communication and learning preferences style is a critical factor in a team's ability to establish a fellowship in that community. A recent study found that there was an 82 percent probability of establishing a fellowship in a least reached community when a team uses the community's language, communication and learning preference style, and when at least one person on the team has high skills in the community's language. This is in comparison to a 7 percent probability of establishing a fellowship when none of these are present.[32]

The Future is Hybrid

The model that is being suggested here for engaging hidden peoples is a transformational approach. This is not a call to abandon the current model of ministry of many Australian churches. Rather, it is a call for embracing hybridity for the sake of the hidden peoples in Australian urban centres where barriers to engaging with them relationally currently exist. Hybridity recognises the potential of followers of Jesus within existing attractional churches and seeks to mobilise, empower and skill them to undertake ministry to hidden peoples.[33]

---

31   Schachtel, Lim, and Wilson in their book, *Changing Lanes*, suggest that it is 'unreasonable to think we can become proficient in many languages of the people' we relate to. This is true if one has a ministry to people from multiple ethnic backgrounds. Andrew Schachtel, Choon-Hwa Lim, and Michael Wilson, *Changing Lanes, Crossing Cultures: Equipping Christians and Churches for Ministry in a Culturally Diverse Society* (Sydney: Great Western Press, 2016), 1249.
32   Adams, Allen, and Fish, 'Seven Fruitful Branches', 3666.
33   www.christianitytoday.com/pastors/2013/spring/hybrid-ministry.html.

The vision for engaging hidden peoples in Australian urban centres embraces the biblical premise of God being on mission, and that the people of God are called to be on mission as God's partners (Psalm 67:1–7; John 20:21; Matthew 18–20). This vision portrays churches and Christian communities as integral to the task of sharing and expressing the gospel with hidden peoples.

Today, some churches are planting second congregations or satellite churches in different suburbs within the same city. This often occurs when a church identifies an opportunity in another suburb, seeks volunteers from the church who are willing to go, secures a building and starts doing a satellite church in a new location. The new church or congregation that is established is in many ways similar in DNA to the sending church—a second home, so to speak.

It is believed that a similar initiative could be used for engaging with hidden peoples, but instead of utilising an attractional model, an initiating church will seek to use a transformational approach. Instead of securing a building and running a parallel service, people will be equipped to build cross-cultural relationships with people who have an already established affinity with each other, due to their sociocultural, linguistic and religious heritage. Their aim is to share deeply in life with people in these communities and in time to share their hope in Jesus, translating the gospel for their new friends, and desiring to see Jesus and the gospel established in different homes, with different traditions, cultures and languages.

What about Christians in Least Reached Communities?

In some communities of hidden peoples in the Australian context Christians are already present, albeit in very small numbers. There are two factors that impact the ability of these Christians to engage other people in their own sociocultural and linguistic communities with the gospel. The first is that there are usually too few Christians who can engage the rest of the community in a significant manner. A second and more significant factor is *cultural distance*. Although Christians may share common affinities in terms of ethnicity, language and culture with other people in their ethnic community, religious distance and historical grievances between religious communities may be too large to cross easily. Christians who desire to engage with other people in their own ethnic communities, who are adherents of other world religions, will need to think through how they can engage in ministry lovingly and sensitively. More especially they will need to grapple, as Paul did in 1 Corinthians 9:19–23, with identifying deeply with the *other* so that they can share deeply with them in contextually appropriate ways.

Which Least Reached People Groups are Hidden in Australian Urban Centres?

The 2016 Census shows that immigrants are coming to live in Australian urban centres in large numbers. Although Sydney and Melbourne receive by far the largest numbers of immigrants, most Australian capital cities have growing immigrant populations.[34]

Due to the constraints of this chapter I am only able to give some very broad details on what is occurring in Greater Melbourne and Greater Sydney, but which I believe is representative of what is taking place in other Australian urban centres.

According to the 2016 Census, Buddhists, Muslims and Hindus are growing religious communities. In Greater Melbourne, there are 170,553 Buddhists, 186,654 Muslims, 128,940 Hindus and 49,601 Sikhs.[35] In Greater Sydney there are 186,037 Buddhists, 253,436 Muslims, 170,161 Hindus and 26,996 Sikhs.[36]

The 2016 Census indicates people's country of origin, religious identity and primary language spoken at home according to suburb and local government boundaries, as well as state and federal electoral boundaries. The available census data does not indicate all ethnic groups and their languages. Rather, it tends to indicate large language groups of people coming from countries and regions.

By way of example, the 2016 Census indicates that in Greater Melbourne there is a large and growing Sri Lankan community with more than 36,000 Sinhala speakers, of whom more than 18,000 are living in the South East.[37] There are also more than 30,000 Turkish people living in Greater Melbourne with more than 15,900 living in the North West.[38]

Greater Sydney also has areas where least reached groups are more concentrated. For example, more than 69,000 Arabic speakers live in the Inner South West and 36,000 in the South West.[39] There are also more than 21,000 Thai speakers living in Greater Sydney, of whom 7,590 live in the City and Inner South, 2,508 in the Inner South West, 1,752 in the Inner West and 1,737 in North Sydney and Hornsby.[40]

---

34   www.abs.gov.au.
35   www.profile.id.com.au/australia/religion?WebID=260.
36   www.profile.id.com.au/australia/religion?WebID=250.
37   www.censusdata.abs.gov.au/census_services/getproduct/census/2016/quickstat.
38   www.censusdata.abs.gov.au/census_services/getproduct/census/2016/quickstat.
39   www.censusdata.abs.gov.au/census_services/getproduct/census/2016/quickstat.
40   www.censusdata.abs.gov.au/census_services/getproduct/census/2016/quickstat.

Where to Go from Here?

As has been shown in this chapter, there are many opportunities for envisioning the gospel at home within the different kinds of homes of the hidden peoples who are present in Australia today.

However, in the time-pressured world in which we live, building capacity in terms of skills, knowledge and the awareness needed for appropriate and effective ministry will require time, intentionality, focus and commitment, as will building and establishing relationships.

Added to this is the reality that many people in Australian churches already have full social networks. People would need to be intentional about engaging with other people who are outside of their normal social networks to develop new friendships, as these will most likely not occur without intention and focus.[41]

The result of seeing people from these least reached communities encountering Jesus, worshipping and glorifying God in ways that express their languages, cultures, traditions and heritages is what the church is on mission for, as is expressed in Habakkuk 2:14 and in John's vision in the book of Revelation (7:9).

Such a venture will require more prayer, thought, planning and research. Regarding research, there is a need to more accurately identify where hidden peoples are living in Australian urban centres. It will also be important to explore the actual affinities that people have with others, and to what extent these require special consideration of language and culture. There is a need to better understand the percentage of people in different communities who still identify their first language as the language they speak in their home, the language they want to communicate in, to hear important information in, and use to talk about deep matters. It is necessary to explore the nature of people's social networks in diasporic communities. It is also necessary to understand which Christian denominations and faith communities are already currently working with communities.

Conclusion

The future of Australia is increasingly diverse. Some people talk of immigrant nations such as Australia being like a melting pot. However, a stew is a better metaphor, as a melting pot implies that we become a uniform blend, whereas a stew retains aspects of our identities, cultures, languages, and even our ways of

---

41 Robin Dunbar says people's social networks consist of around 150 people, which includes five intimate friends, fifteen good friends and fifty friends and the rest are acquaintances. Robin Dunbar, 'The Magic Number', *RSA Journal* 156, no. 5541 (Spring 2010), 16, 18.

worshipping God, while also flavouring each of the other parts.[42] This diverse Australia includes many hidden peoples making their homes in the suburbs of our major cities. This is a great opportunity for the church, and we need to embrace it as a gift from God. What remains is for us to take hold of the opportunity, to continue to seek God's guidance and to mobilise ourselves to minister appropriately and effectively so that hidden peoples can have the opportunity of hearing and experiencing the gospel without having to leave their cultural, linguistic and relational homes.

---

42 Patty Lane, *A Beginner's Guide to Crossing Cultures: Making Friends in a Multicultural World* (Downers Grove: IVP, 2002), 15.

BIBLIOGRAPHY

Adams, Eric, Don Allen, and Bob Fish. 'Seven Fruitful Branches.' In *From Seed To Fruit: Global Trends, Fruitful Practices, and Emerging Issues among Muslims*, edited by J. Dudley Woodberry. Pasadena: William Carey Library, 2008.

Australian Bureau of Statistics. www.abs.gov.au. Accessed May 2016–June 2017.

Barret, David B., George T. Kurian, and Todd M. Johnson. *World Christian Encyclopaedia*. Oxford: Oxford University Press, 2001.

Barret, David. *World Christian Encyclopedia*. Oxford: Oxford University Press, 1982.

Cole, Neil. *Organic Church: Growing Faith Where Life Happens*. San Francisco: Jossey-Bass, 2005.

Colgate, Jack. 'Making Storying Meaningful, Part 1: Relational Bible Storying and Scripture Use in Oral Muslim Contexts.' *International Journal of Frontier Missiology* 25, no. 3 (Fall 2008): 135–42.

Datema, Dave. 'Defining "Unreached": A Short History.' *International Journal of Frontier Missiology* 33, no. 2 (2016): 45–71.

Dunbar, Robin. 'The Magic Number.' *RSA Journal* 156, no. 5541 (Spring 2010): 16–19.

Frost, Michael, and Alan Hirsch. *The Shaping of Things to Come*. Erina: Strand and Peabody: Hendrickson, 2003.

Gray, Andrea, and Leath Gray. 'Attractional and Transformational Models of Planting.' In *From Seed To Fruit: Global Trends, Fruitful Practices, and Emerging Issues among Muslims*, edited by J. Dudley Woodberry. Pasadena: William Carey Library, 2008.

Hirsch, Alan. *The Forgotten Ways*. Grand Rapids: Brazos, 2006.

Howell, Brian. 'Multiculturalism, Immigration and the North American Church: Rethinking Contextualisation.' *Missiology: An International Review* 39, no. 1 (January 2011): 79–85.

Johnstone, Patrick. *Operation World*. Downers Grove: Intervarsity Press, 2010.

Joshua Project. www.joshuaproject.net.

Lane, Patty. *A Beginner's Guide to Crossing Cultures: Making Friends in a Multicultural World*. Downers Grove: IVP, 2002.

Piper, John. www.desiringgod.org/articles/unreached-peoples#panta.

www.profile.id.com.au/australia. (An Australian demographics resource website.)

Reisacher, Evelyne. *Joyful Witness in the Muslim World: Sharing the Gospel in Everyday Encounters*. Grand Rapids: Baker Academic, 2016.

Rynkiewich, Michael. 'The World in My Parish: Rethinking the Standard Missiological Model.' *Missiology: An International Review* 30, no. 3 (July 2002): 301–21.

Schachtel, Andrew, Choon-Hwa Lim, and Michael Wilson. *Changing Lanes, Crossing Cultures: Equipping Christians and Churches for Ministry in a Culturally Diverse Society*. Sydney: Great Western Press, 2016.

The Age. www.theage.com.au.

Winter, Ralph. www.missionfrontiers.org/issue/article/waving-the-flag-for-hidden-peoples.

Winter, Ralph, and Bruce Koch. 'Finishing the Task: The Unreached Peoples Challenge.' In *Perspectives: On the World Christian Movement*, edited by Ralph D. Winter and Steven C. Hawthorne. 4th ed. Pasadena: William Carey Library, 2009.

SECTION THREE:
IMAGINATION AND REIMAGINATION:
FINDING HOME IN THE BIBLICAL TEXT

Chapter 11

PRESERVING HOME: SEEKING *SHALOM*

Deborah Storie

The so-called international refugee or immigration crisis preoccupies the media and engenders heated public debate. In destination countries, some people feel angry, others are frightened, many are concerned and confused. Here in Australia, as in New Zealand, Canada and the United States, some of us recognise that we or our ancestors were immigrants and do our best to welcome those now seeking new homes.

And yet, and yet . . . How often do we look beneath, behind and beyond the immigration crisis to ask why so many people are on the move? What forces and factors rendered their original homes untenable? When—*if*—we ask these questions, we discover that the things that make destination countries such attractive places to call home are inseparably connected to the structures and systems that destroy home elsewhere.

This chapter is an experiment in 'intercultural exegesis' in which I read Luke 19:1–27 (the story of Zacchaeus and the parable told in Jericho) in the light of the global immigration crisis. Intercultural exegesis, as Justin Ukpong practises it:

> involves entering into the text with critical awareness about the contemporary context and allowing it to evoke in the reader appropriate reactions, responses and commitments about the context.[1]

---

1   Justin S. Ukpong, 'Developments in Biblical Interpretation in Africa: Historical and Hermeneutical Directions', in *Voices from the Margins: Interpreting the Bible in the Third*

Entering the text this way, readers traverse three horizons in their imaginations—the worlds behind, of, and in front of, the text. Ideally, such readings release the perceptive (discerning, intuitive), generative (creative, constructive) and responsive (empathetic, compassionate, ethical) dimensions of cognition, create space for the untrammelled play of associations, emotions and ideas, and stimulate readers' curiosity, hope and doubt.[2] This multifaceted interpretive process depends on rigorous analyses of the context of the text and of the context of the reader.[3] We come to the text with questions raised by our context, and expect the text in context to question, challenge and move us to respond. Our readings become ethical when we move from reading, to solidarity, to committed response.

The study proceeds as follows. After briefly considering how Jesus's parables functioned as pastoral acts of prophetic imagination, I describe dominant and alternative traditions of interpretation of the parable of Luke 19:12–27; remember Jericho, one of the Herodian cities 'dis-named' by the Gospels;[4] and recall several scriptural echoes in Luke 19:1–27. I then offer a first-person reading of the text in which I imagine hearing the parable as if among those to whom it was first addressed. Returning to our world in front of the text, I reimagine how we are enmeshed and complicit in structures of power and exclusion by delineating some of the complex interrelated forces and factors beneath, behind and beyond the immigration crisis. Finally, I draw insights from others who affirm the alternative tradition of interpreting the parable told in Jericho to consider how this might inform and shape a more adequate Christian response to contemporary immigration and related crises.

    World, ed. R. S. Sugirtharajah (Maryknoll, NY: Orbis, 2006), 60.

2   On the role of imaginative engagement with biblical texts in ethical formation and practice, see Stanley Hauerwas and David Burrell, eds., 'From System to Story: An Alternative Pattern for Rationality in Ethics', in *Why Narrative? Readings in Narrative Theology* (Grand Rapids: Eerdmans, 1989), 158–90; Paul Ricoeur, 'Toward a Narrative Theology: Its Necessity, Its Resources, Its Difficulties', in *Figuring the Sacred: Religion, Narrative and Imagination* (Minneapolis: Fortress, 1995), 236–48; Trevor Hart, 'Imagination and Responsible Reading', in *Renewing Biblical Interpretation*, eds. Craig Bartholomew, Colin Greene, and Karl Moller (Carlisle: Paternoster and Zondervan, 2000), 308–34; Margaret Somerville, *The Ethical Imagination: Journeys of the Human Spirit* (Melbourne: Melbourne University Press, 2007).

3   Justin S. Ukpong, 'The Parable of the Shrewd Manager (Luke 16:1–13): An Essay in Inculturation Biblical Hermeneutic', *Semeia* 73 (1996).

4   On the Gospels 'dis-naming' imperial cities, see Keith Dyer's chapter in this volume. See also Marianne Sawicki, 'Spatial Management of Gender and Labor in Greco-Roman Galilee', in *Archaeology and the Galilee: Texts and Contexts in the Graeco-Roman and Byzantine Periods*, eds. Douglas R. Edwards and C. Thomas McCollough (Atlanta: Scholars Press, 1997) 7–28.

The Parables of Jesus—Pastoral Acts of Prophetic Imagination

Like the prophets before him, Jesus didn't perform parables in a vacuum. His parables addressed particular people in particular places at particular times, often in response to a question, a challenge, a complaint or grumble. The prophets of Israel, as Walter Brueggemann understands them, were Spirit-inspired poets of enormous imagination who saw the present as it was yet called it into question by remembering the past and imagining the future of God's promise: 'New imagination evoked new realities in community'.[5] Brueggemann describes Jesus's way of teaching through parables as:

> a pastoral act of prophetic imagination [that] invited his listeners out beyond the visible realities of Roman law and the ways in which Jewish law had grown restrictive in his time . . . [Jesus] tells parables consistent with the rabbinic tradition [that] serve to conjure alternative social realities. They are specific, but they are open-ended. The listener, when the story is ended, is not instructed and does not know what to do. The stories intend to characterize an alternative society which he calls 'kingdom of God' but the stories do not offer blue-prints, budgets or programs. They only tease the listeners to begin to turn loose of the givens of the day and to live toward new possibilities.[6]

For those with ears to hear, Jesus's parables, poetic visions and other forms of enigmatic speech unveiled realities that 'the powers that be' concealed and evoked futures that 'the powers' denied.

A Parable Told in Jericho

According to Luke (19:1–27), Jesus, his disciples and other pilgrims had entered and were passing through Jericho *en route* to Jerusalem for Passover when Jesus told a parable (vv. 12–27) to 'all those' who saw and heard his interaction with a ruling tribute collector—Zacchaeus. The dominant interpretive tradition of this parable assumes that the parabolic nobleman/king represents Jesus or God and, thereby, shields him from any critique. Having allegorised the nobleman/king, interpreters inevitably allegorise other dimensions of the parable—slaves and

---

5   Walter Brueggemann, *Hopeful Imagination: Prophetic Voices in Exile* (Philadelphia: Fortress, 1986), 2.
6   Brueggemann, *Hopeful Imagination*, 97.

slavery, imperial rule, client kings, tribute, money, profit and interest—that had real and fiercely contested meaning in first-century Palestine.

An alternative interpretive tradition neither allegorises the parable nor assumes its nobleman/king good. It reads the parable as a 'stylized fictional but realistic account of daily life' which resonated with experiences, memories and hopes shared by many of its early hearers.[7] Read this way, the parable calls the surrounding economy of power and exclusion into question and invites all those listening to serve a different king and to imagine and live toward a different kingdom.

Remembering Jericho

First-century Jericho—its royal estates, aqueducts, slaves and plantations, extravagant buildings, gardens and pools—advertised wealth, conspicuous consumption and the play of power. Jericho was a summer retreat favoured by the Herods and other Jewish and Roman elites. It was also a major administrative, tribute, trade and agricultural centre, one of the cities to which Rome deployed additional troops at times, such as Passover, when uprisings were feared. Jericho epitomised and embodied the consequences of imperial domination and Herodian ambition. A different picture emerges if we penetrate the city's glossy facade and look beyond the shadows of its walls. Within the city limits, beggary, prostitution, hunger, squalor, slavery and coercion were the brutal lot of economic outcasts. Beyond the city and its plantations, villages and countryside spoke of dispossession, desiccation and fear, their water consumed by Jericho's aqueducts, their forests denuded by its greed. The prosperity and pleasures of Jericho came at a cost. The city that enriched a few impoverished many.

Jericho, in an earlier incarnation, looms large in the Scriptures of Israel. Remember the stories? The prostitute's house and the scarlet thread (Josh 2:1–21). The commander of the Lord's army who met Joshua, Jesus's namesake, outside Jericho, commanding him, like Moses, to remove his sandals: he stood on holy ground (Josh 6:13–15). Remember how Jericho's walls fell at a shout (6:20)? Remember how Joshua declared, 'Cursed before God be anyone who tries to build this city—this Jericho!' (Josh 6:22)? Remember Achan and the Valley of Achor (Josh 7)?

In Jericho, the history and hopes of first-century Jews collided with the humiliation of their present experience. Jericho remembered was the city conquered by miracle, the memory and hope of divine intervention, and the promise of land and dignity home. Jericho experienced was a tangible reminder of the triumph of

---

7   Luise Schottroff, *The Parables of Jesus* (Minneapolis: Fortress, 2006), 225.

imperial politics, economics and religion, and of the subjugation and dispossession of the Jews.

Remembering the Scriptures

According to Luke, Jesus tells a parable to all those who grumbled, 'He has gone in to be with a sinful man' (Luke 19:7), and heard Jesus proclaim: 'Today salvation has come to this house . . . the Son of Humanity came to seek and to save that which is lost' (Luke 19:9–10). Echoes of Scripture hover just beneath the surface of the narrative, resonate through Jesus's words, and reverberate through the story's geographical and temporal moorings (Jericho, Passover). No wonder those listening were full of expectation and supposed that the kingdom of God was to appear immediately (19:11)!

We often miss scriptural allusions because our imaginations are insufficiently shaped by the Scriptures of Israel (Jesus's 'Bible') and because modern English versions seldom retain connections between New Testament texts and their Old Testament precedents. The NRSV, for example, translates Jesus's self-designation 'the Son of Humanity' (Greek: *ho huis ho anthropos*) as 'the Son of Man' yet renders the divine address to Ezekiel 'son of humanity' (Hebrew: *ben adam;* Greek: *huis anthropos*) as 'mortal'.[8] Jesus's words 'came to seek and to save that which is lost' are straight from an oracle in which Ezekiel envisages the 'good shepherd' that the LORD would send to judge and to save:

> I will seek the lost, and I will bring back the strayed, and I will bind up the injured, and I will strengthen the weak, but the fat and the strong I will destroy. I will feed them with justice (Ezek 34:16).

These and other connections open the way to hear the parable told in Jericho as a creative rendition (implicit exegesis or 'riff') of Ezekiel's oracle against the shepherds in the light of Zacchaeus's role as a ruling tribute collector and the situation and recent history of Judea and Galilee.[9]

---

8   Jesus refers to himself as the Son of Humanity eighty-one times in the Gospels.
9   On implicit exegesis, see Michael Fishbane, 'Revelation and Tradition: Aspects of Inner Biblical Exegesis', *Journal of Biblical Literature* 99, no. 3 (1980).

Hearing the Parable as if among Those Listening in Jericho

Keeping these things in mind, let us now follow Kenneth Bailey's advice and imagine ourselves into the story *as if* among those to whom Jesus first told the parable.[10] For the purposes of this experiment, I read *as if* I were a disciple.

We join Jesus and his disciples approaching Jericho (Luke 18:35). The road is crowded with pilgrims, soldiers, tax collectors, traders, beggars, slaves, labourers searching for work. Not everyone is travelling. On each side of the road, slaves tend plantations, bent double, sweating under the blazing sun. Other slaves, barely visible through the dust, toil on construction sites, aqueducts, storehouses, villas. Jericho's massive walls loom ahead.

Did you hear that? Some idiot beggar yells, 'Jesus, Son of David, have mercy on me!' Here, in the shadow of the city walls, soldiers are everywhere. 'For pity's sake, be silent! Do you want to get us killed?' But he shouts even louder, 'Jesus, Son of David, have mercy on me!' Jesus stops, speaks with him, and heals him with a word. Amazing!

The once-blind man and an excited throng accompany us into Jericho. Hardly the way to keep a low profile! Then, inside Jericho, what does Jesus do? He goes straight up to the ruling tribute collector of Jericho, Zacchaeus, the last person we want to be noticed by or seen with, and invites himself, and all of us, to his house.

With 'all who saw it' we grumble: 'He has gone in to stay with a sinful man' (19:7). It's not that we mind being ceremonially unclean. We're Jesus's mob, not scribes nor Pharisees. We've hung with Jesus long enough to expect him to break purity codes—and quite enjoy it! But breaking bread with a ruling tribute collector? That breaks one boundary too far.

Ruling tribute collectors inspire fear and resentment for good reason. We all know families evicted from ancestral plots, children sold into bonded labour, wives and daughters forced into prostitution, fathers thrown into prison, and homes destroyed because of tribute debts foreclosed. Besides which, hasn't Jesus just said that he'll be handed over to the Romans (Luke 18:31–33)? Who better to do that than Zacchaeus, a Jew grown sleek on Jewish blood, a collaborator?

Zacchaeus welcomes Jesus, rejoicing. I wonder: is Jesus enacting the parable of the Prodigal Father (Luke 15:11–32)? That parable asked the scribes and Pharisees a question. Were they like the elder brother? Did they resent Jesus's radical hospitality and forgiveness, the demonstration of God's grace? We are

---

10 Kenneth E. Bailey, *Jesus through Middle Eastern Eyes: Cultural Studies in the Gospels* (London: SPCK, 2008), 283.

disciples, not scribes nor Pharisees, but in this case, our answer is: Yes—we do resent it. And, no! We will *not* join *this* party. Zacchaeus did not squander his own inheritance; he squandered our inheritance from the LORD (Ps 127:3), our lives and those of our children.

Listen! Zacchaeus is speaking.

> See, half my possessions, Lord, I give to the poor; and if I have defrauded anything I give back fourfold (19:8).

His possessions? *If* he has defrauded anyone? As far as Rome is concerned, tribute collection is, and is expected to be, a profitable business: Zacchaeus is entitled to whatever he can extract in addition to contracted tribute. As far as we, God's people, are concerned, Roman rule and tribute are fraudulent through and through: The earth is the LORD's and *everything* in it (Psalm 24:1).

Then, before anyone can speak, Jesus says:

> Today salvation has come to this house, because he too is a son of Abraham. For the Son of Humanity came to seek and to save that which is lost (19:9–10).

What! Zacchaeus may have been born a son of Abraham, but he sold that birthright years ago. As for seeking and saving the lost, the prophet envisioned thin, weak, hunted sheep being saved, not the fat, strong sheep that ravaged the flock, pushed others aside, trampled the pasture and muddied the waters (Ezek 34:11–19). Zacchaeus might talk big, but he hasn't changed yet. Even if he *is* sincere, his best efforts will not redeem land lost to debt, restore years lost to prison, or return children lost to hunger, disease and bonded labour. The ruling tribute collector should be fed justice (Ezek 34:16), justice of a relentlessly retributive kind.

'Today salvation has come . . .' Recalling the vision with which Ezekiel's oracle ends (Ezek 34:22–31), all the longings the Scriptures inspire surge through our hearts. We are filled with expectation: Might this be the day? Will God now restore Israel? What will happen in Jerusalem this Passover? Is the kingdom about to appear immediately (Luke 19:11)?

Listen! Jesus is telling a parable.

> A certain person of noble birth travelled to a far country to take hold of a kingdom for himself and return. He called ten of his slaves, and gave to them ten *minas* (about 200 *denarii*) and said to them, 'Turn a profit until I come'. But the citizens of that place hated him and sent a delegation after him, saying, 'We do not want this one to reign over us'. And on his return, having taken the kingdom, he said to summon those slaves, to whom he had given the silver, in order that he

might know what they had gained by trading. The first came forward and said, 'Lord, your *mina* has earned ten *minas* more'. He said to him, 'Well done, good slave! Because in a lesser thing you have been faithful, be in authority over ten cities'. And the second came, saying, 'Your *mina*, Lord, has made five *minas*'. He said to him, 'And you, be over five cities'. And the other came, saying, 'Lord, see your *mina*, which I wrapped in a cloth, for I fear you, since you are a harsh person; you take up what you did not deposit, and reap what you did not sow'. He said to him, 'Out of your mouth I judge you, you evil slave! You knew that I am a harsh person, taking up what I did not put down and reaping what I did not sow? Why then did you not give my silver on the table? And when I came, I could have collected it with interest'. And to the bystanders he said, 'Take up from him the *mina* and give it to the one who has ten *minas*'. And they said to him, 'Lord, he has ten *minas*!' 'I tell you that to all who have more will be given; from those who have not that which they have will be taken away. But as for these enemies of mine who did not want me to reign over them—bring them here and slaughter them in my presence (Luke 19:12–26).

'Listening *as if* in Jericho, we know this story. We've been there before. The parable is crammed with the social and political distinctions of our world: an ambitious slave owner; a far country that apportions kingdoms; citizens who hate those who would rule over them; and slaves—slaves who turn profits and slaves who rule over cities. Herod the Great, his sons Archelaus, Antipas and Philip, all went to Rome to get their kingdoms. Fearing that Archelaus would be even worse than his father, our leaders sent a delegation to Rome to oppose him but Archelaus got the kingdom, returned from Rome, and slaughtered his opponents.[11] The possibility that the nobleman/king might be benevolent, the first two slaves good, and the third slave evil, would never occur to *us*.

The parable is realistic. It resonates with our experiences and collective memories of subjugation and dispossession. When a nobleman gains ruling power, we tremble. When a ruler's slaves turn a profit, we lose the little that we have. We are not surprised that the first two slaves report such large profits or that those found 'faithful' are deployed, still slaves, to rule over cities. With each slave act, 'good' slaves replicate the reign of terror and strengthen the system that enslaves them—and us. With each act of obedience, they—and we—have more reason to fear. How did they turn such profits? In what did they trade? Tribute? Debt? Land?

---

[11] You can read the full story as told by Josephus in his *Antiquities of the Jews*, 17.299–318; *Jewish War*, 2.80–94. Flavius Josephus, *The Works of Josephus: Complete and Unabridged*, trans. William Whiston (Peabody: Hendrickson, 1987).

Sex? Slaves? We don't need to speculate. We've experienced Herodian economics. We shudder at the human consequences turning such profits inevitably involve.

We *are* surprised when the third slave breaks the pattern and does not report, 'Your *mina* has made two more'. The slave admits he is afraid. Yet, with every reason to fear, he does not submit to fear. He does not prevaricate, feign subservience, flatter, or plead for mercy. He cuts through the fiction that money 'makes' money, that 'money works', and unmasks the slave owner's malevolence and greed (19:21–21). What slave would openly declare his owner morally bankrupt? What slave would tell his owner that he, not his owner, decides what to do? No slave who values their skin. Who—slave, freed person or citizen—dreams of defying those who dominate them? Who yearns to speak truth to power? Everyone we know. We admire the slave's audacity and fear for his life.

Predictably, the slave owner is angry (19:22–23). Why doesn't he disown the damning description? Does he not hear the *Torah* sound through the slave's words? If the slave owner misses these allusions, he may genuinely consider the slave confused and stupid. If he does catch the scriptural allusions, he appears to have no qualms about mocking the *Torah*. He chastises the slave for not giving his silver on the (moneylenders') table so that he could have collected it with interest (19:23).[12] He feels entitled to take up what he did not deposit and reap what he did not sow. He has forgotten how to blush (Jer 6:15; 8:12).

Or is the slave owner afraid? The noncompliant slave ruptures the transcript of slavery by showing that slaves need not always obey. Were other slaves to take their *minas* out of circulation, the slave owner's wealth would be scattered. Were others to resist his edicts, his enemies would not die. Were citizens, slaves and bystanders to unite, the king's rule would disintegrate. The slave owner/king commands a slaughter (19:26–27). His command addresses everyone and no-one. Does he no longer expect to be obeyed?

Or perhaps, just perhaps, the slave's words prompt him to question the foundations and consequences of his reign. Once raised, such questions are not easily silenced.

The parable ends with the fate of the resisting citizens, the slaves and the slave-owner/king unresolved. Even if the dissidents are slaughtered, the prophetic voice is not silenced. Their blood cries out—the earth cries out—*Ishmael*, God hears.

---

[12] The word 'interest' (Gk: tokos) occurs only here and in the somewhat similar parable of Matthew 25:31–46 in the New Testament. In the Greek version of the Old Testament, tokos occurs eighteen times, always as something prohibited or in lists of behaviours that unrighteous people practice and from which righteous people refrain.

Listening *as if* in Jericho, the parable terrifies and challenges us. It questions everything, dictates nothing, and resolves none of our dilemmas. We have changed but the external realities that constrain our lives have not. The empire still takes all it can and gives nothing back. Ultimately, this is not the way things will be, yet, for the foreseeable future, this is how they are.

Zacchaeus has placed the city in grave danger. It is one thing to repent quietly—Caesar, Herod and their armies might ignore that—but such public declarations are rarely tolerated. Should the people of Jericho prepare for a swift and bloody reprisal? Remembering Exodus in the shadow of Rome, how should we anticipate God's reign? Will we, like the Hebrew slaves, grumble and drag our feet, reluctant to leave the bondage we know for the promise and command of God? Or will we, together with Zacchaeus, find courage to serve a different king and live toward a different kingdom?

As Jesus leaves Jericho and goes on ahead (19:28), we remember how Jesus took us aside and warned us:

> See, we are going up to Jerusalem, and everything that is written about the Son of Humanity by the prophets will be accomplished. For he will be handed over to the Gentiles; and he will be mocked and insulted and spat upon. After they have flogged him, they will kill him (Luke 18:31–33).

Slave owners as dangerous as Zacchaeus rule that city and their orders are too often obeyed. What will the ruling priests and leaders of the people do when the Son of Humanity prophesies against the city and its false shepherds? When we reach Jerusalem, will we disciples have the courage to choose whom we serve? We remember Isaiah:

> Thus, says the Lord, 'Maintain justice, and do what is right, for soon my salvation will come, and my deliverance be revealed' (Isa 56:1).

Could it be that when and how God's reign arrives depends on us?

Reimagining Our World

We do not live in first-century Palestine and Jesus did not tell this parable because we supposed the reign of God was about to appear immediately. Our social locations (well watered and well shaded; well fed, well educated and well protected) and most of our life experiences attune us to appreciate the beauty and comforts of Jericho without noticing its less savoury aspects. Our foundational cultural assumptions coincide with those of slave owners rather than slaves. We expect to enjoy all that the world has to offer. The imperial account of Jericho makes sense to us.

The International Organisation for Migration reports that 244 million people lived outside their home countries in 2015.[13] Many were economic refugees hoping to enhance their livelihoods and send money back home. Many others, including sixty-five million forcibly displaced people, faced extreme conditions without work, land, water, income or purposeful activity to sustain them. Whether or not these people qualify as refugees, their original homes no longer give life and liberty. For today's economic outcasts, immigration to countries like Australia is often the simplest and most effective way to improve their livelihoods—or even to stay alive.

The United Nations' 2016 *Human Development Report* highlights mutually reinforcing problems: deepening inequality, entrenched human deprivation, increasing violence, and widespread environmental degradation.[14] Global and regional inequalities are increasing as more and more of the world's resources are channelled to produce products and services for the wealthy few. Economists calls this the 'deepening of capitalism'.[15] Chasms of income, opportunity, life experience and expectations separate rich and poor within as well as between countries.[16] The geography and complexion of imperialism have changed but empires still give more to 'the haves' and take from 'the have nots' the little that they had.

The World Wildlife Fund estimates that the planet passed the ecological break-even point in the early 1970s.[17] Since then, we have used more resources than the planet can replace and produced more waste than it can absorb. Our economic systems normalise destructive commercial-industrial practices and promote irresponsible patterns of consumption that undermine essential ecosystems; the ecosystems that sustain food production and maintain fresh water, forests and air, regulate climate and ameliorate infection and disease. The collective ecological footprint of destination societies, towards which so many look in the hope of making a home, destroys homes elsewhere.

Australia contributes to all these crises. The Australian Government goes to extreme lengths to deter those fleeing conflict or poverty, deploys troops to fight in distant conflicts, recently cut Overseas Development Assistance (ODA) to record lows,[18] and promotes ever-escalating levels of consumption and waste production here at home. Eight out of ten Australians are among the 10 percent of the world's

---

13   IOM, *Global Migration Trends Fact Sheet* (2015).
14   UNDP, *Human Development Report 2016: Human Development for Everyone* (New York: UNDP, 2016).
15   Ankie Hoogvelt, *Globalization and the Postcolonial World* (London: Palgrave, 2001).
16   Branko Milanovic, *Global Inequality* (Cambridge, MA: Harvard University Press, 2016).
17   Graphs, charts and further details available from World Wildlife Fund, *Living Planet Report 2012* (Gland, Switzerland: WWF, 2012).
18   https://www.lowyinstitute.org/issues/australian-foreign-aid, accessed June 15, 2017.

population who control 90 percent of global resources.[19] Per capita, Australians consume and pollute more than most other countries.[20] Like the Herods, we are 'lovers of luxury'. We build some of the largest houses with the fewest people living in them.[21] Australians have inordinate appetites for air travel.[22] Our ecological footprints are among the heaviest on earth.

In 1974, the Lausanne Covenant called affluent Christians to live simply 'in order to contribute more generously to both relief and evangelism'.[23] Half a century later, the call to live simply is more urgent than ever. Not primarily to enable generous giving, essential as that is, but because neither the earth nor our souls can withstand the escalating levels of consumption to which we've grown accustomed and to which we feel entitled.

In 2008, Jonathan Bonk's editorial for the *International Bulletin of Missionary Research* confessed:

> The gospel of plenty, carried obediently to the uttermost parts of the earth by its emissaries, is at last being appropriated by the vast populations of the non-Western world. Too late, those of us who have been its chief beneficiaries and advocates now realize that this 'good news' could doom the planet . . . Only now are . . . missiologists starting to realize that their strategies for saving the world have been framed

---

19 Anthony Shorrocks, James B. Davies, and Rodrigo Lluberas, *Global Wealth Data Book* (Zurich: Credit Suisse, 2016). The two out of ten Australians outside this top income bracket are likely to be indigenous, non-English speaking, living with mental or physical disabilities or addicted to gambling, alcohol or other drugs.

20 World Wildlife Fund, *Living Planet Report 2014* (Gland, Switzerland, 2014), 38–39.

21 Australian Bureau of Statistics, '4130.0—Housing Occupancy and Costs, 2015–16' (2017); CBA, 'CommSec Home Size Trends Report', in *CommSEC Economic Insights* (November 17, 2017).

22 The Australian Bureau of Statistics reports that nearly 10,000,000 Australians travelled overseas in 2016 for a holiday (60%), visits to friends and relatives (24%) and business (6%). ABS, '3401.0—Overseas Arrivals and Departures, Australia, Dec 2016' (2017). Over 61,000,000 domestic flights were taken within Australia in the year ending June 2017. Department of Infrastructure and Rural Development, 'Aviation: Domestic Activity 2016–2017' (Commonwealth of Australia, 2017). The amount of (domestic and international) travel is highly variable: over half of those who travelled took one return trip a year; around 10 percent of travellers taking domestic trips at least once a month; and less than 5 percent of travellers taking more than one international trip. 'Sky High: Australians' Air Travel Habits' (Roy Morgan Research, 2016). I have not been able to find an estimate of the proportion of Australians who have never flown. In 2003, a survey found that 18 percent of people in the US had never flown. US Department of Transportation, 'Airline Passenger Travel', *Omnibus: Bureau of Transportation Statistics* 3, no. 3 (2003). I have not been able to find the source of a widely cited estimate that less than 20 percent of the world's population has ever travelled by plane.

23 The Lausanne Covenant and Papers from the 1974 International Congress on World Evangelisation are available from https://www.lausanne.org.

within a theological cocoon that prevented them from adequately understanding the end result of their civilization's notions of progress, development, and the social material destiny of humankind. The planet is simply too small to accommodate large numbers of human beings who think and live as we do.[24]

Affirming the Alternative Interpretive Tradition

Social location shapes our imaginations but does not determine our commitments. We are responsible for the consequences of our interpretations. We can choose how to read.

If we listen to the parable within an imperial framework, we see a world that works: a ruler acting as entitled, faithful slaves serving well, a stupid slave being enlightened by his master. Read this way, the parable sounds a warning to serve the empire and its vassals wholeheartedly. But this is not the only way to read.

Merrill Kitchen reads the parable within an interpretive framework created by Jesus's wilderness contest with the devil (Luke 4:1–13) and 'Nazareth Manifesto' (4:16–21).[25] On her reading, the parabolic nobleman serves as a satanic figure, an antitype for Christ; the obedient slaves as those who serve powers that oppose the reign of God: the noncompliant slave as one who speaks truth to power and pays the cost, prefiguring Christ; and the dissident citizens stand in continuity with the prophetic voice of Israel, the righteous who suffer for the sake of justice. Kitchen explains that the parable functions rhetorically by placing 'the concepts of judgment and enslavement in juxtaposition' to reflect the 'ever-present struggle' between the reigns of God and of human rulers.[26] The parable challenges readers:

> to reassess their presuppositions and review their allegiances. They must choose the God with whom they will align themselves. Will it be the god of wealth, power and status . . .? Or will it be the God of Israel . . .?[27]

---

24 Jonathan J. Bonk, 'Mission and the Groaning of Creation', *International Bulletin of Missionary Research* 32, no. 4 (2008): 170.

25 Merrill A. Kitchen, 'The Parable of the Pounds: A Reading of Luke 19:11–28 within the Social and Narrative Framework of the Gospel of Luke' (MTh thesis, Melbourne College of Divinity, 1993). See also her 'Rereading the Parable of the Pounds: A Social and Narrative Analysis of Luke 19:11–28', in *Prophecy and Passion: Essays in Honor of Athol Gill*, ed. David Neville (Adelaide: Adelaide Theological Forum, 2002), 227–46.

26 Kitchen, 'Rereading the Parable', 232–37, 245.

27 Kitchen, 'The Parable of the Pounds', 151–52.

Elizabeth Dowling reads the parable within the interpretive framework of Jesus's sermon at Nazareth (4:16–21) and the brutal realities of imperial rule and slavery in the Gospel world.[28] The parable tells a frighteningly realistic story about the abuse of power and the consequences of opposing oppression.

Luise Schottroff holds that the parable is interpreted by Jesus's 'previous encounter with Zacchaeus and his departure for Jerusalem where he will be killed by . . . imperial power and where—according to Luke—he will rise again'.[29] On her reading, the parable describes 'the economic and political structure of an exploitative kingship [from] the perspective of people that reluctantly bear this governance and desire its end'. It challenges 'beneficiaries of Western wealth' 'to practice the repentance of the rich' and resist analogous forms of economic and political exploitation in a world 'of growing militarism and intensifying economic imperialism'.

Sylvia Keesmaat and Brian Walsh read the parable through a triple lens of its narrative context, Jesus's teaching about economic relations, and the Scriptures of Israel.[30] Reading in the aftermath of the 2008 economic crisis, they notice how the fictional nobleman's values and practices reflect the values and practices of actual rulers condemned by the prophets, and how the third slave and dissident citizens do what discipleship requires. They hear in the parable a call to return to a 'crucifixion economics . . . of restraint'.

Preserving Home: Seeking Shalom

Read in the light of today's ecological, social, economic and political crises, the parable Jesus told in Jericho still calls surrounding economies of power and exclusion into question and invites those listening to serve a different king and to imagine and live toward a different kingdom. The parable challenges us to do more than welcome those seeking new homes. It calls us to look beneath, behind and beyond the presenting problem to interrogate underlying structures of violence and exclusion, repent of our complicity in them, renounce the false gods of our age, and imagine and live towards a different future. We must reimagine 'home' in order to preserve the home—the *Shalom*—of others.

---

28 Elizabeth Dowling, 'Taking Away the Pound: Women, Theology and the Parable of the Pounds in the Gospel of Luke' (PhD thesis, Melbourne College of Divinity, 2005). See also her *Taking Away the Pound: Women, Theology and the Parable of the Pounds in the Gospel of Luke* (London: T&T Clark, 2007).

29 Here and following, Schottroff, *Parables*, 181–87.

30 Brian Walsh and Sylvia Keesmaat, 'Outside of a Small Circle of Friends: Jesus and the Justice of God', in *Jesus, Paul and the People of God: A Theological Dialogue with N. T. Wright*, eds. Nicholas Perrin and Richard B. Hays (Downers Grove: IVP, 2011), 66–88.

Our economic and ecological violence is rarely intentional or overt. Faceless systems and structures take for us what we did not deposit and reap for us what we did not sow. Our nation worships the false gods of acquisition, competition, comfort and security. Our ruling priests assure us that it is possible to 'exploit the market' without exploiting people or the environment. Unable to imagine Jubilee, we speak the language of obedient slaves and accept the lie that 'money makes money', that 'money works', and are blind to the true cost of turning such profits: degraded lands, rivers and forests; debt, displacement and imprisonment; hunger, prostitution, bonded labour and slavery. Millions are slaughtered but not in our presence. They die, largely unnoticed, offstage.

The prophet speaks directly to us:

> Is it not enough for you to feed on the good pasture, but you must tread down with your feet the rest of your pasture? When you drink of clear water, must you foul the rest with your feet? And must my sheep eat what you have trodden with your feet, and drink what you have fouled with your feet (Ezekiel 34:18–19)?

It is our lifestyles, our palatial air-conditioned houses, our air travel and cars, our disposable throwaway everything that despoil the planet, trampling the pastures, fouling the waters, destroying our home. We are cut to the heart . . . but will we repent and believe the good news (Acts 2:37–38)?

Look! The kingdom is approaching. It has drawn near and is even among us. We are filled with expectation! The promise is for us and our children (Acts 2:39), as is the question, 'Will we reimagine home in order to preserve home for others? Will we live simply that others may simply live?'

BIBLIOGRAPHY

Australian Bureau of Statistics. '3401.0—Overseas Arrivals and Departures, Australia, Dec 2016.' Accessed October 11, 2018. www.abs.gov.au/AUSSTATS/abs@.nsf/Previousproducts/3401.0Feature%20Article1Dec%202016?opendocument&tabname=Summary&prodno=3401.0&issue=Dec%202016&num=&view=.

Australian Bureau of Statistics. '4130.0—Housing Occupancy and Costs, 2015–16.' Accessed October 11, 2017. http://www.abs.gov.au/ausstats/abs@.nsf/mf/4130.0.

Bailey, Kenneth E. *Jesus through Middle Eastern Eyes: Cultural Studies in the Gospels*. London: SPCK, 2008.

Bonk, Jonathan J. 'Mission and the Groaning of Creation.' *International Bulletin of Missionary Research* 32, no. 4 (2008): 169–70.

Brueggemann, Walter. *Hopeful Imagination: Prophetic Voices in Exile*. Philadelphia: Fortress, 1986.

Commonwealth Bank of Australia. 'CommSec Home Size Trends Report.' *CommSec Economic Insights* (November 2017). Accessed October 10, 2018. https://www.commsec.com.au/content/dam/EN/ResearchNews/ECOReport.20.11.17_Biggest%20homes_size-fall.pdf.

Department of Infrastructure and Rural Development. 'Aviation: Domestic Activity 2016–2017.' Commonwealth of Australia, 2017. Accessed August 20, 2017. https://bitre.gov.au/publications/ongoing/files/domestic_airline_activity_2016-2017.pdf.

Dowling, Elizabeth. 'Taking Away the Pound: Women, Theology and the Parable of the Pounds in the Gospel of Luke.' PhD thesis, Melbourne College of Divinity, 2005.

Dowling, Elizabeth. *Taking Away the Pound: Women, Theology and the Parable of the Pounds in the Gospel of Luke*. London: T&T Clark, 2007.

Fishbane, Michael. 'Revelation and Tradition: Aspects of Inner Biblical Exegesis.' *Journal of Biblical Literature* 99, no. 3 (1980): 343–61.

Hart, Trevor. 'Imagination and Responsible Reading.' In *Renewing Biblical Interpretation*, edited by Craig Bartholomew, Colin Greene, and Karl Moller, 308–34. Carlisle: Paternoster and Zondervan, 2000.

Hauerwas, Stanley, and David Burrell, eds. 'From System to Story: An Alternative Pattern for Rationality in Ethics.' In *Why Narrative? Readings in Narrative Theology*, 158–90. Grand Rapids: Eerdmans, 1989.

Hoogvelt, Ankie. *Globalization and the Postcolonial World*. London: Palgrave, 2001.

International Organisation for Migration. *World Migration Report 2015: Migrants and Cities*. Geneva: IOM, 2015. Accessed June 20, 2017. https://www.iom.int/world-migration-report-2015.

International Organisation for Migration. *Global Migration Trends Fact Sheet 2015*. Geneva: IOM, 2015. Accessed June 20, 2017. https://publications.iom.int/books/global-migration-trends-factsheet-2015.

Josephus, Flavius. *The Works of Josephus: Complete and Unabridged*. Translated by William Whiston. Peabody: Hendrickson, 1987.

Kitchen, Merrill A. 'The Parable of the Pounds: A Reading of Luke 19:11–28 within the Social and Narrative Framework of the Gospel of Luke.' MTh thesis, Melbourne College of Divinity, 1993.

Kitchen, Merrill A. 'Rereading the Parable of the Pounds: A Social and Narrative Analysis of Luke 19:11–28.' In *Prophecy and Passion: Essays in Honor of Athol Gill*, edited by David Neville, 227–46. Adelaide: Adelaide Theological Forum, 2002.

Milanovic, Branko. *Global Inequality*. Cambridge, MA: Havard University Press, 2016.

Ricoeur, Paul. 'Toward a Narrative Theology: Its Necessity, Its Resources, Its Difficulties.' In *Figuring the Sacred: Religion, Narrative and Imagination*, 236–48. Minneapolis: Fortress, 1995.

Roy Morgan Research. 'Sky High: Australians' Air Travel Habits' (2016). Accessed June 15, 2017. http://www.roymorgan.com/findings/7084-sky-high-australians-air-travel-habits-201612091252.

Sawicki, Marianne. 'Spatial Management of Gender and Labor in Greco-Roman Galilee.' In *Archaeology and the Galilee: Texts and Contexts in the Graeco-Roman and Byzantine Periods*, edited by Douglas Edwards and C. Thomas McCollough, 7–28. Atlanta: Scholars Press, 1997.

Schottroff, Luise. *The Parables of Jesus*. Minneapolis: Fortress, 2006.

Shorrocks, Anthony, James B. Davies, and Rodrigo Lluberas. *Global Wealth Data Book 2016*. Zurich: Credit Suisse, 2016.

Somerville, Margaret. *The Ethical Imagination: Journeys of the Human Spirit*. Melbourne: Melbourne University Press, 2007.

Stephan, André, and Robert Crawford. 'Size Does Matter: Australia's Addiction to Big Houses Is Blowing the Energy Budget.' *The Conversation* (December 14, 2016). Accessed October 11, 2018. https://theconversation.com/size-does-matter-australias-addiction-to-big-houses-is-blowing-the-energy-budget-70271.

Stockholm International Peace Research Institute. *SIPRI Year Book 2016 Summary: Armaments, Disarmament and International Security.* Oxford: Oxford University Press, 2016.

Tyers, Roger. 'It's Time to Wake Up to the Devastating Impact Flying Has on the Environment.' *The Conversation* (January 15, 2017). Accessed June 15, 2017. https://theconversation.com/its-time-to-wake-up-to-the-devastating-impact-flying-has-on-the-environment-70953.

United Nations Development Program. *Human Development Report 2016: Human Development for Everyone*. New York: UNDP, 2016. Accessed June 17, 2017. www.hdr.undp.org/sites/default/files/2016_human_development_report.pdf.

Ukpong, Justin S. 'Developments in Biblical Interpretation in Africa: Historical and Hermeneutical Directions.' In *Voices from the Margins: Interpreting the Bible in the Third World*, edited by R. S. Sugirtharajah, 49–63. Maryknoll, NY: Orbis, 2006.

Ukpong, Justin S. 'The Parable of the Shrewd Manager (Luke 16:1–13): An Essay in Inculturation Biblical Hermeneutic.' *Semeia* 73 (1996): 189–210.

US Department of Transportation. 'Airline Passenger Travel.' *Omnibus: Bureau of Transportation Statistics* 3, no. 3 (2003). Accessed June 20, 2017. https://www.bts.gov/archive/publications/omnistats/volume_03_issue_03/entire.

Walsh, Brian, and Sylvia Keesmaat. '"Outside of a Small Circle of Friends": Jesus and the Justice of God.' In *Jesus, Paul and the People of God: A Theological Dialogue with N. T. Wright*, edited by Nicholas Perrin and Richard B. Hays, 66–88. Downers Grove: IVP, 2011.

World Wildlife Fund. *Living Planet Report 2012*. Gland, Switzerland: WWF, 2012. Accessed Oct 11, 2018. http://wwf.panda.org/knowledge_hub/all_publications/living_planet_report_timeline/lpr_2012/.

Chapter 12

INDIGENOUS HOMEMAKING AS PUBLIC THEOLOGY IN THE WORDS AND DEEDS OF MAORI LEADER, WIREMU TAMIHANA

Steve Taylor

Homes are essential to being human. Physically, they are meant to provide us with safety.[1] Psychologically, they protect our identity and nurture our values. At the same time, homes are easily imagined. They can be understood as privatised, reduced to a nuclear family in a gated community. They can be romanticised, as safe havens of emotional harmony. Homes thus emerge as complex. They are a reality yet require care in their imagining.

There are some rich, yet surprising insights when we consider home in relation to New Zealand history. Maori call Aotearoa New Zealand home. As a culture, they have a deep sense of identity, linked with concepts like whenua. The word means both land and placenta and communicates a deep sense of connection with place as home, through birth and ancestral connection.

Equally, Maori have had to respond to multiple moments of home invasion. The threat of home invasion can be direct, as an armed person bangs on our door.

---

[1] A key resource in this chapter is Vincent O'Malley, *The Great War for New Zealand: Waikato 1800–2000* (Wellington: Bridget Williams Books, 2016). I am grateful to O'Malley not only for the book but also for the online communication that encouraged my initial hunches.

The threat can also be indirect, as different values and new sets of beliefs challenge established patterns. Maori in Aotearoa New Zealand home have faced both. Threats have been direct, with guns, and indirect, with the arrival of many diverse values, aspirations and beliefs. What insights for Christian faith are evident in the response of Maori to home invasion? What could this contribute to a reimagining of home?

These questions will be considered in relation to the life and witness of Maori chief, Wiremu Tamihana Tarapipi Te Waharoa, who during the 1850s and 1860s, in the Waikato area, reimagined home in response to the arrival of colonisation. For Tamihana, home is lived in planting an alternative indigenous community, in leadership reorganisation and in public speechmaking. A rich set of insights emerge as his theology and practice is read in light of translation theory and his use of Ephesians as a reading strategy of ethical action.

Further clarification emerges as Tamihana's reimagining of home is considered alongside the work of Pacific missiologist, Seforosa Carroll. A public missiology of homemaking as embodying relational movements, dwelling in place and intentional homemaking practices becomes evident. Homemaking, as theorised and practised by Tamihana, thus becomes an exemplar of a public missology of homemaking. Read in dialogue with a range of Christian expressions of gospel in culture, Tamihana's indigenous responses are in fact a dynamic, creative, contextual and imaginative way of following Christ.

Biography as Missiology

Wiremu Tamihana is a historical individual and approaching him raises the methodological question of how to work missiologically with history lived in individual lives? What is the way to respect original context and make contemporary applications while avoiding hagiography and dehistoricised data? To reflect missiologically on the life of Wiremu Tamihana, I will use an approach that I am calling biography as missiology.[2] This involves paying attention to lives, to biography, in order to find narratives that might remake our understandings of missiology. It is an application of the work of theologian, James McClendon, refracted for a specifically missiological purpose. In *Biography as Theology: How Life Stories Can Remake Today's Theology* McClendon argues that the study of biography can remake theology, by paying attention to lives, seeking narratives

---

2   I have taken a similar approach in Steve Taylor, 'Jesus as the Divine Tracker: An Indigenous Experiment in a Post-Colonial Atonement Theology' (Paper presented at the Australian and New Zealand Association of Theological Schools conference, University of Divinity, Melbourne July 3–6, 2016).

that guide theology's faithful evolution. We do so to be more faithful to 'the age now being born'.[3]

This approach is not hagiography. It is based on the critical capacities expected in any study, along with a set of analytical and generative skills consistent with the tasks involved in application to a contemporary age. It assumes revelation is embedded in, and refracted through, the work of the divine in human lives. This comes through the observation of character in the individual and the community. For McClendon, character involves the:

> level at which one's person, with its continuities, its interconnections, its integrity, is intimately involved in one's deeds. By being the persons we are, we are able to do what we do, and conversely, by those very deeds we form or re-form our own characters . . . character is paradoxically both the cause and consequence of what we do.[4]

The focus on 'ethics of character-in-community' is used in the search for convictions, the 'tenacious beliefs which when held give definiteness to the character of a person or of a community, so that if they were surrendered, the person or community would be significantly changed'.[5] These convictions originate from the work of the divine in human lives. The task of biography as missiology is thus to carefully examine and sensitively articulate these traces of the divine as they are embodied in human life, both individually and in community.

In sum, McClendon is my methodological impetus. Biography as missiology expects theology and ethics to speak to each other. Missiology takes shape in the lives, or in this case, the homes of the people in its community of concern. There is no *a priori* segregation of ethics from theology proper.[6] This is essential to any articulation of a missiology that seeks to reimagine home. It is congruent with the essential interplay between identity and ethics in the human experience of home. As I will argue, it makes sense of Tamihana and demonstrates appreciation for him as a theologian in both deed and word.

Strangers at the Door

Early contact between Maori as indigenous peoples and the empires of Europe began with sailors. Dutchman, Abel Tasman, explored the coastline in 1642. James Cook followed with visits in 1769 to 1770, 1773 and 1777. Maori watched Cook

---

[3] James McClendon, *Biography as Theology: How Life Stories Can Remake Today's Theology* (Nashville: Abingdon, 1974), 37–38.
[4] McClendon, *Biography as Theology*, 30–31.
[5] McClendon, *Biography as Theology*, 29, 34.
[6] McClendon, *Biography as Theology*, 36.

and his crew. One account is told by Te Horeta, a twelve-year-old boy.[7] When Cook and his crew stepped onto the white sands of Te Whanganui-o-Hei (Mercury Bay), they were stepping onto his home. Over centuries Maori had developed a 'custom of living'. This involved moving from block to block, using fire to farm the fern and cultivate their boundaries, 'so that it might not be taken from us by some other tribe'.[8] When Cook stepped onto the foreshore, for Maori he was stepping onto home. In the account of Te Horeta, there is fear at the sudden appearance of strange white visitors, who he called 'goblins'.[9] There is also curiosity and surprising benefits as food is shared and knowledge exchanged.

Explorers like Abel Tasman and James Cook were followed by missionaries, sealers and whalers. Perched on the edges of Aotearoa, essentially at the mercy of indigenous peoples, over time increasing numbers, introduced disease and the use of superior technologies ensured the increasing exertion of colonial power.

A key moment in the history of New Zealand is 1840, when the *Treaty of Waitangi* was signed. It was, and is, a contested document. The Treaty is written in both Maori and English. The Maori version of the Treaty uses the language of *te tino rangatiratanga*, translated as full chieftainship, for Maori over their lands (Article 2), while acknowledging the *kawanatanga*, translated as governorship, of the British Crown (Article 1). For indigenous Maori, sovereignty was not ceded, but maintained by indigenous people.

The Crown was placed under increased pressure through the 1850s and 1860s by a growing settler population, migrants from the British Empire, with a lust for land. This placed pressure on the Crown to secure more land from Maori, who believed that the Treaty gave them the right not to sell if they did not want to. It is these pressures that resulted in what was effectively a civil war in New Zealand in 1861. The Crown gave Waikato Maori an ultimatum: their land would remain their own 'so long only as they are strong enough to keep it; might and not right will become their sole title'.[10] One response to this direct threat of home invasion was provided by Maori chief, Wiremu Tamihana.

---

7   Alex Calder, ed., 'Discoveries: Te Horeta Te Taniwha: An Account of Cook's Visit', in *The Writing of New Zealand: Inventions and Identities* (Auckland: Reed, 1993), 26–30.

8   Calder, 'Discoveries', 26.

9   Calder, 'Discoveries', 26.

10 O'Malley, *The Great War for New Zealand*, 141, citing 'Declaration by the Governor to the Natives Assembled at Ngaruawahia, 21 May, 1861', GBPP, [3040], 72.

Wiremu Tamihana: Reimagining Home in Distinctive Community

Wiremu Tamihana was born around 1805, at Tamahere, near Hamilton. He was the second son of Ngati Haua chief, Te Waharoa.[11] His mother was Rangi Te Wiwini. His education was at a missionary school and he was baptised in 1839.[12] After the death of his father, Wiremu Tamihana, now as chief of his tribe, led his people in the building of new, and what seem to be distinctly Christian, villages. The first was named Te Tapiri, the second Peria. Te Tapiri had a church that seated one thousand people.[13]

Peria had a church, post office, a school educating one hundred children and a flour mill. There were gardens with maize, potatoes and kumara, orchards and fields of wheat. It was named after the people of Berea in Acts 17:10–12 and was, according to *Te Ara*, 'a model Christian community'.[14] The name of the village suggests the importance of Scripture. It also suggests the value of discernment. The Bereans receive the message with eagerness, yet commit to a daily examination of the Scriptures for themselves. This suggests a distinct identity, distinct from that of the arriving missionaries, that remains under the authority of Scripture.[15]

The application of a methodology of biography as missiology points to one consequence of the encounter between British and Maori as being the formation of Christian communities. At Peria, Maori formed new homes and sought to express in their own cultural patterns what the examination of Scripture meant.

---

11 For a description of the life of Te Waharoa, see Peter Lineham, 'Te Waharoa's War and Missionary Visions of Peace', in *Saints and Stirrers: Christianity, Conflict, and Peacemaking in New Zealand, 1814–1945*, ed. Geoffrey Troughton (Wellington: Victoria University Press, 2017), 50–51, 56–57.

12 For a description of Wiremu Tamihana's early years, see Lineham, 'Te Waharoa's War', 58–61.

13 Athol Anderson, Judith Binney, and Aroha Harris, *Tangata Whenua: A History* (Wellington: Bridget Williams, Wellington, 2015), 175.

14 *Te Ara: The Encyclopedia of New Zealand*, 'Wiremu Tamihana Tarapipipi Te Waharoa', accessed October 3, 2017, https://teara.govt.nz/en/biographies/1t82/te-waharoa-wiremu-tamihana-tarapipipi. Thanks to Rosemary Dewerse, for assistance in noting both Te Tapiri and Peria.

15 The creation of distinct communities by indigenous people is also evident as a response following colonisation in other nations, including Australia, South Africa and Papua New Guinea. In Australia, Boyce notes the native village concept practised in the Kat River settlement of Cape Colony and the Owenite community at Lanark in Scotland. James Boyce, *1835: The Founding of Melbourne and the Conquest of Australia* (Victoria: Black Inc, 2012), 181–83. Courtney Handman describes the important role of Christian villages in *Critical Christianity: Translation and Denominational Conflict in Papua New Guinea* (California: University of California Press, 2015), 24–26.

Wiremu Tamihana: Reimagining Home in Reworking Patterns of Leadership

When the Treaty was signed in 1840 at Waitangi, the initial signatories included forty Maori chiefs. Over the next months, another five hundred chiefs signed, as copies were taken around the country. This provides an important insight into Maori organisational leadership. In 1840, there was no concept of a Maori nation. Rather, sub-tribes, called *hapu*, consisting of a few hundred to a thousand people, were the 'effective social and political unit of Maori society'.[16]

By 1861, Tamihana was arguing the need for a Maori King, one overarching chief. It was an idea adapted from Europe that would enable Maori to maintain the promised *te tino rangatiratanga*, full chieftainship of the Treaty. Maori believed it did not 'challenge the overarching authority of the Crown but instead sought to preserve . . . the self-governance seemingly promised in the Treaty'.[17] It would provide a cohesive sense of identity. For Hill and O'Malley, the *Kingitanga* is 'an incontestable historical actor' in Maori history and resistance.[18] For Lineham, the *Kingitanga* is a 'Maori Christian peace movement based on scriptural principles'.[19]

In this, Tamihana is a highly significant factor. As chief of Ngati Haua, he was involved in the ceremony that installed the first Maori King. This involved the act of placing a Bible over the king's head, to indicate the authority of God and the authority of Scripture in the Maori King movement. For this reason, Wiremu Tamihana became known by the title 'Kingmaker', by Pakeha. The chief of Ngati Haua continues in the present to play this role. At every coronation of a Maori King, the leader of Ngati Haua places the Bible on the head of the incoming king.

Maori culture places great value on tradition. This makes the organisational changes of this period even more startling. The appointment of a Maori King and the development of rituals of coronation stand as a testimony to the overwhelming pressures being brought to bear by British colonisation. They also demonstrate the creativity of Maori and their ability to innovate in response to the British Empire.

The application of a methodology of biography as missiology points to a second consequence of the encounter between British and Maori: a new theology of church and state. Maori articulated a public theology in which kings stand under

---

16   Richard S. Hill and Vincent O'Malley, *The Maori Quest for Rangatiratanga/Autonomy, 1840–2000*, Occasional Papers 4 (Wellington: Treaty of Waitangi Research Unit, Stout Research Centre, Victoria University of Wellington, 2000), 2.
17   Hill and O'Malley, *The Maori Quest for Rangatiratanga/Autonomy*, 2000, 5.
18   Hill and O'Malley, *The Maori Quest for Rangatiratanga/Autonomy*, 2000, 24.
19   Lineham, 'Te Waharoa's War', 62.

the authority of Scripture. This theology and practice of sovereignty is revealed in a speech Tamihana gave in 1861.

Wiremu Tamihana: Reimagining Home in Public Political Speechmaking[20]

The occasion was a visit by the New Zealand Government to Maori in the Waikato. The context was the swelling numbers of settlers, driven by a lust for land. The land of the Waikato was being expertly farmed by local Maori, who were confidently selling produce to the booming town of Auckland.

The speeches are recorded in history, in the Great Britain Parliamentary Papers. The Crown issued an ultimatum to Waikato Maori, as noted above: 'retain your land only as long as you are strong enough to keep it'. A response, by Wiremu Tamihana is recorded. It is a peculiar afterlife of British Law, to find a Maori contextual theology of sovereignty located in Great Britain Parliamentary Papers. The title is distressing, with the use of the word 'disturbance' as a descriptor to what would result in the death of 4 percent of Maori in Waikato.

This speech provides insight into the resources used as Tamihana seeks to reimagine home.[21] It is a rich and complex theology. Elsewhere I have used three hermeneutical strategies—the Wesleyan quadrilateral, an indigenous place-based narrative and feminist standpoint epistemologies—to examine the speech. In this chapter, given the theme of home, I want to pay particular attention to the implications of Tamihana's use of Scripture. In articulating his theology of home, Tamihana cites Ephesians 2:13. The use of Ephesians has some important insights for missiology. These are accessed as we consider themes relating to Bible translation, indigenous reading strategies and household codes as a biblical genre.

---

20   I am indebted to Hone Te Rire, who provided insightful feedback when this material was first presented at a Knox Centre for Ministry and Leadership Theological Reflection block course in Dunedin, February 2017.

21   Using the speech needs some cautionary footnotes. It is introduced as a 'translation of the Reply of Wiremu Tamehana [sic]'. Hence there are natural questions about the accuracy of the translation. In addition, we are drawing on a written production of what is an oral output. However, theologies of sovereignty regularly utilise some material. Indeed, the Parliamentary Papers are predominantly a written record of speeches. In addition, Christian theology has a long tradition of drawing on the written production of oral sayings. The Gospels are an obvious example, as are Paul's letters when Paul is dictating to a scribe. So too are theologies drawn from Augustine's sermons, which come to us as a record taken by Augustine's scribe.

Ephesians and a History of Translation

The first printing press arrived in New Zealand in January 1835. Within a month, parts of the Bible were being printed in the Maori language. The first book of the Bible translated and printed was Ephesians. So, in February 1835, one month after its arrival, some two thousand copies of a Maori translation of Ephesians and Philippians rolled off the printing press.

A first copy, with corrections in the hand of the translator, William Williams (1800–1878), can be viewed at the National Library in Wellington.[22] The entire New Testament was printed by 1837. This translation of the Bible allowed Maori to read Scripture for themselves. Biography as missiology and a third result of the encounter between British and Maori are that Scriptures were being heard 'in our own native language'.[23]

What is the impact of hearing or reading about home in one's own language? Research into the impact of translation points to the unintended consequences that result from translation, including the formation of cultural identities. Lawrence Venuti examines the interplay between what is domestic and what is foreign in relation to translation and documents an intriguing tension.[24] Translation works by domesticating, 'foreign texts, inscribing them with linguistic and cultural values that are intelligible to specific domestic constituencies'.[25] Indeed, the more domesticated, the more like the home of the receiving culture, the more successful the translation. At the same time, it can usher in significant cultural change. Translations become 'ethical acts that can introduce significant difference into . . . culture'.[26]

Venuti engages with translations in general, from Bible translations to modern Japanese novels.[27] His work provides a helpful frame, first in examining Tamihana's use of Scripture, and second, in reflecting on how the translation of Scripture shaped Maori culture. For Venuti, one of the most significant results of translation

---

[22] The first copy, with corrections in the hand of the translator, William Williams (1800–1878), are located at the National Library in Wellington. Ruth Lightbourne, 'Shipwreck Bible, Soldier's Bible, First New Testament in Maori, and More . . .', accessed January 24, 2017, https://natlib.govt.nz/blog/posts/shipwreck-bible-soldier-s-bible-first-new-testament-in-maori-and-more.

[23] Acts 2:8, NRSV.

[24] Lawrence Venuti, *Scandals of Translation: Towards an Ethics of Difference* (London: Routledge, 1998).

[25] Venuti, *Scandals of Translation*, 67.

[26] Venuti, *Scandals of Translation*, 87.

[27] See also Lawrence Venuti, *The Translator's Invisibility: A History of Translation* (London and New York: Routledge, 1995).

is the formation of cultural identities, often unintended.[28] This is double-edged, involving stereotyping the foreign culture from which the translation comes. It also 'constructs a domestic subject . . . a translation can be powerful in maintaining or revising the hierarchy of values in the translating culture'.[29] This is shaped by the decisions of the translator and the detail of the translation and can thus be controlled by those translating. It is also shaped by reader reception, including the uses made of the translation by cultural and social groupings and thus cannot be controlled by those translating. Translations can result in a reimagining of home.

This is evident in the way Tamihana reads Scripture. When we consider Tamihana's use of Ephesians, what becomes clear is the way that he has reversed foreign and domestic. In other words, a foreign translation, domesticated into *te reo*, the Maori language, is read in ways that locate the Crown as foreign. It becomes an intriguing example of Venuti's 'ethical acts that can introduce significant difference into . . . culture'.[30]

Reading Strategies and Ephesians

What are Tamihana's reading strategies? How is home being reimagined? Tamihana cites Ephesians 2:13, stating 'My only connexion with you is through Christ: Ephesians 2 c., 13v'. He is standing in front of the Crown, responding to their speech, which includes the inflammatory words: 'retain your land only as long as you are strong enough to keep it'.[31]

The words from Ephesians as used by Tamihana, 'But now in Christ Jesus you who once were far away have been brought near through the blood of Christ" were written originally to a Gentile audience who were themselves newcomers to Christian faith. Ralph Martin in his *Ephesians* commentary describes them as standing outside God's covenant with Israel, having no rights as citizens of God's special nation.[32] When Tamihana uses Ephesians, the implication is that British citizens were once far away, physically, back in England, with no rights as citizens of Aotearoa New Zealand. They have been 'brought near by the blood of Christ'. This has two implications for sovereignty. First, that the British are here by the purpose and design of Christ. Second, that the behaviour of those who were once

---

28 Venuti, *Scandals of Translation*, 67–87.
29 Venuti, *Scandals of Translation*, 68.
30 Venuti, *Scandals of Translation*, 87.
31 O'Malley, *The Great War*, 143, citing 'Memorandum on Our Relations with Waikato, 3 May 1861', GBPP, 1862 [3040], 51.
32 Ephesians 2:13, NRSV. Ralph Martin, *Ephesians, Colossians, and Philemon* (Louisville: John Knox Press, 1991), 32–33.

far away should reflect that of Christ. It should originate from the gift, appreciate grace and exhibit the sacrifice as evident in the blood of Christ.[33]

It is likely that a British citizen, journeying to New Zealand, would consider Maori 'far off'. Tamihana reverses notions of what is domestic and what is foreign. Tamihana has taken the foreign translation, likely used by the British to reference Maori as foreign, and has inverted the categories. This aligns Maori as traditional owners of the gospel and in a continuity with Israel. It suggests interactions shaped not by the power of being 'strong enough' to either keep or take land, but by a set of 'ethical acts' shaped by the blood of Christ. The 'foreign' British, 'once far off' have been brought here by the purpose and design of Christ. They should exhibit behaviour that is consistent with the ways of Christ.

In other words, home has been reimagined. Maori read Scripture as the original homeowners. That shapes how they see visitors and how visitors should see them. Both peoples, foreign and domestic have been invited into a new ethical code, in which each other is treated in ways consistent with the grace and gift of God that brings all people who were once far off to this land. Such is the power of translation.

Tamihana only uses one verse from Ephesians. Yet the theme of reimagining home invites us to consider how home is being understood in other parts of the letter, particularly in the household codes of Ephesians 5:21–6:9.

Ephesians and Household Codes

The wider sociocultural context used a form of literature, known as household codes, in constructing understandings of home. Household codes were used by philosophers from Aristotle's *Politics 1* onward, in writing about household management. They involved a form, in which an imperative verb was paired with reciprocal responsibilities, followed by a reason clause to provide justification. Scripture like Colossians 3:18–4:1; 1 Peter 2:18–3:7; and early Christian literature like the letter from Ignatius to Polycarp 4:1–5:1 and from Polycarp to the Philippians 4:2–6:1 are similar both in form and in a focus on how relationships in homes function.

Ephesians 5:21–6:9 shares the form, including paired responsibilities and a focus on relationships in marriage, between parents and children, and in

---

33   For a discussion of Ephesians in relation to housecodes—the *Haustafeln*—and the interplay between Tamihana's alternative Christian community and his use of Ephesians, and his integration of Christology and ethics see Steve Taylor, 'Converting Kings? Theologies of Church and State in the Encounter between British and Maori' (paper presented at the Reimagining Home, Australian Association of Mission Studies conference, Whitley College, July 2–5, 2017).

employment.[34] For biblical scholar, Margaret MacDonald, a feature of Ephesians is how it links 'the household teaching with the ethical teaching concerning walking in the world in a manner distinct from the Gentiles'.[35] This has two important implications in relation to a reimagining of home. First is the interrelationship between theology and ethics. The Christ of Ephesians chapter 2 shapes the ethics of the home. Second, the task of Ephesians includes identity formation, including in distinctive domestic relationships.[36] For MacDonald, the household codes of Ephesians 'need to be understood in light of the realities of an emerging Christianity in competition with other social groups and subject to hostility from outsiders'.[37] It is a way of doing what Venuti argues can be a consequence of translation: 'maintaining or revising the hierarchy of values in the translating culture'.[38] Christians live distinctly in their homes, their ethics shaped by their theology.

Ephesians is thus a homemaking narrative, with a Christology that prepares the reader to have a 'standpoint' in which to negotiate the complex relationships of the empire—both Roman and the eighteenth-century British Crown. The book resources homemaking as a public theology of empire resistance.

This is exactly what Tamihana is doing. His reading strategy in relation to Ephesians 2:13, in which Christ shapes ethics, in his case of how to live in this home of Aotearoa New Zealand, is consistent with what the author of Ephesians was seeking. Scripture, now translated into Maori, is being deployed by Tamihana to revise the values of the cultures both foreign (empire) and domestic (Maori).

To return to McClendon's biography as theology: there is no *a priori* segregation of ethics from theology proper. Theology indeed enters into 'the actual shape of the lives of the people in its community of concern', enabling us to be more faithful to 'the age now being born'.[39] This suggests that homes can be distinctive, as a public theology of empire resistance, calling all inhabitants to live under Christ. This trajectory, of homemaking imagined as a public theology of

---

34 Scholars are divided on whether the household codes section of Ephesians begins at 5:21 or with the next verse, 5:22. I follow MacDonald, who emphasises the ways in which 5:21 is thematically related to what follows, in Margaret Y. MacDonald, *Colossians, Ephesians* (Collegeville, Minnesota: Liturgical Press, 2000), 325.

35 MacDonald, *Colossians, Ephesians*, 326.

36 For helpful discussion of implications in relation to slavery and patriarchy, see MacDonald 165–66, including the way the NT is addressing all directly, guaranteeing a place and offering a guide for living. 'With God there is no partiality; in the final judgement no one group . . . would experience favouritism . . . when understood within their context, texts that appear only to reinforce conventional attitudes may in fact include elements that challenge the status quo.' MacDonald, *Colossians, Ephesians*, 166, 168.

37 MacDonald, *Colossians, Ephesians*, 169.

38 Venuti, *Scandals of Translation*, 68.

39 McClendon, *Biography as Theology*, 36, 37.

resistance, can be developed further when brought into conversation with Pacific missiologist, Seforosa Carroll.

Reimagining Home as Contemporary Missiology

Seforosa Carroll is an indigenous (Fiji-born Rotuman) woman. She draws on her experiences of migration to explore homemaking as mission.[40] For Carroll, homemaking is 'the redemptive practice of making the ideal of home possible for all'.[41] She draws on feminist geographer, Linda McDowell, in a gendered reading in which home is more than a physical structure.[42] The home, as a place of connection and dialogical relationship[43] invites us to the redemptive task of homemaking in reconciling, renewing and transforming places and spaces.[44] Placed alongside Tamihana's biography as missiology, in particular his speech, she develops frameworks by which to imagine a public missiology of homemaking.

Carroll argues that homemaking is based on relational movements. This involves relationships within the home. It also involves the movements of those migrating to make a home and the interplay between guests and hosts in the visiting of the home of another. Thus, a place—the home—is conceived as a movement of relationships. Homes are never only physically located either here and there. They always involve coming and going, welcoming and being welcomed. In other words, home is not privatised and is not to be reduced to a nuclear family in a gated community.

What is interesting is how relational movements are central to Tamihana's speech. He begins with a *waiata*, a song, in which he references the voyage of the original *Te Awara* canoe to New Zealand.[45] Thus Tamihana locates homemaking

---

40   Seforosa Carroll, 'Homemaking: Reclaiming the Ideal of Home as a Framework for Hosting Cultural and Religious Diversity,' in Colonial Contexts and Postcolonial Theology: Storyweaving in the Asia-Pacific, ed. Mark G. Brett and Jione Havea (London: Palgrave Macmillan, 2014), 219–30.

41   Carroll, 'Homemaking', 224.

42   Carroll, 'Homemaking', 221, citing Linda McDowell, *Gender, Identity and Place: Understanding Feminist Geographies* (Cambridge: Polity Press, 1999).

43   Carroll, 'Homemaking', 223.

44   Carroll, 'Homemaking', 221.

45   *Te Arawa* and its crew left Hawaiki after a conflict over food resources involving Houmaitawhiti and his sons, Tamatekapua and Whakatūria, against the chiefs Toi and Uenuku. When Whakatūria was killed, Tamatekapua departed on the *Arawa*, having kidnapped Ngātoroirangi (Ngātoro) from the *Tainui* canoe to act as his navigator. He also abducted Whakaotirangi, the wife of Ruaeo, a prominent man of the village. While at sea Tamatekapua also tried to seduce Ngātoro's wife. In retribution Ngātoro threatened to destroy the canoe in Te Korokoro-o-te-Parata (the whirlpool of Te Parata) but relented at the crew's pleading. According to some accounts the canoe was saved by a mystical shark (arawa), for which the

in migration: his people—first people—have like these second—colonising people—migrated and learnt to live in a new home. The experience of Maori is of homemaking as a relational movement.

Carroll also argues that homemaking is about dwelling in relationships with people and place. She describes the work done by homemakers, of how 'newcomers invest their energies in what they build', they 'dwell by setting down roots in a particular place'.[46] It is consistent with the instructions of Jeremiah 29:5–7, to build houses, to plant gardens and to invest in relationships. In other words, home is not to be romanticised because it allows a contextual and place-based engagement.

We see a similar expectation in Tamihana's speech: 'Look; there are two stores of . . . shops. The goods in one store are sold; those of the other are not sold . . . So, with the consent of one chief, that which belonged to another did not go by such consent being given'. People who 'were once far off . . .' are expected to invest in place making. New arrivals can engage in commerce alongside existing inhabitants. There can be two shops, different, yet able to live side by side, with all peoples enjoying the benefits of diversity. This is a public, commercialised, representation of the dwelling dimensions of homemaking in which newcomers are invited to set up shop—distinctively, mutually.

Tamihana's words bring into sharp relief the actual commercial dimensions of his time. Prior to the Waikato War, Maori had supplied extensive produce to Auckland. By 1853, eighteen Maori-owned wheat mills were being constructed in the Waikato district.[47] The British Government provided the schooner *Albert* to make twice-weekly runs to carry the produce from the Waikato to Auckland. Tamihana's description of trade between two shops is an accurate description. So, Tamihana's speech locates homemaking, whether for Maori or British, as having public, commercialised dimensions, in which newcomers and all-comers are challenged to participate distinctively and in mutuality.

Third, Carroll argues for intentional homemaking practices 'in a way that relies upon certain regular, trusted habits of behaviour'.[48] This returns us to the household codes and work of theologian, Miroslav Volf, who has identified in household codes a set of missiological insights around gospel and culture as practices of distinctive difference.[49] While Greek household codes were culturally addressed

---

canoe was named. 'Te Arawa and Tainui', accessed April 19, 2017, http://www.teara.govt.nz/en/canoe-traditions/page-5. My thanks to Hone Te Riri, who provided this insight during a KCML Theological Reflection class.

46 Carroll, 'Homemaking', 225.
47 O'Malley, *The Great War for New Zealand*, 54.
48 Carroll, 'Homemaking', 226.
49 The following discussion is based on my working with the biblical text and with John H. Elliot, *1 Peter: A New Translation with Introduction and Commentary* (New York:

to men, the household codes, for example in 1 Peter 3:1, addressed wives directly (' . . . in the same way, you wives . . .' GNB). While in Greek household codes, women were viewed as the property of men, the household codes, for example in 1 Peter 3:2, understood women as responsible moral agents who can influence their husbands by their behaviour. While Greek household codes encouraged individuals to behave as if society were watching them, the household codes, for example in 1 Peter 3:4, expected individuals to behave as if God was watching (' . . . which is of greatest value in God's sight . . .' GNB). In Scripture, the genre of household codes is utilised, yet simultaneously subverted by advocating a distinctive Christian lifestyle. For Volf, this provides a generative set of insights regarding the lived practice of contemporary mission. The household codes offer a 'complex interplay of commensurability and incommensurability [that] suggests . . . there is no single proper way for Christians to relate to a given culture as a whole. Instead, there are numerous ways of accepting, rejecting, subverting or transforming various aspects of a culture'.[50] This affirms the essence of homemaking as trusted habits of behaviour (Carroll) and ethical acts (MacDonald). They affirm the creative plurality of Tamihana's reimagining of home, as a complex interplay of numerous ways of accepting, rejecting, subverting or transforming various aspects of a culture. This becomes more apparent when we place Tamihana's reimagining of alternative indigenous community, in leadership reorganisation and in public speechmaking alongside a range of Christian expressions of gospel in culture, in particular the work of Walter Brueggemann.

Homemaking as Plural Practices

Biblical scholar Walter Brueggmann finds in a range of Old Testament passages a different imagination regarding the relationship between church and society.[51] What is instructive is to realise that Tamihana is in fact using each of these Old Testament approaches in different ways in his reimagining of home.

    Doubleday, 2000). However, it was Volf who initiated my exploration with his argument that the household codes in 1 Peter are 'an example of differentiated acceptance and rejection of the surrounding [Hellenistic] culture . . . We would have to take into account the possibility of either rejecting or accommodating to particular aspects of the surrounding culture in a piece-meal fashion. That is, I think, what we actually find in 1 Peter'. Miroslav Volf, 'Soft Difference: Theological Reflections on the Relation between Church and Culture in 1 Peter', accessed October 23, 2017, http://www.pas.rochester.edu/~tim/study/Miroslav%20Volf%201%20Peter.pdf.

50   Volf, 'Soft Difference', page 13 of 17 from online version.

51   Walter Brueggemann, 'The Bible and Mission: Some Interdisciplinary Implications for Teaching', *Missiology* 10 (1989): 397–412.

An *alternative community* is evident in Hosea 2:14–18. This is a textual fragment, set in the midst of a poem, which draws on the metaphors of divorce and remarriage. In this text, there is simultaneously both complete loss of relationship and the complete gift of relationships. God takes, and God gives. The hinge (vv. 14–15) is unexpected. God intervenes and there is disarmament and environmental hope (2:16–18). The suggestion is of living a life that views society differently, in which there is peace, environment health and interconnectedness with God. 'The church simply exists in society in such a way that people should become aware of the transitoriness, relativity and fundamental inadequacy of *all* political programs and solutions.'[52] In relation to Tamihana, this is the vision of Peria. It makes no attempt to lobby for reform, nor confront society. It stands apart from the British Empire, offering a different way of being.

A *reformationist* approach is evident in Deuteronomy 19:1–10, where legislation is proposed to establish cities of refuge. It expects that workplace accidents will happen and proposes a framework by which a public hospitality as an alternative to vengeance might be enacted. This is a reformationist approach, which assumes society is open to change, that systems and structures can be aligned, and that culture will listen to the church. Tamihana's organisation of leadership is shaped by a similar vision, that in structural reform. The work of the *Kingitanga* movement assumes that Maori society is open to change, and that systems and structures can be aligned to provide a coherent voice for Maori people.

A *Constantinian* approach is evident in 1 Kings 4:20–28. A story is told of success, of wealth and wellbeing. People are happy, safe and well fed. A key claim made by the text in verse 25 is *shalom*, that everyone is safe under their 'vine and fig tree'. Thus, this text links faith, church and a way of being in society.[53] Such a model is a danger in the role of Scripture in the appointing of a Maori King. The Bible might signal a set of values but might slide into a fusion of church and state.

A *liberationist* approach is evident in 1 Samuel 2:1–10. Israel is transitioning from a loose affiliation of tribes led by charismatic judges, to that of a king, living in a centralised place. In the midst of this societal transition, we hear the song of a barren mother. It is the cry of a woman who will become the mother of the last of

---

52 David Bosch, 'God's Reign and the Rulers of This World: Missiological Reflections on Church–State Relationships', in *The Good News of the Kingdom: Mission Theology for the Third Millennium*, ed. Charles Van Engen and Dean Gilliland (Maryknoll: Orbis, 1993), 89–95, 92.

53 Brueggemann notes that while the text suggests a society of peace and harmony the discerning reader is left with a nagging suspicion. Who pays for the system? Who is doing the forced labour of 1 Kings 4:6? For Brueggemann the text suggests a Constantinian model, yet equally the text asks some nagging questions about the impact of such a model in all of society. Walter Brueggemann, 'The Bible and Mission'.

the judges. Hannah means 'grace, free gift' and the song she sings is of surprise. The song anticipates a new social reality, in which roles are swiftly reversed and there is an upside-down kingdom. This vision is communicated not in legislation, but in the poetry of a woman unable to conceive in a patriarchal world. Change does not come through structural reform or through existing leaders, but in singing of a new reality.

This sort of approach is not immediately evident in Tamihana's public theology of home. However, over time it has become his legacy. For New Zealand historian, Vincent O'Malley, we examine our past, the horror of New Zealand's Great War, and find 'buried within this tale of loss and waste . . . some uplifting elements . . . the principled idealism and bicultural vision of Wiremu Tamihana'.[54] This is a reversal, the hearing a different song, a voice from Down Under offering a vision of public homemaking. It is congruent with Tamihana's Christology from Ephesians 2, that in the blood of Christ is ' . . . our peace; in his flesh he has made both groups into one and has broken down the dividing wall, that is the hostility between us'.[55] This is radical reimagining of home.

Reimagining Home for Original Hearers

What might this theology have meant for original hearers, both Maori and British? For Maori, it offered a vision of home for that new time and place. This vision came with agency. In the face of the threat of home invasion, they could make choices by adopting a range of proactive postures. These included forming their own communities shaped by Christian faith, seeking to reform their own systems of leadership and public speechmaking. This agency was also subversive. Maori could read Scripture for themselves. God had been detached from Britain. Indeed, the resources from the empire, of Scripture, were being used back against the Crown, calling everyone to a standard based not around culture but around God.

For the British, it called them to account. They were being invited to look in the mirror of Scripture and their own political categories, all recorded for perpetuity in their own legal documents (the Great Britain Parliamentary Papers). They were being offered a vision of home in which all peoples could belong, a way of settling in which distinct identities in different cultural settlements could be retained, all within an overarching framework of justice as marked by the sacrifice of Christ.

Sadly, Tamihana's reimagining of home proved unable to hold back the power of the empire. The history is told in Vincent O'Malley's *The Great War for New*

---

54   O'Malley, *The Great War*, 13.
55   Ephesians 2:14, NRSV.

Zealand.⁵⁶ The war in the Waikato that resulted brought twelve thousand British troops to New Zealand, more than were stationed in all of England. The results included the killing of 4 percent of the Maori population of the Waikato, including disturbingly high numbers of women and children.⁵⁷ Some forty years later, over 3,500 Maori remained landless through land confiscation. Such experiences of dispossession would have a catastrophic future impact on Maori ability to be at home in their own land.

Despite Tamihana's inability to hold back the tides of the empire, his work offers a valuable set of resources. He reminds us of the power of Scripture translated in reconceived categories for home. He points to the dynamics of contextualisation and demonstrates how a dynamic culture can creatively respond to imperialism.

Conclusion

The theme of home yields rich insights when it is examined through diverse cultural lens, in this case in relation to New Zealand history. Methodologically, an approach of biography as missiology has been used in researching the life of Maori leader, Wiremu Tamihana. In word and deed his reimagining of home has been outlined: in planting an alternative indigenous community, in leadership reorganisation and in public speechmaking as a set of ethical acts shaped by a christological ethic. Translation theory has clarified Tamihana's reading of Scripture, including the reversing of what is foreign and domestic, and a household code shaped by Christology. What Wiremu Tamihana offers is a theology of homemaking as a public theology of empire resistance.

The richness of Tamihana's work has been enhanced by conversation with Pacific missiologist, Seforosa Carroll, and Walter Brueggemann's outlining of a range of missiological postures in the Old Testament. Using Carroll has clarified how Tamihana's reimagining of home embodies relational movements, expects a dwelling in place and offers a set of intentional homemaking practices. Using Brueggemann has made clear that Tamihana's reimagining of home included a plurality of responses to a dominant culture: alternative in community, reformationist in leadership reorganisation and potentially Constantinian in the *Kingitanga* movement. In the death of so many Maori in New Zealand's Great War, it has become liberationist, offering a dominant culture a reversing and life-giving vision of home reimagined in the harmony of Christ.

---

56   O'Malley, *The Great War*.
57   World War I killed around 1.7 percent of the NZ population, mainly male. Hence the assertion by O'Malley that the Waikato War is truly New Zealand's Great War of Waikato. O'Malley, *The Great War*, 370.

Tamihana's public theology of homemaking affirms that home need not be privatised nor romanticised but can function as a public missiology speaking to issues of migration, place making and befriending the other. His theology offers significant resources for those seeking to reimagine home in response to dominant cultures, in encouraging a Christology interwoven with ethics and the use of place-based readings to reverse categories of what is foreign and domestic. It affirms the importance of the work of contemporary missiologist, Seforosa Carroll, and reminds us of the plurality of postures by which Christianity might engage culture.

It suggests that creative responses to the empire can emerge through the ongoing renegotiation that happens as people move in the tides of history. A flexible justice-making is encouraged, one that uses the translations from the empire in resistance against the empire. Above all, it invites us to honour a Maori theologian, Wiremu Tamihana, who in word and deed offered a public, dynamic, creative, contextual and imaginative reimagining of home.

> Gracious and eternal God,
> as we honour Wiremu Tamihana,
> keep us honourable and fair
> in our dealings with each other,
> true servants of the Prince of peace.[58]

---

58 Wiremu Tamihana, Prophet, Kingmaker, 1866, *New Zealand Prayer Book: He Karakia Mihinare o Aotearoa* (Auckland: William Collins Publishers, 1997).

BIBLIOGRAPHY

Anderson, Athol, Judith Binney, and Aroha Harris. *Tangata Whenua: A History*. Wellington: Bridget Williams, Wellington, 2015.

Bosch, David. 'God's Reign and the Rulers of This World: Missiological Reflections on Church–State Relationships', in *The Good News of the Kingdom: Mission Theology for the Third Millennium*, edited by Charles Van Engen and Dean Gilliland. Maryknoll: Orbis, 1993.

Boyce, James. *1835: The Founding of Melbourne and the Conquest of Australia*. Victoria: Black Inc, 2012.

Brueggemann, Walter. 'The Bible and Mission: Some Interdisciplinary Implications for Teaching.' *Missiology* 10 (1989): 397–412.

Calder, Alex, ed. 'Discoveries: Te Horeta Te Taniwha: An Account of Cook's Visit.' In *The Writing of New Zealand: Inventions and Identities*, 26–30. Auckland: Reed, 1993.

Carroll, Seforosa. 'Homemaking: Reclaiming the Ideal of Home as a Framework for Hosting Cultural and Religious Diversity.' In *Colonial Contexts and Postcolonial Theology: Storyweaving in the Asia-Pacific*, edited by Mark G. Brett and Jione Havea. London: Palgrave Macmillan, 2014.

Elliot, John H. *1 Peter: A New Translation with Introduction and Commentary*. New York: Doubleday, 2000.

Handman, Courtney. *Critical Christianity: Translation and Denominational Conflict in Papua New Guinea*. California: University of California Press, 2015.

Hill, Richard S., and Vincent O'Malley. *The Maori Quest for Rangatiratanga/Autonomy, 1840–2000*. Occasional Papers 4. Wellington: Treaty of Waitangi Research Unit, Stout Research Centre, Victoria University of Wellington, 2000.

Lightbourne, Ruth. 'Shipwreck Bible, Soldier's Bible, First New Testament in Maori, and More . . .' Accessed January 24, 2017. https://natlib.govt.nz/blog/posts/shipwreck-bible-soldier-s-bible-first-new-testament-in-maori-and-more.

Lineham, Peter. 'Te Waharoa's War and Missionary Visions of Peace.' In *Saints and Stirrers: Christianity, Conflict, and Peacemaking in New Zealand, 1814–1945*, edited by Geoffrey Troughton, 47–62. Wellington: Victoria University Press, 2017.

MacDonald, Margaret Y. *Colossians, Ephesians*. Collegeville, Minnesota: Liturgical Press, 2000.

Martin, Ralph. *Ephesians, Colossians, and Philemon*. Louisville: John Knox Press, 1991.

McClendon, James. *Biography as Theology: How Life Stories Can Remake Today's Theology*. Nashville: Abingdon, 1974.

O'Malley, Vincent. *The Great War for New Zealand: Waikato 1800–2000*. Wellington: Bridget Williams Books, 2016.

Taylor, Steve. 'Jesus as the Divine Tracker: An Indigenous Experiment in a Post-Colonial Atonement Theology.' Paper Presented at the Australian and New Zealand Association of Theological Schools Conference, University of Divinity, Melbourne July 3–6, 2016.

Taylor, Steve. 'Converting Kings? Theologies of Church and State in the Encounter between British and Maori.' Paper Presented at the Reimagining Home, Australian Association of Mission Studies Conference, Whitley College, July 2–5, 2017.

Te Ara: The Encyclopedia of New Zealand. 'Wiremu Tamihana Tarapipipi Te Waharoa.' Accessed October 3, 2017. https://teara.govt.nz/en/biographies/1t82/te-waharoa-wiremu-tamihana-tarapipipi.

'Te Arawa and Tainui.' Accessed April 19, 2017. http://www.teara.govt.nz/en/canoe-traditions/page-5.

Venuti, Lawrence. *Scandals of Translation: Towards an Ethics of Difference*. London: Routledge, 1998.

Venuti, Lawrence. *The Translator's Invisibility: A History of Translation*. London and New York: Routledge, 1995.

Volf, Miroslav. 'Soft Difference: Theological Reflections on the Relation between Church and Culture in 1 Peter.' Accessed October 23, 2017. http://www.pas.rochester.edu/~tim/study/Miroslav%20Volf%201%20Peter.pdf.

'Wiremu Tamihana, Prophet, Kingmaker, 1866.' *New Zealand Prayer Book: He Karakia Mihinare o Aotearoa*. Auckland: William Collins Publishers, 1997.

Chapter 13

READING ROMANS IN MULTICULTURAL AUSTRALIA

Siu Fung Wu

I moved to Melbourne in the late 1980s. I migrated to Australia because I hated my home in Hong Kong. We lived in a tiny apartment in an overcrowded, badly polluted British colony. I could hardly cope with the noise and the cramped living conditions. It was oppressive. Of course, home is more than a physical dwelling. It is also about close family relationships. Unfortunately, ours was a dysfunctional family, with many domestic issues—because of the time pressure of a very busy urban life and the economic struggles of being factory workers (or what some may call in the West 'sweatshop workers'). So, it was wonderful to live in Australia. I thank God for the clean air I breathe and the physical space I have in this affluent country. Having my own bedroom, and indeed, a bed of my own, for example, was a luxury I did not have.

But what I never imagined was that, after twenty years, I would find myself missing my life in Hong Kong. To my surprise, the noise, the smell and the high-rises that make the city a concrete jungle make me feel at home. Yet, I realise that I no longer belong to that city. I only know a few people there. In fact, I cannot afford to live there, for it is a very expensive place to live nowadays. I have a dual identity, in that I am an ethnic Chinese from a British colony who has migrated to Australia; yet I do not have a home that I fully identify with.

So, I need to reimagine home! And this is where Paul's letter to the Romans comes to the rescue. Indeed, it provides me, and the church, with valuable resources to be residents in multicultural Australia.

About two thousand years ago, Paul, a Jew, wrote to the Jesus-followers in Rome, who lived in a socially hierarchical and culturally diverse society. He addressed his audience as *adelphoi*, that is, 'sisters and brothers' (e.g. Rom 1:13; 7:1, 4; 12:1; 14:10, 13, 15, 21; 15:14, 30; 16:17). Given his Jew–Gentile audience, Paul's usage of the term *adelphos* ('sister/brother') was counterintuitive because Jews would not normally use it to address Gentiles. In Rom 8:29, Paul says that believers are to be conformed to the image of the Son, in order that Christ may be the firstborn 'among many *adelphoi*', or 'within a large family', as the NRSV puts it. Then in 12:10 he exhorts the multicultural house churches to love one another with sibling affection. The themes around conformity with the Son's image, believers being a family in Christ, and the call to love each other as siblings are important resources for Jesus-followers in multicultural Australia to imagine home together. More specifically, in this chapter I will propose that Paul's letter invites believers to embody Christ's self-giving love by sharing one another's affliction. For just as the Son of God made his home in this world, so are his followers called to envision a home without ethnic boundaries as love-centred siblings in Christ.[1] In the following we will study several relevant texts in Romans and reflect on their implications for multicultural Australia today. But first, we will take a look at the social backgrounds of the residents of Rome.

What Do Ancient Rome and Multicultural Australia Have in Common?

In Australia, we commonly read Romans as if Paul's audience was like us. But it is vital to realise that the house churches in Rome consisted of people from diverse cultural and socio-economic backgrounds, which is very different from a typical middle-class church in the West today.

The twenty-six names in Rom 16:3–16 provide us with helpful information about Paul's audience.[2] Peter Lampe suggests that many of the twenty-six were

---

[1] I will not directly deal with the *geographic* systems and structures that create barriers in a multicultural society, which is of course in itself an important issue. For a good discussion, see David P. Leong, *Race and Place: How Urban Geography Shapes the Journey to Reconciliation* (Downers Grove, IL: IVP), 2017.

[2] Peter Lampe, 'The Roman Christians of Romans 16', in *The Roman Debate*, ed. Karl Donfried (Peabody: Hendrickson, 1991), 216–28; Robert Jewett, *Romans* (Hermeneia; Minneapolis: Fortress, 2007), 951–53.

immigrants.³ It is probable that fourteen of them were not born in Rome and that three of them might have been Jews.⁴ Importantly, close to two-thirds of the twenty-six people were of slave origin (30 percent slaves and 30 percent freed people, that is, former slaves).⁵ In addition, Lampe estimates that nine of them were women, out of which up to seven were in active service in the church.⁶ On the other hand, out of the seventeen men, only up to five were active. According to Bruce Longenecker, about 65 percent of the Christ-followers in Pauline house churches lived at or below subsistence level, and 25 percent had the basic resources to sustain life.⁷

The diversity of the Christians in Romans 16 was characteristic of the society in Rome. The following features of life in Rome serve to illustrate the daily reality faced by Paul's audience. The society in Rome was intensely hierarchical. Gender, social status and education largely determined one's fortunes and destiny. Rome was also a multi-faith society, with people worshipping different household gods, the gods at the temples and the emperor himself. It was a multicultural city, with Jewish, Greek and African immigrants, in addition to native Romans.⁸ Racial tension was inevitable. Judaism was called 'a barbarous superstition', Greeks received slurs and Africans were despised.⁹ Thanks to the success of Roman military conquests, a large portion of Rome's population consisted of war captives and their descendants. They served as slaves and provided cheap labour for the city's prosperous economy. In fact, slaves made up about 25 to 40 percent of Rome's population. Slavery, of course, involved exploitation. Owners used slaves for sexual pleasure and the Roman whip (*flagellum*) was used to punish slaves by inflicting deep wounds in their flesh.¹⁰ Steve Friesen's poverty scale for Graeco-Roman urbanism shows that the majority of the population in the Roman Empire lived at or below subsistence level (68 percent) and there were many at near-subsistence level (about 22 percent).¹¹ In Rome, the poor often resided in the dwellings at the back of the shops, or on the upper floors of the tenement houses

---

3   Lampe, 'The Roman Christians', 226–27. Colin Kruse, Paul's *Letter to the Romans* (PTNC; Grand Rapids: Eerdmans, 2012), 574–75, provides a handy summary of Lampe's work.

4   Lampe, 'The Roman Christians', 224–25, 227.

5   Lampe, 'The Roman Christians', 228; cf. Jewett, *Romans*, 953.

6   Lampe, 'The Roman Christians', 222.

7   Bruce Longenecker, *Remember the Poor* (Grand Rapids: Eerdmans, 2010), 294–96.

8   See the discussion in Siu Fung Wu, *Suffering in Romans* (Eugene: Pickwick, 2015), 34–35.

9   James Jeffers, *Conflicts at Rome* (Minneapolis: Fortress, 1991),106; R. B. Edwards, 'Rome: Overview', in *Dictionary of New Testament Background*, eds. Craig A. Evans and Stanley E. Porter (Leicester: IVP, 2000), 1014; Wu, *Suffering in Romans*, 34.

10 Wu, *Suffering in Romans*, 35–38, 234.

11 Steven Friesen, 'Poverty in Pauline Studies: Beyond the So-Called New Consensus', *Journal for the Study of New Testament* 26 (2004): 340–47.

(which were small, damp, unhygienic, cold in winter and hot in summer), while the poorest of the poor lived on the streets or in urban slums.[12]

What do the diverse audience of Paul and the society they lived in have to do with us today? Much in every way! In case we are not aware, parts of Melbourne, Sydney and other Australian cities are not unlike ancient Rome. We are very multicultural, especially in the suburbs that are not dominated by white Australians, Chinese, or any one particular ethnic group. Ours is a multi-faith society, with many Muslims, Buddhists and people of other faiths. There are asylum seekers who have very limited financial resources, without any certainty of whether they will be allowed to stay in Australia. The poor and marginalised are certainly among us. Every night more than 105,000 Australians are homeless.[13] Many live with mental illness or a severe disability, who want to work but are unable to do so.

Therefore, in many ways the society in ancient Rome is similar to ours today. In addition, not a few migrants have come from places where life was comparable to that of Paul's audience. I, for example, grew up in a district that was a small reflection of ancient Rome, with homeless people, beggars and unsafe streets not far from home. And I used to worship half a dozen household gods, in addition to worshipping my ancestors, which was essential to family honour and solidarity. Former refugees know only too well the experience of persecution, the horror of war and forced displacement in their countries of origin. Many migrants have a non-Christian faith background. They are familiar with cultures that are much more religious than Australia, where the spiritual and the physical are understood as inseparable. In short, Romans was just as relevant to its first audience as it is to Christians in multicultural Australia today.

Siblings in Christ in a Multicultural Society

What would Paul's teaching in Romans mean to his audience in Rome and to us today? In the following I will discuss a number of selected texts in the letter. Our special focus will, however, be on Rom 8:29.

> For those whom he foreknew, he also predestined to be conformed to the image of his Son, that he would be the firstborn among many *adelphoi*.[14]

---

12   Jewett, *Romans*, 53–55; Paul Trebilco, 'Early Christian Communities in the Greco-Roman City', *Ex Auditu* 29: 27–28; Wu, *Suffering in Romans*, 30–31.
13   See http://www.homelessnessaustralia.org.au/sites/homelessnessaus/files/2017-07/Homelessness%20in%20Australiav2.pdf, accessed September 28, 2017.
14   All Scripture translations are mine, unless otherwise stated.

The foreknowledge and election of God here are matters of much debate. But for our purposes, there is no need to engage in the argument except to note that, from Paul's Jewish vantage point, the 'fact that YHWH has the prerogative and power to decide and know in advance is assumed in the Scripture (see Gen 18:19; Jer 1:5; Amos 3:2)'.[15] Paul's point is that conformity with the Son's image has long been God's predetermined purpose.

The Greek word *adelphoi*, that is, 'sisters and brothers', in Rom 8:29b deserves much attention. Kyu Seop Kim's recent study on the Old Testament and Jewish literature helpfully concludes the following.

> In short, sibling language in Jewish literature highlights ethnic insider designation as a member of the family of Abraham. The notion of a brother often referred to the concept of a fictive kinship relationship in the symbolic world of Israel. Israelites' brotherhood distinguished them from Gentiles and foreigners, and assigned solidarity as a family member sharing a common blood relationship and ancestry. Therefore, sibling titles do not refer to a regional, but to an ethnic concept (e.g. 2 Macc 1:1), and Gentiles were not designated as brother(s) by Jews with the exception of proselytes.[16]

Thus, Paul's multiple use of *adelphos* in Romans to address his audience is quite remarkable, for he is a Jew and his audience includes both Jews *and* Gentiles (Rom 1:13; 7:1, 4; 12:1; 14:10, 13, 15, 21; 15:14, 30; 16:17).[17] Scholars often, rightly, affirm that siblingship in antiquity and in Paul signifies a strong sense of group identity, belonging and solidarity.[18] In particular, Kar Yong Lim highlights the

---

15 Wu, *Suffering in Romans*, 159.

16 Kyu Seop Kim, 'Reframing Paul's Sibling Language in Light of Jewish Epistolary Forms of Address', *HTS Theological Studies* 71, no. 1 (2015): 3. Likewise, in a separate study on the Book of Acts, Aaron Kuecker, *The Spirit and the 'Other'* (London: T&T Clark, 2011), 187, concludes that the word *adelphoi* was used by the Jews to refer to their own kindred, not the Gentiles. He says that prior to the (so-called) Jerusalem Council in Acts 15, '*no non-Israelite is ever categorized as a "brother" of an Israelite*' (emphasis original). See also the discussion by David G. Horrell, 'From ἀδελφοί to οἶκος θεοῦ: Social Transformation in Pauline Christianity', *Journal of Biblical Literature* 120, no. 2 (2001): 293–311, especially 296–97, 299–304.

17 Most recent commentators believe that the addressees of Romans consisted of a mixed group of Jews and Gentiles. See, e.g., the recent discussion in Stanley Porter, *The Letter to the Romans* (Sheffield: Sheffield Phoenix Press, 2015), 5–10.

18 See, e.g., Reidar Aasgaard, *'My Beloved Brothers and Sisters': Christian Siblingship in Paul* (London: T&T Clark, 2004), especially 306–7; Kar Yong Lim, *Metaphors and Social Identity Formation in Paul's Letters to the Corinthians* (Eugene: Pickwick, 2017), 51–92, especially 63–71, 74.

significance of Paul's use of sibling language in light of the fact that in the Roman social world such language was used only among social equals.

> Now that the rich and poor, master and slave, and Jews and gentiles—even though they were not social equals—were all addressed as 'brothers and sisters' suggests that *Paul deliberately used sibling imagery to create and affirm a social group that was markedly different from other groups in the Roman Empire*.[19]

Also, Abera Mengestu emphasises the notion of kinship and the boundary-crossing nature of Paul's sibling language. He helpfully highlights the following.

> By applying sibling language to Jews and Gentiles . . . Paul is 'reordering relationships' and dissolving boundaries.[20]

> Using kingship language, Paul develops a narrative of networks of familial relationships that coalesce to image the emerging of community Christ-followers as the family that belongs to God.[21]

> Paul utilizes very well the dynamic and versatile nature of kinship that makes non-kin in one situation kin in another. He uses it both in stable and crisis situations to construct boundaries and also to create unity.[22]

In light of the above, Paul's use of the term *adelphos* indicates that he sees no boundary between Jewish and Gentile believers. And importantly, the term conveys a real sense of kinship, solidarity and unity among Christ-followers. It is not surprising, then, in Romans 14, that Paul uses *adelphos* to deal with the intergroup conflict between the strong and the weak concerning food practices.

Paul says:

> Why do you pass judgment on your *adelphon*? Or you, why do you despise your *adelphon*? For we will all stand before the judgment seat of God (Rom 14:10).

---

19 Lim, *Metaphors*, 74. *Emphasis added*. Here Lim refers to Joseph Hellerman, *Ancient Church as Family* (Minneapolis: Fortress, 2001), 22–23.

20 Abera M. Mengestu, *God as Father in Paul: Kinship Language and Identity Formation in Early Christianity* (Eugene: Pickwick, 2013), 201. Note that Mengestu disagrees with Aasgaard in that the latter seems to disregard the 'fictive family' construction (200).

21 Mengestu, *God as Father in Paul*, 203. *Emphasis added*. Mengestu's study includes a number of familial terms in Paul, not only *adelphos*.

22 Mengestu, *God as Father in Paul*, 203.

> Therefore, let us not pass judgment on one another, but rather determine not to put a stumbling block or hindrance in the way of an *adelphō* (Rom 14:13).

> If your *adelphos* is grieved by what you eat, you are no longer walking in love. Do not by what you eat destroy the one *for whom Christ died* (Rom 14:15; emphasis added).

> It is good not to eat meat or drink wine or do anything by which your *adelphos* stumbles (Rom 14:21).

Apparently, in the house churches there were those who believed that they could eat anything, while others ate vegetables only (14:2). In practice, this most likely meant that they were not able to share meals together. Given the honour and shame culture of the ancient world, Paul was very much aware of the importance of meal sharing, for it signified their unity and respect for one another. It is, therefore, vital for him to urge his audience to welcome one another and to refrain from quarrelling over opinions (14:1).

In the verses above, he exhorts his readers not to pass judgement on or despise each other, or to cause anyone to stumble. In each case he uses the term *adelphos* to convey the fact that they are siblings and hence that there is a need for unity. In other words, there should be solidarity and harmony between Jesus-followers precisely because they are siblings in Christ.

At this point it should be noted that the sibling language implies that, at least within Romans, Paul does not convey any sense of hierarchical relationship between Christ-followers. Of course, the worldview of the people of Rome was that relationship within a family was hierarchical. The head of a family was the father, the *paterfamilias*, who had control over the estate and the properties of the family. The wife was inferior to the husband, and the slaves had the lowest status in the household. The Roman emperor was effectively the benevolent father of Rome. My sense is that in his letters Paul subverts this hierarchical worldview by the self-giving love of Christ in his letters.[23] I am aware of the debate on this matter,

---

23 For example, if we assume Pauline authorship of Ephesians, then the household code in Eph 5:22–33 may suggest a hierarchical structure. But the *mutual submission* out of *reverence for Christ* in Eph 5:21, the mention of Christ's self-giving love in 5:25 and the emphasis on believers' lives being determined by Christ's death in 1:20; 2:1, 5, 16; 5:14 signify the fact that Jesus's cruciform love should shape all human relationships. This, in turn, subverts the Roman sense of hierarchical structure by removing the power imbalance within the familial relationship among believers.

especially in terms of gender equality.²⁴ But *as far as Romans goes*, there seems to be no hierarchical relationship between the children of God at all, precisely because they are all siblings in Christ.²⁵

Yes, God is the *Abba* Father, and Christ is the firstborn (Rom 8:15, 29). But *all believers* are children of God, heirs of God, and coheirs with Christ (Rom 8:14–17).²⁶ All are adopted into God's family, whether Jew or Gentile (8:15, 23; 9:4). There is no indication that ethnicity or gender determines a person's status in the family of God. Decisively for me, the Greek word for 'one another' (*allēlōn*) appears most frequently in the section Rom 12:1–15:13, which is also the place where the sibling relationship between believers is evoked frequently (Rom 12:1, 5, 10, 16; 13:8; 14:10, 13, 15, 19, 21; 15:5, 7).²⁷ The word 'one another' indicates *mutuality and solidarity, not hierarchy*. In view of this, when Paul says in Rom 8:29 that the Son of God is the firstborn among many *adelphoi*, he refers to the Jew–Gentile multicultural family of God, where Christ is the firstborn and its members share lives together with a strong sense of kinship, solidarity and corporate identity.²⁸

This would have challenged the multicultural house churches to adopt an alternative worldview from that of the prevailing culture in imperial Rome. The Gentile believers had been incorporated into the family of Abraham according to God's promise to the patriarch (4:1–25; see also 11:11–32). Indeed, the new Christ-community now constituted a new humanity in Christ (Rom 5:1–21). There should be no ethnic and gender boundaries in this community.

This invites us to read Romans afresh in multicultural Australia. Imagine that we are not simply members of a local church, but also brothers and sisters of a family. Imagine that our friends in the migrant churches in our neighbourhood are not only migrants but also our siblings in Christ. Let us picture the indigenous peoples of this land as our brothers and sisters and envision a real sense of solidarity. Imagine that you are a migrant like me, someone who left home to find a new

---

24 I believe in biblical gender equality. I also find Cynthia Long Westfall's *Paul and Gender: Reclaiming the Apostle's Vision for Men and Women in Christ* (Grand Rapids: Baker, 2016) helpful.

25 The fact that Junia is an apostle, Phoebe is a *diakonos* ('deacon' or 'minister') and Prisca is a co-worker in Christ is very important in Romans when it comes to the role of women.

26 The fact that Paul uses *huios* ('son') and *teknon* ('child') interchangeably in Rom 8:14, 16–17, 19, 21 suggests that the apostle sees no distinction between male and female when it comes to the believers' status as God's children. But see also Jewett, Romans, 500–502 for his proposal that the use of *teknon* indicates Paul's emphasis on gender inclusivity. Jewett may well be right here.

27 The term *allēlōn* appears nine times in Rom 12:5, 10, 16; 13:8; 14:13, 19; 15:5, 7, and *adelphos* six times in 12:1; 14:10, 13, 15, 21.

28 See Mengestu, *God as Father*, 190–94. Cf. Aasgaard, 'My Beloved', 137–50.

home. How wonderful is it that there are siblings in Christ in the church? Perhaps you know some of the asylum seekers and refugees in Australia, like the ones in my own church community, who have been separated from their families. To be part of the family of God means that they are not so much victims of violence, but our siblings in Christ, whom Jesus died for.

The biblical text enables us to reimagine life in multicultural Australia. It calls for a fresh evaluation of our understanding of our roles and vocations as members of the church. Monocultural churches, white or non-white, need to consider ways to welcome people of other cultural backgrounds and to connect with churches of other cultures. All of us should actively engage in reconciliation with indigenous Australians. We are to develop an awareness and understanding of the plight of asylum seekers and refugees, and find ways to walk with them rather than succumbing to the fear politics in Australia that work against them. And let us welcome the new migrants in our midst, especially those who lack English competency and other resources to overcome the cultural barriers in settling into this country. In addition, I would like to suggest that we should intentionally ensure that the leadership of our churches, Christian organisations and theological colleges have a multicultural composition, and that people of both genders and from a spectrum of socio-economic backgrounds are represented. Our leadership make-up is a reflection of our theology and the health of the church as a whole, and it determines whether we can fulfil the mission of God in a rapidly changing society.

To Be Conformed to the Image of the Son Together Without Ethnic Boundaries

The formation of a family of God, however, is inseparable from the image bearing of believers. Paul says in Rom 8:29 that the children of God are 'to be conformed to the image of his Son, that he would be the firstborn among many *adelphoi*'.

The term 'firstborn' (Greek: *prōtotokos*) may point to YHWH's relationship with Israel in the Exodus story, as in Exod 4:22–23. At the same time, Douglas Campbell and Gordon Fee have rightly alerted us to the allusion to Ps 89:26–27, noting that the words 'father' (*patēr*) and 'firstborn' (*prōtotokos*) appear in the psalm (88:27–28 LXX).[29] Commentaries on the psalm often recognise the

---

29 Douglas A. Campbell, 'Story of Jesus in Romans and Galatians', in *Narrative Dynamics in Paul*, ed. Bruce W. Longenecker (Louisville: Westminster John Knox, 2002), 116; Gordon D. Fee, *Pauline Christology* (Peabody: Hendrickson, 2007), 250–51. Also, in the Exodus tradition, Israel is said to be YHWH's firstborn (Exod 4:22, 23), and so the Son's being the 'firstborn among many *adelphoi*' in Rom 8:29 probably refers to Christ being the firstborn of a new people of God.

references to YHWH's promise to David in 2 Sam 7:10–15 (see Ps 89:19–37).[30] Given the anointing of David in Ps 89:20, the reference to the Davidic covenant in Ps 89:28, the mention of Jesus as the son of David in Rom 1:3 and the fact that Jesus is the Christ (that is, 'the anointed one') in Paul's letters, Rom 8:29 may allude to the Davidic sonship of Jesus, with the implication that believers are being incorporated into the people of God through the Davidic covenant.

But this allusion must be understood together with a more important imagery, namely, the 'image' (*eikōn*) of the Son in Rom 8:29. The explicit and extensive reference to Adam in Rom 5:12–21 and the repeated mention of the creation in Rom 8:19–23 make it likely that in Rom 8:29 the creation accounts in Genesis are evoked. The term 'image' reminds us of Gen 1:26–27, which says that human beings are made in God's image. These interlinked thematic and linguistic connections mean that we should take note of the motif of believers being image bearers of God.[31] Just as the future resurrection calls for steadfastness and faithful labour on the part of believers in this life (1 Cor 15:48), so are the children of God encouraged to display God's glory as image bearers as they groan with the creation and anticipate the future cosmic renewal in expectant hope (Rom 8:18–30).[32]

Jesus is the image of God (2 Cor 4:4; cf. Col 3:15). And, in 2 Cor 3:18, Paul speaks of the transformation of believers into God's image through the Spirit. Likewise, the apostle talks about the empowerment of the Spirit in Rom 8:1–17. Also, as I have argued elsewhere, the believers' conformity to the image of the Son in Rom 8:29 is about the process of transformation into God's image, which has started in this age and will be consummated at the final renewal of the entire creation.[33] According to ancient worldview (and the worldview of many cultures today), the images of the gods in the temples represented the characteristics of the gods themselves. Similarly, the image of a ruler—such as the image of Caesar on the Roman coins and temple statues—represented the honour of the ruler,

---

30   Craig Broyles, *Psalms* (Peabody: Hendrickson, 1999), 357; John Goldingay, *Psalms 42–89* (Peabody: Hendrickson, 2001), 677–81; Wu, *Suffering in Romans*, 161–62.

31   Wu, *Suffering in Romans*, 160. See also Jewett, *Romans*, 529; James D. G. Dunn, *Romans 1–8* (WBC; Dallas: Word, 1988), 483; Brendan Byrne, *Romans* (Collegeville, The Liturgical Press, 1996), 272–73; F. F. Bruce, *Romans* (Leicester: IVP, 1985), 167.

32   Here I am not in total agreement with the view of John Kilner, *Dignity and Destiny: Humanity in the Image of God* (Grand Rapids: Eerdmans, 2015), 236, that Rom 8:29 primarily refers to a future fulfilment of image bearing. But I really appreciate Kilner's conclusion that the 'New Testament is more concerned about Christians focusing on becoming conformed to the image of Christ (Rom. 8:29) than about pointing people back to Adam ... In Christ, the old *adam* is not being made better, but a new humanity is created for the purpose of a much greater renewal (Col. 3:9–10)' (275).

33   Wu, *Suffering in Romans*, 159–62. Cf. Jewett, *Romans*, 528–29; Dunn, *Romans 1–8*, 483; Michael Gorman, 'Romans: The First Christian Treatise on Theosis', *Journal of Theological Interpretation* 5 (2011): 26.

who, in turn, was considered to be the agent of the gods. Hence, several scholars today rightly think that the notion that human beings are God's image bearers means that they are his representatives, or vice-regents, on earth.[34] In light of this, the conformity to the image of the Son and him being the firstborn among many siblings means that all believers are God's representatives and vice-regents.

If my interpretation is right, then *there is no superior race or ethnicity within the multicultural Jew–Gentile family of God*. Paul's argument in Rom 9–11 seems to bear this out, where he says that there is no room for the Gentiles to be arrogant despite their inclusion into God's people and the Jews' disobedience (11:13–32). For Paul, all believers are renewed image bearers of God. No-one can claim superiority.

Imagine what this means in Australia today. We who are newcomers to this land, white or non-white, cannot, in our wildest dreams, think that we are superior to indigenous Australians, who are the traditional custodians of the land. The early newcomers, the British, are not superior to the Italians, the Greeks, or the Vietnamese. The Chinese doctors and accountants are not superior to the Aussie battlers. The professional migrants with fluent English are not superior to the refugees who speak little or no English. God is impartial. Salvation is available to all by grace and all those who believe in Christ can participate in that salvation (Rom 3:22). Being renewed imager bearers of God, believers should not have any us-and-them mentality.

Participation in Christ

We will soon discuss how in practice the multicultural Jesus-community may live as siblings in Christ. But before that, it is important to take a closer look at what it means to be conformed to the image of the Son. In my view, this sharing of Christ's identity and participation in him is a key theme in Romans. This theme is prominent in Rom 6:1–11, where Paul speaks of sharing in Christ's death, burial and life. Believers have been baptised into and crucified with Christ. They have died with him and will live with him. They have been united with him. Crucially, the imagery of family is vividly displayed in Rom 8:14–17, where the notion of participation in Christ is also the strongest. Paul says that those who are led by the

---

34 See Wu, *Suffering in Romans*, 170–73; J. Richard Middleton, *The Liberating Image: The Imago Dei in Genesis 1* (Grand Rapids: Brazos Press, 2013), 58–60; Watts, 'The New Exodus/ New Creational Restoration of the Image of God', in *What Does it Mean To Be Saved*, ed. John Stackhouse, 21; John Walton, *Genesis 1 as Ancient Cosmology* (Winona Lake, IN: Eisenbrauns, 2011), 192; Greg Beale, *The Temple and the Church's Mission* (Leicester: Apollos, 2004), 81; Jon D. Levenson, 'Temple and the World', *The Journal of Religion* 64 (1984): 297.

Spirit are the children of God, and by the Spirit they cry out *Abba*, Father. They are heirs of God. Once the familial relationship between God and the believers is clearly spelt out, Paul says the following in Rom 8:17:

> And if children, then heirs, heirs of God and joint-heirs with Christ, provided that we suffer with Christ, in order that we may also be glorified with him.

In the Greek, the words for 'joint-heirs', 'we suffer with' and 'we may be glorified with' (*sygklēronomoi, sympaschomen* and *syndoxasthōmen*) have the same prefix (*syn* or *sym*)—a prefix that means 'together with'. Hence, effectively they represent the concepts of 'coheirs', 'co-suffer', and 'being co-glorified'. This concentrated vocabulary of participation indicates that Paul intends to strongly emphasise the call to share in Christ's suffering and glorification. Followers of Jesus are God's children. They are siblings in the family of God living in solidarity with one another. Christ is the firstborn, and believers are coheirs with him. If we see conformity with the Son holistically and understand it as a transformation that involves the whole person and community, then it most likely includes participating in his death and resurrection, as well as partaking in his suffering and glory—that is, the whole package, so to speak. The outworking of this transformation, in turn, needs to involve every sphere of life, both as individuals and as a community. To be God's representatives on earth, and as people led by the Spirit, Jesus-followers are called to share in Christ's suffering, so that they may reflect his glory as his image bearers, both in their life orientation and daily behaviour.

Sibling Love in Practice

What does this mean in practice? The answer is found in Rom 12:1–15:13. I have chosen to highlight three specific matters that are particularly relevant. But before that, I need to mention the remarkably strong links between 12:1–15:13 and our key verse 8:29. To start with, Paul uses the word *adelphos* multiple times in 12:1–15:13 to address his audience (12:1; 14:10, 13, 15, 21). The term is, of course, also a keyword in 8:29. Thus, the word connects 8:29 with 12:1–15:13.

But importantly, there seems to be a clear echo of 8:29 in Rom 12:2a.

> Do not be conformed to this age, but be transformed by the renewal of the mind (12:2a).

The language of conformity and transformation harks back to the 'being conformed to the image of the Son' in Rom 8:29. The verbal link is quite clear if we put the Greek terms side-by-side.

8:29 *symmorphos*

12:2a *syschēmatizō*

12:2a *metamorphoō*

Indeed, given the fact that Rom 12:1–2 introduces the section of 12:1–15:13, these words connect 8:29 with the whole section through the theme of transformation. In other words, the process of transformation as God's renewed image bearers is to be worked out in the communal life of believers, which is the subject matter of 12:1–15:13. Also, the Greek terms for 'think' and 'mind' (*phroneō, phronēma, phrovimos, pronoeō, nous*) appear frequently in both Rom 8:5–8, 27 and 12:1–15:13 (five times in chapter 8 and nine times in chapters 12–15). And they refer to a Spirit-inspired mindset, or pattern of thinking, that determines how believers may live in community. This further indicates that Romans 8 and 12–15 are closely connected, in that the transformation of believers involves a Spirit-led thinking process.

In light of this, to be conformed to the image of the Son, to be siblings in Christ, Jesus-followers partake in a process of Spirit-led transformation as a multicultural family of God, sharing their corporate life together. Now, let us consider what it means in practice.

First, Paul envisions a community of mutual love where people share one another's suffering. This is highlighted in the following verses in Romans 12.

> Love one another with sibling affection. Outdo one another in showing honour (Rom 12:10).

> Rejoice with those who rejoice, weep with those who weep (Rom 12:15).

These two verses convey a strong sense of mutuality and solidarity. The word for 'sibling affection' in 12:10 is *philadelphia*, which means the love of brothers and sisters. As siblings in Christ, Jesus-followers are to love and honour one another. There is a real sense of togetherness that happens only in a home—not a dysfunctional home but an authentic love-centred home—where members see the sharing of their joy and sorrow as participation in the suffering of Christ himself.

Given the cultural and socio-economic diversity of Paul's audience in Rome, his words would have been simultaneously counterintuitive and comforting. The notion of mutual honouring would have been quite striking given their honour and shame culture. Christians of Roman stock were called not to despise the Africans and the Jews in their midst. Nor should the (relatively) well-to-do look down on the poor. Indeed, the slave owners should not treat their slaves with disrespect.

Rather, they were all urged to earnestly show honour to each other, as if they are people of the same kin. Imagine how comforting it would have been for those who suffered from socio-economic hardship and oppression. The poor would find support. The homeless would experience love. And the slaves would find solace in the Christ-community.

Second, Paul exhorts the Roman house churches to share their lives with strangers. In Rom 12:13, Paul asks his audience to pursue hospitality. The Greek for 'hospitality' is *philoxenia*, which means 'love of strangers' (cf. Heb 13:2).[35] But we must note that hospitality is not simply about giving and generosity. Nor is it about asking people to go to church meetings. In light of the fact that the church is actually a family of God, hospitality is also an invitation to a 'home'. It is about people who have experienced the hospitality of God embodying his hospitality in the world. For the early Christians in Rome, it would have been about welcoming strangers—regardless of their ethnicity and socio-economic status, and whether they were Christ-followers or not—so that they might see what a multicultural Christ-community looks like, and how believers shared their lives as siblings in Christ.[36]

Third, Paul urges the multicultural house churches to live in harmony in Rom 14:1–15:13. There is some debate about the identity of 'the weak' and 'the strong', and the exact problem Paul is dealing with in this passage. I have stated my view elsewhere (which is fairly similar to the majority position). Here is a summary.

> The issue in 14:1–15:13 is the intergroup conflict concerning the observance of Jewish dietary laws and Sabbath-keeping. The 'weak' are those who observe those laws, and the 'strong' are those who do not. In particular, I tend to agree with John Barclay's proposal that Paul's teaching protects the weak by urging the strong not to despise them, and in doing so allows for a 'Jewish Christianity' that observes the Jewish law. At the same time, by identifying himself as someone among the strong, Paul advocates for the validity of a 'Gentilized Christianity', where law-observance is not needed. With this, Paul's teaching aims at promoting social cohesion within a Jew–Gentile

---

35 See Stanley E. Porter, *The Letter to the Romans* (Sheffield: Sheffield Phoenix Press, 2015), 239; Toews, *Romans* (Scottdale, PA: Herald Press, 2004), 305.

36 While some say that Rom 12:13 refers to relationships within the Christ-community only, I think the hospitality in this verse refers to relationships within *and* outside the community. Cf. Trebilco, 'Early Christian Communities', 42, n. 63.

community, where the Jewish law serves as an important social-religious identity marker.[37]

What is the basis of this call for social cohesion? The answer lies in Paul's conviction that believers are to participate in Christ's death and life, which is vividly demonstrated by Paul's words in the following passages.[38]

> We do not live to ourselves, and we do not die to ourselves. If we live, we live to the Lord, and if we die, we die to the Lord; so then, whether we live or whether we die, we are the Lord's. For to this end Christ died and lived again, so that he might be Lord of both the dead and the living (Rom 14:7–9).

> If your *brother or sister* [*adelphos*] is being injured by what you eat, *you are no longer walking in love*. Do not let what you eat cause the ruin of one *for whom Christ died* (Rom 14:15).

> We who are strong ought to put up with the failings of the weak, and not to please ourselves. Each of us must please our neighbour for the good purpose of building up the neighbour. For Christ did not please himself; but, as it is written, 'The insults of those who insult you have fallen on me' (Rom 15:1–3).

To be united with Christ in his life and death means that members of the Jew–Gentile community needed to live in love and harmony, despite their different cultural-religious practices. They had to remember that they were renewed image bearers of God, who were called to reflect his glory in their lives. Disharmony would have meant that they were not walking in love. In practice, their insistence on adhering to their own cultural-religious practices would have meant that they could not share meals together and hence they were not honouring one another. Paul's advice was that those who were strong should welcome the weak and bear with their failings. And they were to model after Christ by not pleasing themselves but their neighbour (14:1; 15:1–3). If the house churches took heed of Paul's

---

37 Siu Fung Wu, 'Participating in God's Purpose by Following the Cruciform Pattern of Christ', *Journal for the Study of Paul and his Letters* 5 (2015), 5–6. The reference to Barclay's view can be found in John M. G. Barclay, *Pauline Churches and Diaspora Jews* (WUNT 275; Tübingen: Mohr Siebeck, 2011), 43–44, 54–56. Similar, but not identical, views can be found in Matera, *Romans* (Paideia; Grand Rapids: Baker, 2010), 309; N. T. Wright, *The Letter to the Romans* (NIB X; Nashville: Abingdon, 2002), 731; Byrne, *Romans*, 403–7. Cf. Kruse, *Romans*, 509–10.

38 The following three Scripture citations (Rom 14:7–9; 14:15; 15:1–3) are taken from the NRSV. Emphasis added.

exhortation, they would welcome one another, with meal sharing being the sign of their kinship and sibling love.

In summary, Romans speaks of a love-centred family of God, where God is the parent, Christ is the firstborn, and the siblings in Christ share their pain and sorrow together. Inspired by the indwelling Spirit, they make their home together and they show hospitality by inviting people to their home. And when there are intercultural conflicts, they seek to walk in sibling love and find ways to sort out their differences. The basis of all these is the call to participate in the death, suffering, resurrection and glory of Christ.

In multicultural Australia, what do mutual love, sharing in suffering, hospitality for strangers and communal harmony mean? I suggest that we start with an outward-looking posture, namely, hospitality, and see what a loving and harmonious community means when it entertains strangers. Let us imagine what happens when Jesus-followers invite people of different cultures and faiths to the family of God. What happens when they see, in the lives of believers, the hope of glory in this world of suffering and violence?

Imagine what hospitality means to the asylum seekers and refugees among us? I suspect it means the safety of a home, as opposed to the danger of an oppressive regime or the peril of war. Imagine what hospitality means to the migrants who struggle to understand English and the Western culture, those living on a low income, those living with a disability and those living with mental illness? I think it means that they are invited to a place of acceptance, love, and honour, as opposed to isolation, humiliation and stigma.

On the other hand, let us think about those who are in positions of socio-economic stability and relative security, by virtue of their education, wealth, or place of birth. Imagine what happens when they offer their hands of friendship to those in need with acts of hospitality? I suspect they will find that giving and hospitality is not so much a matter of generosity towards the helpless. It is, instead, a genuine sharing of pain and solidarity with them. It is an offering of 'home for the homeless', metaphorically and literally.

The fact is, a love-centred family of God that cultivates sibling love is a beautiful home for both its members and outsiders, for such a 'home' is where believers seek to be conformed to the image of the self-giving Son of God, who died for humanity.

Jesus Made His Home Among Us

As I conclude, I must mention that everything above depends on one thing in Rom 8:3, where it says that God sent his Son in the likeness of sinful flesh and to deal with sin (8:3b). There is a lot of debate around this verse. But my sense is that most would agree that it speaks of, among other things, God sending his Son to become a human being, so as to set believers free from the bondage of sin and death through his death and resurrection (see the immediate context of 8:1–17 and Paul's argument in Rom 5–8). We may say that, in a real sense, the Son of God made his home on earth by becoming a human. Outside Paul's letters, John's Gospel makes this clear. The Word became flesh and made his dwelling among us, full of grace and truth (John 1:14). Christians should never lose sight of the sacrifice that Christ made on the Roman cross, which was a symbol of shame, humiliation, oppression and violence. Christ made his home in this world of chaos and sorrow, to accomplish God's purpose of salvation for humanity.

I mentioned that I came to Australia because I hated my noisy, cramped, tiny and dysfunctional home in East Asia. But I often imagine that Jesus came to my home. He came, despite the oppressive condition of the dwelling, or the brokenness of the family. He came, despite the yelling, the shouting and the violence in the neighbourhood. He listened to the frustration and the tears. He cried with us and encouraged us. He was willing to live among us. It is Christ's self-giving 'homemaking' that ultimately gives me a sense of belonging—that is, belonging to his family—wherever I live, and no matter how I struggle with my identity as a bicultural person.

Just as God sent his Son to make his home on earth so that we can be God's children, so are we called to embody the family of God in the world. The Son of God, who is *the* image bearer of God, made his dwelling among us and showed us who God is. Likewise, we, who are called to be conformed to the image of the Son, are to reflect the glory of God in this world by modelling after his self-sacrificing cruciform love. If we think that the mission of the church is simply about inviting people to our church buildings, then we miss the point all together. Instead, it is about living out Christ's cross-shaped love in the market places, among the poor and marginalised, so that the homeless may find home.

BIBLIOGRAPHY

Aasgaard, Reidar. *'My Beloved Brothers and Sisters': Christian Siblingship in Paul*. London: T&T Clark, 2004.

Barclay, John M. G. *Pauline Churches and Diaspora Jews*. WUNT 275; Tübingen: Mohr Siebeck, 2011.

Broyles, Craig C. *Psalms*. NIBC. Peabody: Hendrickson, 1999.

Byrne, Brendan. *Romans*. Sacra Pagina 6. Collegeville: Liturgical, 1996.

Campbell, Douglas A. 'Story of Jesus in Romans and Galatians.' In *Narrative Dynamics in Paul*, edited by Bruce W. Longenecker. Louisville: Westminster John Knox, 2002.

Dunn, James D. G. *Romans 1–8*. WBC 38A. Dallas: Word, 1988.

Edwards, R. B., M. Reasoner, and S. E. Porter. 'Rome: Overview.' In *DNTB*, edited by Craig A. Evans and Stanley E. Porter, 1010–18. Leicester: IVP, 2000.

Fee, Gordon D. *Pauline Christology*. Peabody: Hendrickson, 2007.

Friesen, Steven. 'Poverty in Pauline Studies: Beyond the So-Called New Consensus.' JSNT 26 (2004) 323–61.

Goldingay, John. *Psalms 42–89*. BCOT 2. Grand Rapids: Baker Academic, 2007.

Gorman, Michael. 'Romans: The First Christian Treatise on Theosis.' *Journal of Theological Interpretation* 5 (2011): 13–34.

Hellerman, Joseph. *Ancient Church as Family*. Minneapolis: Fortress, 2001.

Horrell, David G. 'From ἀδελφοί to οἶκος θεοῦ: Social Transformation in Pauline Christianity.' *Journal of Biblical Literature* 120, no. 2 (2001): 293–311.

Jeffers, James S. *Conflicts at Rome*. Minneapolis: Fortress, 1991.

Jewett, Robert. *Romans: A Commentary*. Hermeneia. Minneapolis: Fortress, 2007.

Kim, Kyu Seop. 'Reframing Paul's Sibling Language in Light of Jewish Epistolary Forms of Address.' *HTS Theological Studies* 71, no. 1 (2015): 1–8.

Kruse, Colin. *Paul's Letter to the Romans*. PTNC. Grand Rapids: Eerdmans, 2012.

Kuecker, Aaron. *The Spirit and the 'Other'*. London: T&T Clark, 2011.

Lampe, Peter. 'The Roman Christian of Romans 16.' In *The Romans Debate*, edited by Karl P. Donfried. Peabody: Hendrickson, 1991.

Lim, Kar Yong. *Metaphors and Social Identity Formation in Paul's Letters to the Corinthians*. Eugene: Pickwick, 2017.

Mengestu, Abera M. *God as Father in Paul: Kinship Language and Identity Formation in Early Christianity*. Eugene: Pickwick, 2013.

Middleton, J. Richard. *The Liberating Image: The Imago Dei in Genesis 1*. Grand Rapids: Brazos Press, 2013.

Leong, David P. *Race and Place: How Urban Geography Shapes the Journey to Reconciliation* (Downers Grove, IL: IVP), 2017.

Levenson, Jon D. 'Temple and the World.' *The Journal of Religion* 64 (1984): 275–98.

Longenecker, Bruce W. *Remember the Poor: Paul, Poverty, and the Greco-Roman World*. Grand Rapids: Eerdmans, 2010.

Trebilco, Paul. 'Early Christian Communities in the Greco-Roman City.' *Ex Auditu* 29 (2013): 25–48.

Walton, John H. *Genesis 1 as Ancient Cosmology*. Winona Lake: Eisenbrauns, 2011.

Watts, Rikk E. 'The New Exodus/New Creational Restoration of the Image of God: A Biblical–Theological Perspective on Salvation.' In *What Does It Mean To Be Saved*, edited by John G. Jr. Stackhouse, 15–42. Grand Rapids: Baker, 2002.

Westfall, Cynthia Long. *Paul and Gender: Reclaiming the Apostle's Vision for Men and Women in Christ*. Grand Rapids: Baker, 2016.

Wright, N. T. *The Letter to the Romans*. NIB X. Nashville: Abingdon, 2002.

Wu, Siu Fung. 'Participating in God's Purpose by Following the Cruciform Pattern of Christ.' *Journal for the Study of Paul and His Letters* 5 (2015): 1–20.

Wu, Siu Fung. *Suffering in Romans*. Eugene: Pickwick, 2015.

Chapter 14

A 'STEAM BOAT' THEOLOGY OF HOME: READING THE GOSPEL OF LUKE WITH CHINESE EYES

Xiaoli Yang

Have you ever walked past a Chinese restaurant where hot steam covers the glass window and wondered what is going on inside on a cold winter's night? Have you ever joined in a Chinese meal, where both the hosts and the guests are eating together around a 'steam boat'? Drawing on the metaphor of a 'steam boat' (*huoguo*, 火锅, a communal hot pot), this chapter develops a Chinese theology of home. It will investigate the etymology of the term 'home' and related terms in the Chinese language and explore the central role of table meals in Chinese home culture. Using the metaphor of a 'steam boat' observed in Chinese culture for over one thousand years, it will look in depth at the essential worldviews embedded in Chinese tradition and offer the reading of the Gospel of Luke from a Chinese perspective,[1] as well as some missiological insights. It will argue that a 'steam boat' theology of home can be developed by identifying relevant contact points and will suggest some possible ways of understanding the gospel within a given culture.

---

1 Some data is taken from Xiaoli Yang, *A Dialogue between Haizi's Poetry and the Gospel of Luke—Chinese Homecoming and the Relationship with Jesus Christ* (Leiden: Brill, 2018).

Cultural Foundations of Words

A study of ancient forms of Chinese characters reveals many examples of the origins of word meanings linked to a cultural context. The following diagrams show the development of the written language of the character 'home'—*Jia*—by depicting a pig-shaped animal under a roof.[2] The character used for roof '宀' (*mian*) is also related to the concept of family. Ancient Chinese people used to breed pigs in their homes, so a pig in a house is a symbol of a home. Domestication was part of agriculture prior to the Shang dynasty (before 1600 BCE).

The word origin of 'home' provides a basis for a Chinese ethics of home based on Confucian teaching. Confucius outlined a period of Grand Union (*datong*, 大同) followed by a period of Small Tranquillity (*xiaokang*, 小康), which is the policy promoted by the current PRC (the People's Republic of China) government. Confucius continues:

> People accumulate articles and exert their strength for their own advantage . . . Their object is to make the walls of their cities and suburbs strong and their ditches and moats secure . . . they frame buildings and measures; lay out the fields and hamlets [for the dwellings of the husbandmen]; adjudge the superiority to men of valour and knowledge; and regulate their achievements with a view to their own advantage . . . This is the period of what we call Small Tranquillity.[3]

The Chinese cultural understanding of home is closely linked to the traditional Confucian understanding of a home, such as building walls, gathering goods, setting boundaries and establishing family prosperity, power and position within one's own territory. The mention of building walls for strength, security and protection suggested in the quotation above shows an inward-looking desire for preservation. Collecting goods and wealth from outside for the benefit of the members within is a common feature of an agricultural society where maintaining a recognisable comfort zone is upheld.

---

2   *The Dictionary of Han Language*, 's.v. 家 (Jia)', http://www.zdic.net/z/18/js/5BB6.htm.
3   Confucius, 'Liji, Li Yun', http://ctext.org/liji/li-yun#n11484, 2.

The concept of home can also be measured by looking at varying degrees of relational life. *Jia* is often used together with *Xiang* (乡), meaning one's homeland or hometown. The ancient character *Xiang*'s formation is like two people facing each other sharing food from a container in the middle, as shown below.[4]

This character depicts a collective sharing of wine and food and symbolises hospitality. The sharing of meals and the breeding of animals within walls are thus important elements of the concept of home in Chinese culture.

Home is also a place where hospitality is offered and life is connected through establishing close relationships, especially over meal tables. As explained, the Chinese character for home, *Jiaxiang* (家乡), denotes a place where a family lives within a closed wall, under the same roof where food is shared and people are entertained. It is closely related to hospitality (*haoke*, 好客), where guests, strangers or travellers are entertained. The ancient character for guests (*ke*, 客) is vividly portrayed as someone bending over to serve a meal under a roof, as shown below:[5]

Each year at the Chinese Spring Festival, a 'reunion of the entire family' (*hejia tuanyuan*, 阖家团圆) eating under the same roof is still seen as the ideal in terms of home and homecoming after a long year of work and study. This strong sense of inclusion can be seen in *He* (阖) which is often used together with *Jia* (家) to mean the whole family. The shape of *He* in the ancient small seal script (*xiaozhuan*, 小篆) is shown below as a person sitting before a dish within a closed door:[6]

---

4   The Dictionary of Han Language, 's.v. 乡 (Xiang) ', http://www.zdic.net/z/15/zy/4E61.htm, accessed November 11, 2013.

5   The Dictionary of Han Language, 's.v. 客 (Ke) ', http://www.zdic.net/z/18/zy/5BA2.htm, accessed November 11, 2013.

6   The Dictionary of Han Language, 's.v. 阖 (He) ', http://www.zdic.net/z/27/zy/9616.htm, accessed February 15, 2013.

From these etymologies, therefore, we can conclude that home for Chinese people is being present in a place that houses their family within a closed wall and is under the same roof where hospitality is offered. This cultural foundation has been reinforced and preserved in the written language throughout the ages.

'Steam Boat' as Table Meals

Table meals are essential elements of daily life in Chinese home culture, not only from an etymological perspective but also from the vantage point of Chinese history. 'People treat meals as heaven' (*min yishi weitian*, '民以食为天') is a common saying for ordinary Chinese. Laozi even thinks that 'a sage seeks to satisfy (the craving of) the belly, not (the insatiable longing of) the eyes' (*shengren weifu bu weimu*, '圣人为腹不为目').[7] One-third of the classic *A Dream of Red Mansions* describes the eating activities of a noble family.[8] Even when Chinese people worship idols, they sacrifice food. The famous national hero, Yue Fei (岳飞, 1103–1142), wrote the poem '壮志饥餐胡虏肉，笑谈渴饮匈奴血' (*zhuangzhi jican hulurou, xiaotan keyin xiongnuxue*) which talks about the joy of eating the enemy's meat and drinking their blood to celebrate the victory. The Italian Jesuit missionary, Matteo Ricci (1552–1610) and his colleagues were fascinated by Chinese table meals and first recorded them in detail for the Western world during the seventeenth century.[9]

Table meals, as complex social events, express one's identity and value. The code associated with meals can connect with layers of information including 'the pattern of social relations, social ranking, group solidarity, and economic transactions'.[10] Meals involve a variety of activities including food preparation, invitation, celebration, sharing, reciprocity and setting social boundaries. The fellowship at the table and the very fact of eating together demonstrate a powerful social function.[11] As a 'timeworn symbol',[12] it is a sign of acceptance, 'friendship,

---

7 Laozi, 老子, 'Dao De Jing', http://ctext.org/dao-de-jing, 12.

8 Xueqin Cao, 曹雪芹, 'Dream of Red Mansions', http://zhidao.baidu.com/question/30114242.html, accessed October 2, 2009.

9 Xiang-Xiang Ji and Qian-Hua Wu, 'Chinese Food in Western Missionaries Eyes of the Ming and Qing Dynasties' (明清之际入华宣教士眼中的中国食物), *Keep Memories of Ancestors' Tables—The Proceedings of 2011 Asian Food Cultural Heritage Forum* (2011), 395–405.

10 Jerome H. Neyrey, 'Ceremonies in Luke-Acts', in *The Social World of Luke-Acts: Models for Interpretation*, ed. Jerome H. Neyrey (Peabody: Hendrickson Publishers, 1991), 362.

11 Adele Reinhartz, 'Reflections on Table Fellowship and Community Identity', *Semeia*, no. 86 (1999), 232.

12 Dennis E. Smith, 'Table Fellowship as a Literary Motif in the Gospel of Luke', *Journal of Biblical Literature* 106, no. 4 (1987): 633.

intimacy and unity'.[13] It is important to know who eats with whom, what one eats or does not eat, when and how often one eats and where one sits to eat in the seating arrangements.

Chinese eating customs, where dishes are shared in the middle of the table, can be seen as an outward expression of communal and collective thinking. The way to eat a Chinese meal— 'a few dishes are put on the table, many pick at the dishes with their own chopsticks' (*jipan dacai zhuoshang fang, zhongren kuaizi fenfen jia*, '几盘大菜桌上放，众人筷子纷纷夹')—is the ideal picture of a whole family sitting around the table and enjoying a meal together. Sitting around a 'steam boat' (*huoguo*, 火锅), commonly used to entertain guests at home in Chinese culture, has been observed for over one thousand years. The raw ingredients are dipped and cooked in a 'steam boat' sitting in the middle of a table. Each person participates and serves food into their dish at the amount and speed they wish. This extremely communal and individualistic metaphor can be used as the lens to appreciate the Gospel of Luke from Chinese perspectives.

Reading the Gospel of Luke as Chinese

THE COLLECTIVE MINDSET

Surrounding a hot 'steam boat' in the middle of a table in a home speaks of the collective mindset of Chinese culture. It is an important element of life shared collectively not only with their ancestors and later generations vertically, but also with their family clan, their state and the country horizontally.

Genealogy

Sharing a meal around a table shows the way that one is linked with both ancestors and with future generations as the person returns to the place of home. It can be a place that connects Chinese people with the past, present and future; hence meals are served not only with the existing family members but also in ancestor worship. Similar to Hebrew genealogies, Chinese family trees speak of the collective memory and life shared through the communal act of sharing a meal together.

In the Gospel of Luke, the Mediterranean culture that Jesus came to live in also demonstrates such high context collectiveness in its thinking. In Luke 3:23–38, Chinese eyes would take notice of the long record of Jesus's genealogy. The

---

13   S. Scott Bartchy, 'Table Fellowship', in *Dictionary of Jesus and the Gospels*, eds. Joel B. Green, Scot McKnight, and I. Howard Marshall (Downers Grove: InterVarsity Press, 1992), 796.

ontological quest for home goes deep into the genealogy of life in the Gospel. The Gospel writers Matthew and Luke show their concern with Jesus's relationship with the roots of humanity by taking into account details of his ancestral origin. Unlike Matthew, who begins with the genealogy of Jesus that descends from Abraham (Matt 1:1), Luke records the long genealogy that ascends from Jesus and traces back to the first man Adam—the human origin, the beginning of all races.[14]

The universality of Jesus's life is signified in Luke's genealogy of life. By going back to the origins of humanity, Luke, with his universalistic concern, intends to show that Jesus comes not only in human body and flesh for the nation of Israel, but also marks a new beginning for all humanity. 'Jesus' special status is a pledge and paradigm of the dignity intended by the Creator', as Brendan Byrne stresses, 'not merely for Israel but for the human race as a whole'.[15] The incarnation and the creation of humanity are deeply connected. In his life and ministry, Jesus purposely fulfils what is originally intended for the first Adam, that is a perfect relationship with God and other human beings. It is in this place that humanity finds the intended life-giving and life-flourishing home.

This would be good news indeed for those who do not have an honourable family line and for those who do not have that sense of place and belonging to a family. In my family genealogy, there are four ministers down the generational line. Together with four moral codes, they are regarded as a glorious family root that we trace, remember and pass onto the next generation. The elderly continue to tell the young about this collective past over table meals. For example, one of my ancestors, Yang Shi (杨时, 1053–1135), was a well-known neo-Confucian philosopher, writer and government minister in the Song dynasty. He started various schools and influenced the later Confucian scholars both domestic and abroad. Volumes of his books can still be found in the library of the University of Melbourne. This honourable genealogy, however, does not include any females, simply because they are not able to carry the family line, just as in Jewish tradition.

Jesus's genealogy in Luke would warm the heart of anyone born into the collective mindset and yet are not included or favoured in the family line. Jesus, born of the Virgin Mary, started a new humanity, in that everyone who responds to him is included and accepted equally in the family of God regardless of their gender, race, ethnicity or culture. In his life and ministry, he constantly embraced women, children, the poor and the marginalised into his family. With a strong

---

14 Joel B. Green, *The Gospel of Luke*, New International Commentary on the New Testament (Grand Rapids: Eerdmans, 1997); C. F. Evans, *Saint Luke*, TPI New Testament Commentaries (London: SCM Press, 1990).

15 Brendan Byrne, *The Hospitality of God: A Reading of Luke's Gospel* (Strathfield: St Pauls Publications, 2000), 41.

connection to the roots of the human race, Luke shows that Jesus is indeed the prototype of what humanity was created for. Jesus represents not only humanity but also a 'new humanity'.[16] Karl Barth shows that he is not only a true man but the true man.[17] This true man—the incarnated Christ—comes to the very world that is created by him and belongs to him. He opens a homecoming path for all people towards where humanity is created to be—a place of restoration, redemption and reconciliation. It is the place of home where Chinese can find their true identity and destiny through their collective identification with Jesus.

Family relationships

Chinese people not only connect with history vertically but also horizontally—they tend to think collectively and value the group and relationships with one another. For Chinese people, harmony and interdependence of the group, including their family or clan, can become the driving force of their decision-making. These major characteristics of harmony, interdependence and situation-centeredness form a collective Chinese identity and character. William Dudykunst and Stella Ting-Toomey define Chinese cultural characteristics as 'collectivism' and 'high context'.[18] In such a culture, people are seen as part of a network rather than as individuals. They rely on each other to save face for one another and for help to be offered.[19] The Chinese ethics of *Li* is expressed within five main relationships (五伦) of human life and society in Mencian tradition—between father and son, ruler and minister, husband and wife, old and young, and friends. The Chinese culture of *Li* can use meal tables as a place to build social networks and enhance relationships between family, neighbours and friends. *Li*, as a form of social ethics based on mutuality, is not self-seeking but is supported by a higher Doctrine of Means (中庸)—seeking the middle way and graciously allowing the other to make their move. To be a part of this human family is very important to Chinese in this collective culture. Yet, the corporate identity can be taken to an extreme in that people can lose the sense of individual identity, the courage for truth-telling, and also carry unnecessary burdens in order to be a part of the group. The corrupted

---

16   Daniel L. Migliore, *Faith Seeking Understanding: An Introduction to Christian Theology*, 2nd ed. (Grand Rapids: W. B. Eerdmans, 2004), 146.
17   Karl Barth, *Church Dogmatics: The Doctrine of Reconciliation*, vol. IV. 2, eds. Geoffrey W. Bromiley and Thomas F. Torrance, trans. Geoffrey W. Bromiley (Edinburgh: T&T Clark, 1958), 27.
18   William Gudykunst and Ting-Toomey Stella, *Culture and Interpersonal Communication* (Newburt Park: Sage, 1988), 43.
19   Maynor Clara Cheng, 'Missionary Wholeness', in *Chinese around the World*, vol. 174, ed. Chinese Coordination Centre of World Evangelism (Hong Kong: The Centre, 2000), 5.

self-seeking *Li* for personal gain is nothing but a hypocritical mask and therefore complicates social relationships.

From this context, Chinese would turn their ears towards Jesus's family and his relationship with them when reading Jesus's story in Luke's Gospel. Jesus identified himself with humanity by having a family of his own and experiencing life and death in the first-century Hebrew culture. Living within the Jewish communal tradition that honours family and community, he respected and honoured his earthly parents in obedience. He grew in wisdom and stature, and in favour with God and people (Luke 2:51–52). He became our true human brother.

Luke describes how Jesus gathers his people to a home in communion with God through faith. When his mother and brothers came to look for him during his ministry, Jesus redefines the meaning of a family: 'My mother and my brothers are those who hear the word of God and do it' (Luke 8:19–21). Again, when a woman in the crowd raised her voice to bless his earthly mother, Jesus repeated that true blessedness lies with those who 'hear the word of God and obey it' (Luke 11:27–28). Jesus's acceptance of people as part of his family is clearly articulated: that whoever does the will of the Father in heaven is his brother and sister and mother. These new members of the household of God will embrace each other as the same spiritual blood flows in their bodies.

The ultimate relational home is to be in communion with God, where the person and God are in fellowship. A new form of relationship is redefined in the family of God, centred on God's provision, power and love. This inclusive home takes no prejudice against one's social or economic status, racial background or gender. Luke emphasises the realised eschatology of the kingdom of God as a homecoming journey towards an inclusive community for both men and women, Jews and Gentiles, and for the strong and the weak. While there are some positive aspects of this culture of home in an agricultural society, the tendency of Chinese culture that values men before women, the old before the young, and the insider before the outsider is challenged by the gospel here.

Jesus is clear about the precedence of love towards one's family versus love towards God. Discipleship demands total abandonment of self, including one's own families. When a man asks to bury his father before following Jesus, Jesus says, 'Let the dead bury their own dead, but you go and proclaim the kingdom of God' (Luke 9:59–60). The kingdom of God takes precedence over all aspects of our lives including families. While affirming that marriage is God-ordained, Jesus never married and speaks of no marriage in heaven. This too would challenge Chinese people to let go of their important relationships and to set the kingdom of God as a priority in their lives.

From this biblical reading, it can be discerned that the grace of Jesus offers unconditional acceptance and love so that the ultimate relational home is with God. It challenges Chinese culture that regards gifts as earned and releases the unnecessary burden of any obligation of recipients to return favour. It also clearly articulates the kingdom value that takes precedence. Chinese Christians today exercise the love of Christ and the traditional *Li* in action, particularly in looking after the elderly and the disadvantaged rural regions where the traditional form of family is breaking down as a result of urbanisation.

While both Chinese and Hebrew cultures demonstrate such high context collectiveness in their thinking both vertically and horizontally, the gospel both affirms and challenges Chinese culture. Today's Western Christianity often presents its faith as a matter of individual decision and individual application. This hallmark of Western Christianity is described by Andrew F. Walls: 'Western thought developed a particular consciousness of the individual as a monad, independent of kin-related identity'.[20] This can be traced back to Friedrich Schleiermacher's *Christian Faith* and Karl Rahner's transcendental theology where individual self (in the language of 'heart' and 'existence') in relation to the inner experience of transcendence is explored deeply in modern soteriology.[21] Jackson Wu examines the uncritical assumption of the Western understanding of the gospel in terms of legal metaphors and centres upon an atomistic view of humanity as individuals.[22] This primacy of individual decision, absolutely crucial to the capture by Christ of other worldviews in Western Christianity, does not mean that the same points of reference apply in the collective Chinese culture.

The beauty of a 'steam boat' analogy is to allow one to preserve their individuality while keeping the corporate identity through the soup cooking in the centre, which symbolises the love of Christ. The biblical account provides a key for loving relationships through other-centred and self-giving sacrificial love. The oneness of the Godhead does not dilute, but instead preserves and strengthens the personality of the Father, of the Son and of the Spirit. It is both individual and corporate, both diverse and coherent, both vertical and horizontal. This trinity is

---

20   Andrew F. Walls, 'Culture and Coherence in Christian History', *Scottish Bulletin of Evangelical Theology* 3, no. 1 (1985): 5.

21   Jürgen Moltmann, *The Way of Jesus Christ: Christology in Messianic Dimensions*, trans. Margaret Kohl (London: SCM Press, 1990), 55–63. He makes the critique on the privatisation of the religion in the West and offers the social and political dimension in the understanding of soteriology.

22   Jackson Wu, *Saving God's Face: A Chinese Contextualization of Salvation through Honor and Shame* (Pasadena: William Carey International University Press, 2013).

not a closed system but an 'open-trinity',[23] which invites and embraces humanity to enter into a covenantal relationship.

In the Western world, the assertion of individual freedom has been taken to an extreme in that people can make individual choices regarding their own happiness and fulfilment without any respect towards higher values and causes. Without transcendental ideas, the postmodern 'means-without-an-end' can only lead to exploitation, competition and personal power. Contemporary Chinese continue to struggle with the Western influx of individualism and their own traditional collectivism; even the way to eat 'steam boat' has changed from sharing a common hot soup in the middle to eating individually from a small soup burner set before each person. The timeless symbol of 'steam boat' can reflect the shift in the way of thinking from collectivism to individualism.

HARMONY AT THE CORE

The hot 'steam boat' is very popular in the winter season, for it warms the body and the heart. One of the keys is to make sure that the heat of the cooked food is balanced with something 'cold', to achieve the harmony of Yin and Yang within one's body. For example, one should have a cold drink like herbal tea to cool down the heat of the body. The soup pot divided into the plain and the chilli sections is called a twin-sided 'steam boat' (*yuanyang huoguo*, 鸳鸯火锅, literally meaning a couple of mandarin ducks—both male and female ducks). Sometimes the shape of the two sides is made as a Daoist Yin–Yang divide, symbolising the harmony of the eating custom. Participants also cook the ingredients with the hot soup in the centre and add any sauce they wish. The goal is not just to fill the belly, but also to achieve some kind of health and wellbeing.

Harmony through the correlation of Yin and Yang has long been regarded as the core of all things in Chinese tradition. Unlike the Western approach of segregation and demarcation of the 'soul/body' under the influence of Hellenism, ancient Chinese regard the soul as an integral part of the Yin and Yang, harmony, health and wellbeing.[24] Laozi says, 'Everything in the universe is born out of being. Being is born out of non-being' (天下万物生于有，有生于无).[25] He continues, 'The Dao gives birth to One, One gives birth to Two, Two gives birth to Three, Three gives birth to the myriad of things. Everything bears yin and embraces yang. The balance of yin and yang produces harmony' (道生一，一生二，二生三，

---

23   Jürgen Moltmann, *The Trinity and the Kingdom: The Doctrine of God* (Minneapolis, MN: Fortress Press, 1993), 94.

24   'Huangdi Neijing, Ling Shu Jing, Benshen'. In *Zhuzi Baijia*, http://ctext.org/huangdi-neijing/ben-shen/ens, 2–3; Confucius, 'Liji, Jiaotesheng', http://ctext.org/liji/jiao-te-sheng/zh, 36.

25   Laozi, 'Dao De Jing', 40.

三生万物。万物负阴而抱阳，冲气以为和).²⁶ The purpose is to achieve unity of heaven and earth and Yin–Yang harmony.

Since ancient times, Chinese have consistently sought to define a similar harmonious home through the pairing of Yin and Yang. Humanity is understood not as an individual entity, but through the coexistence and harmony of Yin and Yang. The simple pair of life is not just male and female, but the creative tension of all things in which all human origins and dignities are summarised and have emerged out of the Creator-like and the mother-like Dao.

The terms 'home' and 'family' in the Chinese language have the same character *Jia* (家). This linguistic point shows a broader ethical implication. Home is not about the physical place but the ontological relationship. As Confucius thinks, life starts from one's heart, then family, community and state. Homecoming is the return to one's own heart, which seeks the truth of life with genuineness and sincerity, in connection with the idea of heaven (天). The highest good for Confucians is 'Heaven and person becoming one' (天人合一) through Yin–Yang harmony.

While many contextual theologians explore the concept of Chinese Dao in connection with the Greek logos (John 1:1), the reading of the Gospel of Luke with Chinese eyes sheds new light. The Yin–Yang concept can help Chinese to understand the two-nature Christ, that is, he is fully human and fully divine. While the monistic unity between heaven and humanity that Chinese traditions hold cannot be reconciled with the Christian Creator-creature distinction, Paulos Zhanzhu Huang offers that a proper understanding of the image of God in humanity as relational, rather than substantial, may help to bridge this gap.[27] While Adam, as the 'Son of God' (Luke 3:38), disobeyed God and lost the relationship with God in the garden of the first home, Jesus, as the 'Son of Man', demonstrated a perfect relationship with God and other human beings. He was in flesh and blood like us, with physical limitations and needs (Luke 2:40–52; John 4:6; 19:28; Matt 21:18; Heb 2:14). He experienced all forms of emotion (Luke 10:21; 7:9; 19:41) and was tempted in every way (Luke 4). But he remained faithful till death—'Father, into your hands I commend my spirit' (Luke 23:46). He can be perceived as 'the first Dao' and 'the perfect Confucian sage', not as a creative energy or principle from below, but rather a personified, relational and speaking God from above who is the source of all creation.

---

26   Laozi, 'Dao De Jing', 42.

27   Paulos Zhanzhu Huang, *Confronting Confucian Understandings of the Christian Doctrine of Salvation: A Systematic Theological Analysis of the Basic Problems in the Confucian–Christian Dialogue* (Leiden: Brill, 2009). He particularly focuses on Confucian–Christian dialogue.

Luke lives in a cross-cultural setting of the first-century Hellenistic world. He demonstrates that Jesus ushers in the kingdom of God that he proclaims and embodies in order to bring harmony between humans and God. At the beginning of his ministry, Jesus's Nazareth manifesto (Luke 4:18) portrays a home of welcome and acceptance especially to the marginalised and oppressed, so that they can find freedom, healing and transformation in the new home of God.

As an educated person who is familiar with both Jewish Scripture and Graeco-Roman literary form, Luke portrays Jesus taking a journey by going up to Jerusalem (Luke 9 to 19). The journey narrative, however, is not about physical progress or arrival, but ongoing experience of the kingdom of God here and now. Jesus's journey is filled with hardship but with the clear purpose of proclaiming and embodying the kingdom of God. He not only demonstrates voluntary powerlessness as the way to grasp reality, he also takes a necessary, downward and controversial journey by way of the cross to show love, truth, justice and peace to his contemporaries. In order to show the divine necessity to be with the poor and care for humanity, Luke is fond of using the Greek term ἔδει, meaning 'it was necessary/binding' or 'must'. It was repeatedly used in Luke-Acts forty-one times out of 102 times in the whole of the New Testament.[28] Jesus's resolution and determination to head towards Jerusalem ('set his face', 9:51) can also be found in the Old Testament prophets.[29] Clearly, Jesus's journey is filled with controversies and hardship, but his resolution is rooted in fulfilling the divine will.[30]

As Jesus embodies the kingdom of God in the way of the cross, he calls for a radical path of brokenness for his disciples. He challenges his followers with the radical abandonment of family (Luke 12:49–53; 14:26; 18:28–30), material goods (Luke 9:3; 10:4; 12:22–23; 14:33; 18:22) and security (Luke 9:24; 12:22–23). This transition is against the natural human tendency to climb the ladder and grab things for one's own needs. The way of brokenness is to deny oneself and carry the cross, following a downward journey with Jesus. In doing so, a new family is created and redefined by the relationship of brotherhood and sisterhood in the kingdom of God.

Reading the suffering and broken way of life in the journey narrative would resonate with Chinese people whose nation has suffered from civil wars, national upheavals and foreign invasion, especially over the last one hundred years. As suffering through Yin–Yang struggles is necessary for one to achieve harmony,

---

28 Earl Richard, *Jesus, One and Many: The Christological Concept of New Testament Authors* (Wilmington: M. Glazier, 1988), 183; To understand the term on a large scale, see John T. Squires, *The Plan of God in Luke-Acts*, Monograph Series (Society for New Testament Studies) 76 (Cambridge: Cambridge University Press, 1993).

29 Jer 21:10; Ezek 6:2; 13:17; 14:8; 15:7; 20:46; 21:2; 25:2; 28:21; 29:2; 38:2.

30 Craig A. Evans, *Luke*, New International Biblical Commentary (Peabody: Hendrickson, 1990), 435.

Jesus could be viewed as the Yang and humanity as the Yin from a Chinese lens. However, from a Christian perspective, the infinite Creator God differs from the finite creature made in the image of God. The understanding of Yin–Yang interaction nevertheless enhances the organic and intimate relationship between God and humanity. The mutuality of the Yin–Yang relationship expresses the need for the other as a complementary part to bring completion and harmony, just as God is in need of humans and humans are in need of God for relationships. Jesus can be understood as the dot of humanity and the dot of divinity, just as Yang has a dot in Yin and Yin has a dot in Yang.[31] Khiok-Khng Yeo asserts that 'through that interaction, the Yin and the Yang are differentiated. In other words, the imago Dei lies within the interpersonal relationship that exists among human(s)'.[32] The Chinese Yin–Yang harmony can be used to understand the relationship between God and humanity. This driving force of the kingdom value becomes the pillar of spirals in the Yin–Yang struggle that brings unity out of diversity.

The Sino mind values the harmony of Yin and Yang—the union of male and female, and then extends to the relationship between parents and children, and to the relationship between brothers and sisters. 'Blood is thicker than water' (血浓于水). Harmony in a home is the key to the prosperity of a nation. 'When a home is in harmony, all affairs will prosper' (家和万事兴), says a Chinese proverb. In this honour and shame culture, Chinese believe that domestic shame should not be made public (家丑不可外扬), as in the English expression, 'Do not wash your dirty linen in public'. Chinese history has shown that for the sake of preserving harmony, a distorted tradition of filial piety becomes an unnecessary obligatory burden for the children of a family. The extreme forms of filial piety and rank, resulting in the practice of ancestor worship, are hindrances to the worship of the one true God. The desire to maintain 'face' with the elderly or people with high status prevents one from expressing truth in unreserved humility. In the same way that Jesus embodies the kingdom of God and challenges the honour and shame culture of the Mediterranean world, he makes an appeal to the Chinese worldview of 'saving one's face' and introduces what it really means to be honourable. It is in the way of the cross and the way of brokenness, through denying oneself and living for God and others. Jesus's countercultural call poses a challenge to the proud, the self-righteous, the rich and those who are spiritually blind, but in actual fact reinforces kingdom values and purpose. Evans calls this 'the gospel paradox in its extreme form'.[33] For Chinese, Christ is best

---

31   Khiok-Khng Yeo, *What Has Jerusalem to Do with Beijing?: Biblical Interpretation from a Chinese Perspective* (Harrisburg: Trinity Press International, 1998), 60.
32   Yeo, *What Has Jerusalem to Do with Beijing?*, 62.
33   Evans, *Saint Luke*, 570.

presented as 'both the shame-bearer for sinners and honour-winner for believers'.[34] The honour and authority of Christ are given in his humble choosing of the lowly place as the servant of all, not in any given status or age. We should seek to have the 'face' of Christ rather than maintaining our 'face'. The 'face' of Christ is reflected in the kingdom of God that he brings; that is to serve and not to be served, even to the cross.

What would it be like if a 'steam boat' in the centre symbolises the upside-down kingdom of God? The self-giving sacrificial love of Christ warms the heart and permeates the ingredients that each person needs and dips into. It is an invitation to break open ready for service. The call for brokenness brings transformation, not for the simple mix of Yin–Yang balance and wellbeing, but a true harmony— shalom of wholeness with God and with humans in relationships.

Hospitality

A 'steam boat' meal is treated as a delicacy and is used to entertain guests. The communalism of Chinese culture expressed in their table fellowship enhances the building of relationships and the fostering of bonds within the community. For without community, life becomes 'rootless, homeless, anchorless'.[35] However, such a bond can create clannishness, nationalism and other forms of exclusiveness.

The etymological root of hospitality in English is 'host' and suggests that the host's identity is connected to a home. The idea of home embodies the identity of the host and an obligation to care for strangers. Derrida raises the probing question of whether our hospitality arises out of a sense of home—either from the security of our own home or the experience of homelessness and displacement.[36] John Koenig denotes that *philoxenia*, the Greek term for hospitality, refers not to a love of strangers, but to 'a delight in the whole guest-host relationship, in the mysterious reversals and gains for all parties'.[37] This in-depth exploration of the host/stranger relationship in the Western scholarship on hospitality deepens what is already understood in Chinese tradition from the etymologies shown earlier.

Chinese culture bears a striking resemblance to ancient and modern Jewish culture that places much emphasis on hospitality around eating and table fellowship. The Chinese mind would immediately pay attention to the many table

---

34 Enoch Wan, 'Practical Contextualization: A Case Study of Evangelising Contemporary Chinese', *Chinese Around the World*, no. 173 (2000): 21.
35 Choan-Seng Song, *Theology from the Womb of Asia* (Maryknoll: Orbis Books, 1986), 123.
36 Jacques Derrida and Anne Dufourmantelle, *Of Hospitality*, Cultural Memory in the Present (Stanford: Stanford University Press, 2000).
37 John Koenig, *New Testament Hospitality: Partnership with Strangers as Promise and Mission*, Overtures to Biblical Theology 17 (Philadelphia: Fortress Press, 1985), 8.

meals recorded in Luke where hospitality is offered by people, yet Jesus turns out to be the host at the table in many incidents.

In Jewish culture, table meals express the social relationship of inclusiveness, equality and mutuality, either for the purpose of friendship, reconciliation, honour or reciprocity. Eating together implies sharing a common set of ideas and values. In table fellowship, one shares his or her life and the blessing of God over the food with others. James D. G. Dunn summarises well that 'in the sharing of everyday food that is blessed before God, human relationships can become an expression of the more fundamental divine-human relationship'.[38] Moreover, hospitality plays an important role in the religious and daily life of first-century Jews. Judaism treats the Sabbath as one of its religious institutions, which is originally set for humans, and hospitality as part of the observance of the Sabbath is practised on the day. The evening meal on the Sabbath is considered to be a time of opening one's home to others.[39] A virtuous Jew would open his house to the poor and the needy.[40]

Influenced by both Jewish tradition and the Greek-Roman symposium culture, Luke records many incidents in meal settings. 'Almost every chapter in Luke has some mention of eating.'[41] This is important remembering that Luke's Gospel is written for the Gentiles and their inclusion in the kingdom. John Koenig thinks that all of the dimensions of hospitality in human life find a place in the New Testament.[42] It is often a banquet in the Bible that is used as an analogy of the coming kingdom. Karris states that Jesus is killed because of the way he

---

38 James D. G. Dunn, 'Jesus, Table-Fellowship, and Qumran', in *Jesus and the Dead Sea Scrolls*, ed. James H. Charlesworth (New York: Doubleday, 1992), 254–55; Joachim Jeremias, *New Testament Theology*, New Testament Library (London: S .C. M. Press, 1971), 115: He states that to invite a man to a meal is an honour, an offer of peace, trust, brotherhood and forgiveness. Sharing a table meant sharing life. In Judaism, table fellowship meant fellowship before God, for the eating of a piece of broken bread by everyone who shared in the meal brings out the fact that they all have a share in the blessing which the master of the house had spoken over the unbroken bread.

39 Darrell L. Bock, *Luke*, 2 vols., Baker Exegetical Commentary on the New Testament (Grand Rapids: Baker Books, 1994), 1256. The Jews customarily had two meals a day but observed three meals on the Sabbath. Guests were invited after the synagogue service around midday to the Sabbath meal, which was prepared the day before and kept warm to avoid breaking the Sabbath (m, Shab 3:1–6; 4:1–2).

40 Koenig, *New Testament Hospitality*, 16–17. For example, the woman who 'had lived a sinful life' can have access to a Pharisee's house (7:36–38).

41 Snodgrass Klyne, 'Common Life with Jesus: The Parable of the Banquet in Luke 14:16–24', in *Common Life in the Early Church: Essays Honoring Graydon F. Snyder*, eds. Julian Victor Hills, Richard B. Gardner, and Graydon F. Snyder (Harrisburg: Trinity Press International, 1998), 186.

42 Koenig, *New Testament Hospitality*, 2.

eats—he associates himself with sinners.[43] Jesus treats meals as times of special sanctity where people from all walks of life could find their true humanity in the presence of God.

The table fellowship of Jesus is used to speak about the inclusion of the marginalised, for example, the prodigal son (Luke 15:11–32), the great banquet (Luke 14:1–14) and the conversion story of Zacchaeus (Luke 19:1–10). Table fellowship becomes the context in which the sharp contrast between the radical inclusiveness of Jesus's ministry and exclusiveness demanded by his opponents is displayed. The table fellowship of Jesus at the banquet is a miniature expression of God's unconditional love for the poor and the outcast. As the host of the table, Jesus attacks the elitist attitudes of the Pharisees who are concerned primarily with status and mutual hospitality, which excluded the poor, the disabled, and the so-called 'sinners'. By doing so, they reveal their own assumptions that these people are already excluded from God's kingdom. Jesus's parable reinforces not only the need for humility exemplified by himself as the servant king but also God's desire for the inclusion of all at his kingdom banquet. He also warns his hearers that they could lose their own place if they continue to take their invitation for granted. Jewish table fellowship, which was meant to symbolise communal equity and love, had deteriorated. Although there were still many positive features, the heart attitude had been lost and as an eschatological symbol, it had also lost its power. Jesus seeks to reverse the honour and shame culture, once again through his own servant attitude. As the king who would serve to the point of death, he not only challenges the existing presuppositions but also points to a radical change of values, that is, to kingdom values, which are to be manifested in his church.

As Jesus radically challenges the Jewish religious presuppositions and the conventional Graeco-Roman traditions of table fellowship and reverses the honour and shame culture of the Mediterranean world, he too challenges Chinese tradition that limits the hospitality to people of similar social status, ranks or business dealings. Table fellowship is used not only to foster existing community bonds but is also used by Jesus to welcome the lost and the marginalised. He not only is present and relates to his contemporaries at the table but also lives out the parables through his life, ministry and death on the cross. The closed door of a home in Chinese culture needs to be wide open to outsiders, therefore creating an inclusive community of God by imitating Jesus who extends hospitality to the lost and forgotten ones. The inward-looking mentality within one's comfort zone needs to be challenged to be radically open to strangers. More so, the constant movement of guest/host reversal towards the centre place opens up new spaces

---

43 Robert J. Karris, *Luke, Artist and Theologian: Luke's Passion Account as Literature* (Mahwah: Paulist Press, 1985), 70.

that allow mutually enriching experience, as well as a new home that transcends time and place.[44] Each person becomes both the guest and the host; each is affirmed to be free to be the other while empowered through mutuality and reciprocity. This newly articulated place challenges our constructed presuppositions through intentional hospitality and demands an ongoing inner movement from a place of comfort to a deepened and renewed self.

The Chinese relational approach, which centres on the table, can in practice be more effective through their inclusion of outsiders in the new community grounded in relational loving hospitality. The 'steam boat', the rich cultural heritage that has been practised for so long, can be used to 'break open' the closed door and self-preserved idea of home in Chinese traditional understanding. It can be a place for hospitality and for the inclusion of the forgotten, the lonely and the lost in our time. With the 'steam boat' analogy, it would be easier for Chinese people living in a 'high context' culture to grasp in comparison to Westerners living in individualistic contexts. This is especially relevant in our technological culture where fast food and smartphones occupy this essential space for conversations and hospitality.

Conclusion

Drawing on the symbol of 'steam boat', this chapter has attempted to develop a potential Chinese theology of home. The ancient Chinese characters reveal that the cultural foundation of home is where a family within a closed wall under the same roof shares food and provides hospitality. Following this cultural premise, the chapter further emphasises the important role of table meals, especially the 'steam boat', in Chinese tradition. While suggesting that sitting around and eating from a 'steam boat' in the centre of a table symbolises the underlying Chinese worldview of a collective mindset, harmony at the core and hospitality, it explores the way of reading the Gospel of Luke within these worldviews. Jesus's inclusive ministry to the marginalised, reversal of the accepted cultural customs and call for radical discipleship both affirm and challenge the traditional Chinese culture. The kingdom values affirm certain aspects of Chinese collective mindset but also challenge its potential for avoiding truthtelling and of extreme forms of filial piety or ancestor worship. Sharing a similar goal to reach harmony, the kingdom of God offers the way of the cross and brokenness to reverse the honour and shame culture. Having a rich cultural tradition of hospitality, the inward-looking closed

---

44 Henri J. M. Nouwen, *Reaching Out: The Three Movements of the Spiritual Life*, 1st ed. (London: Collins, 1976), 47; Parker J. Palmer, *The Company of Strangers: Christians and the Renewal of America's Public Life* (New York: Crossroad, 1981), 65.

door of Chinese home culture needs to be broken open to strangers and to the poor, especially those who are not of a similar social status or are not able to reciprocate.

In contrast to the emphasis on the doctrine of 'justification by faith' as expressed in Romans and Galatians, and common to the Protestant Reformation tradition, the gospel can focus on family, honour, harmony and relationship, which are at the core of the traditional Chinese culture of home. For the eating culture of 'steam boat' that values honour and shame, hospitality and community can become the very place where the church can show what it means to become a home of true belonging. It is a place centred in the love of Christ (the steam boat in the centre) that warms the body and the heart through the way of brokenness, a place that includes people equally regardless of their gender, race and ethnicity, a place that affirms both corporate and individual identities, a place of hospitality that welcomes strangers and outsiders. In doing so, the joy of sharing a 'steam boat' can extend to the Eucharist, becoming a foretaste of a future heavenly banquet. The 'steam boat' meal becomes an image of union between human beings, and between human beings and God. The message of the gospel is therefore 'transformed, yet recognisable' in the Chinese home culture.

BIBLIOGRAPHY

Bartchy, S. Scott. 'Table Fellowship.' In *Dictionary of Jesus and the Gospels*, edited by Joel B. Green, Scot McKnight, and I. Howard Marshall. Downers Grove: InterVarsity Press, 1992.

Barth, Karl. *Church Dogmatics: The Doctrine of Reconciliation*. Vol. IV. 2. Translated by Geoffrey W. Bromiley. Edited by Geoffrey W. Bromiley and Thomas F. Torrance. Edinburgh: T&T Clark, 1958.

Bock, Darrell L. *Luke*. 2 vols. Baker Exegetical Commentary on the New Testament. Grand Rapids: Baker Books, 1994.

Byrne, Brendan. *The Hospitality of God: A Reading of Luke's Gospel*. Strathfield: St Pauls Publications, 2000.

Cao, Xueqin, 曹雪芹. 'Dream of Red Mansions.' http://zhidao.baidu.com/question/30114242.html. Accessed October 2, 2009.

Cheng, Maynor Clara. 'Missionary Wholeness.' In *Chinese around the World*, vol. 174, edited by Chinese Coordination Centre of World Evangelism, 3–7. Hong Kong: The Centre, 2000.

Confucius. 'Liji, Jiaotesheng.' http://ctext.org/liji/jiao-te-sheng/zh.

Confucius. 'Liji, Li Yun.' http://ctext.org/liji/li-yun - n11484.

Derrida, Jacques, and Anne Dufourmantelle. *Of Hospitality, Cultural Memory in the Present*. Stanford: Stanford University Press, 2000.

The Dictionary of Han Language. 's.v. 客 (Ke).' http://www.zdic.net/z/18/zy/5BA2.htm. Accessed November 11, 2013.

The Dictionary of Han Language. 's.v. 家 (Jia).' http://www.zdic.net/z/18/js/5BB6.htm.

The Dictionary of Han Language. 's.v. 乡 (Xiang).' http://www.zdic.net/z/15/zy/4E61.htm. Accessed November 11, 2013.

The Dictionary of Han Language. 's.v. 阖 (He).' http://www.zdic.net/z/27/zy/9616.htm. Accessed February 15, 2013.

Dunn, James D. G. 'Jesus, Table-Fellowship, and Qumran.' In *Jesus and the Dead Sea Scrolls*, edited by James H. Charlesworth. New York: Doubleday, 1992.

Evans, C. F. *Saint Luke*. TPI New Testament Commentaries. London: SCM Press, 1990.

Evans, Craig A. *Luke*. New International Biblical Commentary. Peabody: Hendrickson, 1990.

Green, Joel B. *The Gospel of Luke*. New International Commentary on the New Testament. Grand Rapids: Eerdmans, 1997.

Gudykunst, William, and Ting-Toomey Stella. *Culture and Interpersonal Communication*. Newburt Park: Sage, 1988.

Huang, Paulos Zhanzhu. *Confronting Confucian Understandings of the Christian Doctrine of Salvation: A Systematic Theological Analysis of the Basic Problems in the Confucian–Christian Dialogue*. Leiden: Brill, 2009.

'Huangdi Neijing, Ling Shu Jing, Benshen.' In *Zhuzi Baijia*.

Jeremias, Joachim. *New Testament Theology*. New Testament Library, London: S. C. M. Press, 1971.

Ji, Xiang-Xiang, and Qian-Hua Wu. 'Chinese Food in Western Missionaries Eyes of the Ming and Qing Dynasties' (明清之际入华宣教士眼中的中国食物). *Keep Memories of Ancestors' Tables—The Proceedings of 2011 Asian Food Cultural Heritage Forum* (2011): 388–420.

Karris, Robert J. *Luke, Artist and Theologian: Luke's Passion Account as Literature.* Mahwah: Paulist Press, 1985.

Klyne, Snodgrass. 'Common Life with Jesus: The Parable of the Banquet in Luke 14:16–24.' In *Common Life in the Early Church: Essays Honoring Graydon F. Snyder*, edited by Julian Victor Hills, Richard B. Gardner, and Graydon F. Snyder, xxx. Harrisburg: Trinity Press International, 1998.

Koenig, John. *New Testament Hospitality: Partnership with Strangers as Promise and Mission.* Overtures to Biblical Theology 17. Philadelphia: Fortress Press, 1985.

Laozi, 老子. 'Dao De Jing.' http://ctext.org/dao-de-jing.

Migliore, Daniel L. *Faith Seeking Understanding: An Introduction to Christian Theology.* 2nd ed. Grand Rapids: W. B. Eerdmans, 2004.

Moltmann, Jürgen. *The Trinity and the Kingdom: The Doctrine of God.* Minneapolis, MN: Fortress Press, 1993.

Moltmann, Jürgen. *The Way of Jesus Christ: Christology in Messianic Dimensions.* Translated by Margaret Kohl. London: SCM Press, 1990.

Neyrey, Jerome H. 'Ceremonies in Luke-Acts.' In *The Social World of Luke-Acts: Models for Interpretation*, edited by Jerome H. Neyrey. Peabody: Hendrickson Publishers, 1991.

Nouwen, Henri J. M. *Reaching Out: The Three Movements of the Spiritual Life.* 1st ed. London: Collins, 1976.

Palmer, Parker J. *The Company of Strangers: Christians and the Renewal of America's Public Life.* New York: Crossroad, 1981.

Reinhartz, Adele. 'Reflections on Table Fellowship and Community Identity.' *Semeia* 86 (1999): 227–33.

Richard, Earl. *Jesus, One and Many: The Christological Concept of New Testament Authors.* Wilmington: M. Glazier, 1988.

Smith, Dennis E. 'Table Fellowship as a Literary Motif in the Gospel of Luke.' *Journal of Biblical Literature* 106, no. 4 (1987): 613–38.

Song, Choan-Seng. *Theology from the Womb of Asia.* Maryknoll: Orbis Books, 1986.

Squires, John T. *The Plan of God in Luke-Acts.* Monograph Series (Society for New Testament Studies) 76. Cambridge: Cambridge University Press, 1993.

Walls, Andrew F. 'Culture and Coherence in Christian History.' *Scottish Bulletin of Evangelical Theology* 3, no. 1 (1985): 1–9.

Wan, Enoch. 'Practical Contextualization: A Case Study of Evangelising Contemporary Chinese.' *Chinese Around the World*, no. 173 (2000): 18–24.

Wu, Jackson. *Saving God's Face: A Chinese Contextualization of Salvation through Honor and Shame.* Pasadena: William Carey International University Press, 2013.

Yang, Xiaoli. *A Dialogue between Haizi's Poetry and the Gospel of Luke—Chinese Homecoming and the Relationship with Jesus Christ, Theology and Mission in World Christianity.* Leiden: Brill, 2018.

Yeo, Khiok-Khng. *What Has Jerusalem to Do with Beijing?: Biblical Interpretation from a Chinese Perspective.* Harrisburg: Trinity Press International, 1998.

Chapter 15

THE LORD'S HOME IN ISAIAH

Eleonora Scott

My first interest in Jesus as a young child was a result of learning that Jesus was preparing a place for his followers in his Father's house so that we could be with him forever. That passage in John 14 made me realise that this was indeed the desire of my heart—to be with Jesus always and to find my home with God. The concept of God dwelling with humanity of course begins with Adam and Eve in Genesis, and is the promised destiny of those who remain faithful to God, as expressed in Revelation 21:3, when John records the words he hears in God's throne room, 'See, the home of God is among mortals. He will dwell with them; they will be his peoples, and God himself will be with them'.[1]

I've always found it astonishing that God invites humans into his home and chooses to dwell with people. What an amazing privilege and blessing to live with God. So, I mourn with the Lord as I read canonical Isaiah, because God's desire to dwell with his people is so clear and yet seems to be so disregarded and disrespected by his covenant family.

Throughout much of the Old Testament, the home of God is physically represented by the temple on Mount Zion in Jerusalem and underlies the notion of God's family, the children of Israel. This is true in Isaiah also, though throughout Isaiah, God's home is under threat from within and without.

---

[1] Scripture references are from the *New Revised Standard Version* unless otherwise noted.

In the Hebrew language of the Old Testament, the term בַּיִת *(bayith)* is used for 'house', 'home' and even family. This term is preferred in the book of Isaiah over the other specific Hebrew words for temple, including מִקְדָּשׁ *(miqddash)*, 'temple or sanctuary', and הֵיכָל *(heycal)*, 'temple or palace'. While these are used only a few times in Isaiah, the term 'house of the Lord' is used more often. This is significant because as Motyer correctly observes, '"temple" is primarily a place for worship; a "house" is primarily where the Lord has come to live among his people (cf. Exod 29:42–46)'.[2] Therefore, I think Isaiah's preference for the phrase 'home of the Lord' probably points to the intimate relationship God desires to have with his people. Other terms in Isaiah associated specifically with the Lord's house include הַר *(har)* mountain, צִיּוֹן Zion, יְרוּשָׁלִַם Jerusalem, Judah יְהוּדָה and לְאַרְצִי Israel. So every time these words appear in Isaiah, we must keep in mind the Lord's home.

I've traced these terms throughout the book of Isaiah in order, firstly, to examine the characteristics of the Lord's home in canonical Isaiah; secondly, to demonstrate the ways the Lord no longer feels at home in Israel; thirdly, to explore the Lord's willingness to continue to make a home among his people despite their sin and imminent exile; and finally, to extrapolate principles relevant for church and mission today. While it would be difficult to sufficiently cover every aspect of the Lord's home in Isaiah, I will here attempt to highlight and summarise what I think is particularly significant.

The Characteristics of the Lord's Home in Isaiah

So, firstly, what are the characteristics of the Lord's home in Isaiah?

In ancient Near Eastern cultures, including Israel, mountains were typically considered the sacred realm of deities.[3] Temples were built in sacred places to provide a spirit house in the dwelling place of the deity.[4] Israel follows this practice, although they knew historically that God's glorious presence, or כָּבוֹד was not limited to a particular place, but spilled out into the world. Israel historically understood that God created the whole world and walked with Adam and Eve in the garden of Eden (Gen 1–3), appeared to Moses in a burning bush and at Mount

---

2 J. Alec Motyer, *Isaiah: An Introduction and Commentary*, vol. 20, Tyndale Old Testament Commentaries (Downers Grove, IL: InterVarsity Press, 1999), 58–59. See also John D. W. Watts, *Isaiah 1–33*, vol. 24, Word Biblical Commentary (Dallas: Word, Incorporated, 1998), 28.

3 Motyer, *Isaiah: An Introduction and Commentary*, 58–59. See also, D. Brent Sandy, 'Mountain Imagery', in *Dictionary of the Old Testament: Prophets*, eds. Mark J. Boda and Gordon J. McConville (Downers Grove, IL; Nottingham, England: IVP Academic; InterVarsity Press, 2012), 556.

4 P. P. Jenson, 'Temple', in *Dictionary of the Old Testament: Prophets*, 769.

Sinai (Exod 3, 19, 24, 31, 34), and led Israel through the wilderness wanderings (Exod 14; Num 14; Deut 5). When Solomon eventually builds the Lord's temple in Jerusalem, he prays, 'But will God indeed dwell on the earth? Even heaven and the highest heaven cannot contain you, much less this house that I have built!' (1 Kings 8:27).

Certainly, also in Isaiah, the Lord's home is not confined to the physical temple. For example, the Lord declares in Isaiah 66:1, 'Heaven is my home and the earth is my footstool. Where is a house you could build to contain me?' Also, the vision in Isaiah 6 indicates that the Lord's home extends well beyond the physical temple, for in this vision God is way too big for his home—just the hem of his robe fills the temple (Isa 6:1). Therefore it is reasonable to conclude that at least some of Israel had a sense that the Lord's home extended beyond Jerusalem.

Nonetheless, in Isaiah, the physical home of the Lord is typically understood as the Jerusalem mountain temple, which is often referred to in Isaiah as Zion. So, for example, Isaiah 8:18 declares that the Lord of hosts dwells on Mount Zion. Throughout Isaiah there are many references to 'the Lord's mountain', meaning the temple, the place where God's presence is made known to Israel, where he lives in their midst (Isa 12:6).

This mountain, or Zion, is described in Isaiah as an exalted and high place, stressing that God is a great and awesome God who deserves to be glorified, especially in his home (cf. Isa 2:1; 8:14; 12:6; 33:5; 52:7). The Lord's home is to be so exalted that any others priding themselves above it will be punished (Isa 2:11–19; 10:12; 24:21–23; 25:9–12; 42:8–17). Such a lofty home is characterised by high values.

The Lord's home as a place of instruction

In Isaiah chapter 2, Isaiah describes a beautiful eschatological vision of the nations coming to the mountain of the Lord's temple in order to worship the Lord and learn from him so they can follow his ways (Isa 2:2–4; cf. Isa 16:1; 18:7; 19:19–25; 27:13; 28:29; 48:17–18).

> In days to come the mountain of the Lord's house
> shall be established as the highest of the mountains,
> and shall be raised above the hills;
> all the nations shall stream to it.
> Many peoples shall come and say,
> 'Come, let us go up to the mountain of the Lord,
> to the house of the God of Jacob;
> that he may teach us his ways and that we may walk in his paths'.

> For out of Zion shall go forth instruction,
> and the word of the Lord from Jerusalem.
> He shall judge between the nations, and shall arbitrate for
> many peoples;
> they shall beat their swords into plowshares, and their spears into
> pruning hooks;
> nation shall not lift up sword against nation, neither shall they learn
> war any more (Isaiah 2:2–4).

It is significant that in Isaiah's depictions of the Lord's home, it is not primarily the physical characteristics that are in focus, but rather the functional and moral characteristics of the Lord's home that are emphasised. So, in Isaiah's vision in chapter two, the Lord's home is the place where God's Word is heard and all are welcome to learn from the Lord. The temple is to be an educational centre where life-giving instruction flows out from it to fill the land.

Furthermore, the result of coming to the Lord's house is peace. For instead of learning war, the nations learn from the Lord—and the implication is that the Lord will teach them his ways of righteousness and peace (cf. Isa 48:18; 54:13). When the world is filled with people who know the Lord, God promises that then 'nothing will hurt or destroy in all my holy mountain' (Isa 11:1). The peace of the Lord has cosmic significance as all creation is renewed by God's Spirit of wisdom and understanding (Isa 11:1–9).

The Lord's home as a refuge

The Lord's home in Isaiah is indeed a refuge of peace, prayer and security (Isa 11:9; 33:6; 52:7; 57:13). So, for example, in Isaiah chapter 37, when King Hezekiah of Judah hears the threats made by the king of Assyria, he goes to the house of the Lord to seek help. The Lord hears Hezekiah's prayer and answers. And for a time, Judah is kept safe as the king of Assyria is suddenly called away and leaves them in peace. God's needy people who put their trust in the Lord will find refuge in the Lord's home (Isa 14:32; 25:4–6; 28:16).

Furthermore, in Isaiah, the Lord's home is a place of prayer that includes all nations and people who are willing to join themselves to the Lord and his family. In Isaiah 2:2–4, the nations stream to the Lord's home, praying that the Lord will teach them his ways. Likewise, the Lord promises in Isaiah 56:7 that foreigners who commit themselves to him will be brought to his holy mountain to rejoice in his house of prayer. God calls his home a house of prayer for all nations, all peoples (Isa 56:7). The Lord promises to adopt into his family home even those nations who oppress Israel, when those nations worship the Lord God by bringing their offerings, sacrifices, vows, pleas and prayers to God (Isa 19:19–25).

The Lord's home as filled with justice, righteousness and holiness

In addition to being a home of instruction, peace, prayer and security, the Lord's home in Isaiah is also filled with justice and righteousness. As Isaiah 33:5 says, 'The Lord is exalted, he dwells on high; he has filled Zion with justice and righteousness' (cf. Isa 45:19–25; 46:13; 50:8; 51:5–8; 56:1; 61:8; 62:1–7). This justice and righteousness will be established by the Messiah King who rules from Jerusalem on the throne of Mount Zion (the Lord's home) according to God's ways—defending the poor and eagerly doing what is right (Isa 9:6–7; 11:4–5; 16:5). Yet also there is a sense in which this justice and righteousness is readily available to all who seek the Lord's help and are willing to heed his teaching, for the Lord himself promises to instruct them (Isa 30:18–22).

The Lord's home is also described in Isaiah as being filled with God's glory and holiness (Isa 6:1–6; cf. Isa 24:23; 46:13). This is seen clearly in Isaiah 6, when Isaiah has a vision of the Lord in his temple. Isaiah 6:1–7 says:

> In the year that King Uzziah died, I saw the Lord sitting on a throne, high and lofty; and the hem of his robe filled the temple. Seraphs were in attendance above him; each had six wings: with two they covered their faces, and with two they covered their feet, and with two they flew. And one called to another and said:
>
> 'Holy, holy, holy is the Lord of hosts; the whole earth is full of his glory.'
>
> The pivots on the thresholds shook at the voices of those who called, and the house filled with smoke . . . Then one of the seraphs flew to me, holding a live coal that had been taken from the altar with a pair of tongs. The seraph touched my mouth with it and said: 'Now that this has touched your lips, your guilt has departed and your sin is blotted out'.

In this vision of Isaiah, God himself is high and lifted up and so full of light and glory that the temple is filled with smoke to shield Isaiah. The Lord is present on his throne, a symbol of God as King and ruler in his home (cf. Isa 24:23). The holiness of the Lord is awesome and his holiness makes the temple, and Isaiah, holy. Those who remain in the Lord's home are made holy by the Lord's glorious presence (Isa 4:3–4; 60:1–7).

So, the Lord's home in Isaiah is characterised by the Lord's glorious presence which brings holiness, righteousness and justice, which gives instruction, peace and security, and which hears and responds to prayer.

But God No Longer Feels at Home in Israel

As wonderful as the Lord's home is, and as amazing as it is that the Lord invites people to dwell with him, Isaiah throughout makes it clear that Israel continually rejects God's home and seeks out other homes. Isaiah depicts Israel as a people far from their true home in God because of their abandonment of him as evidenced by their idolatry, injustice, violence and greed (Isa 1:3–8; 57:3–9). They have allowed foreign invaders to overtake God's home as they fill the land with idols (Isa 2:8; 42:8).

What is happening in the spiritual realm—Israel's separation from the Lord—will be expressed in the physical realm as their god-substitutes fail them (Isa 65:1–7). When Israel's enemies trample down and destroy the temple (Isa 63:18; 64:10), they are merely acting out how Israel has consistently degraded the Lord's home. The Lord will allow Israel to experience the consequences of their abandonment of their true home in the Lord.

As Isaiah 65:11–12 says (*my* translation):

> You who forsake the Lord
> and forget the mountain of my holiness,
> who set the table for Gad, the god of Luck,
> and who fill jugs of wine for Meni, the god of Destiny,
> I will count out the sword for all of you,
> and you will bow down to the butcher,
> because I called but you did not answer,
> and I spoke but you did not listen;
> instead you manufactured evil,
> and chose what is displeasing in my eyes.

Instead of exalting God in his home, Israel has ignored God's teaching, sought refuge from other so-called 'gods', and disregarded justice, righteousness and holiness. The very things that characterise the Lord's home are absent. Consequently, the Lord no longer feels at home in Israel and warns them that he will abandon them to the consequences of abandoning him. Sadly, Israel has become an 'anti-home', and its people an 'anti-family'.

No longer interested in the Lord's instruction

The Lord's home is meant to be a place of instruction in the ways of the Lord, but Israel has become a place that is no longer interested in the Lord's instruction. Indeed, Israel seeks guidance from those who consult the dead rather than seeking guidance from God (Isa 8:18–22). Instead of seeking God's way of peace, Israel studies war (Isa 2:4, 7). Though the Lord persists in instructing Israel, they heed only the call of alcohol (Isa 28:7–13). Instead of going to the temple with teachable hearts, Israel makes a farce of the worship they bring to the house of the Lord and they no longer seek to please him (Isa 29:13–14; 58:2–5; 66:3). They no longer listen to the Lord's guidance and instruction (Isa 28:12; 42:18–20).

God's family have disowned him and abandoned his ways. In practice they have exiled the Lord from his home. Because Israel no longer listens to the Lord, they are cut off from the Lord, so the Lord will no longer listen to them (Isa 59:2). Their rejection of the Lord leads to their exile from the Lord's home (Isa 5:24; 30:12–14; 48:17–19; 65:12; 66:4).

Seeking security from elsewhere

The Lord's home in Isaiah is supposed to be a refuge of peace, prayer and security for both Israel and the nations, but Israel abandons the Lord's refuge and they seek help and security elsewhere. Israel makes alliances with foreign powers apart from God (Isa 2:6; 30:1–5, 15–17; 31:1–3). Rather than remaining content with Mount Zion, Israel seeks out the home of idols and looks to them for help instead of trusting the Lord alone (Isa 2:8; 41:29; 44:9; 45:20–21; 46:6–7; 57:5–9). Their abandonment of the Lord and their persistent wickedness make peace elusive (Isa 48:18, 22; 57:21). So, the Lord makes it clear that Israel must face the consequences of their turning away from the Lord because they trust in what is only dust, which cannot provide them shelter (Isa 27:8–11; 40:17; 65:2–7).

No justice, no righteousness, no holiness

Jerusalem was once the home of justice and righteousness, but Israel defiles the Lord's home with murder, rebellion and injustice (Isa 1:21–23; 10:1–2; 32:6–7; 59:4–8). The Lord searches for justice and righteousness in Israel, but instead finds oppression and violence (Isa 5:7; 28:17; 59:14–16). The Lord's home has become unrecognisable. Israel has forgotten the Lord's home (Isa 65:11). The implication is that the Lord no longer feels at home in Israel (Isa 5:7, 16; 59:4–15). God no longer feels at home in Jerusalem because Israel has ignored the Lord and treated him as a stranger, and even as an enemy (Isa 1:2–5; 17:10; 22:11; 30:9; 63:10; 65:2–3, 11).

By their lack of justice, righteousness, faithfulness and compassion in Israel, Israel has in effect exiled the Lord from his home. In doing so, Israel has abandoned its own home in the Lord. Their evicting of the Lord and dismissing of the Lord's instruction is what inevitably leads to their own exile from their home as they are enslaved by their stubborn sin (Isa 52:4–5). Their only hope is to return to the Lord as their home and to live in the Lord's home, seeking refuge in him alone (Isa 30:15; 31:6).

The Lord's Willingness to Make a Home among His People Despite Their Sin

While Isaiah warns the people of Judah and Israel of their impending war and exile, Isaiah also provides glimpses of hope that the Lord is still willing to make a home among his sinful and rebellious people (Isa 30:18).

The Lord's invitation to restore his home

The Lord sees everything that Israel has done, all of their sinful rebellion, and yet he declares, 'I will heal you' (Isa 57:18). The Lord recognises how shameful Israel has become and yet he promises, 'I will help you' (Isa 41:14). To blind and faithless Israel, the Lord says, 'I will not forsake you' (Isa 42:16). To those who carried idols that could not save them, the Lord cries out, 'I will carry you and save you' (Isa 46:4). Not only will the Lord give Israel's rulers a heart for justice (Isa 28:5–6), but also God himself will restore justice and will personally rescue his family (Isa 33:22; 44:21–23; 59:16–20; 63:5–9, 16).

For the sake of his glory, the Lord will do what it takes to once again make his home with his people in Jerusalem (Isa 33:5; 57:18–19). God even invites Israel's oppressors—represented by Cyrus—to restore the Lord's home and rebuild Jerusalem (Isa 14:2; 44:26–28; 45:13–14; 60:10). This is a complete reversal of circumstances. Moreover, the Lord is not just concerned for his home in Israel, but also demonstrates his care for the whole cosmos, for the Lord will renew all creation and restore joy to his home (Isa 55:11–13; 65:17–19).

Although Israel will be punished for their sins, the Lord will not abandon them, for he still desires to make his home with them. The Lord promises to ransom Israel and to personally go with them through every difficulty they face (Isa 43:1–2). Throughout Isaiah, the Lord invites Israel to return to him and his home, and he makes it clear that he is ready to forgive all who turn to him (Isa 1:18–19; 33:24; 44:23; 54:7–8; 55:7; 58:6–14).

The Lord calls Israel to repent, and commands them, 'Wash yourselves; make yourselves clean; remove the evil of your doings from before my eyes; cease to do evil' (Isa 1:16). At the same time, the Lord beckons Israel to come to him in order to be cleansed and forgiven: 'Come now, let us argue it out, says the Lord: though your sins are like scarlet, they shall be like snow; though they are red like crimson, they shall become like wool' (Isa 1:18). Indeed, the Lord invites Israel to return to him so that he may generously forgive them (Isa 55:7). The Lord's home is a shelter and refuge of peace. He will cleanse Israel and restore his home by justice and righteousness (Isa 1:25–27; 33:15–16, 20; 58:10–14).

The Lord returns home

Just as the Lord is greater than Israel's sin and rebellion, the Lord is powerful enough to renovate and rebuild his home in Israel. Furthermore, the Lord is gracious enough to make his presence known and to return to his people. A redeemer will come to Israel to renew the covenant and the Lord's Spirit will remain with them, restoring the Lord's home with them (Isa 32:1–2, 15–18; 57:14–15; 59:19–21). God's Spirit will dwell with his people once more and will enable his servants to do his will (Isa 44:1–5; 61:1–2; cf. Isa 11:1–9; 42:1–7).

Isaiah 52:8–10 expresses the joy of seeing the Lord return home, bringing redemption and victory with him:

> Listen! Your sentinels lift up their voices,
> together they sing for joy;
> for in plain sight they see
> the return of the Lord to Zion.
> Break forth together into singing,
> you ruins of Jerusalem;
> for the Lord has comforted his people,
> he has redeemed Jerusalem.
> The Lord has bared his holy arm
> before the eyes of all the nations;
> and all the ends of the earth shall see
> the salvation of our God.

The Lord returns to Zion! He comes back home! His return signifies his reconciliation with his children and his willingness to bring them home. So, Israel is given the good news that their Saviour is coming and will smooth the way for them to return to home with him (Isa 62:10–12).

The Lord preserves a remnant to return to his home

The Lord promises to preserve a remnant who will live in his home (Isa 65:9) and the Lord himself will lead this remnant home (Isa 11:15–16). Just as the Lord delivers Jerusalem from the king of Assyria when Hezekiah prayed in the Lord's home in Isaiah chapter 37, so the Lord then promises to deliver and preserve a faithful remnant to survive the exile. As Isaiah 37:32 says (*my* translation), 'For a remnant will go out from Jerusalem and survivors from the mountain of Zion. The passion of the Lord of hosts will make this happen!' The remnant who experience this promised restoration will realign themselves with the Lord and be counted as God's family and live with him (Isa 44:5).

Thus, the book of Isaiah closes in chapter 66 with the surviving remnant declaring the glory of the Lord to the nations, and the nations responding by bringing the children of the Lord to the home of the Lord as an offering.

Isaiah 66:20 says (*my* translation):

> They will bring all of your family from all of the nations as an offering to the Lord, on horses and chariots and in wagons and on mules and on camels, to the mountain of my holiness, Jerusalem, says the Lord. So, they will bring the children of Israel as an offering in a clean vessel to the house of the Lord.

Thus, Isaiah confirms that the Lord's home will be restored as a place of holiness, peace, righteousness, and justice—a place where God is once again worshipped and glorified, and where his Word is heard and proclaimed so that the knowledge of him fills the earth and welcomes others into his family.

Implications for Church and Mission Today

I find it striking how 'gospel-like' the story of the Lord's home in Isaiah is. We, like Israel, are sinful sheep who have a tendency to stray from our true home in God (Isa 53:6). And yet the Lord has gone to great lengths to call us to repentance, to redeem us and forgive those who come home to him (Isa 55:7; 63:7–9). As God's people, we are invited to dwell with God by his Spirit, and as we allow God's Spirit to guide us, we begin to embody those values that characterise the Lord's home (Isa 44:1–5; 61:1–2).

According to Isaiah, God feels at home where his name is honoured, his justice shown, his righteousness revealed, his Word heard and followed, and his holiness and peace sought after. This means that we, like Israel, must beware of any ways that we forsake the Lord and make him feel unwelcome in our lives, work, ministries and churches. When God looks at us, will he find justice? Will he see his righteousness displayed? Will he examine in us the characteristics that are consistent with his home? These are questions that we as Christians must ask of ourselves, our churches and our mission work.

Isaiah's depiction of the home of the Lord reminds us of God's willingness to make his home with his people—the church as the new Israel (Eph 2:1–16). No other home can substitute for the Lord's home, and God is worthy of welcome into our hearts and lives. Through Jesus, God's home took on flesh to demonstrate his great love for us and bring us redemption and victory over our bondage to sin and death. As we trust in Christ, by his Spirit, the Lord makes his home in our hearts (Eph 3:17). We as God's people today must remain mindful that God is making his home among us—now by his Spirit, and one day in glory in all its fullness. Isaiah then challenges us to make God feel at home in our hearts.

Additionally, Isaiah reiterates the importance of God's Word for church and mission. There is no other 'home' apart from the Lord's home where people can receive his teaching. Because God's home is among us, so the church must be a place where all are welcome to learn from the Lord's instruction through his Word. And just as in Isaiah, God's Word flows from his home to all the earth, so today the church is charged with the task of sending out God's Word and making him known throughout the world.

Just as Isaiah declares that God gathers together a remnant and calls the nations to bring them as an offering to his home, so too today God is gathering together a people from every nation, language and people group to be brought home to him to dwell with him forever.

Passages like Isaiah 2:1–4 and 11:1–9 provide excellent motivation for theological education, for peace is the result of the wisdom and instruction that comes from the Lord. When we dedicate ourselves to learning God's Word, coming to know the Lord more and allowing God's Spirit of wisdom and understanding to teach us his ways, then there are cosmic consequences resulting in relationships of all kinds being healed and renewed. God invites us to join him in his work of filling the world with people who know him as Lord.

I wonder also if we would take better care of the earth if we regarded it as the Lord's home (Isa 66:1). We are guests in the Lord's home, and good guests treat their host's home with respect and care. While it is true that in Isaiah the Lord promises to renew all of creation, the fact remains that God chooses this world for us to dwell in now. This should spur us on to environmental good deeds.

In canonical Isaiah, the Lord's home is described as exalted and holy, while remaining a refuge of peace for those who trust in the Lord and cry out to him. In Isaiah, the Lord's home is physically represented by the temple on Mount Zion in Jerusalem, but it is not bound to one place as the Lord's home also fills the whole heavens and all of the earth. Isaiah demonstrates that the Lord's home is wherever his Word, his justice and his righteousness are made known—and wherever these are ignored or rejected, God no longer feels at home. However, God is faithful to cleanse his home by bringing judgement, preserving a remnant of those who are faithful and restoring his home through the work of his chosen servants. The Lord's home is with all those who commit themselves to him and love to honour him (Isa 56:6–8).

BIBLIOGRAPHY

Jenson, P. P. 'Temple.' In *Dictionary of the Old Testament: Prophets*, edited by Mark J. Boda and Gordon J. McConville. Downers Grove, IL; Nottingham, England: IVP Academic; InterVarsity Press, 2012.

Motyer, J. Alec. *Isaiah: An Introduction and Commentary*. Vol. 20. Tyndale Old Testament Commentaries. Downers Grove, IL: InterVarsity Press, 1999.

Sandy, D. Brent. 'Mountain Imagery.' In *Dictionary of the Old Testament: Prophets*, edited by Mark J. Boda and Gordon J. McConville. Downers Grove, IL; Nottingham, England: IVP Academic; InterVarsity Press, 2012.

Watts, John D. W. *Isaiah 1–33*. Vol. 24. Word Biblical Commentary. Dallas: Word, Incorporated, 1998.

Chapter 16

POLIS AND *TOPOS*: REIMAGINING 'HOME' IN MARK'S NARRATIVE

Keith Dyer

On the opening night of the AAMS Conference as Terry Le Blanc was challenging us to begin our theology with Genesis 1 rather than with Genesis 3 and the fall, it was appropriate that the painting titled 'The Creation Story' by Linda Napurrula Walker of Yuendemu was hanging just to his right-hand side, affirming everything he was saying in full colour. The painting is not just a theology of creation, but a cosmology and an ecotheology, showing the sun, moon and stars, and not only human bum prints in the sand, but also the divine imprint and the tracks of the emu and the dingo—the whole of creation embodying the image of the Trinity.[1] This got me wondering what it would look like if we had the patience to represent the movement of people and animals in the Gospels in the same way—a kind of Google satellite map of the places (*topoi*) and cities (*poleis*) the Jesus traditions tell us about—or don't.

---

1   Many similar indigenous Australian artworks can be found in Louise Sherman and Christobel Mattingley, *Our Mob, God's Story. Aboriginal and Torres Strait Islander Artists Share Their Faith*, eds Max Conlon, Gail Naden, Glenny Naden and Inawantji Scales (Art Selection) (Sydney: Bible Society Australia, 2017), an award-winning compilation for the 200th anniversary of the Bible Society in Australia.

Polis and *Topos* in Mark

The Gospel of Mark begins with Jesus heading south to be baptised by John in the Jordan (1:9–11), then traditionally, thrust west of Jericho into the wilderness by the Spirit to be tested, where angels ministered to him and the wild animals were with him (1:12–13). Then he goes back to the region of Galilee after the arrest of John the Baptist (1:14–15) and initiates multiple trips across the Sea of Galilee, trying to get his disciples to go to the 'other side'—the non-Jewish side (4:35ff), then straight back 'home' (5:21); to Bethsaida (6:45)—a failed attempt, then back 'home' in Gennesaret (6:53). He walked them the long way around to the Decapolis (7:31) after being challenged by the Syro-Phoenician woman that even Gentiles could claim the crumbs (7:28), then straight back 'home' (8:10, briefly); then to the 'other side' again (8:13–21), with stern words in the boat about bread for Jews *and* Gentiles. Then they head up north to Mount Hermon for the transfiguration, back south to Jericho and finally to Jerusalem (see map 1).

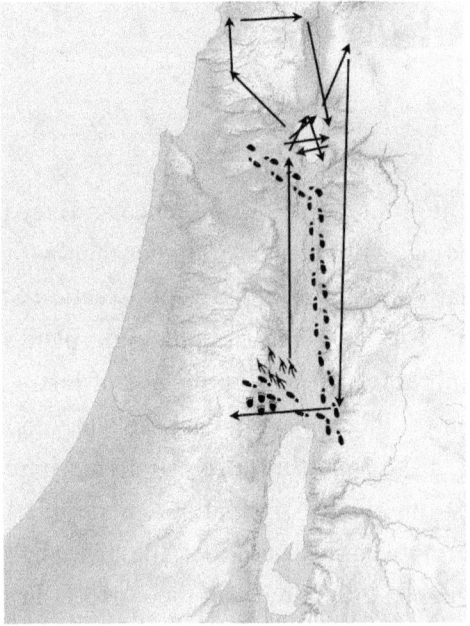

Map 1: A 'bird's-eye' view of Mark's narrative (with arrows replacing footprints)

(Eric Gaba—Wikimedia Commons user: Sting)

What might these tracks in the sand (and sea) tell us about the places where Jesus felt at home—or created home—for his followers? What if we could put the tracks of the Romans in one colour, the religious leaders in a different colour, and the earliest inhabitants in another? How might the tracks of each Gospel differ, and what would that tell us?

Destro and Pesce have done something similar to this in a recent publication—not by using tracks and footprints, but by plotting the distinctive named locations in each Gospel as a way of showing the places (the *topoi*) of Jesus and the memories of his movements recorded by his followers.[2]

The named locations in Mark fall within three areas: north and east of the Sea of Galilee (from Tyre to the Decapolis); around Nazareth; and around Jerusalem and Jericho.

The distinctive names in John focus further north in the Galilee itself (Cana) and include more of Samaria (Jacob's well).

Luke's distinctive traditions also include part of Samaria, and Emmaus in the south-west, and Acts extends the area to include Joppa and Caesarea Maritima.

Matthew's distinctive locations (*topoi*) extend further into Syria than any of the other Gospels. We should note that Matthew and Luke both include Mark's references to Nazareth, the Sea of Galilee, and to Jerusalem as well—and both also add their distinctive versions of the Bethlehem birth traditions.

The authors (Destro and Pesce) undertake this analysis to try and locate the sources behind each Gospel (asking: from which communities might the evangelists have gathered their stories of Jesus?), but I'm more interested in what it tells us about where Jesus felt 'at home' and where he created spaces for his followers, according to the earliest memories of those followers.

In particular, why is it that on a political map of first-century Graeco-Roman Palestine,[3] the largest cities are avoided altogether in the biblical narrative, and particularly so in Mark? The major Graeco-Roman centres of power (often administered through the Herodian dynasty), do not even rate a mention in Mark (and mostly not in the rest of the New Testament either). Sepphoris, Tiberias, Hippus and Scythopolis are never named; Caesarea Philippi is mentioned indirectly; and even the more ancient and traditional Jewish cities of Jericho and Jerusalem do not fare well in Mark's narrative.

Some of these Graeco-Roman cities (Scythopolis, Hippus, Caesarea Maritima, Caesarea Philippi, Gerasa—but not the more Jewish ones) had temples

---

[2] Adriana Destro and Mauro Pesce, *From Jesus to His First Followers: Continuity and Discontinuity* (Leiden; Boston: Brill, 2017), see the maps from page 175 onwards.

[3] Indeed, a map of the major first-century archaeological sites remaining today would raise the same question. Christian visitors to the 'Holy Land' often miss the extraordinary tension between the archaeological remains and the New Testament texts because they tend to conflate the fifth-century (and later) churches and sacred sites with the first-century stories, and often ignore the 'non-biblical' first-century sites altogether. To be ignorant of the historical context of texts is the first step towards docetism—a spiritualisation of the text that ignores what we can know of its life setting.

to the Graeco-Roman deities in them, and in the case of the two cities named after Caesar, even temples dedicated to the emperor. On the flagstones around such temples and their altars are often engraved place markers for the citizens of the town to participate in the civic religion. In particular, we find the recurring word *TOPOS* (typically in uncial script), followed by a noun in the genitive, as in: place of the potters, place of the freedmen, place of the women, and so on.

There are similar inscriptions, sometimes abbreviated, in the great theatres of the ancient Mediterranean world. At the theatre in Miletus (Acts 20:15–17; 2 Tim 4:20) is the famous scrawl marking the *topos* of the Jews and Godfearers. Of course, those who get the shaded front seats between the columns have no need to mark their place by scratching on the rock—it is theirs by birth and/or by power.

The exact translation of the Miletus inscription is still disputed. Is one group or two implied—that is, does 'Godfearers' qualify the Jews or signify a separate group of Gentile Godfearers, as in Acts? Whichever may be the case, at least it suggests that in Roman times, somewhere around the first century, such groups found their *topos*, their place in public life (a bit like a corporate box at the MCG or SCG). Did these 'fearers of God' turn up only for high drama and music, or for the gladiatorial contests too? Did they have a *topos* at a temple also, or only at the synagogue?

So again I am left wondering by Mark's account, where the *topoi* of Jesus and his followers were in the cities of Galilee and beyond?

Topoi of Jesus and His Followers

Nazareth and Sepphoris today are the opposite in size to what they once were, but they are still visible from each other and less than one hour's walk apart. After being destroyed by the Romans because of a rebellion after the death of Herod the Great, Sepphoris was rebuilt as the administrative centre (or 'capital' city) for Herod Antipas in the early years of the first century.

Many scholars have speculated that a young Jewish *tektōn* (builder, stonemason, carpenter; 6:3) and his father from the small nearby village of Nazareth would have worked on the building sites of Sepphoris. There certainly wasn't much work to be had in the small village of Nazareth at that time. Perhaps they worked on the Graeco-Roman theatre at Sepphoris, and we may wonder whether anyone from Nazareth found a *topos* in the seating there. But Mark, and indeed the whole New Testament, never even mentions the place, not even when after his rejection at his hometown we're told that Jesus was 'going around the villages in a circle teaching' (6:6b). Yet somehow, Jesus (or Mark) managed to miss the town Josephus called 'the jewel of all Galilee', or what some think was referred to in

Matthew as 'the city set on a hill that could not be hid' (Matt 5:14)—except in Mark's narrative, apparently.

Some time when Jesus was in his twenties, Herod Antipas moved his headquarters from Sepphoris to Tiberias, newly built on the Sea of Galilee to control and tax the thriving fishing industry. Yet amidst the many crossings of the sea between Mark 4 and 9, somehow the seafarers manage to avoid all contact with the new capital city of Tiberias and its busy taxation agents—since it too is never mentioned in Mark, even though then, as now, the city dominates the whole lake. Since at least two of these crossings were at night, one wonders how much 'rendering to Caesar' (12:17) was being done by the motley crew in the boat.

At the turning point of the Gospel narrative, just before the transfiguration, Jesus takes his disciples on an unusual journey northwards to the 'villages of Caesarea Philippi' (8:27)—the ancient equivalent of visiting the outer suburbs of a capital city, and not the city itself. In that specific, but rather unlikely location, he asks the big questions about his identity: 'Who do people say I am?' and 'Who do you think I am?' (8:27–30).

The outskirts (or villages) of Caesarea Philippi are the precise location of the only Temple of Caesar cult that we know of on 'Jewish' lands apart from Caesarea Maritima, on the coast. The Augusteum of Omrit may date its foundation to Herod the Great, and it was certainly operational at the time of Jesus's visit to the area, as the coins of Philip's tetrarchy demonstrate. Also nearby was an ancient shrine to Pan, the Greek god of the wild.

Somewhere in the shadow of a temple proclaiming Caesar as Son of God, and Pan as god of wild things, Peter makes his declaration that Jesus is the anointed one, but his subsequent comments rebuking Jesus indicate that he misunderstands what that might mean (8:32–33). At this stage Peter could not comprehend that Jesus could say (openly!) that he must suffer greatly and die.

As Jesus heads south from the nearby Mount of Transfiguration (where the divine voice affirms Jesus, not Caesar, as Son, 9:7), the narrative skirts around two more prominent cities of the Decapolis, Hippus and Scythopolis, both of which fail to rate a mention. Eventually, Jesus reaches the ancient city of Jericho. There the narrative equivalent of the 'drive-by shooting' occurs—or rather, doesn't occur. Nothing happens in Jericho, notwithstanding its significance as the winter capital of Judea and playground of the rich and famous. The Herods built no fewer than three fabulous palaces beside the road leading out of Jericho to Jerusalem. The remains are still there today. But no-one in Mark's account pays any attention to them.

Instead, after blinking and missing Jericho altogether, the story pays attention to a blind beggar by the road: 'And they come into Jericho. And he was departing from Jericho—and his disciples and a sizeable crowd—Bartimaeus son of Timaeus, a blind beggar, was sitting by the roadside' (10:46).

The location nearby of the pools where the last Hasmonean prince was drowned at his father Herod's orders provides the unseen backdrop to the beggar who cries out to the son of David, much to the consternation of the crowd. And it is the beggar who ends up following the Messiah resolutely to Jerusalem (10:52), where Jesus mounts a donkey and heads towards the greatest Herodian monument of all (11:1–19).

Again, we have another metaphorical 'drive-by shooting', as (seemingly) Jesus mistimes his entry abysmally—and after glancing around the magnificent temple, he leaves to stay overnight outside the city altogether (11:11). There is no place, no *topos*, for him there—so Jesus prefers to stay in the nearby village of Bethany.

The journey the next day, past the barren fig tree and into the barren temple, is not just metaphorically violent, things really do turn nasty, culminating ultimately in Jesus's pronouncement of doom on the temple (this Herodian monument will not have a stone to stand on; 13:2) and later on in the charges brought against him at his trial, 'He said: "Destroy this man-made temple and in three days I will build another not made by human hands"' (14:58).

Mark reports Jesus's words of judgement on the temple as occurring on the Mount of Olives, 'over-against the Temple mount' (13:3).

What are we to make of the *topoi* of Mark's narrative? Some twenty-eight places are named explicitly; an additional four seem to be unnamed deliberately (Sepphoris, Tiberias, Scythopolis, Hippus); and a further three are named indirectly, or perhaps, dis-named (Caesarea Philippi, Jericho, Jerusalem/Temple). (See map 2.)

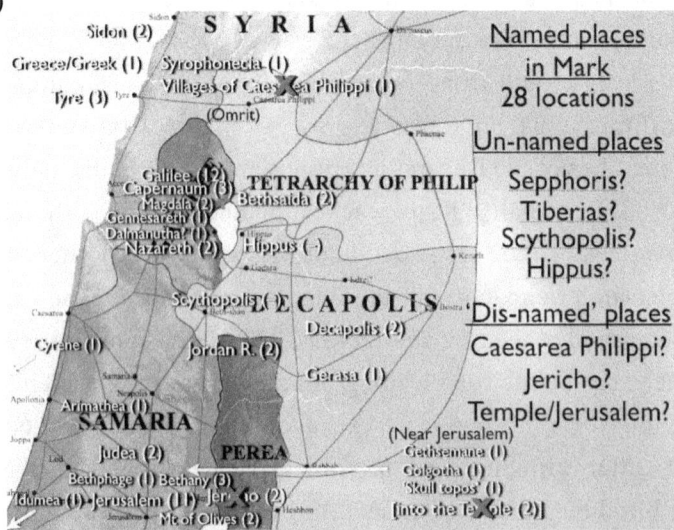

Map 2: Map of named locations in Mark's Gospel (based on Accordance Maps)

Of course, this is an argument from silence. But it is a silence that becomes deafening for those who live nearby these centres of power, or even those who have a distant knowledge of the powers and places that control first-century Palestine.

Finding Place

I continue to wonder where the early followers of Jesus found their place within the cultures of their day, amidst the monumental architecture of Herod and the Caesars. More specifically, does the text of Mark give us any indication of its orientation towards or against the dominant powers and the material expression of that power? I'm not seeking specific archaeological connections here. I understand that we have *no* inscriptional or material evidence for Christians in the first two centuries—apart from the many papyrus fragments of the NT ('many' compared with other first- and second-century writings). What I'm seeking is evidence from the text that relates to our general knowledge of the material culture of the day, and that intersects (or doesn't!) with the various *topoi* engraved in stone or recorded in texts such that we might imagine the social location of early Jesus followers. Mark seems to give us some clues here. The use of *topos* itself in Mark is distinctive, and in particular the phrase 'desert(ed) place' (or 'wilderness place'), which is used as a positive location in the beginnings of the Markan narrative and also further on in the narrative.[4]

Topos is also used in more mundane contexts in Mark (6:11; 13:8), but clearly the dominant *topoi* of Jesus Christ are the desert/wilderness (1:35, 45; 6:31, 32, 35), and ultimately, the final two *topoi* in Mark reveal the potency of the term: the *place* of crucifixion (15:22) and the *place* of the empty tomb (16:6).

The *topoi* of Mark's narrative world suggest a deliberate relativising and even avoidance of the monumental material culture of (Herodian) kingdoms and (Roman) empire. This subversive use of place and space is thoroughly consistent with the social imaginary embodied in Jesus's teaching and life. This is made most explicit in the critique of the powerful in Mark and the emphasis on servant leadership:

> And summoning them, Jesus says to them, 'You know that those who think they have hegemony over the nations lord it over them, and their great ones are tyrants over them. It is not to be so among you; but whoever wishes to become great among you must be your servant, and

---

[4] Compare Mark's five uses of *desert(ed) topos/topoi* with Matthew's two, Luke's two and in Josephus four times (but the latter only using it negatively as the place of exile, three times, or the place where the Essenes dug their private latrines). The wilderness is a good place in Mark's narrative.

whoever wishes to be first among you must be slave of all. For the son of humanity came not to be served but to serve, and to give his life a ransom for many (Mark 10:42–45).

Note that in Mark only the angels (1:13), the women (1:31; 15:40–41) and Jesus (10:45) put into practice this service (= ministry, in Latin); the disciples never quite get there! Simon Peter's mother-in-law serves or ministers (*diakonein*) to Jesus (1:31), as is also said of the women at the cross, who were ministering to Jesus all the way from Galilee (15:40–41). For Mark, the question is not can women be ministers, but can men?

At the entrance to the Community Church of Saint Mark in Clifton Hill, Melbourne, ten minutes' drive to the east of us here at Whitley College—where Athol Gill founded the House of the Gentle Bunyip—there is a wonderful double-sided commemorative stained-glass screen erected in his honour.

As we enter the church building, we are greeted at the door by the early morning sun of the eighth day, resurrection Sunday. After entering and looking back, we see eight scenes from the Gospel of Mark. But the scene that resonates most with what we have been exploring here is set in one of those wilderness places that Jesus found to be so close to God, and a home for a new community.

Image 4: Mark 6:41, 'He blessed and broke the loaves'(Artwork: David Wong, Community Church of St Mark, Clifton Hill)

In Mark chapter 6, we are told it was a lonely place/*topos* in the wilderness (three times we are told this), yet nevertheless, five thousand people find their way there and begin to feel hungry! We know the story well, but unfortunately our translators miss the comic mimicry, the delightful satire that takes place there by the Sea of Galilee. The usual translations read something like:

> 6:39–41: Then he ordered them all to sit down in groups on the green grass. So they sat down in groups of hundreds and of fifties. Taking the five loaves and the two fish, he looked up to heaven, and blessed and broke the loaves, and gave them to his disciples to set before the people; and he divided the two fish among them all.

If we pay more attention to the Greek text, we could read verse 39 as:

> 6:39: Then he ordered them all to *recline symposium by symposium* on the green grass.

This is the only place in the New Testament where the Greek word for the evening dinner party and entertainment of the wealthy and free (the *symposion*) is used, and it refers to the moment where Jesus provides simple food from God's abundance for the common people who find their place, their *topos*, in the wilderness far from the economics and politics of power in the cities.

Home among the Powerless

What are we to make of this avoidance of the centres of power in Mark's narrative? I think it does strongly affirm the rural and village focus of the ministry of some of the earliest followers of Jesus, if not Jesus himself. But this should not be interpreted as a biblical basis for abandoning urban mission—the *polis*/the city makes a very strong comeback in the writings of Luke and Paul, at least.

More significantly, I think we can see not just an avoidance, but a powerful implied critique of the dominant culture, the world of the colonisers, the violence of the Herodians and Romans. The Gospel belongs with the powerless, and unless we learn to read and celebrate with them, we shall not understand the upside-down nature of the *Basileia* of God at all, let alone enter it and find our home there.

BIBLIOGRAPHY

Destro, Adriana, and Mauro Pesce. *From Jesus to His First Followers: Continuity and Discontinuity.* Leiden; Boston: Brill, 2017.

Sherman, Louise, and Christobel Mattingley. *Our Mob, God's Story. Aboriginal and Torres Strait Islander Artists Share Their Faith.* Edited by Max Conlon, Gail Naden, Glenny Naden, and Inawantji Scales (Art Selection). Sydney: Bible Society Australia, 2017.

SECTION FOUR:
HOME AND THE MISSIONARY EXPERIENCE

Chapter 17

MAKING BENGAL HOME, 1882–1931

Rosalind M. Gooden

By the end of 1887, the jubilee year of Queen Victoria, eleven Australasian women had left Australia and New Zealand to live and work in East Bengal, British India, with five autonomous colonial Baptist missionary societies. Six of them came from South Australia, three from Victoria, one from Queensland and another from New Zealand. They were all single and under thirty at the time they left. To varying degrees, they made home in Bengal.[1]

Let me introduce them to you—the pioneers, Marie Gilbert and Ellen Arnold (South Australia); the 'Five Barley Loaves', Martha Plested (Queensland), Marion Fuller and Ruth Wilkin (Victorians), Alice Pappin (South Australia) along with Arnold; Rosalie MacGeorge (a New Zealander); and four of the 'Jubilee Five', Jessie Clelland (Victoria), Annie Newcombe (Victoria for New Zealand), Agnes Pearce (South Australia) and Fanny Denness (South Australia for New South Wales).

Linda Wilson, in examining the place of women in dissenting churches during the Industrial Revolution in Britain, suggests that while there was a

---

1 I have just completed my doctoral studies: '"Mothers in the Lord", Australasian Baptist Women Missionaries at the Intersection of Cultural Contexts 1882–1931', relating to the experiences of single Baptist women missionaries from the Antipodean colonial situation to the equally colonial situation of British India in the period 1882–1931. Mine was a historical study from an interdisciplinary perspective of the missiology of this group of single women, who were part of the modern zenana mission movement which grew after the 1850s.

separation of sphere for men in the dirty workplace and women in the home, there also developed a safe sphere for women outside the home for ministry.[2] Women were able to emerge and minister in hospitals, churches, mission halls and dwellings. Wilson refers to this as the third sphere, accepted in the life of churches. While families were tending to move out of industrial areas into leafy suburbs, women were finding new opportunities for service. At the same time, the factories were supplying households with more goods, reducing the need for domestic labour, increasing the need for industrial labour and freeing women for such service. Nursing and teaching were attracting female participants. There was a sense of *kyros* (opportune time). Changed circumstances were providing new possibilities. The zenana mission movement of which the eleven Australasian women were a part was a logical extension of this third safe sphere. But it needed new concepts of home.

Relocating Home

Silas Mead, the father of Australasian Baptist Missions, early in his ministry in Flinders Street Baptist Church, Adelaide, was a strong advocate of churches having deaconesses, appointed by each congregation as an integral structure of the church's ministry. They fitted Wilson's safe sphere of accepted women's ministry. It was from this church that the first two of the eleven women were sent. Zenana workers were a logical result of this third sphere, but without the possibility of them living at home under the guardianship of their father, so there was a redefining of the concept of women's ministry and of home.

These women in India were often referred to as 'zenana missionaries', where 'zenana' referred to the segregated women's quarters of wealthy Indian homes. Initially they were all young women under thirty in order that they still had the capacity to learn a foreign language. Their role was perceived as evangelists in those places where male missionaries could not go. Their sphere was shaped by the segregated society of India, rather than the emerging colonial life. It was women's work with women, and from 1882–1931 there was significant growth in the numbers of women so appointed. The eleven were only the vanguard: by 1931 there were another fifty-five Australian single women who had served in Bengal.

But the significance of this initial group was that they arrived before any of these colonial societies sent any men.

---

2   Linda Wilson, *Constrained by Zeal: Female Spirituality amongst Nonconformists 1825–1875* (Carlisle, UK: Paternoster Press, 2000).

Mission Miss Sahibs

The women who went to Bengal were referred to as Mission Miss Sahibs. In mission literature, the custom was to use the given and family name of single workers, but married women were more usually referred to by either their husband's given name or his initials. However, the more precise term was to indicate their identity. 'Mission' indicated their missionary identity (usually describing a member of an organised missionary society of which there were a number in British India). 'Miss' was the gendered term for the burgeoning group of single women missionaries. The final term, 'Sahib', described a foreigner, usually linked to the ruling power. British and Australasian colonials were indistinguishable by most Indians.

This zenana work had earlier developed within the Baptist Missionary Society (BMS) with the formation of the Baptist Zenana Mission (BZM) in 1857. In fact, the 'Carey tradition' of the BMS consisted mainly of married women in England who formed the BZM to support work among women of India. They were guided and informed by the wives of the (male) missionaries who supervised single women or widows to go into the Indian zenanas. It was felt that such single women got their validation from that supervision. This women's work was simply an adjunct to the main BMS work done by the men. The BZM had gradually built residences for such women, but interestingly when the first two of the group, Arnold and Gilbert, went to stay in Calcutta, they lived with the BMS Kerry family and not in the newly built zenana workers' home. Doubtless, Mrs Kerry was their mentor and supervisor, and not the experienced zenana workers who are mentioned in Arnold's diary for 1883.

These eleven Australian and New Zealand single women were sent out by five autonomous Baptist missionary societies. Both Victorian and South Australian Baptists had been supporting Bengali preachers in Bengal for eighteen years, whereas the other colonies and New Zealand formed their societies to send their own workers.

Rules for marriage of missionaries

The missions required that the prospective wives for their male appointees wait until their husbands-to-be had completed two year's language studies before they could join them and marry. In fact, when Abia Neville wanted to marry Ruth Wilkin, and she had long completed her language exams and already served a full term, they still had to wait. So, the single women sent first were senior to the wives by up to eight years and there was no way that Annie Summers, the first fiancée to arrive, could supervise and validate the work of those experienced eleven, particularly Arnold who was one of the pioneers.

Following Jesus in someone else's country

These women spent years in East Bengal, India and, over time, became not just 'accepting outsiders' of the cultures to which they related, but 'accepted outsiders' by the communities in which they chose to live. Relationships and belonging were key concepts for them and these are certainly part of the basic concept of home.

Experiences of Home

Some, but not all, of them had negative experiences in their own homes in Australasia. Arnold, Wilkin, Pearce, MacGeorge and Newcombe were all from well-to-do families, their fathers middle-class working men. Arnold's father was a jeweller from the Birmingham Jewellers' Quarter who had moved his family out to suburbia. He lost much of his wealth in investments above the Goyder line in South Australia. Wilkin's father was a successful businessman in Castlemaine, Victoria. MacGeorge's family were longstanding members of Hanover Street Church in Dunedin. Newcombe's father migrated to Castlemaine in 1849 and became a very successful timber merchant, moving around Victorian country towns. Pearce's father established his retail business in Kapunda and later entered South Australian politics.On the other hand, Pappin (Mead) was from a large blended family, her father remarrying after the death of her mother and fathering a further seven children. She was glad to escape to Teachers College in Adelaide. Plested was orphaned in Norfolk, UK, at the age of ten, and had only migrated to Queensland to be near her married sister a few months before responding to the call of God and leaving for India. Fuller would seem to have been orphaned by the time her group known as the 'Five Barley Loaves' left for Bengal. Denness came from a dysfunctional family, where her parents had taken each other through the SA courts for child abuse and debts. Gilbert's father had filed for bankruptcy for his public house while she was a child and he had died before she applied for service. There are no details for Clelland. Basically all of these women came out of a patriarchal image of home.

Expatriate Images and Experiences of Indian Homes

The expatriate images of Indian homes were often negative. Frances Ridley Havergal, a contemporary popular hymn writer, wrote a poem 'Lines on Indian

Zenana Work',[3] with its appeal to British women to leave their home to reach their 'sisters' in foreign lands. The emphasis was on relationships. She talks of Indian women as sisters, a family relationship. She wrote:

> Oh! For a clarion voice to reach and stir their rest,
> With story of Sister's woes, gathering day by day.
>
> Over the Indian homes (sepulchres rather than rest),
> Till they rouse in the strength of the Lord, and roll the stone away.
>
> Sisters! Yea and they lie not by the side of the road,
> But hidden in loathsome caves, in crushed and quivering throngs
>
> Down-trodden, degraded, and dark, beneath the invisible load
> Of centuries, echoing groans, black with inherited wrongs.
>
> Is it too great a thing? Will not alone rise and go,
> Laying her joys aside, as the Master laid them down?
>
> Seeking His lone and lost in the veiled abodes of woe,
> Winning His Indian Gems to shine in His glorious crown.

Thus, Havergal portrayed her English racist perception of Indian homes as 'sepulchres' not 'rest', 'loathsome caves', and 'veiled abodes of woe', 'degraded', 'dark' and 'black'. On the other hand, Havergal's image of home for those missionaries comes from another verse:

> *Sisters!* Ye who have known the Elder Brother's love;
> Ye who have sat at His feet, and leant on His gracious breast,
> Whose hearts are glad with the hope of His own blest home above,
> Will you not seek them out, and lead them to Him for rest?

Here are dimensions of personal relationship with Christ in their past—'the Elder Brother's love', 'the sitting at his feet', 'the leaning on his gracious breast', and also of the future 'hope of his blest home above'. It was a call to lead the women to Christ for rest.

These negative images could be multiplied a hundredfold from the Antipodean missionary literature—'caged birds', 'frogs in a well', to name a couple.

I doubt if these missionary women thought in terms of migration. In general, their families had already experienced the rigors of long migration. This was one reason why Silas Mead, the first minister of Flinders Street Baptist Church and

---

3   See the appendix at the end of this chapter for her whole poem.

the inspiration of Baptist missions in the Antipodes, believed that colonials would make effective missionaries. They, or their kin, had experienced separation from families, familiar locations and their known circumstances. They had adjusted to a different climate, social situation and economic possibilities. They had spent months in dangerous travel in restricted quarters, and Australasia was closer to these traditional mission fields of the modern mission movement—India, China and the Pacific Islands.

At that time, there were some strong expectations that they were making a lifetime commitment to single missionary service. However, there is little evidence that these expectations were shaped by the structures of the Roman Catholic vows and the living arrangements of religious orders despite the fact that Mary Mackillop, the first Australian Roman Catholic saint and founder of the Josephites is a South Australian contemporary of these women.

They were required to set up households of two or three women, one for each society or location. Wilkin arriving in Mymensingh with her companion Fuller wrote:

> Oh! The novelty and the interest there is when two young people start housekeeping. What an amount of romance centres in the tiny teapot that just holds enough for two. I will not tire you with details nor tell of the numerous discussions as where we should put what, nor who should say grace and who conduct family worship. Nor about our first servants and how we expected them to be such models of propriety and found they were not . . .[4]

She could be describing a newlywed couple. It was a family or home model; small households with assigned roles and mainly male servants.

General Christian sentiment tended to put high expectations on such workers. In June 1890, a poem appeared handwritten in a round-robin letter between the Australasian Baptist missionaries in Bengal, India. Arnold had copied it as a part of her six-page contribution for that month's letter and obviously expressed something of her ideals of single missionary service. She acknowledged the poem as 'Impromptu by ALOE'. There is no indication of how, where or when she got hold of it. But such a quote was consistent with their custom of including quotable quotes, which they wanted to share.

This poem 'Impromptu by ALOE' had been written by Charlotte Marie Tucker around 1876 in her second year in India and was an attempt to define the life of single women missionaries. She had written it so early in her career that it can also be considered a reflection of some of the culture stress of her early days

---

4   Ruth Wilkin, *Gleanings from a Foreign Field* (Geelong, VIC: H. Thacker, 1891), 9.

in India. By 1875, Tucker was already a successful author known as ALOE (A Lady of England). She was in her fifties and went to India as a self-supporting missionary with the Indian Female Normal School and Instruction Society, later joining the Church Missionary Society Zenana Mission. She served initially in Amritsar and later at Batala, Punjab, never returning to England. She died in the Punjab in 1893, having served seventeen years and producing literature for the mission. She expressed the hope that she would become a pioneer and proof of the value of older women joining missionary teams. She did not believe, as a number of societies did, that it was counterproductive to send people over thirty years of age because of their inability to learn the vernacular.[5] In fact, before leaving for India she spent time proving that she could learn another language. Her financial independence meant that no mission funds were likely to be wasted if she broke down and she believed that she had the health necessary for the Indian climate. Her seventeen years of service is ample proof of her justified hopes. The poem is full of musts and oughts—an interesting picture of expected habits of home life.[6] It starts with:

> The Mission Miss Sahibs[7] must never complain,
> The Mission Miss Sahibs must temper restrain,
> Must not be fanciful, foolish or vain:
>
> The Mission Miss Sahibs must work might and main,
> and therefore good nourishment should not disdain,
> for danger is great of them going insane.

India's climate was recognised as demanding for Westerners, with regular holidays taken in the mountains and the belief that Westerners needed to live in *pucca* buildings and be served by numerous servants who lived in adjacent quarters. The zenana women certainly found the idea of employing servants a difficult one and discussed it deeply in their round robin letter. Abia Neville records the following in his history of the VBFM.

> Whilst Miss Fuller was touring in Birisiri and Tangail, the other two (Wilkin and Seymour) dismissed nearly all the servants of the house, in the hope that thereby they might be able to live in simpler style,

---

5   The China Inland Mission at the time of the Boxer Revolution in China was faced with the dilemma that because of the revolution they were forced to delay the departure of several missionaries. In the time of the delay several had their thirtieth birthday and the mission debated the wisdom of sending newcomers of that age to the field.
6   For the full poem, see the appendix.
7   In the printed version, they are referred to as Miss Sahibas, which is a feminine Western Indian expression rather than what Arnold used in Bengal.

and so bring themselves into closer fellowship with the people. The purpose was a noble one, and worthy of all honour.[8]

Fear of 'Fishing Fleeters' or of Missionaries 'Stepping Out of Their Proper Domain'

In India, during the British Raj there was a custom of single women going to India for the winter season in the hope of finding a husband. They were known as 'Fishing Fleeters'.[9] Mrs Timothy Richard in China did not approve of single women missionaries. They were likely to marry and be a waste of money. As a result, the BZM did not appoint single women to work in China for a number of years.

Missions developed their own specific rules to discourage desertion of the missionary call. They imposed a financial bond for a full first term and expected a payback of the proportion of allowances and travel costs if the missionary did not fulfil the first term. If the single woman decided to marry her choice of husband needed to be acceptable to the society if she was to remain in service. Of this group we are considering, three married, or 'stepped out of their proper domain' as ALOE put it. Pearce married Kiddell, the British advisor to the Maharajah of Mayurbhunj at the end of her second year. She subsequently disappeared from the mission records, apart from a cryptic comment that if she changed her mind the SABMS would be happy for her to continue. There is also a record of the repayment of the financial bond by her father.[10] Wilkin, after eight years of zenana service married Abia Neville, the second man sent out from Australia, and Pappin married Cecil Mead after ten years of zenana service. These two continued their service for more than another thirty years, as experienced, fluent missionary wives.

The experience of these women can be characterised with reference to understanding, reconciling, encountering and transforming. Moreover, they embraced differences, moving towards each other, sharing God's stories interculturally and encountering God in community development.[11] Each are practices and expressions of home and reflect the commitment these women made in Bengal, as did women in mission service elsewhere.

8　　Abia Neville, *White unto Harvest: An Account of the Mission in Mymensing, East Bengal* (Geelong, VIC: H. Thacker, 1898), 63.

9　　Ann De Courcy, *The Fishing Fleet Husband—Hunting in the Raj* (London: Weidenfeld and Nicolson, 2012).

10　　There is a fascinating story of their contribution to Mayurbhanj in a private family history written by her daughter—with another twenty years spent in India.

11　　These activities were all mentioned on the brief sent to paper presenters of the AAMS 'Reimagining Home' conference, Melbourne, 2017.

Bengali View of Home

Within the Bengali community there are two words for residence. One is *Basha* বাসা and the other *bari* বাড়ী. Both are translated as home, but there is a significant difference. The first is more the place of living, while *bari* is the family home. This distinction needs to be coupled with a recognition that the Bengali concept of family is not nuclear but extended, with very defined roles and responsibilities. In Bengal for a woman, as in most of India, relationships are more important than personal identity—she is somebody's daughter, sister, child, wife, mother, maternal aunt, paternal aunt, grandmother etc. After childbirth, a mother is referred to as her oldest son's mother. A daughter was expected to leave the family home and go and live with her husband's family, and her position in that family would be dependent on her husband's place in his family. Some daughters-in-law were allowed to joke with their fathers-in-law, others were not. The eldest son's wife had more important responsibilities than wives of younger sons. Where a family had no sons to bring a wife into the home, but only daughters, the family had to find a potential husband who was willing to come and live with his in-laws in order to provide support for their old age. Daughters were expected to be married in their birth order. Arranged marriages were viewed with favour and often the women missionaries undertook this responsibility of matchmaking. The missionaries struggled with child marriages that removed young girls from the opportunity for education. They also struggled with the custom of permanent widowhood and found caste among Hindus distasteful. Becoming accepting outsiders was a demanding task and took time, even years.

Another concept of home is often that of hospitality, of sharing food. But among Bengalis the concept of eating together was not that of sharing a meal together, but of providing appropriate food for family and guests and serving them. Even as church communities slowly grew, the eating of what they called love feasts was segregated, so that people were served and did not help themselves. In a culture of pageantry and memorial events Christmas was celebrated with special food, singing and pageants, as was Good Friday and Easter Sunday. These communal events were symbols of the gospel.

Family names

Most women missionaries were usually called *mashima* or maternal aunt, regardless of their marital status. Although an occasional one was *pishima*, paternal aunt;

younger women may be *didi* (big sister in the Hindu/Christian community) or *Bhabi* (among Muslims).[12]

Living arrangements

Initially, the first two women, Gilbert and Arnold, spent their first year living in Calcutta in the home of Rev George Kerry while he organised the building for them in the town of Faridpur, where there were already Bengali preachers supported by the SABMS. Once the building was ready they moved to the town, and Gilbert stayed there while Arnold was invalided home and recruited more workers. SABMS extended the Faridpur house so that the Five Barley Loaves could live together and learn the language. MacGeorge joined them as did Denness, Newcombe and Pearce. By this time Fuller and Wilkin had moved to Mymensingh to establish zenana work for the VBFM. Initially they shared the only missions house with the Ellisons, a BMS couple, then set up a household for just the two of them. About the same time Arnold moved to Comilla to initiate work for the NSWBMS.

As soon as the latest arrivals, the Jubilee Five, were in Bengal at the end of 1887, the group came together for a convention. They were twelve single missionaries; eleven women and one man. Arising out of their convention, they felt the need to inform their missions of an important issue. Rosalie MacGeorge, in taking minutes, recorded the following three resolutions:

1. The inadvisability of living in homes of other married missionaries.
2. The inadvisability of so large a number of lady agents having to wait to have new stations opened up by others whether European or Bengalees.
3. The propriety of building the Mission houses for gentlemen missionaries at some distance from any zenana house, so as to avoid any appearance of evil.

In a more detailed joint letter written to their committees on January 2, 1888, the six senior women stated:

> We the undersigned feel that the time has come to express our opinion to our Committees on a subject that vitally affects the working of our Australian Zenana Missions . . . not to be published, (as might cause misunderstandings at home) and also with great diffidence, since we are all aware of the fact that missionaries much older and more experienced than ourselves (though not engaged in zenana work) differ from us on this point.

---

12 These women worked almost exclusively with Hindu communities or Christians from that background; in their own writing I have not found bhabi used.

It has been said that it is an advantage to place Zenana Missionaries in a home with married missionaries, but our experience points to an entirely contrary conclusion, since in every instance where we have lived or stayed for any time under the same roof with brethren and their wives we have been hindered from entertaining Bengali ladies, on account of the gentleman being on the premises and have also been subjected to the most insulting and vile questions and remarks about our moral characters by the people among whom we work.[13]

On this later subject, we feel very strongly indeed but cannot enter into details. It is therefore our wish that Australian Zenana Missionaries may not be placed in the same named circumstances as we feel such conditions handicap our work in every direction. These remarks apply to living with any married people.

Further if separate houses are erected in the same station for zenana and other Missions they should be in our opinion, a good distance apart, so as to avoid all appearance of evil, and to allow each department of work to go on uninterruptedly.

After a station has been approved of by our father [an interesting term to use. Kerry was the agent for the SABMS] and advisor, Rev G Kerry, we think it advisable that Australian Zenana Missionaries should be allowed to proceed to such new fields in companies of at least two, to open up their own work without waiting for married missionaries to precede them, as the present disproportion of the numbers of our men and women workers is likely to continue for some time. There being now a good many zenana missionaries in the country we can always depend on each other's help in time of sickness or necessity.[14] With earnest prayers that our individual Committees may be guided at every step in their responsible work.

We remain, Yours in the service,

---

13 Their experiences had been with the Kerrys in Calcutta, Fuller and Wilkin with the BMS Ellisons in Mymensingh, and Arnold in Comilla with the Jewsons. MacGeorge had tried to board with a Bengali family in exchange for tutoring their children, which she believed was a better method than being thought to receive payment from the government.

14 Organisationally they were autonomous missions. The workers in India were more ready for federation than the colonial Baptists.

> Signed Martha Plested, Ellen Arnold, Alice G Pappin, Marion Fuller, Rosalie MacGeorge, Ruth Wilkin.

Here was a culturally framed insight that was to shape these missions as they developed, even though there was also a tendency later to retreat into walled compounds in the face of anti-British agitation. Bengal under British rule was a volatile situation with boycotts of British goods, strikes and unrest, particularly after the partitioning of Bengal in 1905, and there developed a tendency for expatriates to retreat into compounds and to institutionalise work in schools and medical clinics, rather than visit the people in their zenanas in the towns. New believers were often extracted from their extended families and the compounds became Christian colonies.

There was a significant number of *Namasudras*, low caste Hindus, living in the *beel* flooded country of Faridpur District, who approached the Faridpur missionaries, particularly Dr Cecil Mead, to help them find social uplift. Mead made it possible for them to gain help with education and several missionaries moved to live among them. The Mead High School is still conducted in that remote village. Several zenana missionaries went and lived among them and founded a home for widows, including child widows. They sought to model a pattern of relationships and to care for the community. A similar home was established at Pabna where a safe roof overhead was required.

Let me conclude with part of a letter from Arnold to Martin, the general secretary of the ABFM, in 1930, just before she defiantly returned to die in Bengal at the end of her long career:

> I've never proposed going back to do my work, because that time has gone, but long ago I told you that when retiring time came it would have to be in India. I gave myself wholeheartedly to God for Bengalees and have in consequence had very much less fellowship with Europeans as you know. Other furloughs have been more endurable because I was able to get about and work for my Bengalees. This time I can't do anything, I am a stranger to my mother's children and only ask to get back to my own little hut, and to die amongst my 'family' or meet the Master in the air with them. There is a breach of love amongst them, which raised its head just as I was leaving and has not healed. One of them writes 'If God bring you back to us then I shall know He answers prayer'—how can I break their faith? I am still praying for distinct guidance and know He will speak to me one way or the other, but the life and training He has brought me through has not brought me to look to any human beings for direction. The passage to Calcutta

costs no more than a funeral here and to drop one's bones into the ocean is far more God honouring than all the poojah[15] that goes on in these 'civilized' lands. I will not bother the missionaries, but just ask them to leave me in peace. The business is not settled yet, I am just waiting and watching, so please don't bother but just pray and digest Acts 21—'Obstinate old man' wasn't he?

After Arnold had served for forty-nine years in Bengal, home for her was a thatched hut by the road, surrounded by, and shared with, her Bible women in a village community. She had moved beyond being merely the accepted outsider. She was buried by the roadside, and her epitaph in Bengali reads:

> Jesus said: I am the way the truth and the life. Ellen Arnold walked this way, preached this truth, lived this life.

Mozir, a Muslim-background believer, was led to Christ as a teenager by Arnold in Pabna, circa 1905. On hearing of her death in 1931, he wrote to the ABFM and described her as his 'mother in the Lord'. Truly a significant relationship of home.

---

15 Poojah (or puja) is ritual worship, a Hindu term.

APPENDIX

Lines on Indian Zenana Work

Frances Ridley Havergal

Oh! For a fiery scroll, and a trumpet of thunder might,
To startle the silken dreams of English women of ease,
Circled with peace and joy and dwelling where truth and light
Are shining fair as the stars and free as the western breeze!

Oh! For a clarion voice to reach and stir their rest,
With story of Sister's woes, gathering day by day.
Over the Indian homes (sepulchres rather than rest),
Till they rouse in the strength of the Lord, and roll the stone away.

Sisters! Scorn not the name, for ye cannot alter the fact;
Deem ye the darker tint of the glowing South shall be
Valid excuse above for the Priest's and Levite's act,
If ye pass on the other side, and say that you did not see.

Sisters! Yea and they lie not by the side of the road,
But hidden in loathsome caves, in crushed and quivering throngs
Down-trodden, degraded, and dark, beneath the invisible load
Of centuries, echoing groans, black with inherited wrongs.

Made like our own strange selves, with memory, mind and will;
Made with a heart to love and a soul to live for ever.
Sisters! Is there no chord vibrating in musical thrill,
At the fall of that gentle word to issue in bright endeavour?

Sisters! Ye who have known the Elder Brother's love;
Ye who have sat at His feet, and leant on His gracious breast,
Whose hearts are glad with the hope of His own blest home above,
Will you not seek them out, and lead them to Him for rest?

Is it too great a thing? Will not alone rise and go,
Laying her joys aside, as the Master laid them down?
Seeking His lone and lost in the veiled abodes of woe,
Winning His Indian Gems to shine in His glorious crown.

Rules and Regulations of the Mission Bungalow
ALOE (A Lady of England)

Charlotte Marie Tucker

The Mission Miss Sahibs [16]must never complain,
The Mission Miss Sahibs must temper restrain,[17]
Must not be fanciful, foolish or vain:
The Mission Miss Sahibs in dress must be plain,[18]
Must furnish their train,[19]
Of two or three languages knowledge attain,
When wearied and puzzled must try, try again;
We cannot learn grammar by leger de main;
The Mission Miss Sahibs must know every lane,
climb ladder-like stairs without fearing a sprain;
The Mission Miss Sahibs must speak very plain,
Must rebuke and encourage, must teach and explain;
The Mission Miss Sahibs must grasp well the reign,
The Mission Miss Sahibs must not look for gain
though doctoring sick folk like Jenner and Quain.
The Mission Miss Sahibs from late hours refrain
for they must rise early and bear a hard strain.
The vigorous cart horses drawing a wain,
that pull well together when yoked twain and twain.
The Mission Miss Sahibs must work might and main,
and therefore good nourishment should not disdain,
for[20] danger is great of them going insane.
The Mission Miss Sahibs must topees retain,
Must guard against sunstroke to health such a bane,
and midst frogs and mosquitoes must patient remain.

---

16   In the printed version, they are referred to as Miss Sahibas, which is a Western Indian expression rather than a Bengali one.
17   A line had been omitted: When 'sust punkah-wala won't pull at the cane'. 'Sust' was noted to mean idle.
18   She had put in double underlining and also written in Bengali besh—very good, excellent.
19   In the poem as printed in Tucker's biography printed in 1895 the word here was 'brain' not 'train'. Agnes Giberne, *A Lady of England: The Life and Letters of Charlotte Maria Tucker* (New York: A. C. Armstrong and Son, 1895).
20   In the printed poem, this is 'or' rather than 'for'.

Yes, even when tormented must smile thro' their pain,
and with courage like that of the knights of Charlemagne.
By Mission Miss Sahibs snakes should be slain.
The Mission Miss Sahibs should sow well the grain.
Dark babies should fondle, dark women should train,
and bubus and begums at times entertain,
Should smile and should soothe, but should not flatter or feign,
And to usefulness thus they hope to attain.

NB. Let all Mission Miss Sahibs *single* remain,
For if not, they step out of their proper domain,
And can never be Mission Miss Sahibs again.

BIBLIOGRAPHY

De Courcy, Ann. *The Fishing Fleet Husband—Hunting in the Raj*. London: Weidenfeld and Nicolson, 2012.

Giberne, Agnes. *A Lady of England: The Life and Letters of Charlotte Maria Tucker*. New York: A. C. Armstrong and Son, 1895.

Gooden, Rosalind M. '"Mothers in the Lord", Australasian Baptist Women Missionaries at the Intersection of Cultural Contexts 1882–1931.' PhD diss.

Neville, Abia. *White unto Harvest: An Account of the Mission in Mymensing, East Bengal*. Geelong, VIC: H. Thacker, 1898.

Wilkin, Ruth. *Gleanings from a Foreign Field*. Geelong, VIC: H. Thacker, 1891.

Wilson, Linda. *Constrained by Zeal: Female Spirituality amongst Nonconformists 1825–1875*. Carlisle, UK: Paternoster Press, 2000.

Chapter 18

OVERSEAS MISSIONARIES AND THEIR FAMILIES: CAN THE HOMECOMINGS FOR THOSE AFFECTED BY TRAUMA BE REIMAGINED?

Linda Devereux

Globally, at any given moment, there are thousands of families involved in church mission work overseas and thousands more who have moved back to their home countries following such service. Some of these missionaries and their families have lived in challenging sociopolitical and geographical situations. By its nature, missionary work overseas can involve risks.[1] However, despite the large numbers of individuals involved, it is generally acknowledged that there is insufficient academic scholarship on the long-term effects of overseas missionary work on missionaries themselves.[2] There is even less understanding of the effects of overseas

---

1   Robert Grant, 'Trauma in Missionary Life', *Missiology: An International Review* 23 (1995).
2   Karen Carr and Frauke C. Schaefer, 'Trauma and Traumatic Stress in Cross-Cultural Missions: How to Promote Resilience', *Evangelical Missions Quarterly* 46, no. 3 (July 2010); Susan Selby, 'Back Home: Distress in Re-Entering Cross-Cultural Missionary Workers and the Development of a Theoretical Framework for Clinical Management' (PhD diss., University of Adelaide, 2011).

missionary work on the children of missionaries.[3] This chapter examines some of the effects of overseas missionary work on missionaries and their families. The information comes, in part, from my interdisciplinary doctoral studies and is based on interviews with missionaries and archival research in the UK and Australia. My focus here is on the following questions:

- What are the long-term effects of challenging overseas work on missionaries?
- What are the effects of these experiences on their children?

Background

I am an insider and an outsider in this research. My parents worked for ten years for the Baptist Missionary Society (BMS) in the United Kingdom (UK). In the 1950s and 60s Dad worked as a doctor at the BMS mission hospital in Yakusu, a small settlement about twenty-five kilometres downriver from Kisangani (which was called Stanleyville while we were there), in what is now the Democratic Republic of the Congo (DRC). Yakusu is situated one degree north of the equator, about 1400 miles inland, high on the northern bank of a wide section of the Congo River. Some say it is very close to the central heart of Africa. It is a mission station with a long history of BMS work. The site was purchased in 1897, ten years after the first Baptist missionaries arrived in Congo, and only two years after King Leopold II of Belgium had been granted Congo as his personal estate. George Grenfell, the earliest BMS missionary in the region, visited the area in the mission steamboat, *Peace*. In a letter to the BMS headquarters in London written from the site, Grenfell predicted that Yakusu and the area around Stanley Falls would be important as a centre of influence over the heart of the continent.[4]

Yakusu mission had a less than prosperous start, however. The early missionaries, like those elsewhere in Congo, were vulnerable to tropical disease. Some died within weeks of arriving, and the average life expectancy for the earliest missionaries while on the field was between two and four years. Half of the BMS missionaries sent to Congo between 1878 and 1887 died.[5] Six of the early Yakusu missionaries are buried in the little cemetery behind the church.

The first hospital was built at Yakusu by the BMS missionary, William Millman, in 1908. However, the medical work really took off after the appointment

---

[3] Stephanie Vandrick, 'The Colonial Legacy and Missionary Kid Memoirs', in *Narrative Research in Applied Linguistics*, ed. Gary Barkhuizen (Cambridge: Cambridge University Press, 2013).

[4] Brian Stanley, *The History of the Baptist Missionary Society 1792–1992* (Edinburgh: T&T Clark, 1992).

[5] Stanley, *The History of the Baptist Missionary Society 1792–1992*.

of Dr Charles Chesterman in 1920. Dr Holmes later joined Chesterman and they worked to virtually eradicate sleeping sickness and other tropical diseases such as yaws from the area. An education program for paramedics, called infirmiers, was also established to train Congolese health care workers to share the skills and work. Chesterman maintained that educating a Congolese workforce was a better way to have a wide effect on the surrounding communities, making teaching and community preventative medicine a priority. Midwifery, maternity and child welfare clinics, and nurse training programs were also established and there was a great need for this work. When the missionaries arrived in the area, two thirds of the children born at Yakusu died within their first year. Dr Stanley Browne joined the team in 1936 and for the next twenty years he researched, treated and virtually eradicated leprosy in the region. He was known worldwide for this work and he built on the international recognition for the medical work at Yakusu established during Dr Chesterman's years at the hospital.

My parents arrived at Yakusu in 1958 with me as a small baby. My dad's medical work included consulting, surgery, teaching in the Congolese health worker training program and providing support and supervision in rural outposts and in the leprosarium on the opposite bank of the river. He, and the other Yakusu staff, also provided health care to missionaries in the region. My mother was also active in medical missionary work. As a laboratory technologist she helped in the Congolese training programs and consulted on difficult cases.

I lived in Yakusu on and off between 1958 and 1964. This intransience was because these years in Congo were punctuated by the Congolese independence struggles, postcolonial violence and political instability exacerbated by cold war meddling by the world's most powerful nations. I was evacuated from the country twice during that time and sent back to my home country of Scotland. Until I was sent there by the British consular representative in July 1960, I had only visited Scotland for a few weeks as a small baby; it was an unfamiliar home. The first evacuation was soon after Congo gained independence from Belgium. There were riots in nearby Stanleyville where several people were killed and so the British women and children were sent back to the UK. We left suddenly, without opportunities for farewells, and without my father. BMS required the men to stay on in Congo to work and to protect the mission resources from threatened communist opportunism.

After this sudden departure from what I had known as home, my family spent eight months living on two separate continents; my mother, my younger brother and I in Scotland, shuttling between the homes of our grandparents, unsure when, and increasingly, if, we would return to Congo. After protracted negotiations with the mission hierarchy, my father finally joined us for a furlough in 1961.

We all went back to Congo in 1962 with a new baby brother and a new determination to stick together as a family; that decision meant that when civil war broke out in 1964 the whole family was caught up in it.

Supporters of Patrice Lumumba, the first Congolese Prime Minister who was murdered by Congolese Government forces aided by Belgian and US agents[6], attempted to set up an alternative government based in Stanleyville. The Simbas, as they called themselves, conscripted an army—including many child soldiers—as they swept across the east and north of the country. In an attempt to gain recognition for their alternative government, and in retaliation for attacks on their army, the Simbas took almost 1,800 expatriates hostage and held them for many months in prisons and under house arrest in and around Stanleyville. Many of these hostages were missionaries[7].

For four months our family, now with four children, was held in Yakusu with very little contact with the outside world. My father and the missionary nurses continued to work under rebel authority; they tried to keep up the hospital work as normally as possible. My mother and my siblings and I were kept to the house under the protection of Simba soldiers. As the weeks went by, 'protection' began to feel like imprisonment. The situation became progressively worse. We were short of food, and some of the bored, frustrated and hungry Simbas resorted to physical and psychological torment of their captives. Our home was searched regularly, our food was often stolen and some of the Simba guards were violent. In her attempts to keep us safe, Mum increasingly kept her children hidden from view inside the house. Towards the end of our confinement, when our lives were being threatened daily by local Simbas and through the radio broadcasts coming from the rebel government headquarters in Stanleyville, my father sedated the two youngest children in our family to keep them quiet and we hid barricaded in a cupboard in our home.

---

6   The Congolese history of these events is contested. See, for instance: Georges Nzongola-Ntalaja, *The Congo from Leopold to Kabila: A People's History* (London and New York: Zed Books, 2007); Jason Stearns, *Dancing in the Glory of Monsters: The Collapse of the Congo and the Great War of Africa* (New York: Public Affairs, 2011); and Susan Williams, *Who Killed Hammerskjold? The UN, the Cold War and White Supremacy in Africa* (London: C Hurst & Co., 2011).

7   A number of accounts of these events have been published. See, for example: Helen Roseveare, *Doctor among Congo Rebels* (London: Lutterworth Press, 1965); David Truby, *Congo Saga: An Authentic Record of the Heroes of the Cross During the Simba Rising* (London: Unevangelised Fields Mission, 1965); and, Jan Verhoeven and Peter Rutten, *Hostages of Makondo* (Queensland: University of Southern Queensland Printing, 2013).

At the end of November 1964, Dragon Rouge, a multinational rescue mission, was put into action[8]. Belgian paratroopers were flown to Stanleyville through British bases on US planes. The Belgian forces were reinforced by Congolese ground troops supported by mercenary soldiers employed by the Congolese Government and funded indirectly by the US.[9] The Belgian paratroopers took over Stanleyville, but as they descended to the airfield the Simbas marched a large group of hostages, men, women and children, into the central square and opened fire on them. About fifty people were killed. Many more were injured. Hundreds of missionaries in outlying areas were also killed in retaliation during the following days and weeks. Thousands of Congolese lost their lives, and millions have died in years of violence and turmoil since.

My family and the four other Yakusu missionaries were rescued by mercenary soldiers led by Mike Hoare, a retired UK army Major and adventurer. I knew, even as a six-year-old, that most people in Congo were not rescued by an army truck full of gun-firing mercenary soldiers, a helicopter and specially chartered planes in an expensive multinational military campaign. We were returned to Scotland just before Christmas 1964. My family is a living example of the unequal politics surrounding international suffering. As Judith Butler argues:

> Lives are supported and maintained differently, and there are radically different ways in which human vulnerability is distributed across the globe. Certain lives will be highly protected . . . other lives will not find such fast and furious support and will not even qualify as 'grievable'.[10]

Until recently, my family talked about these events infrequently, and in fairly general terms. At the time, of course, there was much discussion within the family and in the local and international media. My father was interviewed on the radio and television and he took part in extensive missionary deputation work all over the UK. He admitted recently that he found these experiences hard because they meant retelling the story, including the loss of many close friends and colleagues, which reinforced his survivor guilt.

---

[8] A detailed description of the Dragon Rouge operation can be found in Fred E. Wagoner, *Dragon Rouge: The Rescue of Hostages in the Congo* (Washington, DC: National Defense University, 1980).

[9] Information on US provision of supplies to the mercenary ground forces was provided to the author during an interview with Mike Hoare in January 2011.

[10] Judith Butler, *Precarious Life: The Powers of Mourning and Violence* (London: Verso, 2004), 32.

At the time, the prevailing wisdom was that it was best not to discuss traumatic events with children.[11] It was assumed children would forget, were resilient and would bounce back from challenging experiences; a kind of what does not kill you will make you stronger attitude which can be very compatible with the expectations in some religious settings. And this has mostly been the case for me. I was supported by loving parents and extended family, a strong church community in Scotland and dedicated school teachers. However, as an adult, I wanted to understand more about the broader circumstances of my childhood. I decided to study missionary work, and in particular the events I have described above, in an academic undertaking as part of my doctoral studies. In the section that follows, I situate my family's experiences within a broader, interdisciplinary scholarship on overseas missionary work.

Overseas Missionary Work in Challenging Contexts

One of the things that surprised me most in my work to understand my family's experiences, a finding corroborated by others, is that despite the thousands of lives touched by overseas missionary work, there is very little academic research on the long-term effects of overseas missionary work on missionaries and their families.[12] There are a number of reasons for this lack of information. Some material has been published informally in religious and mission newsletters and websites rather than in mainstream academic publications; it has been published where those who might need it may find it. In addition, much of the scholarship in the Western academic tradition tends to be non-religious, perhaps to the point of 'secularist bias'. Missionaries, it seems, have been excluded, 'dismissed as an embarrassment to the Western Scientific culture'.[13]

There are, of course, many different missionary settings and some missionaries and their families live in challenging sociopolitical and geographical situations. Often, religious or faith-based groups are the only ones prepared to go to the most demanding situations. This is still the case in the DRC where many of the organisations which provide long-term support are church-based. By its nature, missionary work overseas can involve risks and missionaries are at greater risk of encountering trauma and tragedy and other critical situations with greater frequency than most in their home communities, including their home churches,

---

11 Jessica Stern, *Denial: A Memoir of Terror* (Harper Collins, 2010).
12 Carr and Schaefer, 'Trauma and Traumatic Stress in Cross-Cultural Missions: How to Promote Resilience'; Dieke Folmer, 'Missionaries and Impact of Trauma' (All Nations Christian College, 2006); Selby, 'Back Home: Distress in Re-Entering Cross-Cultural Missionary Workers and the Development of a Theoretical Framework for Clinical Management '.
13 Alex McKay, 'Towards a History of Medical Missions', *Medical History* 51, no. 4 (2007): 548.

and, in some cases, executives in mission agencies.[14] The geographical, cultural and political environments in which missionaries live are often affected by poverty, disease, violence, political instability and social oppression.[15] In addition, missionaries frequently work in demanding cross-cultural situations. Individuals may work long hours, but still be faced with more than can be done with the time and resources available;[16] this may lead to missionaries making excruciating, even life and death, decisions about how to allocate resources and services.[17] In one study of missionaries in Africa, 74 percent identified seeing needs that they were unable to meet as a source of stress.[18] In addition to facing these ethical dilemmas that they would not face in their home countries, missionaries also report experiencing role ambiguity, loneliness and isolation.[19] Moreover, missionaries, along with others who return to their home countries after service overseas, may experience re-entry stress.[20]

As a result of these factors, many missionaries suffer a variety of physical and psychological injuries.[21] As mentioned previously, large numbers of the early missionaries to Africa died from tropical diseases and it seems that this was an expected risk of early missionary service.[22] Contemporary missionaries, global health workers and others including aid workers continue to work in countries where they are exposed to significant health risks and disease as the publicity surrounding US missionaries infected by the Ebola virus a few years ago demonstrates.[23] In a number of countries around the world access to food supplies, medicines, electricity and other services is unreliable. Many missionaries work

---

14   Jeanne L. Jensma, 'Critical Incident Intervention with Missionaries: A Comprehensive Approach', *Journal of Psychology and Theology* 27, no. 2 (1999).
15   Grant, 'Trauma in Missionary Life'; Jensma, 'Critical Incident Intervention with Missionaries: A Comprehensive Approach'.
16   Karen Carr, 'Trauma and Post-Traumatic Stress Disorder among Missionaries', *Evangelical Missions Quarterly* (1994).
17   Catherine Hamlin and John Little, *The Hospital by the River: A Story of Hope* (Australia: Pan Macmillan Australia Pty Ltd, 2001).
18   Joan Carter, 'Missionary Stressors and Implications for Care', *Journal of Psychology and Theology* 27, no. 2 (1999).
19   Folmer, 'Missionaries and Impact of Trauma'.
20   Selby, 'Back Home: Distress in Re-Entering Cross-Cultural Missionary Workers and the Development of a Theoretical Framework for Clinical Management'.
21   Carr and Schaefer, 'Trauma and Traumatic Stress in Cross-Cultural Missions: How to Promote Resilience'; Grant, 'Trauma in Missionary Life'.
22   Stanley, *The History of the Baptist Missionary Society 1792–1992*.
23   Tamara Audi, Cameron McWhirter, and Betsy McKay, 'Ebola Virus Infects a Third American Missionary: Doctor's Plight in Liberia Shines Light on Risks and Ethical Choices for Missionaries', *The Wall Street Journal* (2014), https://www.wsj.com/articles/ebola-sickens-a-third-american-missionary-1409700251.

in areas without a safe, reliable supply of drinking water. Studies of overseas workers, including missionaries, suggest that many are not adequately prepared for these risks to their personal health.[24] They may not take adequate pre-service preparation to protect themselves against disease and they may underestimate the dangers of everyday living in a foreign country. For instance, vehicle accidents alone are a major contributor to death and disability for overseas workers in a number of countries where they serve.[25]

Although there are few studies examining the health of missionaries, in one examination of the health of 212 UK missionaries examined by a GP when they returned home a number of serious physical and psychiatric difficulties were identified. Malaria, diarrhoea and giardiasis were the commonest serious problems followed by psychiatric difficulties. Ten percent of the missionaries in the study were repatriated early for health problems. Sixty percent of these were for mental health problems despite the fact that each individual had been carefully screened before being accepted for work overseas.[26] The authors argue that the attrition reflects the major stresses, both social and work-related, experienced by overseas missionaries. Similarly, in a US study the prevalence of basic preventative health measures for missionaries' children in sub-Saharan Africa was reviewed. There were, according to the authors, roughly 27,000 Protestant North American missionaries with 28,000 children serving overseas at the time and these missionary children did not receive the 'necessary preventative health services' required for the countries where their parents worked. In particular, immunisations and water treatment for cooking and drinking were inadequate.[27] The authors of each of these studies suggest that missionary societies could take more care of the health of their overseas missionaries.[28]

Missionary work can be challenging for other reasons. Host countries may experience frequent changes of authority, changes to administrative systems, civil unrest, rebel army activity and lawlessness.[29] Living and working in such

---

24   Claire Panosian, 'Courting Danger While Doing Good—Protecting Global Health Workers from Harm', *The New England Journal of Medicine* 363, no. 26 (2010).
25   Claire Panosian, 'Courting Danger While Doing Good'.
26   Roger Peppiatt and Peter Byass, 'A Survey of the Health of British Missionaries', *British Journal of General Practice* 41 (1991).
27   T. L. Dwelle, 'Inadequate Basic Preventive Health Measures: Survey of Missionary Children in Sub-Saharan Africa', *Pediatrics* 95 (1995).
28   T. L. Dwelle, 'Inadequate Basic Preventive Health Measures'; Peppiatt and Byass, 'A Survey of the Health of British Missionaries'.
29   Grant, 'Trauma in Missionary Life'; Frauke C. Schaefer et al., 'Traumatic Events and Posttraumatic Stress in Cross-Cultural Mission Assignments', *Journal of Traumatic Stress* 20, no. 4 (2007).

situations exposes missionaries to personal danger and to witnessing violence.[30] Occasionally, where violence becomes life threatening, missionaries are evacuated from situations of conflict in the host country. Evacuation can lead to mixed feelings and reactions and has been shown to be a source of stress.[31] There is usually a sense of relief at surviving, but this is often accompanied by intense pain as a result of being separated from indigenous colleagues and work. These emotions can be compounded by the loss of work, identity, community, possessions, pets and home.[32] After living and working closely with a like-minded community with shared goals and beliefs, evacuated missionaries may find themselves alone, or living and working with people who do not share their worldview. A number of those I interviewed found this extremely hard after their rescue from DRC. One nurse commented that she continues to feel very sorry for survivors of hostage situations when they are returned home, because she understands something of the struggle they face trying to fit in where nobody understands what they have been through. She felt very isolated when she returned to the UK. After living closely with others, sharing a home with another nurse, she found living with her mother and then in nursing quarters in a busy metropolitan hospital challenging.

Even when they do not leave a country in dramatic circumstances, missionaries often miss their overseas work when they return home.[33] The world in their passport country has moved on without them, social connections have been lost and as a result some individuals experience disorientation in formerly familiar settings. Missionaries miss doing work that was clearly important and making a difference to the lives of others in obvious ways, or they may experience a sense of failure because they were not able to do enough or make enough of a difference on the mission field.[34] Some never fully adjust to life at 'home' and continue to live in the past, glorifying the country where they lived as a missionary and becoming overly critical of their passport country.[35] Sending organisations and/or missionaries themselves may not recognise these challenges as significant. For instance, multiple goodbyes, missing significant family events at home,

---

30 Carr, 'Trauma and Post-Traumatic Stress Disorder among Missionaries'.

31 Schaefer et al., 'Traumatic Events and Posttraumatic Stress in Cross-Cultural Mission Assignments'.

32 Carr and Schaefer, 'Trauma and Traumatic Stress in Cross-Cultural Missions: How to Promote Resilience'.

33 Folmer, 'Missionaries and Impact of Trauma'; Alison Palmer, 'Issues Facing Returning Missionaries and How Spiritual Direction Can Help', *Spiritual Growth Ministries* (1999); Selby, 'Back Home: Distress in Re-Entering Cross-Cultural Missionary Workers and the Development of a Theoretical Framework for Clinical Management'.

34 Grant, 'Trauma in Missionary Life'; Palmer, 'Issues Facing Returning Missionaries and How Spiritual Direction Can Help'.

35 Palmer, 'Issues Facing Returning Missionaries and How Spiritual Direction Can Help'.

cancellation of long-term projects, serious conflicts, or changes in roles can be seen as normal parts of the missionary job description.[36] However, many missionaries experience unresolved grief as a result of these experiences.[37]

In addition to the challenges discussed above, it is clear that by the nature of their work some missionaries have been exposed to trauma.[38] According to Grant, a psychiatrist who has worked with missionaries over many years, trauma is caused by 'overwhelming life experiences which one cannot integrate into one's belief systems'.[39] Others suggest trauma can result from powerful and upsetting incidents, usually life-threatening, or posing a significant threat to one's physical or psychological wellbeing.[40] There are different types of trauma. Some trauma responses may result from one-off catastrophic events such as natural disasters; others are the result of human-initiated actions such as civil war or terrorism.[41] However, human-made disasters such as wars and civil unrest can have a longer lasting impact on the affected individuals than natural disasters.[42] Other sources of trauma are episodic, more like a repetitive strain type of stress injury which can be brought about through chronic exposure to unresolved challenges.[43] For missionaries, this type of trauma can result from the demands of working long hours in challenging cross-cultural situations, always short of resources, and faced with more needs and demands than can ever be met. Episodic trauma, although it can be normalised when individuals are exposed to certain experiences over a long period of time, can lead to damaging responses such as feelings of being unable to cope with reality and/or a sense of losing one's identity.[44]

At the time a trauma is experienced individuals may react in a variety of ways, such as through the fight or flight response.[45] Those traumatised in a situation

---

36 Karen Carr, 'Crisis Intervention for Missionaries', *Evangelical Missions Quarterly* (1997).
37 Selby, 'Back Home: Distress in Re-Entering Cross-Cultural Missionary Workers and the Development of a Theoretical Framework for Clinical Management'.
38 Selby, 'Back Home: Distress in Re-Entering Cross-Cultural Missionary Workers and the Development of a Theoretical Framework for Clinical Management'. Drawing on the work of Doka, 1989.
39 Grant, 'Trauma in Missionary Life', 73.
40 Australian Psychological Association, 'Understanding and Managing Psychological Trauma', https://www.psychology.org.au/publications/tip_sheets/trauma/.
41 Vamik Volkan, *Killing in the Name of Identity: A Study of Bloody Conflict* (Charlottesville Virginia: Pitchstone Publishing, 2006).
42 L. McCowan, 'A Social Work Approach to Post Genocide Trauma Recovery for the Rwandese Community' (Masters University of Newcastle, 1996).
43 A. Dirk Moses, 'Genocide and the Terror of History', *Parallax* 17, no. 4 (2011).
44 Grant, 'Trauma in Missionary Life'.
45 Bruce Perry and Maia Szalavitz, *The Boy Who Was Raised as a Dog and Other Stories from a Child Psychiatrist's Notebook* (New York: Basic Books, 2006); Volkan, *Killing in the Name of Identity: A Study of Bloody Conflict*.

where they are powerless may freeze.⁴⁶ For example, young children, especially those too small to respond, may try to be unseen as a form of protection from attack. In the longer term, exposure to trauma can lead to effects such as impulsive behaviours, psychic numbing, flashbacks, hypervigilance, irresolvable stress, sleep disturbances and nightmares, startle responses, feeling unsafe, inability to concentrate and remember, bouts of depression, crying, rage, social isolation and estrangement.⁴⁷ Responses vary from individual to individual, but for many survivors, the contours of the universe are forever changed.⁴⁸

Exposure to trauma is now widely accepted to contribute to serious long-term psychological consequences in some individuals. However, in a review study of literature on trauma—where data from many different studies is re-examined and combined to develop a broader understanding—D'Andrea et al. found that trauma exposure could affect physical health in much more profound ways than previously thought. They report:

> Trauma exposure negatively affects the majority of the body's systems. It disrupts gastrointestinal, cardiovascular, immunological and reproductive functioning, the musculoskeletal system and brain structure and functioning. In addition, the risk of developing future medical disease is far greater following exposure to trauma.⁴⁹

The researchers conclude that taken together, the existing literature 'demonstrates that trauma leads to chronic impairment in . . . psychological and physical functioning'.⁵⁰

Despite a great deal of international interest in trauma in many different fields, at the time of submitting my thesis, I found only one published study in an academic journal that examined trauma in missionaries. Carr and Schaefer compare the experience of missionaries working in Europe with a group of missionaries working in West Africa.⁵¹ Two hundred and fifty-six participants completed surveys

---

46   Perry and Szalavitz, *The Boy Who Was Raised as a Dog and Other Stories from a Child Psychiatrist's Notebook*.
47   Grant, 'Trauma in Missionary Life'; Volkan, *Killing in the Name of Identity: A Study of Bloody Conflict*.
48   Carolyn Nordstrom, *A Different Kind of War Story* (Philadelphia: University of Pennsylvania, 1997).
49   Wendy D'Andrea et al., 'Physical Health Problems after Single Trauma Exposure: When Stress Takes Root in the Body', *Journal of the American Psychiatric Nurses Association* 17, no. 6 (2011): 387.
50   Wendy D'Andrea et al., 'Physical Health Problems after Single Trauma Exposure'.
51   Carr and Schaefer, 'Trauma and Traumatic Stress in Cross-Cultural Missions: How to Promote Resilience'.

about traumatic events, current post-traumatic stress and symptoms of anxiety. Resilience and functioning were also examined.

They found that:
- The rates of traumatic events were considerably higher in the West African setting
- A higher frequency of traumatic events was associated with higher rates of post-traumatic stress.

However, interestingly, the study suggests that given the number of traumatic incidents experienced by missionaries, the degree of post-traumatic stress was lower than anticipated; it was lower than for other population groups. The authors suggest that this might be due to a 'healthy missionary effect' related to volunteering and may be similar to a 'healthy warrior effect' identified in studies of combat veterans. This resilience among missionaries is supported by another study which shows that a strong sense of vocation for missionary work was a protective factor for individuals.[52]

I found these discussions relevant to my research for several reasons. Firstly, the notion of the 'healthy missionary effect' was supported by my research. Each of my interviewees was a deeply committed individual with a strong sense of vocation and a desire to help others through their life and work. Most, even in retirement, were still actively involved in their church and/or local communities. None regretted their missionary work and most had gone back overseas. All were generous in their assessments of other people's actions, including those that had negatively affected them. If they had regrets it was about things like wishing they could have done more, or understood the effects of colonialism better, or had more of an understanding of how their reactions to trauma affected their ability to serve.

However, and this is one of the key arguments in this chapter, the research discussed above draws parallels between the physical and psychological reactions of missionaries to their experiences of stress and trauma with those of combat veterans. One significant difference between soldiers and missionaries is that soldiers do not, to my knowledge, take their children with them to the battlefield. Secondly, though the missionaries themselves may feel strongly called to the work, and this may be a protective factor for them, this may not be true for their children. How are the children of missionaries affected by these experiences?

The answer is, that we do not have enough information to know. There is even less scholarship, less published peer-reviewed research, on the effects of overseas missionary work on the children of missionaries than there is on their

---

52   Carr, 'Crisis Intervention for Missionaries'.

parents. The work of understanding trauma and its health effects on the children of missionaries is an area that deserves further investigation.

Third Culture Kids and Missionary Kids

There is a body of research about a group of young people called 'third culture kids' (TCKs).[53] TCKs are described as children who have spent a significant part of their growing up years in a country that is not their parents' home culture. Missionary children (MKs), or mishkids, are a subset of TCKs which also includes groups such as the children of military personnel, diplomats, overseas aid workers, and business men and women. These studies suggest that there are lasting effects for many of these young people, both positive and negative, as a result of growing up in a culture that is different to their parents' home culture.[54] Although these children report being very adaptable and flexible, 'home' can be a slippery concept. Many TCKs experience a great deal of mobility with numerous moves to different homes in their early years resulting in more changes than many children in their home countries.[55] TCKs may come to feel at home 'everywhere and nowhere'. They tend to experience lives punctuated by moving, adapting, surviving, coping and constantly feeling different to others—both in their adopted country and in their passport country.[56] Some may even come to feel that they are 'hidden sacrifices' to the work of the church.[57] Many studies of TCK, in common with the studies of missionaries described above, identify grief and loss as significant issues for these children. The third culture community is filled with people who come and go, leading to a loss of community and relationships.[58] Large numbers of MKs, according to Walters and Auton-Cuff, 'experience more loss before they graduate from high school than

---

[53] See, for instance, David Pollock and Ruth Van Reken, *Third Culture Kids: Growing up among Worlds* (Boston: Nicholas Brealey Publishing, 2009); and 'Third Culture Kids', *Families in Global Transition* (2010).

[54] Pamela Davis et al., 'Evaluating Impact of Transition Seminars on Missionary Kids' Depression, Anxiety, Stress and Well-Being', *Journal of Psychology and Theology* 38, no. 3 (2010).

[55] Kate A. Walters and Faith P. Auton-Cuff, 'A Story to Tell: The Identity Development of Women Growing up as Third Culture Kids', *Mental Health, Religion and Culture* 12, no. 7 (2009).

[56] Walters and Auton-Cuff, 'A Story to Tell: The Identity Development of Women Growing up as Third Culture Kids'.

[57] J. Marshall et al., *Mission and Motherhood: The Hidden Sacrifice. A Snapshot of Yakusu Missionary Mothers*, 5 vols. (San Bernardo CA: Jane Marshall, 2013).

[58] Walters and Auton-Cuff, 'A Story to Tell: The Identity Development of Women Growing up as Third Culture Kids'.

most people experience throughout their lives'.⁵⁹ This can be a particular issue for children who move quickly due to a natural disaster or political crisis in the host country, or for those who leave their overseas home with little notice,⁶⁰ but moving can be hard for children in any situation.⁶¹ Having to change to a different school means that children will need to adjust to new teachers, new classmates and new social norms. These issues are compounded when they also involve adjusting to a new country and a new culture, perhaps even to a new language. In several studies, MKs reported that moves were particularly challenging if they took place without parents and siblings, such as going to boarding school or to university in their passport country.⁶² Some organisations including missionary societies and international schools run re-entry training programs that aim to help TCKs with re-entry issues. However, this support is not universally available, and some have noted that such programs tend to be US-focused.⁶³

Growing up in cross-cultural mission settings can thus expose children to unique psychological stressors and, like their parents, the children of missionaries are sometimes exposed to social and natural traumas. Children living overseas may be more vulnerable to the effects of parental stress because they lack access to close extended family and also because of the pressure on missionaries to have 'good kids' who will be good witnesses for the church.⁶⁴ In addition, children who experience high mobility due to changes in location, furloughs, changes in mission staff and time spent in boarding schools may experience a disruption of nurturing interactions and as a consequence may have trouble developing deep and trusting relationships.⁶⁵ The lack of supportive relationships can be problematic for children who do experience stress or trauma because it is known that healthy

---

59 Walters and Auton-Cuff, 'A Story to Tell: The Identity Development of Women Growing up as Third Culture Kids', 756.

60 Davis et al., 'Evaluating Impact of Transition Seminars on Missionary Kids' Depression, Anxiety, Stress and Well-Being'.

61 Walters and Auton-Cuff, 'A Story to Tell: The Identity Development of Women Growing up as Third Culture Kids'.

62 Walters and Auton-Cuff, 'A Story to Tell: The Identity Development of Women Growing up as Third Culture Kids'.

63 Lauren Purnell and Elizabeth Hoban, 'The Lived Experience of Third Culture Kids Transitioning into University Life in Australia', *International Journal of Intercultural Relations* 41 (2014).

64 Lynette H. Bikos et al., 'A Consensual Qualitative Investigation into the Repatriation Experiences of Young Adult, Missionary Kids', *Mental Health, Religion and Culture* 12, no. 7 (2009).

65 Christopher H. Rosik and K. L. Kilbourne-Young, 'Dissociative Disorders in Adult Missionary Kids: Report on Five Cases', *Journal of Psychology and Theology* 27, no. 2 (1999).

relationships have a positive effect on their ability to recover and thrive.[66] For many missionary children, as it was for my siblings and I, extended family, even in another country, become an important source of stability.

Children who have witnessed trauma and suffering in the course of living overseas can have long-term health effects as a result of these experiences. In one study of TCKs—some of whom were MKs—the researchers found that these children had an increased stress response 'akin to [those] of combat veterans' as a result of traumatic experiences.[67]

And worryingly, a number of studies suggest that trauma may have longer-lasting effects on the underdeveloped brain of a child than it does on the adult brain.[68] In the large review study on trauma by D'Andrea et al. discussed earlier, the authors consider the physical and psychological implications of trauma on children. They conclude that the repetitive strain types of trauma are significant because they 'occur repeatedly *over key developmental periods*, thereby increasing the likelihood of negative outcomes via chronic activation of stress response systems' in children.[69]

The return to the passport country can be a challenging time for TCKs. They may feel vulnerable and unsure about their place in a culture that is supposed to be home, but which often feels alien. Some TCKs experience the adjustment as a form of silencing their previous life. Pollock and Van Recken who undertook some of the earliest and most influential work on the lived experience of TCKs have identified and labelled three groups of behaviours common to TCKs as they re-enter their passport country.[70] These labels—chameleons, screamers and wallflowers—have made their way into much of the literature and popular information produced for TCKs and their families.

Chameleons, as the name suggests, are experts at blending in, on being like those around them. They may, consciously or unconsciously, hide or downplay previous behaviours to fit into the new environment. Screamers, in contrast, react against people and situations which they find foreign, and they may consciously act differently to those around them; they do not feel as if they fit in and they may choose to act in ways that set them apart from others, perhaps even adopting extreme

---

66 Perry and Szalavitz, *The Boy Who Was Raised as a Dog and Other Stories from a Child Psychiatrist's Notebook*.
67 Rosik and Kilbourne-Young, 'Dissociative Disorders in Adult Missionary Kids: Report on Five Cases', 165.
68 J. D. Bremner, 'Traumatic Stress: Effects on the Brain', *Dialogues in Clinical Neuroscience* 8, no. 4 (2006).
69 D'Andrea et al., 'Physical Health Problems after Single Trauma Exposure: When Stress Takes Root in the Body'.
70 Pollock and Van Reken, *Third Culture Kids: Growing up among Worlds*, 87.

behaviour to create distance between themselves and those they meet. Screamers may act out because they fear rejection, and/or they may be so committed to the values and beliefs that they have adopted from their host country that they reject what they see as inferior moral codes in their passport country. Wallflowers tend to withdraw. Pollock and Van Reken (drawing on the work of Schaetti, 2000) suggest that wallflowers are acutely aware of their status as a stranger in an unfamiliar land.[71] They sit on the sidelines and passively observe their new surroundings, trying to understand how to engage with the behaviours of new groups of people in new and unfamiliar settings. They may take time to engage, or perhaps choose to disengage altogether. Becoming a wallflower, Pollock and Van Reken suggest, is the most commonly reported reaction, although most TCKs adopt various aspects of the three roles and may fluctuate between them depending on the situation they are in.

It occurs to me, drawing on my own lived experience of being a TCK, and through my increased understanding of trauma in missionary communities, that each of these three labels entail drawbacks for TCKs and I am surprised by the lack of critique of these taken-for-granted categories in the literature. Each one has the potential to disempower and/or distance the third culture individual from others at a time when they may be most in need of close and nurturing relationships. Reducing TCKs capacity to engage constructively, they reinforce an uncritical acceptance of hegemonic discourses of difference and othering.

To explain further, although the skills of the chameleon are valued and many TCKs appreciate their ability to adapt to new settings and new situations, it is an approach that may mask self-denial and an insecure sense of self. The chameleon can be so focused on others, helping them to feel comfortable through focusing on their needs, that they may deny or minimise their own. They may not be aware of their own needs or know how to ask for help. Chameleons might not easily take steps to recognise and deal with their own emotional pain. Some may feel unable to share the foreign parts of themselves and others report feeling 'fake' as they struggle to develop a sense of who they are in a challenging new setting.[72] Moreover, chameleons do not threaten hegemonic discourse because they learn to adapt. They do not challenge the majority to be more inclusive of those in the minority.

Screamers may find that they alienate others, reinforcing mistrust of individuals who are different to the majority. Their assertive, perhaps even aggressive, persona is likely to draw criticism and drive away others. It may

---

71   Pollock and Van Reken, *Third Culture Kids: Growing up among Worlds*, 87.
72   Walters and Auton-Cuff, 'A Story to Tell: The Identity Development of Women Growing up as Third Culture Kids', 766.

result in social sanctions which leave the TCK isolated and unsupported. Such alienation can be detrimental to individuals who rely on relationships to develop their sense of self.[73]

Wallflowers, in common with chameleons, do not pose a threat to the status quo; they do not tend to openly challenge others or the taken-for-granted power relationships. 'Good' TCKs, Walters and Auton Cuff suggest, may learn not to make a fuss or to draw attention to their feelings or needs. A quiet and uncomplaining demeanour may be viewed positively, and such behaviours may even be encouraged in some settings. Pollock and Van Reken, drawing on the work of Unseem, suggest TCKs may be pressured to be 'little ambassadors', 'little missionaries' or 'little soldiers' because people around them, including their parents, can expect the children's behaviour to be consistent with the goals and values of the organisational system for which the parents work.[74] However, prolonged disengagement from a wallflower is likely to frustrate those who do try to include them; individuals in the host country may give up trying to engage wallflowers if they feel repeatedly rebuffed.

In addition, and more worryingly, each of these three groups of behaviours may mask symptoms of trauma, particularly if those in authority come to regard them as 'normal' for TCKs. The chameleon role may come easily to those who have developed hypervigilant behaviours in response to trauma. Wallflower behaviours may mask dissociative responses. The child or adolescent who feels powerless and confused may feel more comfortable withdrawing physically and psychologically. In contrast, screamers may act out their anger as they attempt to deal with unresolved feelings of grief, loss or rage resulting from changed life circumstances over which they have no control. More research is needed to critique the ways in which what have been promoted as typical responses of MKs to re-entry may be symptomatic of young people in need of more professional care and support.

Conclusion

By its nature, overseas missionary work will involve risks. This is something that missionaries would be aware of and which, it is hoped, would be addressed in missionary training and through support and debriefing during and following missionary work. However, none of the missionaries that I interviewed received any counselling following their service and they all reported that any follow-up

---

[73] Walters and Auton-Cuff, 'A Story to Tell: The Identity Development of Women Growing up as Third Culture Kids', 758.

[74] Pollock and Van Reken, *Third Culture Kids: Growing up among Worlds*.

was left to their home churches and communities, rather than being offered through their sending organisations. Of course, my work reports on events which took place in the 1960s when there was far less appreciation of the potential lasting effects of trauma. Missionary organisations will no doubt have changed their member care in the intervening years. However, this research and the studies by others reported here suggest that more needs to be done to understand the long-term effects of missionary work on missionaries and their families. Studies suggest that trauma changes the developing child's brain differently at different stages, and in addition, repetitive trauma may change a child's brain repeatedly and permanently. Furthermore, children may not have the same protective, 'healthy missionary effect' that their parents have through their strong sense of vocation for their work and a growing body of evidence suggests that that there are multiple long-term physical and psychological consequences resulting from traumatic experiences. In addition, if missionaries themselves are stressed, or dealing with their own exposure to trauma, they may be less able to protect and support their children.

There are clearly costs associated with providing support to returning missionaries and their families, and this needs to be built into the costs of missionary work, as it is for some other groups of overseas workers. Although such care may seem expensive on the surface, comparisons with other organisations that invest in debriefing, such as the FBI, demonstrate the cost effectiveness of retaining well-functioning staff.[75] There is also potential for collaborative efforts on the part of mission organisations to share the costs of supporting missionaries who serve in overseas countries.[76]

Finally, although I am aware that it is difficult for under-resourced organisations to contemplate allocating scarce resources to the care of missionaries and their families, there are most likely great, and *under-reported*, costs to individual missionaries and to their children as a result of their work overseas. Better knowledge of these issues could empower those of us who come into contact with missionaries and their families to support them more effectively. This understanding would then help us to deal compassionately with other groups such as refugees, returned service personnel and aid workers who may also have been exposed to trauma and long-term stress. I am a firm believer that such knowledge leads to greater understanding, which can enable us all to be more effective sources of support and healing, thereby creating welcoming homes and homecomings for those in need in our communities.

---

75 Jensma, 'Critical Incident Intervention with Missionaries: A Comprehensive Approach'.
76 Carr and Schaefer, 'Trauma and Traumatic Stress in Cross-Cultural Missions: How to Promote Resilience'.

BIBLIOGRAPHY

Audi, Tamara, Cameron McWhirter, and Betsy McKay. 'Ebola Virus Infects a Third American Missionary: Doctor's Plight in Liberia Shines Light on Risks and Ethical Choices for Missionaries.' *The Wall Street Journal* (2014). https://www.wsj.com/articles/ebola-sickens-a-third-american-missionary-1409700251.

Australian Psychological Association. 'Understanding and Managing Psychological Trauma.' https://www.psychology.org.au/publications/tip_sheets/trauma/.

Bikos, Lynette H., Julia Kocheleva, David King, Glenna C. Chang, Anne McKenzie, Chris Roenicke, Victoria Campbell, and Katrina Eckard. 'A Consensual Qualitative Investigation into the Repatriation Experiences of Young Adult, Missionary Kids.' *Mental Health, Religion and Culture* 12, no. 7 (2009): 735–54.

Bremner, J. Douglas. 'Traumatic Stress: Effects on the Brain.' *Dialogues in Clinical Neuroscience* 8, no. 4 (2006): 445–61.

Butler, Judith. *Precarious Life: The Powers of Mourning and Violence.* London: Verso, 2004.

Carr, Karen. 'Crisis Intervention for Missionaries.' *Evangelical Missions Quarterly* (October 1997).

Carr, Karen. 'Trauma and Post-Traumatic Stress Disorder among Missionaries.' *Evangelical Missions Quarterly* (July 1994).

Carr, Karen, and Frauke C. Schaefer. 'Trauma and Traumatic Stress in Cross-Cultural Missions: How to Promote Resilience.' *Evangelical Missions Quarterly* 46, no. 3 (July 2010): 278–85.

Carter, Joan. 'Missionary Stressors and Implications for Care.' *Journal of Psychology and Theology* 27, no. 2 (1999): 171–80.

D'Andrea, Wendy, Ritu Sharma, Amanda D. Zelechoski, and Joseph Spinazzola. 'Physical Health Problems After Single Trauma Exposure: When Stress Takes Root in the Body.' *Journal of the American Psychiatric Nurses Association* 17, no. 6 (2011): 378–92.

Davis, Pamela, Kristel Headley, Tracey Bazemore, Jaclyn Cervo, Pamela Sickinger, Melissa Windham, and Mark C. Rehfuss. 'Evaluating Impact of Transition Seminars on Missionary Kids' Depression, Anxiety, Stress and Well-Being.' *Journal of Psychology and Theology* 38, no. 3 (2010): 186–94.

Dwelle, T. L. 'Inadequate Basic Preventive Health Measures: Survey of Missionary Children in Sub-Saharan Africa.' *Pediatrics* 95 (1995): 733–37.

Folmer, Dieke. 'Missionaries and Impact of Trauma.' All Nations Christian College, 2006.

Grant, Robert. 'Trauma in Missionary Life.' *Missiology: An International Review* 23 (1995): 23–71.

Hamlin, Catherine, and John Little. *The Hospital by the River: A Story of Hope.* Australia: Pan Macmillan Australia Pty Ltd, 2001.

Jensma, Jeanne, L. 'Critical Incident Intervention with Missionaries: A Comprehensive Approach.' *Journal of Psychology and Theology* 27, no. 2 (1999): 130.

Marshall, Jane, Mary Taylor, Hazel Phillips, and Derek Browne. *Mission and Motherhood: The Hidden Sacrifice. A Snapshot of Yakusu Missionary Mothers.* 5 vols. San Bernardo CA: Jane Marshall, 2013.

McCowan, Leanne. 'A Social Work Approach to Post Genocide Trauma Recovery for the Rwandese Community.' Masters Thesis, University of Newcastle, 1996.

McKay, Alex. 'Towards a History of Medical Missions.' *Medical History* 51, no. 4 (2007): 547–51.

Moses, A. Dirk. 'Genocide and the Terror of History.' *Parallax* 17, no. 4 (2011): 90–108.

Nordstrom, Carolyn. *A Different Kind of War Story.* Philadelphia: University of Pennsylvania, 1997.

Palmer, Alison. 'Issues Facing Returning Missionaries and How Spiritual Direction Can Help.' *Spiritual Growth Ministries* (1999): 1–8.

Panosian, Claire. 'Courting Danger While Doing Good—Protecting Global Health Workers from Harm.' *The New England Journal of Medicine* 363, no. 26 (2010): 2484–85.

Peppiatt, Roger, and Peter Byass. 'A Survey of the Health of British Missionaries.' *British Journal of General Practice* 41 (1991): 159–62.

Perry, Bruce, and Maia Szalavitz. *The Boy Who Was Raised as a Dog and Other Stories from a Child Psychiatrist's Notebook.* New York: Basic Books, 2006.

Pollock, David, and Ruth Van Reken. 'Third Culture Kids.' *Families in Global Transition* (2010): 636–43.

Pollock, David, and Ruth Van Reken. *Third Culture Kids: Growing up among Worlds.* Boston: Nicholas Brealey Publishing, 2009.

Purnell, Lauren, and Elizabeth Hoban. 'The Lived Experience of Third Culture Kids Transitioning into University Life in Australia.' *International Journal of Intercultural Relations* 41 (2014): 80–90.

Rosik, Christopher H., and K. L. Kilbourne-Young. 'Dissociative Disorders in Adult Missionary Kids: Report on Five Cases.' *Journal of Psychology and Theology* 27, no. 2 (1999): 163–70.

Schaefer, Frauke C., Dan G. Blazer, Karen F. Carr, Kathryn M. Connor, Bruce Burchett, Charles A. Schaefer, and Jonathan R. T. Davidson. 'Traumatic Events and Posttraumatic Stress in Cross-Cultural Mission Assignments.' *Journal of Traumatic Stress* 20, no. 4 (2007): 529–39.

Selby, Susan. 'Back Home: Distress in Re-Entering Cross-Cultural Missionary Workers and the Development of a Theoretical Framework for Clinical Management.' PhD diss., University of Adelaide, 2011.

Stanley, Brian. *The History of the Baptist Missionary Society 1792–1992.* Edinburgh: T&T Clark, 1992.

Stern, Jessica. *Denial: A Memoir of Terror.* Harper Collins, 2010.

Vandrick, Stephanie. 'The Colonial Legacy and Missionary Kid Memoirs.' In *Narrative Research in Applied Linguistics*, edited by Gary Barkhuizen. Cambridge: Cambridge University Press, 2013.

Volkan, Vamik. *Killing in the Name of Identity: A Study of Bloody Conflict.* Charlottesville Virginia: Pitchstone Publishing, 2006.

Walters, Kate A., and Faith P. Auton-Cuff. 'A Story to Tell: The Identity Development of Women Growing up as Third Culture Kids.' *Mental Health, Religion and Culture* 12, no. 7 (2009): 755–72.

Chapter 19

BUILDING CHURCH HOMES ACROSS CULTURAL BARRIERS:
BIBLICAL GUIDELINES WITH EXAMPLES FROM THE MUSLIM WORLD

J. Dudley Woodberry

A common chorus is 'This world is not my home; I'm just a passing through'. However, Scripture adds another dimension: 'Seek the welfare of the city where I have sent you into exile, for in its welfare you will find your welfare' (Jer 29:7). The 'exiles' of our day includes the flood of refugees from lands in turmoil to more developed countries and the reverse flow of Christian workers into lands of need. Our challenge is how to develop church homes for both groups of 'exiles'.

My wife, Roberta, and I have been reading a book during this trip to Australia entitled, 'A Long Way Home', which has also been made into a movie. You probably know the story since it is about a poor Indian boy who falls asleep on a train and wakes up across the country not knowing where his home is. Subsequently, he is adopted by an Australian family and taken to live in Tasmania. Although his living conditions improve dramatically, he longs to find his 'home'. After years of searching he finally finds his mother and his 'home' in India. Our task is to see how we can develop church homes as we serve in other cultures and provide church homes for refugees as they come to live with us. We find guidelines throughout the Bible.

Biblical Guidelines

We find guidelines both by examples and precepts. Terms for God are borrowed from neighbours, such as *El* and *Theo*, and given new meaning, and God uses familiar concepts such as 'covenant' to reveal his will. Paul in turn to the Jew became a Jew, to those under the law as one under the law. He became all things to all people that by all means he might save some (1 Cor 9:19–23).

When Jews followed Jesus in Judea, they did their 'Jewish worship' in the synagogue and their additional 'Christian worship' in homes. When persecution led to the scattering of the Jewish Christians, Gentiles were converted who did not have the same pre-Christian background. Barnabas and Paul taught the Jewish and Gentile followers of Jesus in Antioch for a year. Three questions arose. Which of the Jewish and pagan practices might they retain? Which should they reject for theological or moral reasons? Which should they reject to facilitate table fellowship between Jews and Gentiles? Since these would apply to all the church, this required the inclusion of all the church leaders.

The conclusions of the Jerusalem Council in Acts 15:19–20 were: (1) Abstain from the pollution of [food offered to] idols [for harmony and so brothers or sisters might not stumble by going against their consciences] (1 Cor 8:1–13); (2) sexual immorality; (3) meat of strangled animals and blood [for harmony since this was against orthodox Jewish practices]. The council listened to the advice of Peter (who was sensitive to the views of Jews but had seen in a vision that he should be free to eat 'unclean' food), and Barnabas (who was a harmoniser), and Paul (a teacher in Antioch with Barnabas), and James (the leader of the church in Jerusalem).

Building church homes was important because this was where Jews and Gentiles ate together and worshipped together. Paul says to the Corinthians that they should eat whatever is sold in the market without raising any questions on the grounds of conscience. This also applies if unbelievers invite a Christian to eat with them. If, however, someone calls attention to the fact that the food has been offered in sacrifice, then they are not to eat it because of sensitivity to the other person's conscience. Christians should not give offense to Jew or Greek or to the church of God (1 Cor 10:23–11:1). Thus, the early church tried to avoid any unnecessary divisions and hence to make it as homelike as possible. Now we turn to examples for the Muslim world with their opportunities and challenges for facilitating church homes.

Examples from the Muslim World

Some time ago when General Motors was considering the possibility of opening a plant in Qairawan, Tunisia, I was asked to orient the proposed directors to living and working in that context. We visited the central mosque there which was built by using and adapting the pillars from various churches and temples. As such it illustrated what happened historically in the development of Islam. Its 'pillars' are adopted and adapted from Christian, Jewish and pagan groups in the region.

We shall first note how the 'pillars of Islam' are adaptations of previous Jewish and Christian forms and then how they may again be used or adapted for biblical worship.[1] There are a number of challenges. First, the forms of worship of Christian churches are often strongly influenced by Greek or Western forms rather than Arabic ones used by Muslims. Also, even the names of biblical people are often different (in Hindi or other languages) than those names in the Qur'an.

Even the traditional Arabic translation of the Bible, by Eli Smith and Cornelius Van Dyck (first published in 1865), adopted some Syriac religious and ecclesiastical terms not seen in Muslim Arabic—for example, Yuhanna rather than Yahya for John and Yesu' rather than Isa for Jesus. And Urdu and Hindi Bibles tend to use Hindi rather than Muslim vocabulary. Hence Muslims do not feel at home using them.

The problem has not only been caused by missionaries and the national churches. In Malaysia, *The Star* (April 5, 1988) reported on a bill passed by the Selangor state government forbidding non-Muslims to use such words as Allah, *rasul* (apostles), *iman* (faith), *nabi* (prophet), *Injil* (Gospel), etc., and such phrases as *Alhamdulillah* (praise God!). The same had been done in five other provinces. I sent documentation to Malaysia showing that all had been used by Christians before Muslims and many were removed from the list, but Allah was still retained even though it is found in a pre-Islamic Christian inscription in Syria in the sixth century.[2] This leads us to consider the extent to which the 'pillars of Islam' may be retained or adapted by Muslims who accept Jesus as Lord and Saviour in the way that many Messianic Jews continue to retain Jewish practices and vocabulary that are compatible with the Christian faith.

---

1 For a more detailed analysis and documentation than is possible here see my 'Contextualization among Muslims', in *The Word Among Us*, ed. Dean Gilliland (Dallas, TX: Word Books, 1989), 281–312.

2 Philip K. Hitti, *History of the Arabs*, 6th ed. (London: Macmillan, 1956), 101.

A. THE CONFESSION OF FAITH (SHAHADA)

'I bear witness that there is no god but God (Allah).' As we have noted, Christian Arabs have used the designation 'Allah' longer than Muslims and still do. It has been considered of Christian Syriac origin.[3] And the Qur'an claims 'your God and our God are one' (29:46 [Cairo ed.]/45 [Fluegel ed.]).

The second half of the confession, 'And Muhammad is the Apostle of God,' most Christians would not affirm. However, al-Ghazali (d. 1111 CE), the most celebrated Sunni theologian, is quoted as saying that it is legitimate for Christians to substitute 'Jesus is the Apostle of God'.[4] Or Christians could substitute a Christian confession such as 'Jesus is Lord' (Rom 10:9).

B. RITUAL PRAYER (SALAT)

The term *salat* ('bowing') which Muslims use for institutionalised prayer has long been used in synagogues and churches. And the ablutions also reflect the Jewish influence (Qur'an 5:6/8; 4:43/46; Exod 30:17–21; 40:30–32). The Friday bath in Islam is similar to the Sabbath bath in Judaism. Both Christian baptism and Muslim proselyte *ghusl* are reinterpretations of Jewish proselyte baptism. If Christian baptism is interpreted as proselyte *ghusl* it might be accepted more easily.

Prayer postures in Islam also replicate Jewish and Christian postures—standing (sura 22:26/27; 1 Kings 8:14, 22; Matt 11:25); bowing (sura 22:26/27; Jewish *keri'a*; genuflection in Roman Catholic mass); prostration with forehead on the ground (*sujud*) (in sura 22:26/27; Gen 22:5; Matt 26:39; Jewish *hishtahawaya* and Eastern Christian prayer); and half kneeling and half sitting (*julus*). Kneeling is biblical (2 Chr 6:17; Acts 20:36).

The content of prayer is also stylistically similar to Jewish and Christian prayers. The repetition of 'God is great' corresponds with 'God is blessed' in the Jewish *tefilla*. The *Fatiha*, the first chapter of the Qur'an, has material similar to Jewish and Christian prayers. In fact, 'the Apostle to Islam', Samuel Zwemer, is reported to have recited it in a public gathering in Calcutta in 1928 and then concluded it with the words 'in Jesus' name, amen'.

Both Christians and Muslims make a distinction between liturgical worship (*salat*) and personal invocation (*du`a*) (e.g., sura 14:40/42; Matt 6:6–13; Acts 4:24–31). Muslims and liturgical Christians focus on the former and non-liturgical

---

3   Arthur Jeffery, *The Foreign Vocabulary of the Quran* (Baroda: Oriental Institute, 1938), 66.
4   Al-Qustas al-Mustaqim, ed. V. Chelhot, 'LaBalance Juste', *Bulletin d'Etudes Orientales* XV (1958): 62; Jamil Saliba and Kamal 'Ayyad, eds., *al-Munqidh min al-dalal (The Deliverer from Error)*, 3rd ed. (Damascus 1358/1939), 101; trans. in W. M. Watt, *The Faith and Practices of al-Ghazali* (London: George Allen and Unwin Ltd., 1953), 39.

Protestants on the latter. There are also Sufis and folk Muslims with Christian counterparts which we shall not discuss here.

The ritual prayer of Muslims includes many themes that Christians share:
1. Witness ('I bear witness that there is no god but God' in the call to prayer; cf. Deut 6:4)
2. God's mercy ('In the name of God the Compassionate, the Merciful' in the Fatiha: cf. Ps 86:5)
3. Praise to God ('Praise be to God' in the Fatiha; cf. Heb. *Halelou Yah* and Christian alleluia)
4. God's sovereignty ('Lord of the worlds' in the Fatiha; cf. Talmudic *Melek ha'olam*, King of the universe)
5. Judgement ('King of the Day of Reckoning' in the Fatiha; cf. Rom 2:2–3; John 5:22; Matt 25:34; 1 Cor 15:24)
6. Worship ('Thee do we worship' in the Fatiha; cf. Exod 24:1. The Hebrew *shaha* and Greek *proskyneo* indicate prostration)
7. Refuge ('To Thee we cry for help' in the Fatiha; cf. Ps 46:1)
8. Guidance ('Guide us in the right paths' in the Fatiha; cf. Pss 31:3; 119:1)
9. God's glory ('Glory to my Lord' in the *ruku*; the nominal form of *sabaha* is used, borrowed from the Hebrew and Aramaic *shabeah* of Jewish worship)
10. God's greatness ('the Great' in the *ruku*; cf. Ps 98:1)
11. God's exaltation ('the Most High' in the *sujud*; cf. Ps 83:18)
12. Petition and intercession (possible in the *du`a*; cf. 1 Tim 2:1).

Christian prayer can include most of Muslim prayer except the emphasis on Muhammad and, for Protestants, prayer for the dead. Muslim prayer cannot include quite as much of Christian prayer because of the references to God as Father, Jesus as Lord, and the Trinity and the crucifixion of Christ.

Some Muslims who accept Christ as Saviour stay for a time in the mosque quietly substituting Jesus for Muhammad in the second part of the confession of faith. Where whole villages have turned to Christ, they often use the former mosque as a church. Others in places like Bangladesh continued a mosque-like worship that was faithful to their new allegiances to Christ. In Damascus, the Church of St. John was divided between Muslims and Christians before the Muslims took it over completely. On the other hand, the Caliph Umar decided not to perform the prayer (*salat*) in the Church of the Holy Sepulcher to guard against it being made into a mosque.

To evaluate the extent to which followers of Christ may appropriately continue to worship in a mosque, it is helpful to determine their functions. We have seen that much of formal Muslim worship, though incomplete, is compatible with Jewish and Christian worship except references to Muhammad. Therefore, some

Muslims who follow Christ remain in the mosque for a time to continue to have contact and influence with their family and friends. They refrain from mentioning Muhammad in the formal liturgy or substitute Jesus in the place of Muhammad in the confession of faith, which the eminent theologian al-Ghazali said was legitimate. They in turn gather with other followers of Christ in celebration of communion, thus following the example of early Jewish believers who went to the temple or synagogue and completed their worship in homes (Acts 2:42–47; 19:8–9; 21:26–29).

C. ALMSGIVING (ZAKAT)

This is the obligatory almsgiving, an Aramaic loan word used by the rabbis for charitable gifts, and in Islam it refers to a prescribed percentage of different kinds of property (2.5% for most). *Sadaqa* is another word for almsgiving from the Hebrew *tsedeq* and is used both for obligatory almsgiving (Qur'an 9:58–60) and for voluntary almsgiving (e.g. Qur'an 2:263/265–264/266). There are parallels with the Bible that giving is not to be seen by people (sura 4:38/42; Matt 6:1–4). However, Protestants in particular would take issue with the qur'anic promise that 'whoever forgoes it [legal retribution] as a free-will offering that shall be to him an expiation [for his own sins]' (sura 5:45/49, 89/90, 95/96). Yet Jesus expected almsgiving to be a regular part of the believer's practice (Matt 6:3).

D. FASTING (SAWM)

Fasting is listed as a characteristic of those who submit to God—that is, true Muslims (sura 33:35). The word *sawm* meant fasting in Judeo-Aramaic suggesting that this was the source of Muslim usage, and the Qur'an makes the prescription to fast a continuation of the prescription for those before them (sura 2:183/179). The practice followed the Jewish one of abstaining from eating and drinking in the daytime but not at night.[5] Moses, Elijah and Jesus all fasted for forty days and nights (Deut 9:9, 18; 1 Kings 19:8; Luke 4:1–2). Jesus expected people to fast (Matt 6:16–18) and Paul fasted frequently (Acts 13:2; 2 Cor 6:6; 11:27). Paul includes going hungry as one of the deprivations he endured so that he could 'put no obstacle in any one's way' (2 Cor 6:3). Lack of fasting is seen by Muslims as being irreligious. This then is one way of helping Muslims feel more 'at home' with our faith.

---

5 W. O. E. Oesterly and G. H. Box, *The Religion and Worship of the Synagogue* (London: Pitman and Sons, 1907), 326, 404.

E. Pilgrimage (*Hajj*)

Although the pilgrimage is an adaption and reinterpretation of pagan rituals, it includes elements that God adopted in the schoolhouse of his children Israel. The word *hajj* is the Hebrew *haj* used in Psalm 81:4 (verse 3 in the English translation) for a sacrifice when the Israelites were in Jerusalem. Likewise, the word *qurban*, frequently used to describe the festival of sacrifice during the pilgrimage, is used for 'offering' or 'consecrated' in Leviticus and Numbers. The Feast of Tabernacles has a number of similarities to the *Hajj*—for example, going seven times around the sanctuary (Ps 26:6) as Muslims do around the Kaaba and standing before God as an act of worship.

The concept of the Mosque of Mecca being *haram* (a sacred place restricted to Muslims—sura 9:28) has its counterpart in the Court of the Gentiles, who were not allowed in the temple. As Muslims on pilgrimage put on white clothing when in a consecrated state, so the Israelite priest put on holy garments (Lev 16:4). Likewise, people do not cut their hair when in a consecrated state as was the case with the biblical Nazarite vow (Num 6:5). If all of these elements were used by God in his schoolhouse for his people, can some of them be adopted or adapted as he gathers a new people for himself?

The lessons will no longer need to be taught in Mecca or Jerusalem, for Jesus told the woman of Samaria that worship will no longer be restricted to specific locations (John 4:20–24). God, however, used pilgrimages to teach his people lessons concerning his holiness and their unity as a people. Today he is using some similar means to do the same. We now turn to adaptations that people, especially from Muslim backgrounds, make to help churches feel more like home.

Adapting the Pillars

Some years ago, a largely Muslim country in South Asia experienced a natural catastrophe. Most of the Christians were not from Islam but from other religious communities. Twenty Christian couples were brought in to help in the relief work, but only one couple had a Muslim background. All their work was appreciated, but the Muslims would not eat their food because the Christians were considered 'unclean' because they did not bathe in the morning when they might have had sexual relations the night before. As the first-century Gentile Christians changed their eating habits so that they could have table fellowship with Jewish Christians, once the Christian workers bathed in the morning the Muslims would eat with them.

However, the Muslim neighbours did not follow Christ until the Christians performed ritual prayers. Subsequently only Muslim converts to Christ were employed. They performed more contextualised worship, and the New Testament was translated using Muslim rather than Hindu vocabulary. They prayed for the sick.

Also important was the fact that some of the Christian workers knew the Qur'an well. The Muslims believed that Muhammad would be an intercessor at the final judgement, but the Christians pointed out that he is not mentioned by name in the Qur'an as an intercessor. They noted that only one whom God approves may intercede (sura 19:87/90; 20:109/108; 53:26/27). However, the *Injil* (Gospel), which the Qur'an affirms, says that God approves of Jesus (Matt 3:17; Mark 1:11; Luke 3:22) and states that he is the only mediator between God and humans (1 Tim 2:5). This fits in with the common interpretation of sura 43:61 as designating that the return of Jesus will be a sign of the last hour.

Some of the Muslim *'ulema* asked the Christians if they believed that Muhammad would be that mediator on judgement day. The Christian spokesman asked, 'Does the Quran say so?' When the *'ulema* could not show a verse that said so, many decided to follow Jesus. Attempts were made to keep families and social units together, if possible, by baptising people only if the head of the family was being baptised. Conversions were normally along family, friendship, or occupational lines. When whole villages followed Christ, the mosque became the church.

Converts developed a contextualised prayer ritual that followed a Muslim form but expressed their new allegiance to God through Jesus. The morning prayer starts with the normal 'intention' (*niya*) to pray but adds 'in the name of my Lord and Saviour Jesus Christ' before the traditional exclamation 'God is great' (or literally 'God is greater'). In the first cycle of prayer Psalm 23 or other biblical passage is recited. The rest of the cycle follows the traditional postures and praises to God although 'all praise to Jesus Christ' may be substituted. Similar biblical additions are made in the subsequent recitations of the prayer plus prayers for their country and Muslims who have not yet confessed Jesus as their Saviour.

Such contextualisation presents many challenges. One is the problem of training leadership for such a creative and rapidly growing movement. Another is how to build bridges to other segments of the church with their distinctives, without inhibiting growth. The demise of the Nestorian Church gives evidence of the results of being isolated. A third problem is how to reuse Muslim forms without retaining common Muslim meanings, such as merit. A fourth is how to avoid an ossified contextualisation that inhibits maturity, an apparent problem of the Jewish believers to whom the Epistle to the Hebrews was written. Despite the dangers, God has been blessing the reuse of those pillars with slight modification to bear the weight of new allegiances to God through Christ.

Home is Where Love and Forgiveness Are

Although every period of Islam has had peaceful and militant expressions, we have seen an increasing militancy since 1979 with the Iranian Revolution led by Ayatollah Khomeini. What was meant to bring the peace of Islamic rule ended up bringing discontent so that when I was privileged to be a guest of Mr. Zarif, the Foreign Minister of Iran, at the beginning of the Nuclear Negotiations, the first time I was alone without a government minder, Iranian citizens approached me to ask about my faith. They wanted something other than religious militancy. They wanted a spiritual home. The Iranian underground church continues to grow rapidly. The Iranian Christians in Southern California meet on an evening during the week so that they can find a church in their community where their children can also feel at home.

When our family lived in Afghanistan, there were very few Afghan Christians. The Russian Soviets gradually took over the country until the Afghans drove them out with help from the UN. But the Afghan factions then began to fight each other until the Taliban took over. During all of this turmoil many Afghans became refugees in Pakistan and some became Christians elsewhere and have since returned to Afghanistan. My wife Roberta and I met two this year. During the Soviet takeover of Afghanistan, they had been sent to Russia as orphans. They got married as teenagers, and then became Christians when they went to Pakistan. They now help other Afghans find a home in the church.

Recently my wife and I were in Lebanon, where we had first met as students years ago. The churches in that land had not reached out to Muslims very much in the past, but with the recent fighting in Iraq and Syria many Muslim refugees had fled to Lebanon for safety, and the Christians were providing for them. The result has been that Muslims are attending Christian churches where they are finding a home to replace the ones they have lost.

In April 2015, twenty-one Egyptian Christians were beheaded on the shore of the Mediterranean in Libya by the Islamic State as the Christians were saying Jesus's name. Immediately the Bible Society in Egypt published a tract of Christian forgiveness and the new life that the twenty-one martyrs now had. On Palm Sunday this year forty more were killed by bombs in two churches, but the Christians forgave them. The response has been the opposite of what the Islamic State expected. So many Muslims are accepting Christ because they want something different. I heard an Egyptian pastor say recently that he baptised ten Muslims in just one service.

Having looked at biblical guidelines for facilitating church homes and at examples from the Muslim world, where do we go from here? In today's world, we have many groups to which we belong. The first-century Christians, as we have seen, had to work on the problem with the Jewish and Gentile believers in Christ. This involved a time of teaching, then consultation, and then a flexibility in adaptation and acceptance under the lordship of Christ. Now there are more varieties and options in a globalised world, but we need to take the same steps. We looked at the first step of teaching. What is essential to our identity?

On the *vertical level,* it is certainly our relationship to God through Jesus Christ. On the *horizontal level,* for the Muslim background believer, it has been and may continue to be, if possible, the Muslim community along the multiple callings we have in a globalised world. Churches likewise are culture based so are a blend of the gospel and the local culture where they have grown. Yet this blend of gospel and local cultures has helped the church be a worldwide church.[6]

Thus, our challenge is how to be true to Christ while being flexible in optional things so that the church is, or becomes, a home for the stranger in our land or for us when we go as strangers to another land. Like the Indian boy who was adopted by Australian parents in Tasmania, we all long for home. May we help others find church homes that will be a foretaste of our future 'home, not made with hands, eternal in the heavens' (2 Cor 5:1).

---

6 See David Greenlee, ed., *Longing for Community* (Pasadena: William Carey Library, 2013), 22–39.

BIBLIOGRAPHY

Al-Mustaqim, Al-Qustas. 'LaBalance Juste.' Edited by V. Chelhot. *Bulletin d'Etudes Orientales* XV (1958): 62.

Hitti, Philip K. *History of the Arabs*. 6th ed. London: Macmillan, 1956.

Greenlee, David, ed. *Longing for Community*. Pasadena: William Carey Library, 2013.

Jeffery, Arthur. *The Foreign Vocabulary of the Quran*. Baroda: Oriental Institute, 1938.

Oesterly, W. O. E., and Box, G. H. *The Religion and Worship of the Synagogue*. London: Pitman and Sons, 1907.

Saliba, Jamil, and 'Ayyad, Kamal, eds. *al-Munqidh min al-dalal (The Deliverer from Error)*. 3rd ed. Damascus 1358/1939, 101. Translation in W. M. Watt, *The Faith and Practices of al-Ghazali*. London: George Allen and Unwin Ltd., 1953.

Woodberry, J. Dudley. 'Contextualization among Muslims.' In *The Word Among Us*, edited by Dean Gilliland. Dallas, TX: Word Books, 1989.

CONCLUSION

ADVANCE AUSTRALIA HOME?

Darren Cronshaw

Thirty years ago, John Smith, founder of God's Squad Christian Motorcycle Club, wrote *Advance Australia Where?*[1] Released during Australia's celebration of the bicentenary of white settlement, the book offered prophetically challenging commentary on Australia's identify crisis, our convict beginnings, mistreatment of Aboriginal people, finding purpose in a materialistic society and the place of God in a 'post-Christian' age. Avoiding clichés and wowserisms, Smith urged reimagining who God is and what really is good news in ways that are relevant to Australia, commenting for example:

> It's not that we haven't presented an Australian God, but that we haven't presented the biblical God—the God of the Bible is relevant to Australia simply because He is God. The key to evangelising Australians is to begin to rectify the shocking images of God we have developed—the God who is a standover merchant, the God who is not interested in wholeness, but who snoops around ready to wallop me when I mess up, the kind of God who says 'no' more than he says 'yes'. They're the images the Aussies have of God. Australians have had the wrong image of God bequeathed to them by a history of neglect and tragedy and a delinquent church.[2]

---

[1] John Smith, *Advance Australia Where? A Lack of Meaning in a Land of Plenty* (Homebush West: ANZEA, 1988).

[2] Smith, *Advance Australia Where?*, 227–28; discussed in Darren Cronshaw, *Credible Witness: Companions, Prophets, Hosts and Other Australian Mission Models* (Melbourne: Urban

Instead of a judgemental and disinterested God, Smith called his readers back to Scripture to see how salvation involves coming under the care of a loving God who longs to be involved in all our life—sex and art, business and family, recreation and justice, politics and sport.[3]

I continue to be challenged by Smith's words and appreciate the content of his writing. Moreover, I am encouraged by his engagement over many decades in questions of what it means to practice radical discipleship in the Australian context. We need to freshly engage the process of reimagining who we are as God's people and how we express mission for each new generation, and in each of the cultural contexts in which we are placed.

Thus, I am encouraged by the dozens of Australian Association for Mission Studies (AAMS) conference participants, presenters and now writers who have been 'reimagining home'. AAMS conference participants are always a thought-provoking combination of Anglo and other cultures, academics, students and practitioners, missiologists and experts from other disciplines. That diversity was especially important as we sought to understand, reconcile and engage with God's stories together in our increasingly diverse and often alienating environment. The issues explored in conference papers and now published chapters included migration, second-generation migrants, environment and ecotheology, economics, rural ministry, indigenous theology, care for missionaries and their families, urban mission and community development. The countries they have been reimagining home for, or cultural contexts they have been reflecting on, included Bengal, India, China, the Pacific Islands, North American First Nations, Aotearoa New Zealand and Australia. Biblical reflection was broad, but engaged in deeper ways with Isaiah, Luke, Romans and Ephesians. In reaching the conclusion, you have read how the writers of this volume point in helpful and life-giving directions about how we can encounter Jesus, experience *shalom*, and be part of a community where we all belong and feel genuinely at home.

The invitation to reimagine home resonates throughout the biblical narrative. The Bible begins with God imagining and then creating the world—in part as a home for people (Genesis 1). God placed man and woman in the garden of Eden as their home (Genesis 2). As part of God's dream for the world, God continued to take an interest in where people made their home. He called Abraham from his country and people to a new homeland. Abraham reimagining home was part of God's call for him to be blessed, in order for all peoples of the earth to be blessed through him (Genesis 12:1–3). Joseph and then his father and brothers needed a new home in Egypt (Genesis 39–50). Eventually, Moses led Israel out of their

---

Neighbours of Hope, 2006), 104.

3 Smith, *Advance Australia Where?*, 195–96.

home of Egypt in Exodus, and Joshua led them to their new home of the Promised Land. God's people had to reimagine home at each step of their journey—what it meant to belong to God and belong to one another in new contexts.

Israel reimagining home was especially challenging when they were carried away in exile. Living in Babylon, far from their beloved temple and everything that reminded them of God's blessings, the prophet Jeremiah urged them to reimagine that place they saw as cursed as their home. They were warned not to imagine that they would be rescued and taken away from it anytime soon, but were to foster family and peace and prosperity where God had placed them:

> This is what the Lord of Heaven's Armies, the God of Israel, says to all the captives he has exiled to Babylon from Jerusalem: 'Build homes, and plan to stay. Plant gardens, and eat the food they produce. Marry and have children. Then find spouses for them so that you may have many grandchildren. Multiply! Do not dwindle away! And work for the peace and prosperity of the city where I sent you into exile. Pray to the Lord for it, for its welfare will determine your welfare' (Jeremiah 29:4–7, New Living Translation).

That is quite a mandate for reimagining home with a vision for community development wherever God sends and places us.

The good news of Christianity is that God in Jesus made his home with people. John explains this incarnational truth: 'the Word became human and made his home among us' (1:14, New Living Translation). The ministry of Jesus brought holistic salvation, including freedom for those who are oppressed:

> The Spirit of the Lord is upon me,
> for he has anointed me to bring Good News to the poor.
> He has sent me to proclaim that captives will be released,
> that the blind will see,
> that the oppressed will be set free,
> and that the time of the Lord's favor has come
> (Luke 4:18–19).

In other words, Jesus came to bring to the poor and oppressed and those in captivity a new home out of the prison they found themselves in.

This encourages me to consider in what ways is the gospel about 'reimagining home'? Early church writers urged Christians to look forward to new heavens and a new earth (2 Peter 3:13). The vision of Revelation includes the truth that one day God's home will be with us, with resulting comfort and alleviation of suffering:

> 'Look, God's home is now among his people! He will live with them, and they will be his people. God himself will be with them. He will wipe every tear from their eyes, and there will be no more death or sorrow or crying or pain. All these things are gone forever' (Revelation 21:3b–4).

Note, however, that the promising hope here is not that we go to heaven, but that God brings God's home of heaven to earth. Tom Wright comments that our hope is that God will make his home with his people: 'filling the city with his life and love, and pouring out grace and healing in the river of life that flows from the city out to the nations'.[4] Furthermore, comments Wright, this points to the work of the redeemed in God's new world—a task of cooperating with God in this work of re-creation:

> So far from sitting on clouds playing harps, as people often imagine, the redeemed people of God in the new world will be the agents of his love going out in new ways, to accomplish new creative tasks, to celebrate and extend the glory of his love.[5]

Unfortunately, sometimes the message that 'this world is not our permanent home; we are looking forward to a home yet to come' (Hebrews 13:14, NLT) has mistakenly led Christians to neglect their responsibility for their home where God has placed them. We are 'citizens of heaven' (Philippians 3:20), but that does not mean we will retire there, or give up on our home on earth.[6] The great hope of Christianity is for the restoration of all things in a new heaven and new earth. And we can cooperate with God in fostering that here and now. Salvation and 'reimagining home' does not look beyond this world, but invites God to foster shalom and wellbeing where we are.

Reimagining home has been part of Australia's ongoing story too. Indigenous people have stewarded the land as home for at least 65,000 years.[7] For them, as we learn for example from reading *Rainbow Spirit Theology*, God was never conceived as up in heaven and separate from the land, but within and shaping the earth. They never saw the land as their home that they owned, but a sacred place to which they belonged.[8]

4　Tom Wright, *Surprised by Hope* (London: SPCK, 2007), 117.

5　Wright, *Surprised by Hope*, 117.

6　N. T. Wright, 'Heaven is Not Our Home', *Christianity Today* (March 24, 2008), http://www.christianitytoday.com/ct/2008/april/heaven-is-not-our-home.html.

7　Ann Gibbons, 'The First Australians Arrived Early', *Science* 357, no. 6348 (July 21, 2017): 238–39.

8　Cf. The Rainbow Spirit Elders, *Rainbow Spirit Theology: Towards an Australian Aboriginal Theology* (Melbourne: HarperCollins, 1997); Jasmine Corowa and Norman Habel, *The*

White settlers—convicts and other early arrivals—had to work out what it meant to make this land home. It was disorienting trying to make sense of a climate that was so different to what they knew 'back home' in the northern hemisphere until they finally realised that the seasons were reversed. The way that the early settlement mistreated Aboriginal people was disastrous. They failed to recognise them as custodians of the land, instead presuming what has since been recognised as the legal myth of *terra nullius*.[9]

Waves of migrants over Australia's history have continued to arrive and reimagine their home in this context. Some of the earliest non-European migrants were the Chinese of the gold rushes. But Australia predominantly preferred Anglo-Celts, or at least Europeans, such as the many European workers who arrived after World War II. The preference for having neighbours who were 'like us' was enmeshed in the White Australia policy, only abolished in 1973, and replaced by an official agenda for multicultural Australia over subsequent decades.[10] The national home we are reimagining is one with Asians and Africans alongside Europeans and Americans, newcomers alongside those who have been here for generations, or—in the case of indigenous Australians—thousands of years. Yet reconciliation with Aboriginal people on the one hand, and multiculturalism with people from all around the world on the other, does not always match the rhetoric we espouse.

We would like to imagine a home of equality and justice where celebrating both our unity and our diversity, as in the popular 1987 song *We are Australian* composed by Bruce Woodley (of *The Seekers*) with Dobe Newton (of *The Bushwackers*), is our experience. The aspiration of that song that recognises the diversity of our origins is that we hope to share a dream and sing together in one voice about how we are all Australian. It captures the imagination of many who call Australia home (though I am admittedly mixing my lyrics or language with another song, Peter Allen's *I Still Call Australia Home.*) Former Victorian Premier, Jeff Kennett, suggested that the national anthem be replaced with *I am Australian*.[11] Yet, despite our aspirations for recognising our indigenous heritage and cultural diversity, there is much work to do before our reality matches our rhetoric.

Rainbow Spirit in Creation: A Reading of Genesis 1 (Collegeville: Liturgical Press, 2000); Darren Cronshaw, 'Reading Rainbow Spirit Theology: Learning from an Australian Aboriginal Theology', *Mission Studies* 32, no. 3 (November 2015): 418–41; Cronshaw, *Credible Witness*, 17–22.

9 Cf. Henry Reynolds, *The Law of the Land* (Ringwood: Penguin, 1987).

10 Mark Lopez, *The Origins of Multiculturalism in Australian Politics 1945–1975* (Melbourne: Melbourne University Press, 2000); Cronshaw, *Credible Witness*, 132–33.

11 Grant McArthur, *'Jeff Kennett Wants National Anthem Changed'*, The Advertiser (February 11, 2011), http://www.adelaidenow.com.au/news/strewth-time-for-dinki-di-anthem/news-story/f190ba8a96a72ef4a2cadb8a421edace.

The history of Australia's national anthems, or anthem-like national songs, reveals interesting insights about how we reimagine our home and express national identity.

God Save the Queen/King was Australia's inherited anthem from Federation in 1901. It resonates strongly with Australia's colonial connections to the British Empire and its sovereign. It also reflects an enmeshed system of religion and politics that pleads with *God* to 'save our gracious Queen' and to 'send her victorious'. The second verse (although not usually sung in Australia) continues the plea to 'scatter her enemies', 'confound their politics' and 'frustrate their knavish tricks'.[12] It is no surprise that there was growing interest through the twentieth century to replace it with an anthem that sounded more at home in Australia.

Whitlam's quest for a national anthem in 1974 attracted 2,500 lyric entries, including, for example, the laconic *Give Me a Home Among the Gumtrees*. In 1977 the Fraser government polled the population with a plebiscite about which of four songs they would like to sing at non-regal occasions. The preference was *Advance Australia Fair* (43 percent), followed by *Waltzing Matilda* (28 percent), *God Save the Queen* (19 percent) and *Song of Australia* (10 percent). *Advance Australia Fair* became the official anthem in 1984.[13]

Written in the 1870s by Peter Dodds McCormack, the original four verses made several mentions of England. The adopted version only had two verses. Thus, in my early years of primary school assemblies I changed from singing 'God save our gracious Queen' to inviting myself and others to rejoice together as Australians in *Advance Australia Fair*. Perhaps because I grew up with it, perhaps because the lyrics resonate strongly with some of Australia's unique geography and history, or perhaps because it evokes memories of significant occasions, singing *Advance Australia Fair* reminds me that I am proud to be an Australian. Take me to the bush, desert or ocean anywhere around our country, and my response is the same—I'm glad to be at home in Australia. Other things also bring out my national pride. I love the perseverance shown by successive generations who have called Australia home. And I celebrate Australian aspirations for justice and a fair go, helping mates, multiculturalism and making the most of summer. It feels appropriate to echo this appreciation with 'Australians all let us rejoice'. Yet I also recognise darkness in the pages of our history. There was no official war against indigenous people, like the American Indians or Aotearoa New Zealand Maoris.

---

12   This work and its copyright are in the public domain.
13   Tony Ward, 'How Advance Australia Fair Waltzed with Matilda and Won', *The Conversation* (January 24, 2014), https://theconversation.com/how-advance-australia-fair-waltzed-with-matilda-and-won-21564.

But the undeclared war against our first nations is a blight for which I feel shame.[14] As a white settler Commonwealth nation we are young—it has been only 230 years since the First Fleet's white settlement and only 117 years since Federation. But Australia's first nations have been here for at least two hundred times more than that. We are *not* all 'young and free', as *Advance Australia Fair* intones. The anthem does not tell our full story. Perhaps it is more inclusive, as has been suggested by Victorian Supreme Court judge, Peter Vickery, to change the phrase to 'in peace and harmony'.[15]

I do not know my ancestors' role, if any, in Aboriginal mistreatment, but I can hear their whisper and I am deeply sorry for what happened—sorry on behalf of my ancestors and for white Australia's poor relations with indigenous people. It may not have been my sin, but I benefit from it. I grieve when I read of labour and property disputes between indigenous and non-indigenous. I sing about the abounding extent of the gifts of nature that are both rich and rare in our country— yet I acknowledge that they are mine to enjoy because yesterday they were taken from someone else.

In addition to massacres and the injustice of land taken while presumed empty, there is the injustice of imported disease (sometimes used intentionally as a kind of germ warfare), abuse of labour, stolen wages, stolen generations, extinction of Tasmanian Aboriginals, slow recognition of indigenous people as worthy of citizenship, and ongoing inequality in health and education. We do not have to probe hard to see the scale of injustices. I will wear a black armband without hesitation. The weight of evidence is overwhelming. Thankfully, throughout white Australian history, there are stories of advocacy for, and respect of, Aboriginal culture. But overall our treatment of Aboriginal people has been far from a balanced sheet, and to suggest that massacres and mistreatment are a fabrication is ludicrous and academically suspect.[16]

I hope that in the twenty-first century 'history's page' we will continue to face the darkness in our history and advance beyond it. We will do well to learn

---

14 Cf. Henry Reynolds, *The Other Side of the Frontier: Aboriginal Resistance to the European Invasion of Australia* (Sydney: UNSW, 2006); *Forgotten War* (Sydney: NewSouth Books, 2012).

15 Renee Viellaris, 'Alternative Version of Advance Australia Fair Recognises Indigenous', *The Courier-Mail* (May 23, 2017), http://www.couriermail.com.au/news/national/alternative-version-of-advance-australia-fair-recognises-indigenous/news-story/187a84db7fcf95535b6b074f85c3cc2d.

16 Robert Manne et al., 'The Inaugural Melbourne Debate, 26 March 1998: "That Australia's Historians Should Wear Black Armbands"', *Melbourne Historical Journal* 26:1 (1998): 1–16; cf. Keith Windschuttle, *The Fabrication of Aboriginal History* (Sydney: Macleay, 2002); Robert Manne, ed., *Whitewash: On Keith Windschuttle's Fabrication of Australian History* (Melbourne: Schwartz, 2003).

from indigenous whispers. It is appropriate as Australians to be proud of much, but also to be appropriately shamed. May that amalgam of pride and shame motivate us toward our best years of relating and working and celebrating together. May the Spirit of God hover over us and draw out our best. I sing *Advance Australia Fair* proudly, but I long for it to reflect wholeness and prosperity for indigenous people as well as for those who have come to these shores more recently.[17]

As an Australian, I learn from Aotearoa New Zealand's history and relationship with indigenous people too. The 'Reimagining Home' conference in Australia welcomed input from Aotearoa New Zealand. In this volume, Steve Taylor's introduction of the Maori chief, Wiremu Tamihana, and his reimagining of home in the face of colonisation, and Kevin Ward's history of church planting among Chinese immigrants, were among the most informative chapters for me. My concluding chapter focuses on Australia, not because it is the only context for reimagining home, but it is where I am placed. How we can advance Australia's home is the main question that I pose here for myself. But in grappling with that question I learn from other contexts. In terms of national anthems, Aotearoa New Zealand has sung *God Defend New Zealand* as its national anthem since 1977 and this is sung first in Maori and then in English. Singing the first verse in Maori must give a rightful sense of pride to Maori people, as well as remind Pākehā (New Zealanders of European descent or any non-Maori) of the indigenous heritage of the land they now share.

Australians might reimagine a home where *Advance Australia Fair* is cause for rejoicing for all Australians. Or there night be an argument for changing the anthem, or at least some of its lyrics, again. Deborah Cheetham, Australian Aboriginal soprano and Associate Dean of Music at University of Melbourne, refused to sing the national anthem at the 2015 AFL Grand Final, largely because of the offensive line 'we are young and free'. In 2009 she helped launch alternative lyrics, written by Judith Durham together with Muti Muti songwriter Kutcha Edwards.[18] These verses seek to celebrate the Dreaming and sacredness of our land, the integration of ancient history and new cultures, and invite us to look towards the future with courage. They invite us to match our rhetoric of celebrating unity and diversity in the home that we share with a reality of showing respect for our ancient history and diverse cultures.

---

17 Previously discussed in Darren Cronshaw, 'Sidebar Column (Darkness—Not Forgotten, by Fiona Hill)', *Witness: The Voice of Victorian Baptists* 91, no. 3 (April 2011): 17.

18 Deborah Cheetham, 'Young and Free? Why I Declined to Sing the National Anthem at the 2015 AFL Grand Final', *The Conversation* (October 20, 2015), https://theconversation.com/young-and-free-why-i-declined-to-sing-the-national-anthem-at-the-2015-afl-grand-final-49234.

BIBLIOGRAPHY

Cheetham, Deborah. 'Young and Free? Why I Declined to Sing the National Anthem at the 2015 AFL Grand Final.' *The Conversation* (October 20, 2015). https://theconversation.com/young-and-free-why-i-declined-to-sing-the-national-anthem-at-the-2015-afl-grand-final-49234.

Corowa, Jasmine, and Habel, Norman. *The Rainbow Spirit in Creation: A Reading of Genesis 1.* Collegeville: Liturgical Press, 2000.

Cronshaw, Darren. *Credible Witness: Companions, Prophets, Hosts and Other Australian Mission Models.* Melbourne: Urban Neighbours of Hope, 2006.

Cronshaw, Darren. 'Sidebar Column (Darkness—Not Forgotten, by Fiona Hill).' *Witness: The Voice of Victorian Baptists* 91, no. 3 (April 2011).

Cronshaw, Darren. 'Reading Rainbow Spirit Theology: Learning from an Australian Aboriginal Theology. *Mission Studies* 32, no. 3 (November 2015): 418–41.

Gibbons, Ann. 'The First Australians Arrived Early.' *Science* 357, no. 6348 (July 21, 2017): 238–39.

Lopez, Mark. *The Origins of Multiculturalism in Australian Politics 1945–1975* (Melbourne: Melbourne University Press, 2000).

Manne, Robert, Stuart Macintyre, Janet McCalman, and Graeme Davison. 'The Inaugural Melbourne Debate, 26 March 1998: "That Australia's Historians Should Wear Black Armbands."' *Melbourne Historical Journal* 26:1 (1998): 1–16.

Manne, Robert, ed. *Whitewash: On Keith Windschuttle's Fabrication of Australian History.* Melbourne: Schwartz, 2003.

McArthur, Grant. 'Jeff Kennett Wants National Anthem Changed.' *The Advertiser* (February 11, 2011). http://www.adelaidenow.com.au/news/strewth-time-for-dinki-di-anthem/news-story/f190ba8a96a72ef4a2cadb8a421edace.

The Rainbow Spirit Elders. *Rainbow Spirit Theology: Towards an Australian Aboriginal Theology.* Melbourne: HarperCollins, 1997.

Reynolds, Henry. *Forgotten War.* Sydney: NewSouth Books, 2012.

Reynolds, Henry. *The Law of the Land.* Ringwood: Penguin, 1987.

Reynolds, Henry. *The Other Side of the Frontier: Aboriginal Resistance to the European Invasion of Australia.* Sydney: UNSW, 2006.

Smith, John. *Advance Australia Where? A Lack of Meaning in a Land of Plenty.* Homebush West: ANZEA, 1988.

Viellaris, Renee. 'Alternative Version of Advance Australia Fair Recognises Indigenous.' *The Courier-Mail* (May 23, 2017). http://www.couriermail.com.au/news/national/alternative-version-of-advance-australia-fair-recognises-indigenous/news-story/187a84db7fcf95535b6b074f85c3cc2d.

Ward, Tony. 'How Advance Australia Fair Waltzed with Matilda and Won.' *The Conversation* (January 24, 2014). https://theconversation.com/how-advance-australia-fair-waltzed-with-matilda-and-won-21564.

Windschuttle, Keith. *The Fabrication of Aboriginal History.* Sydney: Macleay, 2002.

Wright, N. T. 'Heaven is Not Our Home.' *Christianity Today* (March 24, 2008). http://www.christianitytoday.com/ct/2008/april/heaven-is-not-our-home.html.

Wright, Tom. *Surprised by Hope.* London: SPCK, 2007.

INFORMATION ABOUT OUR CONTRIBUTORS AND EDITORS

Reimagining Home

Sharmila Blair is studying a Masters in Pastoral Care at the University of Divinity. She currently works as a classroom music teacher in two Melbourne Catholic schools. She served as a missionary with Frontiers for two years in South-East Asia and in Melbourne for a further thirteen years with Urban Neighbours of Hope prior to returning to teaching in 2016. She sees music teaching as a tool for engaging students and for developing their social and emotional wellbeing.

Seforosa Carroll is a Uniting Church minister and a fellow of the Public and Contextual Theology Research Centre, Charles Sturt University. She works at UnitingWorld, the international partnerships agency of the Uniting Church Assembly, where she is engaged with theological research, resourcing and training in climate change, disaster preparedness and gender. Her research interests lie in Christian theologies of other faiths, interfaith dialogue, migration and diaspora, cross cultural/postcolonial theologies and feminism. Currently she is engaging with climate-induced migration in the Pacific.

INFORMATION ABOUT OUR CONTRIBUTORS AND EDITORS

Michael Chu is assistant professor and chaplain of China Graduate School of Theology, Hong Kong. He teaches preaching, pastoral theology, leadership and conflict resolution. He was a pastor at Northern District Chinese Christian Church, Sydney, for twenty-five years and has been an adjunct lecturer at the Chinese Theological College, Australia. His research interests include intercultural pastoral leadership, leadership development and preaching.

Jonathan Cornford is the co-founder of Manna Gum, a ministry in 'good news economics'. He is a member of the Research School for Religion and Social Policy at the University of Divinity and writes extensively about discipleship in the sphere of economic and material life, including *Coming Back to Earth*, a collection of essays on climate change, agriculture, urban living and the ethics of eating. Jonathan lives in Bendigo with his wife and two daughters, where they are members of Seeds, a small missional community.

Darren Cronshaw is a Baptist pastor, Professor of Missional Leadership with the Australian College of Ministries and honorary chaplain at Swinburne University, Melbourne. His research interests include missional leadership and spirituality, public and contextual theology, theology of work and vocation, congregational transformation, theological education and interfaith dialogue. His latest book is *Dangerous Prayer* (Paternoster, 2017). Darren serves on the AAMS committee and the executive committee of the International Association for Mission Studies.

Linda Devereux is an independent researcher and writer and Adjunct Research Fellow in the School of Theology at Charles Sturt University, Canberra. As a child, Linda lived in the Democratic Republic of the Congo where her parents were medical missionaries with the UK Baptist Missionary Society. Her recent doctoral work is an examination of the effects of overseas missionary work on the children and families of missionaries. Linda researches transcultural childhood and the experiences of third culture kids and is currently writing a book on boarding school.

Rosemary Dewerse has worked in theological education in Aotearoa New Zealand, Australia and Central Asia in areas of formation, hermeneutics, intercultural engagement, contextual theology and mission. She is the current Chair of Interserve New Zealand. Rosemary, with Darren Cronshaw, edited *We are Pilgrims: Mission from, in and with the Margins of our Diverse World* for AAMS (2015) and has written or edited many songs, articles and books.

Keith Dyer teaches New Testament at Whitley College, Melbourne, and is an Associate Professor of the University of Divinity. His publications are mainly on the Gospel of Mark and the book of Revelation, and he has a special interest in interpreting biblical texts in their earliest contexts as a guide to understanding them better today. He has taught at various levels in the Solomon Islands, Switzerland and the USA and enjoys travel, music and sport, and extending hospitality with his family and friends.

René Erwich was appointed Principal of Whitley College, Melbourne, in 2017 after working as a research professor in Practical Theology in the Netherlands. His focus in teaching and research sits at the intersection of faith, religious practices and society. His work in preaching, teaching and writing is motivated by the creation of connections and the integration of the realities of today's world with the realities of the gospel of the kingdom. He is interested in new forms of church, theology and media, human sexuality and theology, and supervised learning. He is an ordained Baptist minister and a registered pastoral supervisor. He is married and together they have four children.

Rosalind Gooden, after training as a secondary teacher, found her opportunities of service as an educator of adults. She spent two decades in East Pakistan/Bangladesh serving the Bengali church, then moved to Melbourne in 1984 to develop new models of mission training for Global Interaction and Missions Interlink. Returning to Adelaide on retirement, she has been researching the early zenana mission movement from the Antipodes. She is easily distracted by family, church and South Australian history, the sorting and preserving of Baptist archives or the making of handmade cards. She also loves teaching conversational English.

INFORMATION ABOUT OUR CONTRIBUTORS AND EDITORS

Deborah Guess is a Research Associate and adjunct teacher at Pilgrim Theological College, University of Divinity. Her main research interest is ecological theology and she is currently writing a book exploring the topic of place from an ecotheological stance. Deborah is interested in the question of how people can live sustainably, and on her small property in Warburton, Victoria, she has owner-built a low-impact house and grows food using permaculture principles. She is a lay Anglican.

Darrell Jackson is the Associate Professor of Missiology, Morling College and the University of Divinity. His research interests lie at the intersection of migration, cultural diversity and theology. His publications span the last twenty years and he continues to write and edit for books and journals, including the *Australian Journal for Mission Studies*, *Vista* and *Lausanne Global Analysis*. He is the Secretary of AAMS.

Edward James has been a cross-cultural worker for twenty-two years in South-Eastern Africa. He is currently a lecturer in Intercultural Studies and a Culture and Language Consultant. His current research interests are contextual ministry with least-reached communities, and intercultural competencies and cultural intelligence required for intercultural engagement. Edward James is a pseudonym.

Mick Pope is a lecturer in meteorology and ecomissiology, a member of the Centre for Research in Religion and Public Policy (RASP) and is completing a MPhil at the University of Divinity. He is the author of several books and papers on ecotheology, including *All Things New: God's Plan to Renew Our World* (2018). Mick is also a black belt in Brazilian Jiu Jitsu.

Stephen Said is a husband, a father, an adjunct lecturer at Whitley College, a martial arts instructor, a blogger and director of an education consultancy. His experience of being a second-generation Maltese migrant born and raised in Melbourne's working class Western Suburbs has resulted in his lifelong fascination with the nexus between culture and spiritual formation through a missiological lens, which is currently the focus of his master's thesis.

Graham Scott is the current Principal and Executive Officer of the Summer Institute of Linguistics Australia. His research interests include Old Testament, linguistics and cross-cultural ministry. He is working towards a PhD in biblical studies, researching discourse analysis in 2 Samuel, through the Brisbane School of Theology. Graham has been a member of Wycliffe Bible Translators for eighteen years and has worked in several cross-cultural contexts, including as the English Pastor of Brisbane Cantonese Christian Church for eight years.

Eleonora Scott has worked as a lecturer at the Summer Institute of Linguistics Australia and she currently serves as a mentor and checker. Her research interests include mission, Old Testament, anthropology, theology and cross-cultural ministry. She is working towards a PhD in biblical studies and theology, researching 'Mission in Isaiah', at the Brisbane School of Theology. Ellie has been a member of Wycliffe Bible Translators for eighteen years and has worked in several cross-cultural contexts, including eight years at Brisbane Cantonese Christian Church.

Mark Short is the National Director of The Bush Church Aid Society, a mission organisation serving in rural, regional and remote Australia. Mark has a PhD in Old Testament from the University of Durham and his research interests include the biblical theology of mission, particularly as it relates to churches in rural contexts. He has published articles exploring the current social and economic context for mission in rural Australia and on church engagement with people from culturally and linguistically diverse backgrounds.

Monica Short is a lecturer and social researcher at Charles Sturt University, and is a volunteer social researcher with Bush Church Aid. Monica's research interests include mutual dialogic exchanges between theologians, sociologists and social workers; personhood; and community engagement. She has authored several publications including two books about the rural church: *Anglican Churches Engaging with People Living with Disabilities* and *Three Anglican Churches Engaging with People from Culturally and Linguistically Diverse Backgrounds*, which are freely available online.

INFORMATION ABOUT OUR CONTRIBUTORS AND EDITORS

Deborah Storie is Adjunct Faculty at Whitley College, Interim Pastor at Footscray Baptist Church and Honorary Postdoctoral Associate at University of Divinity. She previously lived and worked in conflict affected regions and is concerned that humanitarian responses often overlook international and global factors that constrain the lives of the poor and drive conflict and displacement. Her research explores interpretive approaches that equip and motivate discipleship responses to Scripture that are responsible with regard to their ecological, social and economic consequences.

Steve Taylor is Principal at Knox Centre for Ministry and Leadership, Dunedin, New Zealand and Senior Lecturer, Flinders University, Adelaide, Australia. He researches in cultural change, including innovation, fresh expressions of church, popular culture and indigenous theologies. Steve is the author of *Built for Change* (2016), *The Out of Bounds Church?* (2005) and *First Expressions*. Married to Lynne and parent to Shannon and Kayli, he enjoys exploring, gardening and coffee.

J. Dudley Woodberry was born in a Presbyterian missionary home in China, met his wife as a student in Beirut, Lebanon, and after his doctoral studies at Harvard University, served as a missionary in Pakistan, a pastor in Kabul, Afghanistan, and Riyadh, Saudi Arabia, and as a professor of Islamic Studies and dean of the School of Intercultural Studies at Fuller Theological Seminary in Pasadena, California. His writings and edited books include *From Seed to Fruit: Global Trends, Fruitful Practices*; *Emerging Issues among Muslims: Muslims and Christians on the Emmaus Road*; and *Missiological Education for the 21st Century*.

Siu Fung Wu came to faith in Christ in East Asia and since then the Scripture has played a major part in his life. He was a factory worker and a software developer, before becoming a pastor in an inner-city church. He then worked in aid and development. He is Lecturer in New Testament Studies at Whitley College and Honorary Postdoctoral Associate at University of Divinity. Although the focus of his research has been on Pauline studies, he has strong interests in intercultural studies, poverty and justice. He is the author of *Suffering in Romans* and the editor of *Suffering in Paul* (forthcoming).

Xiaoli Yang is a Postdoctoral Associate and Adjunct Lecturer of the University of Divinity, Melbourne. She is a pastor, mentor and poet, and has served in Australia and Asia over the last twenty years. She has published journal articles, book chapters and bilingual poetry for both academic and general readers. Her most recent publications include *A Dialogue between Haizi's Poetry and the Gospel of Luke—Chinese Homecoming and the Relationship with Jesus Christ, Theology and Mission in World Christianity*, and book chapters including 'Poetry as Theology—A Creative Path' and 'Verse by Verse: The Use of Poetry in Advanced Theological Education'.

www.ingramcontent.com/pod-product-compliance
Lightning Source LLC
Chambersburg PA
CBHW060457010526
44118CB00018B/2445